KU-520-159

ANCIENT AND CLASSICAL ARCHITECTURE

SIMPSON'S HISTORY OF ARCHITECTURAL DEVELOPMENT

New Edition

Volume I

ANCIENT AND CLASSICAL ARCHITECTURE

by

Hugh Plommer

Volume II

EARLY CHRISTIAN, BYZANTINE AND ROMANESQUE ARCHITECTURE

by

Cecil Stewart

Volume III

GOTHIC ARCHITECTURE

by

Cecil Stewart

Volume IV

RENAISSANCE ARCHITECTURE

by

J. Quentin Hughes

and

Norbert Lynton

Volume V

NINETEENTH AND TWENTIETH CENTURY ARCHITECTURE

by

Thomas Howarth

and

Frank Jenkins

Simpson's History of
Architectural Development
Vol. I

ANCIENT AND CLASSICAL ARCHITECTURE

by
Hugh Plommer

LONGMANS

LONGMANS, GREEN AND CO LTD
48 Grosvenor Street, London W.1
*Associated companies, branches and representatives
throughout the world*

B56   15073

*This Edition first published 1956
Second Impression by photolithography 1961
Third Impression by photolithography 1963
Fourth Impression by photolithography 1964*

HERTFORDSHIRE
COUNTY LIBRARY
720.9
2803544

*Made and printed by offset in Great Britain by
William Clowes and Sons, Limited, London and Beccles*

TO MY MOTHER

CONTENTS

PART I   ARCHITECTURE BEFORE GREECE

Chapter   *page*
  I   HISTORICAL INTRODUCTION   1
        1   The Primitive Background   1
        2   Prehellenic History   4

 II   EGYPTIAN ARCHITECTURE   15
        1   The Old Kingdom   16
        2   The Middle Kingdom   26
        3   The New Kingdom   28
        4   The Ptolemaic Age   42
        5   Building Science and Decoration .   .   .   45

III   ARCHITECTURE OUTSIDE EGYPT   56
        1   Sumer   56
        2   Assyria and Later Babylonia   .   .   .   65
        3   The Bronze Age in the Aegean   .   .   .   72
        4   Other Prehellenic Styles   89
        5   The Transmission of the Forms .   .   . 100

PART II   GREECE

 IV   THE HISTORICAL SETTING   107
        1   Summary of Greek History 107
        2   Conditions of Life and Types of Building . 112

  V   THE GREEK ORDERS   124
        1   Introductory   124
        2   The Doric Temple   128
        3   The Ionic Temple   158
        4   The Designing of Individual Buildings .   . 172

 VI   ARCHITECTURAL DEVELOPMENT 600–300 B.C. .   . 182
        1   Greek Buildings: Temples 182
        2   Other Greek Buildings   196
        3   Achaemenid Architecture   212
        4   Other Contemporaries 220

PART III   ARCHITECTURE AFTER GREECE

Chapter   *page*

VII   THE HELLENISTIC AGE 322–31 B.C. 231
  1   General History. 231
  2   Earlier Hellenistic Architecture, down to
      200 B.C. 235
  3   Later Hellenistic Architecture, 200–80 B.C. . 248
  4   The First Roman Style, 80–30 B.C. . . 265

VIII   THE CHARACTER OF ROMAN ARCHITECTURE . . 282
  1   The Roman Empire, 31 B.C.–A.D. 330 . . 282
  2   Roman Building Methods 287
  3   Roman Ornament: the Orders . . . 303

IX   THE BUILDINGS OF THE HIGH EMPIRE . . . 314
  1   Civic Buildings 314
  2   Baths 338
  3   Places of Amusement 344
  4   Private Buildings 351

X   THE TRANSFORMATION OF CLASSICAL ARCHITECTURE . 356

    ARCHITECTURAL GLOSSARY 367

    INDEX 372

PLATES

facing page 16

1   A house at Trelleborg, Jutland (*National Museum, Copenhagen*)
Zoser's Colonnade, Sakkara (*Dept. of Antiquities, Cairo*)

facing page 17

2   Granite Temple, Gizeh (*Reproduced from Jéquier, 'Temples Memphites et Thébains', by permission of Editions Morancé*)
Pylons at Edfou (*J. G. Griffith*)

facing page 32

3   Tomb at Beni Hasan : exterior
Tomb at Beni Hasan : interior
(*Photographs reproduced from Jéquier, 'Temples Memphites et Thébains', by permission of Editions Morancé*)

facing page 33

4   The Great Temple, Deir-el-Bahari (*Reproduced from Jéquier, 'Temples Memphites et Thébains', by permission of Editions Morancé*)

facing page 64

5   Columns of the High Gate, Uruk
General view : restored
(*Both reproduced from 'Preussische Akademie der Wissenschaften: Phil. Hist. Klasse, Abhandlungen 1932', Nr. 2*)

facing page 65

6   Ziggurat at Ur : front view (*Sir Leonard Woolley and British Museum*)
Pavement at Khorsabad (*Mansell Collection*)

facing page 80

7   Postern Gate, Mycenae (*author*)
    Columns of the Temple of Ceres, Paestum (*author*)

facing page 81

8   Blocks of column bases, Senjirli (*Reproduced from Von
    Luschan, 'Ausgrabungen in Sendschirli', Berlin,* 1898)
    Nimrud Ivory, showing Temple Courtesan (*British Museum*)

facing page 160

9   Propylaea and Pinakotheke, Athens (*author*)
    South Peristyle of Parthenon (*author*)

facing page 161

10 West elevation of Parthenon: restored (*Reproduced from a
    drawing by A. Mennim*)

facing page 176

11 Sanctuary of Marmaria, Delphi (*author*)

facing page 177

12 Temple of Poseidon, Paestum: two interior views (*author*)

facing page 224

13 North Porch of Erechtheum, Athens (*Alison Frantz*)

facing page 225

14 Monument of Lysicrates (*Reproduced from Stuart and Revett,
    'Antiquities of Athens',* 1761)

facing page 240

15 Column drums from Temple of Poseidon, Sunium (*author*)
    Corinthian capital, Orange (*author*)

facing page 241

16 Theatre of Epidaurus (*J. G. Griffith*)
    Tomb della Pietrera, Vetulonia (*R. M. Cook*)

facing page 272

17   East Curtain, Aigosthena (*R. M. Cook*)
     House of the Faun, Pompeii (*author*)

facing page 273

18   Decoration in Second Pompeian style, House of Livia, Rome
     (*Reproduced from 'Monumenti Inediti, publicati dell'
     Instituto'*

facing page 288

19   Terrace above Great Ramp, Praeneste (*Eric Southern*)

facing page 288

19   Pseudo-pendentives, Baths of Caracalla, Rome (*author*)

facing page 289

20   Temple of Concord, Rome: interior, restored (*Reproduced
     from a drawing by A. Mennim*)

facing page 304

21   Arch of Titus, Rome (*Mansell Collection*)

facing page 305

22   Pantheon, Rome (*Mansell Collection*)
     Profile of length of Pantheon at Rome (*Reproduced from
     Desgodetz, 'Ancient Buildings of Rome', 1795*)

facing page 320

23   Amphitheatre of Pozzuoli (*Anderson*)
     Cortile in Insula of Serapis, Ostia (*author*)

facing page 321

24   Mosaic on arch-soffit, Baths of the Seven Sages, Ostia (*J. B.
     Ward Perkins*)

LINE ILLUSTRATIONS

FIG.   *Page*
  1 Building at Mosul (F. Oelmann, *Haus und Hof im Altertum*,
     Berlin, 1927, Fig. 60b. By permission of Messrs.
     Walter de Gruyter & Co. Berlin)   1
  2 Apulian Trulli (F. Oelmann, *op. cit.*, Figs. 6a, 6b. By per-
     mission of Messrs. Walter de Gruyter & Co., Berlin)   .   2
  3 (a) (b) Dragon House, Mt. Ocha (after F. B. Johnson, in
     AJA, pp. 398 ff.)   3
  4 Egyptian Mastaba (G. A. Reisner, *Giza Necropolis*, I, Cam-
     bridge Mass., 1942, Fig. 153. By permission of Harvard
     University Press)   19
  5 Pyramid of Sahure, Abusir. Cross-section (Somers
     Clarke and R. Engelbach, *Ancient Egyptian Masonry*,
     Oxford, 1930, Fig. 135. By permission of Mrs. Engle-
     bach and Oxford University Press)   20
  6 The Great Pyramid (Simpson Vol. I, 1905, corrected with
     the aid of Clarke and Engelbach and I. E. S. Edwards,
     The Pyramids of Egypt, Harmondsworth, 1952)   .   .   22
  7 Second Pyramid, Embalming and Offering Temples (after
     Jéquier, *Temples Memphites et Thébains*, Paris, 1920,
     Pl. 2)   24
  8 Brick Pyramid, Abydos (after Perrot and Chipiez, Tome I,
     Paris, 1882, Fig. 162)   26
  9 Pylon of Rameses I, foundations (Clarke and Engelbach, *op.
     cit.*, Fig. 67. By permission of Mrs. Engelbach and
     Oxford University Press)   29
 10 Plan of Luxor (W. Otto, *Handbuch der Archäologie*, Munich,
     1939, p. 568)   32
 11 Great Temple of Karnak at Thebes (Simpson, Vol. I, 1905)   32
 12 In the Hypostyle Hall, Karnak (Simpson, Vol. I, 1905)   .   33
 13 Temple of the Kings, Abydos (A. St. G. Caulfeild, *The
     Temple of the Kings at Abydos*, London, 1902, Pl.
     XXIV. By permission of the British School of Egyptian
     Archaeology)   35
 14 Roof-joint, Abydos (Clarke and Engelbach, *op cit.*, Fig. 175.
     By permission of Mrs. Engelbach and the Oxford Uni-
     versity Press)   36
 15 Temple of Deir-el-Bahari, Axonometric (E. Naville, *Temple
     of Deir-el-Bahari*, Part VI, London, 1908, Pl. CLXIX.
     By permission of the Egypt Exploration Society) .   .   37
 16 Small Temple, Abu-Simbel (Simpson, Vol. I, 1905) .   .   40

FIG.   *Page*
17   The House of the Vizier Nekht (Peet and Woolley, *City of
     Akhenaten*, I, London, 1923, Pl. III. By permission of the
     Egypt Exploration Society)   42
18   View of the Inner Court, Edfou (Simpson, Vol. I, 1905)   .   44
19   Tomb of Rameses IV.   Modern Plan and Section and
     Papyrus Plan (Clarke and Engelbach, *op. cit.*, Fig. 49.
     By permission of Mrs. Engelbach and the Oxford Uni-
     versity Press)   46
20   Egyptian brick arch (Clarke and Engelbach, *op. cit.*, Fig. 216.
     By permission of Mrs. Engelbach and the Oxford Uni-
     versity Press)   51
21   Vault constructed without centering (Clarke and Engelbach,
     op. cit., Fig. 214.   By permission of Mrs. Engelbach and
     the Oxford University Press)   51
22   Egyptian roll and gorge (Simpson, Vol. I, 1905)   .   .   52
23   Old Kingdom Capitals, Abusir : (i) Dactyliform, (ii) Papyri-
     form (L. Borchardt, *Grobdenkmal des Königs Sahu-re*, I,
     Leipzig, 1907, Blätter 9 and 11. By permission of
     J. C. Hinrichs Verlag)   53
24   Red Temple at Uruk, plan (*Preussische Akademie der Wissen-
     schaften Berlin : Phil. Hist. Klasse, Abhandlungen* 1932, Nr.
     2 (Jordan), Abb. 2.   By permission of J. C. Hinrichs
     Verlag.)   57
25   Plan of High Gate, Uruk (*Preussische Akademie der Wissen-
     schaften Berlin, op. cit.*, Abb. 1.   By permission of J. C.
     Hinrichs Verlag)   58
26   King Gudea's plan and instruments (L. W. King, *History of
     Sumer and Akkad*, London, 1923, Figs. 64 and 65)   .   61
27   Reed wall, Al 'Ubaid (after C. L. Woolley and H. R. Hall,
     Al 'Ubaid, Oxford, 1927)   62
28   Courtyard of private house, Ur (C. L. Woolley, *Excavations
     at Ur*, London, 1954.   By permission of Messrs. Ernest
     Benn Ltd.)   63
29   House at Fara (F. Wachtsmuth, *Der Raum*, I, Marburg,
     1929, Abb. 7.   By permission of the author and Verlag
     des Kunstgeschichtlichen Seminars)   65
30   Plan of Palace, Khorsabad (Lubke, *Geschichte der Architec-
     ture*, I, 1884)   68
31   Babylon, Palace of Nebuchadnezzar : (i) The Ensemble,
     (ii) The State Apartments (R Koldewey, *Babylon*,
     London, 1914, Figs. 43 and 46. By permission of
     Messrs. Macmillan & Co. Ltd.)   71
32   Caravanserai at Cnossus (after Evans, *Palace of Minos*, II,
     Fig. 49.   By permission of Messrs. Macmillan & Co. Ltd.)   74
33   Plan of State Apartments, Cnossus (Evans, *Palace of Minos*,
     II, Plan C.   Plan by W. G. Newton and Theodore Fyfe.
     By permission of Messrs. Macmillan & Co. Ltd.)   .   76

FIG.   *Page*

34   King's Private Suite, Cnossus (A. M. Mennim; constructed from data in Evans) 78

35   Temple Tomb at Cnossus and Egyptian tomb compared (A. Persson, *New Tombs at Dendra*, Oxford, 1942, Fig. 121. By permission of Kungl. Humanistiska Vetenskapssamfundet, Sweden) 80

36   Mycenae, Treasury of Atreus (*British School Annual*, XXV (1923), Pl. LVI. By permission of British School of Archaeology) 83

37   The Doric Column and its prototypes (author) . . 85

38   Plan of Palace, Tiryns (K. Mueller, *Tiryns*, Augsburg, 1930, Bund III, Tafel 4) 87

39   Hairpin Arch, Boghazkoi (O. Puchstein, *Boghazkoi, Leipzig*, 1912, Abb. 46. By permission of J. C. Hinrichs Verlag) 90

40   Plan of Palace I, Boghazkoi (Puchstein, *op. cit.*, Abb. 108. By permission of J. C. Hinrichs Verlag) . . . 91

41   Door-jamb. Boghazkoi (Puchstein, *op. cit.*, Abb. 74. By permission of J. C. Hinrichs Verlag) . . . 92

42   Tibetan loggia-buildings (F. Oelmann, *Haus und Hof im Altertum*, Berlin, 1927, Abb. 57. By permission of Walter de Gruyter & Co. Berlin) 94

43   'Third Temple' Alalakh (*Antiquaries' Journal*, 1950, p. 10, Fig. 5. By permission of the Society of Antiquaries, London) 95

44   Tell Halaf, cross-section of front loggia (M. von Oppenheim, *Tell Halaf*, Trs. by G. Wheeler, London (1932), p. 136. By permission of Messrs. G. P. Putnam's Sons) . . 97

45   Site plan of Temple of Aphaia, Aegina (after A. Furtwaengler, *Aigina*, Munich, 1906) 119

46   Profile and decoration of Greek mouldings (author) . 127

47   Temple of Poseidon, Cape Sunium : Axonometric (author, cf. *British School Annual*, 1950) 129

48   Temple of Poseidon, Paestum : Metopes of Pronaos (author) 142

49   Alternative cross-sections, Temple G, Selinus (author) . 144

50   Doric capital, Tiryns (after H. Schliemann, *Tiryns*, London, 1886, p. 293) 148

51   Athena Alea, Tegea (Clemmensen, *Tégée*, Paris, 1924, Pl. XVIII) 149

52   Athens, Sima of Old Temple of Athena (Allan Marquand, *Greek Architecture*, London, 1909, Fig. 296. By permission of the Macmillan Company, New York) . 157

53   Ionic corner-capital : mirror-plan (Allan Marquand, *op cit.*, Fig. 313. By permission of the Macmillan Company, New York) 162

54   Priene, Temple of Athena Polias : section through tympanum (Wiegand-Schrader, *Priene*, Berlin, 1904, Abb. 67. By permission of Prof. Dr. Th. Wiegand) . . 164

FIG. Page

55 Priene, Temple of Athena Polias : section through ceiling
(Wiegand-Schrader, *op. cit.*, Abb. 68. By permission of
Prof. Dr. Th. Wiegand) 165

56 Early Corinthian capitals (after H. Klumbach, *Tarentiner
Grabkunst*, Reutlingen, 1937, and C. R. Cockerell, *Aegina
and Bassae*, London, 1861) 170

57 The Arsenal, Piraeus : after Choisy (A. M. Mennim, after
Choisy, *Études Epigraphiques*, Paris, 1884, Pl. 1) . . 173

58 Athens ; Propylaea from South-west (Baumgarten, Poland
and Wagner, *Die Hellenische Kultur*, 1913 Ed., Fig. 343.
By permission of B. G. Teubner, Leipzig) . . . 176

59 Propylaea section through central gable (W. B. Dinsmoor
in *AJA*, 1910, Fig. 6. By permission of the Editor,
AJA) 177

60 Propylaea : central gable, north elevation (Dinsmoor, *loc. cit.*,
Fig. 4. By permission of the Editor, *AJA*) . . 178

61 Corinthian capital, Epidaurus (W. R. Lethaby, *Greek
Buildings*, London, 1908, Fig. 172. By permission of
B. T. Batsford Ltd.). 196

62 Athenian Stoa, Delphi (P. Amandry, *La Colonne des Naxiens
et le Portique des Athéniens*, Paris, 1953, Fig. 7. By permission of Editions de Boccard, Paris) . . . 199

63 Double Stoa, Magnesia (Allan Marquand, *op. cit.*, Fig. 361.
By permission of the Macmillan Company, New York) . 200

64 Grouped megara, Larisa (Boehlau and Schefold, *Larisa am
Hermos*, Berlin, 1940, Vol. I, Abb. 7. By permission of
Messrs. Walter de Gruyter & Co.) 201

65 House at Priene (Wiegand-Schrader, *Priene*, Abb. 298/9.
By permission of Prof. Th. Wiegand) . . . 203

66 Villa of Good Fortune, Olynthus (D. M. Robinson and J. W.
Graham, *Excavations at Olynthus*, VIII, Pl. 85, 2. By
permission of the Johns Hopkins Press, Baltimore) . 205

67 Theatre at Epidaurus (Simpson, Vol. I, 1905) . . 207

68 Persepolis Terrace (in *JHS*, 1951, p. 113. By permission
of the Oriental Institute, Chicago University) . . 215

69 Persepolis, column of Apadana (Simpson, Vol. I, 1905) . 218

70 Naqshi Rustum, tomb (after F. Bell, *Early Architecture in
Western Asia*) 219

71 Lycian tomb (Simpson, Vol. I, 1905) 221

72 Tuscan temple plan, after Wiegand (D. S. Robertson, *Greek
and Roman Architecture*, Fig. 88. By permission of
Verlag F. Bruckmann, K.G., Munich) . . . 224

73 Tuscan temple, conjectural elevation (author—based on A.
Andrén, *Architectural Terracottas from Etrusco-Italic
Temples*, Lund, 1940) 226

74 Centre of Priene, plan (Wiegand-Schrader, *Priene*, Pl. II.
By permission of Prof. Th. Wiegand) . . . 237

FIG.   *Page*

75 First Pompeian Style (Mau-Kelsey, *Pompeii*, London, 1899, Fig. 21) 240

76 Hellenistic engaged order at Ptolemais' Cyrenaica (after G. Pesce, *Il Palazzo delle Colonne in Tolemaide di Cirenaica*, Rome, 1951) 242

77 Altar of Athena, Priene : detail (Wiegand-Schrader, *Priene*, Abb. 96. By permission of Prof. Th. Wiegand) . . 244

78 Hypostyle Hall, Delos (Vallois and Poulsen, *Delos* II, 2, Paris, 1914, Pl. I. By permission of Éditions de Boccard, Paris) 250

79 Delian house, plan (Allan Marquand, *Greek Architecture*, Fig. 387. By permission of the Macmillan Company New York) 252

80 Pompeian house, exterior (after Mau-Kelsey, *Pompeii*, Fig. 109) 254

81 Pompeian house, interior (after Mau-Kelsey, *Pompeii*, Fig. 130) 255

82 Pompeii, House of the Faun, plan (after Mau-Kelsey, *Pompeii*, Fig. 132) 256

83 Pompeii, House of Faun, longitudinal section (after Mau-Kelsey, *Pompeii*, Fig. 136) 257

84 Corinthian capital, Praeneste (A. M. Mennim, after R. Delbrueck, *Die Hellenistische Bauten in Latium* I, Abb. 74) 260

85 Arched entrance to Agora, Priene (Wiegand-Schrader, *Priene*, Abb. 200. By permission of Prof. Th. Wiegand) 261

86 Lower Gymnasium, Priene (Wiegand-Schrader, *Priene*, Abb. 273. By permission of Prof. Th. Wiegand) . . 263

87 Basilica, Praeneste (A. M. Mennim, after Delbrueck, *op. cit.*, I. Taf. XVII) 267

88 Roman model of a stage-building (A. M. Mennim, after O. Benndorf in *JOeI*, 1902) 268

89 Tilted capital, Praeneste (author) 270

90 Stabian Thermae, Pompeii (Mau-Kelsey, *Pompeii*, Fig. 81) 274

91 Villa of the Papyri, Herculaneum : after Weber (author) . 275

92 Tower of the Winds, lanceolate capital (author, after Stuart and Revett, *Antiquities of Athens*, Vol. I, Ch. III) . . 277

93 Tower of the Winds, internal cornice (Stuart and Revett, Vol. I, *op. cit.*, Ch. III, Pl. IX) 277

94 Lesser Propylon, Eleusis (A. M. Mennim, after *Unedited Antiquities of Attica*, London, 1817, Ch. III) . . 279

95 Rome, Throne Room of Domitian (author, after Wachtsmuth, *Der Raum*, Marburg, 1929, Bd. I) . . 290

96 Rome, Temple of Castor, entablature (Simpson, Vol. I, 1905) 291

97 Brick-faced concrete (Simpson, Vol. I, 1905, after Middleton, *Remains of Ancient Rome*, London, 1892) . . 293

98 Opus reticulatum (Simpson, Vol. I, 1905, after Middleton) 294

99 Brick arches (Simpson, Vol. I, 1905, after Middleton) . 295

FIG.   *Page*

100   Intersecting vaults (from Choisy) (Simpson, Vol. I, 1905) . 297

101   Stone barrel vault, 'Baths of Diana', Nîmes (Simpson, Vol. I, 1905) 300

102   Portico of Pantheon, roof according to Serlio (Serlio, *Third Booke*, London, 1611, 4th Ch., Folio 3 verso) . . 301

103   Portico of Pantheon, roof according to Dosio (author, after R. Lanciani, *Ruins and Excavations of Ancient Rome*, London, 1897, Fig. 188) 302

104   The Roman orders (Simpson, Vol. I, 1905) . . . 307

105   Colosseum, elevation and part-section (Simpson, Vol. I, 1905) 311

106   The Fourth Pompeian Style (Simpson, Vol. I, 1905) . 312

107   Rome, Forum of Trajan (Simpson, Vol. I, 1905, after Lanciani) 318

108   The Great Sanctuary, Baalbeck (D. S. Robertson, *Greek and Roman Architecture*, Fig. 95. By permission of Prof. Th. Wiegand) 320

109   Basilica of Trajan, cross-section (Simpson, Vol. I, 1905) . 322

110   Temple of Venus and Rome (Lanciani, *Ruins and Excavations of Ancient Rome*, London, 1897, p. 197. By permission of Messrs. Macmillan & Co. Ltd.) 326

111   Maison Carrée, Nîmes (Simpson, Vol. I, 1905) . . 328

112   The Pantheon and its predecessor (author, after Lanciani, *op. cit.*, Fig. 185. By permission of Messrs. Macmillan & Co. Ltd.) 331

113   Arch of Orange, short side (not to scale : sculpture omitted) (author) 337

114   Central Baths, Pompeii (Mau-Kelsey, *Pompeii*, Fig. 89) . 339

115   Thermae of Caracalla (J. H. Middleton, *Remains of Ancient Rome*, II, Fig. 76. By permission of Messrs. A. & C. Black Ltd.) 340

116   Colosseum, plan at four levels (J. H. Middleton, *op. cit.*, Fig. 59. By permission of Messrs. A. & C. Black Ltd.) . 348

117   Hatra, general plan (author, after Wachtsmuth, *Der Raum*, I, Abb. 53) 357

118   Hatra, section through Iwan (author, after Wachtsmuth, *op. cit.*, Abb. 54) 358

119   Hadrian's Villa, semi-dome (Simpson, Vol. I, 1905) . . 360

120   Rome, 'Temple of Minerva Medica' (Simpson, Vol. I, 1905) 362

121   Arcading in the Palace of Diocletian, Spalato (Simpson, Vol. I, 1905) 364

PREFACE TO THE REVISED EDITION

SINCE Simpson's original publication of this volume in 1900, the discoveries of archaeologists have everywhere proceeded at a notable pace. Remains of an early civilisation, the existence of which had been hardly suspected, gradually appeared in Crete in the years after 1900, while long vistas were opened after 1920 into the origins of civilisation in Mesopotamia. Now we are even beginning to trace the links between early Crete and Mesopotamia, so far has our knowledge advanced. The dates and connections of the Hittite and North Syrian monuments have now been much more securely fixed, and it is far easier than it was to appraise the cultural character of Assyria. In the field of Classical Archaeology, excavation at sites such as Olynthus and Priene has given us for the first time some knowledge of Greek town-planning: while Ostia has presented us with a far clearer picture than we could ever have hoped to obtain of a trading centre in the Roman Empire. We have learnt something new even of such well-trodden cities as Rome and Athens—places of which even the most trivial detail has importance, so great are their merits and their fame. I find it hard to recollect that, when Simpson wrote, el Amarna and Delos, the larger parts even of Olympia and Delphi were still below ground; and that the Hellenistic Age, that central period between Alexander and Augustus, was still unknown to architects and almost unknown to scholars.

It has therefore been necessary to rewrite the whole volume, keeping only those illustrations of Simpson's which still seem pertinent. Simpson's section on Roman construction and its aesthetic consequences seems to me at once the most admirable and the least dated in the former volume, and I should like here to confess my debt to it. In the Roman chapters, too, I could follow to some extent in my own work the outlines of Simpson's arrangement.

The student who approaches the Ancient World is appalled by the number and complexity of its cultures and their attendant artistic styles. If he perseveres, he becomes aware that these are themselves often a simplification made by art critics from an

enormous and increasing mass of reports, written in many
languages and compiled, not always with too much science or
scholarly co-operation, from the survey or sometimes the bare
memory of excavated sites.   Important criticisms of these reports
often appear in periodicals normally inaccessible.   In most cases,
moreover, it is absurd to call the sites 'ruins'.   They are rather
the thin wraiths of their ancient selves, often the thinner the more
important the cities that they represent.   For often, of course, the
greatest ancient cities occupied the natural centres of their
regions.   Therefore, when repeatedly destroyed in the Dark Ages
or the twentieth century, they have risen in ever worse squalor
from their ruins.   In Rome itself, 'quod non fecerunt barbari,
fecerunt Barberini' (a destruction that continues today, and
embraces the very buildings of the Barberini): while in the Agora
of Athens one is fortunate to find above the cutting for the
foundations even two or three battered blocks from the whole of
an ancient stoa.   On the other hand, ancient buildings that are
still reasonably complete, such as the Great Pyramid or the
Pantheon, can be counted on the fingers.   The specialist's
potential knowledge may be of an order altogether different from
that available in 1900.   But even he still knows virtually nothing
of such topics as Greek temple interiors.   The new information is
still scattered and tantalisingly insubstantial.   How is one to
assess it fairly, and present to students those conclusions which one
considers the best established and the most beneficial?

However, classical scholars may never shirk the duty of ex-
pounding in each generation their honest conception of classical
art.   It had virtues, simplicity, symmetry, politeness, always hard
to achieve, and discarded in no age more completely or more
disastrously than in our own.   Whatever we may not know of it,
we still know that it has inspired the greatest artists—Mantegna,
Raphael, Poussin—of our culture, and that its creators were at
once so like and so unlike ourselves, that we cannot truly know
ourselves without having sought to know them.

Following what I conceive to have been Simpson's intention, I
have written this book chiefly for students who have learnt neither
Greek nor Latin, and who are unlikely to have grasped the general
pattern of Ancient History.   Certain consequences have followed.

(1) I have devoted considerable space to political history.
Before one can begin to understand a building, one must know
whose programme it was designed to satisfy, and at what stage of

human knowledge and belief. One conceives, for instance, a rather false picture of the Parthenon, if one is told, as I was once told by an eminent modern architect, that it was designed by slaves. Again, one should know why there exists that strange gap, ignored in so many textbooks, between Classical Greek and Classical Roman Architecture. Were architects asleep or not during this Hellenistic period?

(2) I have aimed at clarity rather than at comprehensiveness, concentrating where I could on excellent representative buildings, such as the temples of the Second Pyramid, or unusual buildings that display high architectural merit, such as the Pantheon or the Athenian Propylaea. I am bound to omit even the most cursory reference to many a newly excavated site.

(3) I have tried to provide my readers with a way of escape from my own rather one-sided views. Too often, when one disbelieves an author and wishes to examine his source, one is given no real clue where to find it. One finds merely an enormous bibliography of the works which he has presumably consulted, and in which one may perhaps hope to find one's needle. To help the enterprising student, I have therefore cited such relevant authorities as I may know at the places where they impinge upon my own discussions. This must serve as my excuse for the large number of short footnotes in this volume, and for the absence of a bibliography other than the short table of abbreviations, at the beginning of my text, of the works that I have habitually consulted for my footnotes. By such means I hope that the reader, when he comes to important topics, such as, say, the meaning of the Greek word *harmonia*, will be able to discover my evidence far more easily than he could from a mere bibliography.

Needless to say, I can provide in this book only the most inadequate series of illustrations—which is, of course, no reflection on my publishers. The truly serious student, to acquire any real knowledge of sites or buildings, must always resort to their official standard publications. I have done my best to give him exact references to these at the appropriate places. In making my own sketches and reproductions from these works, I have been unable to secure that uniformity in the scale and method of illustration so useful in the second volume of this series. I have, however, attempted, wherever possible, to give scales in both feet and metres. Of one or two buildings, such as the Arch of Orange, I have made a quick sketch, not having the time or the means for detailed measurement. These sketches seemed worth inclusion, as being sufficient to illustrate one or two of my arguments. Perhaps I shall one day be able to offer a sounder, more uniform series of illustrations.

I have received help and encouragement from a great number of friends, all of whom I cannot possibly name here. On my Egyptian sections I was much helped by Mr. Alan Rowe, while my account of Early Asia and the Bronze Age in the Aegean has benefited (not, I fear, as greatly as he would have wished) from the astringent criticism of Mr. Sinclair Hood. Professor J. M. C. Toynbee and Mr. Robert Cook performed the same service for my Classical sections. Mr. Cecil Stewart showed forbearance toward my last chapter, where my uncompromising Romanism is hardly to his taste. Mr. W. A. Eden discussed with me many passages of my work as it proceeded—we hoped in those days that we might be allowed to teach some students, even in modern Britain, a few sound classical principles, extracted by candid historical inquiry. The correction of my galley proofs was shared by Mr. Peter Salway and Mr. Richard Schwarz, to both of whom I am most grateful. In studying ancient architecture, one cannot afford to ignore the sumptuous and elegant publications made one or two centuries ago; and I must here thank Mr. A. de M. Chesterman, who, in the midst of all his heavy and fruitful work at Nostell, so kindly bore with me while I explored the Priory's copies of Piranesi, Dodwell and *Herculaneum*.

For several illustrations, of which I was not capable myself, I have drawn on the professional skill of Mr. Michael Mennim. Certain photographs I owe to Mr. John Griffith, Mr. Eric Southern, Miss Allison Frantz and Mr. J. B. Ward Perkins. This book is the better for them.

To conclude, I wish to thank Longmans, especially Miss Evans and Mr. Blagden, for the efficiency with which they have seen this book through the press. It is good to find publishers who still hold before themselves the ideal 'Denique, sit quod vis, simplex dumtaxat et unum', and who strive to reach it even with the results of modern archaeological inquiry.

HUGH PLOMMER

Cambridge
   October 1955

CHIEF AUTHORITIES USED,
WITH ABBREVIATIONS

AA=Archaeologisches Institut des Deutschen Reiches. Archäologischer Anzeiger (Beiblatt zum Jahrbuch). Berlin, 1889– (in progress).

AJA (American Journal of Archaeology)=American Journal of Archaeology, Second Series; Baltimore, Boston and Norwood, 1897– (in progress).

AM=Mittheilungen des Deutschen Archaeologischen Instituts in Athen, Athen, 1876–1937.

Antiquities of Ionia=Antiquities of Ionia, published by the Society of Dilettanti, 5 vols., London, 1769–1915.

Antiquity=Antiquity. A Quarterly Review of Archaeology, Gloucester, 1927– (in progress).

Archaeologia=Archaeologia. Proceedings of the Society of Antiquaries of London, Vols. 51– : London, 1888– (in progress).

Atkinson and Bagenal= R. Atkinson and P. E. Hope Bagenal, *Theory and Elements of Architecture*, London, 1926.

Bell=E. Bell, *Early Architecture in Western Asia*, London, 1924.

BSA=(British School Annual)=Annual of the British School at Athens; London, 1894– (in progress).

BCH (Bulletin de Correspondance Hellénique)=Bulletin de Correspondance Hellénique, Athens and Paris, 1877– (in progress).

CAH (Cambridge Ancient History)=The Cambridge Ancient History, Vols. I–XII, Cambridge, 1923–39.

Childe=V. Gordon Childe, *New Light on the Most Ancient East*, 4th Edition, London, 1952.

Clarke and Engelbach=Somers Clarke and R. Engelbach, *Ancient Egyptian Masonry*, Oxford, 1930.

Delbrueck, *Hellenistische Bauten* (Delbrueck)=R. Delbrueck, *Hellenistiche Bauten in Latium*, 2 vols., Strassburg, 1907–12.

Délos=Exploration archéologique de Délos faite par l'école française d'Athènes, Paris, 1909– (in progress).

Dinsmoor=W. B. Dinsmoor, *The Architecture of Ancient Greece*, London, 1950.

Fergusson=James Fergusson, *History of Architecture*, 3 vols., London, 1865–7 (and subsequent editions).

FD (Fouilles de Delphes)=Fouilles de Delphes executées par ordre du gouvernement français et publiées . . . avec le concours des directeurs de l'École d'Athènes, Tomes I–V, Paris, 1907– (in progress).

Hesperia= Hesperia. Journal of the American School of Classical Studies at Athens, Athens, 1931– (in progress).

Iraq=Iraq (The journal of the British School of Archaeology in Iraq), London, 1934– (in progress).

Jahrbuch (JdI)=Archaeologisches Institut des Deutschen Reiches. Jahrbuch, &c., Berlin, 1888–   (in progress).

JOeI=Oesterreichisches Archäologisches Institut. Jahreshefte, &c. Vienna, 1898–   (in progress).

JHS (Journal of Hellenic Studies)=Journal of Hellenic Studies, London, 1880–   (in progress).

JRS (Journal of Roman Studies)=Journal of Roman Studies, London, 1911–   (in progress).

JRIBA=Journal of the Royal Institute of British Architects, Third Series, London, 1894–   (in progress).

KP (Koldewey and Puchstein)=R. Koldewey and O. Puchstein, *Die Griechischen Tempel in Unteritalien und Sicilien*, 2 vols. Berlin, 1899.

KIB (Kunstgeschichte in Bildern)=Kunstgeschichte in Bildern: I. Das Altertum, Ed. F. Winter, Leipsic, n.d.

Lanciani, *Ruins=*R. Lanciani, *The Ruins and Excavations of Ancient Rome*; London and New York, 1897.

Lethaby=W. R. Lethaby, *Architecture*, London (1912).

Lethaby, *Greek Buildings=*W. R. Lethaby, *Greek Buildings represented by fragments in the British Museum*, London, 1908.

MAAR=American Academy in Rome. Memoirs, Bergamo, 1915– (in progress).

Mau-Kelsey=A. Mau, *Pompeii, its Life and Art*. Translated into English by F. W. Kelsey. 2nd Edition, London and New York, 1902.

NS=Notizie degli Scavi. Series V, Vols. 1–21 (Milan, 1904–24); Series VI, Milan, 1925–   (in progress).

Olympia=Olympia. Die Ergebnisse der von dem deutschen Reich veranstalteten Ausgrabung, Edd. E. Curtius and F. Adler, 5 vols. of text and 4 of plates, Berlin, 1890–7.

*PM (Palace of Minos)=*Sir Arthur Evans, *The Palace of Minos at Knossos*, 4 vols.+Index Volume, London, 1921–36.

Perrot and Chipiez=G. Perrot and C. Chipiez, *Histoire de l'Art dans l'Antiquité*, 10 vols., Paris, 1882–1914.

RA=Revue Archéologique: sixième série, Paris, 1933–   (in progress).

Robertson=D. S. Robertson, *A Handbook of Greek and Roman Architecture*, 2nd Edition, Cambridge, 1943.

RM (Roemische Mittheilungen)=Mittheilungen des (Kaiserlich) Deutschen Archaeologischen Instituts, Roemische Abtheilung, Rome, 1886– .

Syria=Syria. Revue d'art oriental et d'archéologie, Paris, 1920– (in progress).

Vitruvius=Vitruvii de Architectura libri decem. Iterum edidit V. Rose, Lipsiae, 1899.

PART ONE

ARCHITECTURE BEFORE GREECE

CHAPTER I

HISTORICAL INTRODUCTION

1. THE PRIMITIVE BACKGROUND

THE buildings of savages, considered on their own merits, have no place in this book. We are concerned with architecture, that is the 'monumental building' of craftsmen conscious of the beauty of certain forms and eager to heighten and perpetuate them. But we must remind ourselves of those immemorial shapes that dominate at all times the primitive buildings in the large climatic zones of the northern hemisphere. Each of these zones, as shown by Oelmann,[1] has two forms of building, based on the round and rectangular plan. Since we are interested, moreover, only in the first development and transmission of our own traditional architecture, the forms of the rainy tropical zone, which also dominate the brilliant, sensitive architecture of Japan, will not concern us. We can confine ourselves to the steppes and the northern forests.

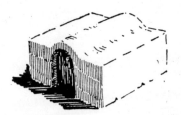

Fig. 1   Building at Mosul.

The typical building of the dry steppe and desert zone of Asia and Africa, where summers are hot and winters cold, has thick walls and a thick, flattened outer roof, supported either on a continuous tunnel vault or on a series of stout transverse arches (see Fig. 1). Mud-brick walls and roofs of beaten earth in these dry climates are the rule. Such forms, natural to Mesopotamia and the deserts of eastern Syria (as shown by the 'Arch of Chosroes' at Ctesiphon and the famous houses of the Hauran),[2] have occasionally made their way westwards and northwards into the Mediterranean Basin. They are seen to perfection in eighteenth- and

[1] *Haus und Hof in Altertum* (Berlin, 1927), pp. 3 ff.
[2] See, for these houses, Robertson, p. 314. Arches, though not complete tunnel vaults, had become common even in the middle-class houses of Ur before 2000 B.C.

nineteenth-century buildings[1] on the dry Greek island of Santorin and are recalled, however distantly, in some of the Roman and Romanesque work of southern France. The thick walls, angular exteriors and vaulted interiors of the desert zone appear, moreover, in some Mediterranean buildings of circular plan, such as the trulli found today in Apulia (see Fig. 2), and, in monumental form, in the beehive tombs of Mycenae and the Egyptian Middle Kingdom.

In the north temperate forests, down to the time of the Vikings, men lived in the 'heroic' style, feasting and drinking round a hearth in long rectangular timber halls, with high roofs, large rafters and massive ridge poles.[2] How far this style invaded the

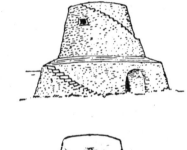

Fig. 2   Apulian Trulli.

Mediterranean at certain times is a matter of controversy. But long houses of apparently northern type, with one open and often one apsidal end, recur in Greece between the third millennium and the seventh century B.C. These are the 'megara', the history of which we shall trace below. The surviving 'dragon houses' (petrified block-houses?) on the Greek island of Euboea (see Fig. 3), together with the account in Vitruvius[3] of the houses of Colchis, on the Black Sea, show that in classical times the Mediterranean was in close touch with a more savage and wasteful timber technique—of laying tree trunks horizontally—always

---

[1] For the date, see Pègues, *Histoire de Santorin* (Paris, 1842), *passim*.

[2] The most beautiful examples we know, certainly the most beautifully grouped, were at Trelleborg in Jutland, of *c.* A.D. 1000. See P. Norlund, *Trelleborg* (Copenhagen, 1948). See Pl. 1.

[3] II, 1, iv. I do not see why Atkinson and Bagenal (Fig. 6) should lay the pyramidal roofs of these blockhouses diagonally. Galiani, in Tom. III of his *Vitruvius* (Naples, 1758), gives a more straightforward picture. The 'Dragon House' of Mt. Ocha in Euboea, with its flat stones and corbelled roof, reminds me of such buildings. The dressing and jointing of its masonry are late classical or Hellenistic, as Johnson cogently argues (*AJA*, 1925, pp. 398–412).

popular in the east forest zone, as shown, for instance, by the later 'tent churches' of Russia.[1]

The Mediterranean, an extraordinarily favoured region, had moderate rainfall, warmer, shorter winters and excellent building stone. So, while solid building was easy and necessary, the thick vaults and earth-packing of the desert were on the whole out of

Fig. 3 (*a*) Dragon House, Mt. Ocha.

Fig. 3 (*b*) Dragon House, Mt. Ocha.

place. Hence both the prevalence of trabeated building, before the Romans discovered concrete, and the suitability of gentle, low-pitched roofs, once the Greeks had invented roof-tiles.

[1] For these, see D. Roden Buxton, *Russian Mediaeval Architecture* (Cambridge, 1934), pp. 36–8.

The student of architecture should sometimes reflect on these immemorial practices, which will help to explain, for instance, even the great high roofs of the French Gothic cathedrals. A little earlier, similar roofs, as steeply pitched and in their way nearly as methodical, had appeared over the stave-churches of Norway.[1]

2. PREHELLENIC HISTORY

Excluding early India and China, human civilisation has at least two primary sources at present irreducible to one, in Egypt and Mesopotamia. Both existed as true civilisations at the beginning of the Bronze Age and were flourishing in the third millennium.[2]

The first civilisations of Egypt and Sumer (southern Mesopotamia), though both in great river-valleys, differ fundamentally.[3] The system of hieroglyphs is long confined to Egypt. The wheel, known from the first in Sumer, remains very scarce in Egypt until the Eighteenth Dynasty. Building bricks, straight-sided in Egypt, were plano-convex in Sumer. Mathematics,[4] religion and the very orientation of the temples differ radically in the two countries. Whereas the normal Egyptian tomb or temple has an axis due east and west, the Sumerian ziggurat is sited with its corners on the cardinal points of the compass.[5] With the lapse of ages the Sumerian towered temples slowly rose on the debris of their predecessors, while the Egyptian, with their colonnades and halls, surrounded by successive towns of mud and reeds, came in time to form great hollows, as Herodotus remarked.[6]

Childe[7] notes some slight interchange about 3000 B.C. at the

[1] On this topic, see Atkinson and Bagenal, p. 37.

[2] Childe distinguishes a civilisation by the existence of real cities and the practice of writing. See especially Childe, pp. 128–9.

[3] The distinctive features of a culture appear in general amazingly early. For instance, Childe (third edition, p. 137) had noted evidence that in Elam, the later Persia, the dead were already exposed in Parsee fashion before 3000 B.C. Why does his fourth edition omit this?

[4] See T. L. Heath, *A Manual of Greek Mathematics* (Oxford, 1931), Chaps. I and II. The Mesopotamian notation was quite different and far more advanced.

[5] See Bell, Chap. IV, e.g. pp. 31–2. Only one Egyptian pyramid, a stepped example, square on plan, at El Kolah (near El Kab), is known to have the Sumerian orientation. It is of the Third Dynasty, and so earlier than the Great Pyramid.

[6] *Histories*, II, 138, ii.

[7] Especially p. 240. I owe to Childe all my information on the predynastic phases in Egypt and Mesopotamia.

very beginning of the First Egyptian Dynasty, when cylinder seals, always used for the ordinary flat seal from the beginning of truly civilised times at least in southern Mesopotamia, make a momentary appearance in Egypt. But this is a trivial flicker. We have no documented synchronism between the two countries before the fourteenth century B.C. The earliest Aegean centres, even those of Crete, developed later than those of Egypt and Sumer. But by 2000 B.C. Crete, at least, had reached such brilliance and independence that we must give it a special place. By then, as Schaeffer says,[1] it was in many things leading the world.

Although Sumer had developed further than Egypt by the end of the fourth millennium,[2] and was soon to win the lead in metal-work that she always retained, two or three hundred years later Egypt had already taken first place in sculpture and monumental architecture. This is not due only to the excellent stone in Egypt. The Sumerians had ingenious, inventive, scientific minds. The Egyptians were the greater artists. The Cretans, some centuries later still, were challenging Sumerian metallurgy and assuming the leadership in ceramics.

The third millennium, then, is a period of advancing cultures. A certain change comes over history when, at the beginning of the second, Anatolia is conquered by new Indo-European races, the Hittites and the Hurrites, and a related people, the Kassites, threaten and finally conquer the Sumerians and Semites of Mesopotamia. The civilised world becomes wider but more stagnant, and the familiar oriental despotisms occupy lands subjected a millennium earlier to the busy conflicts of traders from small kingdoms and cities. Crete retained its enterprise for a few more centuries. But its culture, with that of its apparent off-shoots, suffered a series of blows, and had disappeared by about 1100 B.C., the beginning of the Iron Age. Egypt and Mesopotamia continued, their real creative age long past, until the days of classical Greece.

[1] *Ugaritica*, III (Paris, 1939), p. 53. Woolley now attributes some features of the later Cretan palaces, notably the 'free use of cement' and the frescoes, to the North Syrian Kingdom of Yamkhad (see *A Forgotten Kingdom*, pp. 76–7). But Crete had already developed much of its characteristic civilisation when it imported these foreign ideas.

[2] See Childe, p. 238. The Royal Tombs at Ur, with their filigreed masterpieces, have now to be dated probably as late as 2500 B.C. (Early Third Dynasty: cf. Childe, p. 151). So in metallurgy Egypt and Sumer were more nearly level about 3000 B.C. than was at one time believed (see, e.g., Childe, third edition, p. 128).

We have sketched the general picture. But to understand these early cultures and their architecture, we must now consider their history in more detail. Each has its own flavour, and, moreover, in the generally decadent period at the end of the second millennium there arise smaller civilisations in the interstices of their predecessors: the Phoenicians, for instance, whose buildings have a certain importance.

In Egypt, successive cultures, culminating in the Gerzean, precede the First Dynasty, the point where written records begin. They seem to be stages in the growth of one people. It is hard to believe with H. R. Hall[1] that the Egyptians were sufficiently civilised by 4240 B.C., to devise the distinctive Egyptian Calendar; and the First Dynasty, of kings from Upper Egypt, seems to have united the country only about 3000 B.C.

Trade at once increased. Egypt, as a powerful economic entity, could at once secure the import of various luxuries, such as cedar wood from Byblos on the coast of Syria. As with other old oriental empires, the long arm of the king could now protect his subjects trading in distant lands. Nor had absolute monarchy, that raised the standards of life so miraculously in one or two generations, yet suffered the moral tarnishing of the next three millennia. Indeed, with all its faults, it alone seemed to offer the world the chance of improvement, until its prestige was at last shattered by a new form of government in the early fifth century B.C. So the erection and decoration of its palaces and official temples engrossed over the ages the labours of its subjects. But it was never more welcome nor more powerful than at the dawn of Egyptian history.

There follows the Old Kingdom of the Pyramid Builders, with its capital at Memphis, near Cairo, which embraced the first six dynasties, down to about 2500 B.C.[2] Through most of this period the Pharaohs devoted all their wealth and all the skill of their architects to ensuring the physical survival for ever of their embalmed bodies and their choicest possessions. Their activities culminated at Gizeh in the Fourth Dynasty, under Cheops and

---

[1] *Cambridge Ancient History*, I, p. 258. For arguments against Hall, see now Childe, p. 4.

[2] No Egyptian dates are satisfactorily established even now before 1580 B.C. (Hall, *op. cit.*, p. 227), the beginning of the Eighteenth Dynasty. For the sequence we have to rely on excerpts from Manetho, a scribe of the third century B.C., supplemented by documents much earlier but very fragmentary.

Chephren.   By the Sixth Dynasty this great attempt was clearly
failing.   The most despotic government could neither defeat the
determination of the tomb-robbers nor make further inroads, for
the cult of the ever-growing numbers of royal and noble dead,
on the starved and depleted labourers.   Before its inevitable collapse, the Old Kingdom had sunk to entrusting the safety of the
dead to magical sentences—the so-called Pyramid Texts.[1]   Never
again was building, or even painted decoration, to reach the scale
and durability that distinguish the work of the Old Kingdom.
Nor was any later age to alter at all seriously the types and canons
it had set.   The Middle Kingdom, erected towards 2000 B.C. on
the ruins of the Old, but with a new capital, Thebes (the modern
Karnak and Luxor), some four hundred miles up the Nile from
Memphis, is distinguished for the classical purity of its language
and the delicacy of its frescoes and jewellery.   Its few extant
buildings show good design and workmanship, but nothing to
rival the Old Kingdom.   It lasted also a shorter time, for the
Eleventh and Twelfth Dynasties only, and at the end, perhaps
during the eighteenth century B.C., was disastrously cut short by
the Hyksos, mysterious conquerors from Asia.   Who these were
and why they left so little but hatred behind them in Egypt, we
may begin to see if we trace Asiatic history to this point.

We can establish no dynastic synchronisms in the early history
of Mesopotamia before about 2350 B.C., when Sargon of Akkad
established his rule over all the cities of Sumer.   A connected
narrative begins only about 2200 B.C., with the great dynasty of Ur.
We are ignorant not from any lack, but from a bewildering
complexity, of records.[2]   Before 2350 B.C. we find numerous
cities, Ur, Eridu, Lagash, Umma, Kish and others, all important,
all independent and all constantly struggling for power and profit.
Thus, although the script punched on clay tablets had already
reached its classical form by 3000 B.C., the cities are too numerous,
their dynasties too short (on an average no more than 100 years),
their annals too biased, their catastrophes and internal revolutions

---

[1] These texts are considered at some length by Breasted, *Religion and
Thought in Ancient Egypt* (London, 1912).   They show the great complexity and occasional sublimity of Egyptian thought on the world of the
dead.

[2] Of the numerous somewhat conflicting chronologies attempted by
modern scholars for all these early civilisations I have found that of
L. Delaporte (*Le Proche-Orient Asiatique* (Paris, 1938)) very convenient.
For synchronisms of cultures before 2350 B.C. the table on Childe,
pp. 232–3, is at present indispensable.

too frequent and complicated and their vast ruins[1] too little explored to allow us more than a few partial glimpses.   Moreover, the Elamites, living in the modern Persia, were always ready, at the first sign of weakness, to overrun and disorganise the whole country.

When, at the end of Sumerian independence and creativeness (about 2100 B.C.), the priestly scribes of Isin attempted to co-ordinate the chronicles of the cities, they did their work so badly that we can trust it in little except, perhaps, the sequence of names within single dynasties.[2]   We do know that they include some historical names in the very early dynasties of their list.   The so-called 'archaic' period, from the earliest of these to the great dynasty of Ur (2200 B.C.), probably lasted about 700 years.

But great, civilised dynasties much older still had disappeared entirely from memory by 2100 B.C.   Queen Shubaid of Ur, for instance, whose death-pit evinces such ghoulish artistry, was apparently forgotten as early as the First Dynasty of Ur,[3] not long after 2500 B.C.   Archaeologists can now trace the emergence of Mesopotamia, with very few gaps, from its original savagery, and have named each successive stage of its culture from the site where it was first identified.

The oldest of all is the rustic culture of Al 'Ubaid, called after the famous site near Ur and remarkable for the beauty of its painted hand-made pottery.   It is followed by another phase first recognised at Uruk (the Biblical Erech), from which date the first monumental temples, the potter's wheel and the earliest sealed accounts.   The succeeding Jemdet Nasr culture, attested through-out lower Mesopotamia, achieves such building triumphs as the

---

[1] Woolley, on p. 1 of his *Royal Cemetery* (London, 1934), calculated that Ur alone, in 2000 B.C., must have had 500,000 inhabitants.   The site of Kish is five miles long (Langdon, *Kish*, IV (Paris, 1924), p. 3). Frankfort has lately tried to deflate the figures for the population of Sumer.   See Childe, p. 168.

[2] Even here they apparently omitted some names.   Thus Woolley found the tablet of King A-Annipadda, son of Mes-Annipadda, in the temple at Al 'Ubaid of the First Dynasty of Ur.   But the Isin lists know only the latter name.   See Childe, third edition, p. 16.   The fourth edition, p. 10, somewhat telescopes these particulars.

[3] Not only had burial customs by then changed completely, but her grave was then hidden from view by the stray burials of commoners above it.   See Woolley, *Royal Cemetery*, pp. 15–16 (but I am not sure how far his arguments are altered by the deflation of the dates.—See above, p. 5, n. 2.).

Temple of Al 'Ubaid. It immediately precedes[1] the earliest kings whose names are found in the Isin lists, and has possible links with the Gerzean phase in Egypt, likewise the immediate predecessor of written history.[2] At its end occurred a widespread flood,[3] and the semi-historical, or 'archaic', phase began about 3000 B.C., perhaps with the dynasty of Kish. For the written history of its seven centuries we still depend chiefly on the monuments discovered by the French[4] at Lagash in Sumer and at Susa, the capital of the Elamites, who stored there the Sumerian trophies they had carried off.

In the 'archaic' age, the Sumerians reached their zenith as an industrial people. Sumer had no natural wealth except in corn, bitumen used as mortar, and a coarse alluvial clay good for nothing but bricks. Palm-trees were too small and rare for any use except as cores of small decorative columns. The few lumps of limestone found near Ur had a limited usefulness. So Sumer had to pay for all her raw materials with manufactured goods, and to build up reserves of capital in special storehouses—the temples.[5] Her priests were kings, her cities theocracies; and temples were to remain the banks of the world down to at least the Hellenistic Age. As the metallurgical centre of the world, she discovered inlaying, soldering, filigree, bronze-casting by *cire perdue* and the use of oxidised metals as a coloured coat for terracotta roof-revetments.[6] The science of hydraulics, especially drainage, was, of course, well understood.

A remarkable early culture much farther north, at Tell Halaf and Arpachiyah, near Aleppo, perhaps anticipated Sumer in some of these discoveries and even in the first serious architecture,[7] but is difficult to date; and the legends of Gilgamesh, like the records of Sargon of Akkad, show that in the third millennium it was Sumer

---

[1] Speaking archaeologically, of course, from the sequence of types of artifacts. As we saw, at Ur the dynasty of the Royal Tombs had been forgotten at the time of the rulers corresponding to the 'First Dynasty of Ur' near the beginning of the Isin lists.

[2] See above, p. 6.

[3] Childe, p. 136.

[4] Their discoveries form the basis for most of King, *History of Sumer and Akkad* (London, 1910), still valuable as a reconstruction of the period half covered by the Isin list.

[5] Childe, p. 124.

[6] See R. Demangel, *La Frise Ionique* (Paris, 1932), p. 58.

[7] Its beautiful pottery seems contemporary with Al 'Ubaid, the first Sumerian epoch of all; and yet it was already building large mud domes, 18 feet in diameter, on stone ground-courses. (See also below, p. 81, n. 4.)

that exploited the cedars of Amanus in north Syria and even the merchandise of Anatolia.[1]   Very early, also, she sent out colonies, notably to Ashur, the nucleus of the later Assyria.   A short, clean-shaven people, naked to the waist and draped below this in a long quilted skirt, the Sumerians are unmistakable on all the monuments of the time in the regions they controlled.

The resentment of the exploited foreigners and the internal disputes of Sumer began about 2400 B.C. to produce their effects. The half-submerged Semites of Mesopotamia asserted themselves, with Sargon of Akkad as their champion, and began to oust Sumerian from the inscribed monuments.   His dynasty was short-lived and followed by renewed Sumerian leadership under the great kings of Ur, and the culmination of Sumerian sculpture under Gudea of Lagash (*c.* 2200 B.C.).   But soon after—before 2050—Ashur asserted her freedom, and a little later still a dynasty of Semitic Amorites, now established at Babylon, conquered Sumer and Akkad and turned them into Babylonia.   In codifying the laws, the Amorite King Hammurabi gathered the last harvest of Sumerian civilisation, and after his dynasty a long barren period began.

The state of Asia Minor in the third millennium is still obscure to us, and was probably backward.   About 2000 B.C. we find small 'concessions' of Assyrian traders there, exploiting the local principalities and protected by the power of the Assyrian king. One such 'concession' was the famous Karum of Kanesh.   By contrast, the Aegean coast seems to have enjoyed the dawn of a native civilisation, to judge from the remains of Early Minoan Crete and the second city of Troy.[2]   Nor was the Cretan culture, then in its Middle Minoan phase, interrupted, like the Egyptian and Babylonian, by the northern invaders of *c.* 1700 B.C.

About that time a group of partly Aryan peoples, represented by the Hittites, Hurrites and Kassites, already, as Woolley has shown, in possession of Aleppo and Alalakh in north Syria, transformed Asia Minor and overran Babylonia, where they founded the long-lived but ignoble Kassite Dynasty.   Egypt, too,

---

[1] See L. Delaporte, *Les Hittites* (Paris, 1936), pp. 39 ff. and Sir Leonard Woolley, *A Forgotten Kingdom*, p. 28.

[2] Crete may have derived some elements from the mysterious culture of Arpachiyah and Tell Halaf, mentioned above (p. 9).   The Halafian domed circles, however, thought by some to be ancestors of the Early Minoan, were not sepulchral.   See M. E. L. Mallowan and J. C. Rose, *Prehistoric Assyria* (Oxford, 1935), p. 34.

after the Middle Kingdom, collapsed before them. We can probably see here the first sensational success of hardy mountaineers over ancient but effete civilisations, a success repeated by Persia and Macedon later.[1] But only the Hittites erected a strong and lasting kingdom this time. The Egyptians expelled the invaders, there called Hyksos, before 1570 B.C.

Meanwhile Crete and her possible trading outposts, the ports of Ugarit and Alalakh in Syria (the last named under a new dynasty), continued their brilliant progress, with merely local and temporary setbacks. Transforming all that they borrowed from Egypt and Asia, the Cretans now entered the Late Minoan phase and made their influence strongly felt, from 1600 B.C. onwards, in some favoured corners of the Aegean world,[2] notably Mycenae and Tiryns. Great roads, carried over bridges and causeways, began to radiate from these Greek centres, as already from Cnossus, the Cretan capital. Crete now led the world in ceramics, rivalled in hydraulic science the Sumerians of 1,000 years before and emulated in the minor arts the masterpieces of Middle Kingdom Egypt. Even her mysterious overthrow, *c.* 1400 B.C., did little immediate harm to the rest of the culture she had led, which developed steadily for another two centuries.

By 1400 B.C. we see a new international balance of power. The Kassites had become Babylonian; the Hittite Kings of Hattusas (Boghazköï, near the modern Ankara) had consolidated an empire, whose culture seems to owe something, particularly in architecture, to its neighbour the Aegean; while the Egyptians, by force of reaction against the Hyksos, had conquered everything as far as the Euphrates. These were the glorious days of the New Kingdom, of Hatshepsut (1501–1479), Thothmes III (1501–1447) and Amenhotep III (1412–1376). The shrunken Kingdom of Mitanni alone remained of the Hurrite nation. The Amarna Tablets, of the earlier fourteenth century, from the archives of Amenhotep IV (Akhnaton), reveal the diplomatic relations of all these powers. For a moment, about 1350 B.C., Egypt weakened, demoralised by the famous heresy of Akhnaton. But our general picture, restored about 1275 B.C. by the treaty of Rameses II and the Hittites, stays much the same down to 1200 B.C., when the

---

[1] No one has described this process more eloquently than Herodotus, in the magnificent conclusion of his *Histories*.

[2] Attempts at present being made serve only to show the difficulty of relating the political histories of Mycenae, Crete and the Syrian outposts.

northern sea-raiders appeared and heralded the Iron Age. Obliterating the Aegean culture and its Syrian outposts, they destroyed the Hittite Empire, overran Egyptian Asia and, though repulsed by Rameses III, reduced Egypt itself to five centuries of exhaustion, broken only by momentary revivals under Sheshonk (950 B.C.) and some Ethiopians (*c.* 720–667). As the date of this barbarian turmoil exactly coincides with that later assigned by the Greeks to the expedition against Troy, the subject of the great Homeric epics, it becomes a nice point to determine whether Homer is writing about the last great Aegean kings of the Bronze Age or about their destroyers.

At the same time Assyria became, for reasons still obscure, a strong military power.[1] Hitherto a watch-dog on the frontier, she turned wolf. Her first great militarist, Tiglath Pileser I, conquered the south-east portion of the ruined Hittite Empire (1110 B.C.). But, for reasons again obscure, she withdrew once more into her shell for another two centuries. These two quiet centuries, marked everywhere by an absence of destructive empires, are vital in the history of civilisation. The Semites of south Syria, now called Phoenicians, became habituated to an alphabet of the form we now use, with the letters standing for radicals, not whole syllables.[2] Their neighbours and near relatives, the Israelites, developed monotheism at the same time. Politically, this age left a complex of small states capable of uniting and strong enough to withstand Assyria until 750 B.C. Even in the arts, Syria between 1100 and 700 has a creative role of some importance. Now was devised that repertory of decoration, common to large buildings and tiny ivories, encountered by the new Aegean settlers, the classical Greeks, when, after five centuries of obscure growth, they first lifted their eyes eastward during the seventh century B.C. The influence of the larger Syrian buildings, known best from Senjirli and Tell Halaf, passed both east and west. A powerful though little-known state, Urartu, arose in Armenia at this time, and was still troubling Assyria in the eighth century.

[1] We find a new dynasty, that of Pashe, replacing the Kassites in Babylon a few years before (1180 B.C.), but we cannot appreciate the significance of the change.
[2] Modern discoveries push back this invention, e.g. at Ugarit, where a Phoenician element was clearly living in the second millennium, having perhaps developed out of Amorite stock during the third (see Schaeffer, *Ugaritica*, III, p. 15). But only now can we detect a general Phoenician culture, with a common use of the Phoenician alphabet.

According to Sidney Smith,[1] it was closely connected not merely by policy but by race and culture with the Syrian league.   He traces motifs that originated in eighth-century Urartu and were transferred through north Syria to the infant civilisation of Greece.[2] The Assyrians themselves lifted many features wholesale from north Syria.

But in an age of fighting kingdoms, the military genius of Assyria at last broke down every enemy.   The century from 750 to 650 is the Assyrian Age.   Sennacherib thoroughly sacked Babylon.   Ashurbanipal not only obliterated Elam, after 2,500 years, but sacked Thebes itself, the capital of Egypt.   As Assyria slowly wore herself down, outlying provinces began to shake off the yoke.   Egypt passed under a native dynasty from Sais in the Delta (666–525 B.C.), and Asia Minor under Lydians ruling at Sardis. Chaldeans from the Persian Gulf were hovering off Babylon, ready to seize it at the first moment of Assyrian weakness. Elsewhere, the miserable people were invaded by Scyths from south Russia and slowly conquered by a new Aryan nation, the Medes, now occupying the mountains of Armenia and north-west Persia, the former land of Urartu.

Between 611 and 605 the Assyrians were annihilated, fighting to the last man.   The Medes seized their northern territories, the Chaldeans, now established in Babylon, their southern.   The Babylonians, under their new regime, set their hands to an extensive, almost feverish restoration of the old cities.   In this age under Nebuchadnezzar they tasted their last real prosperity; and the Near East enjoyed up to 550 B.C. a perfect balance of power between Saite Egypt, Lydia, Media and Babylonia.

Then a small Aryan power, Persia, which had grown up in the derelict centre of Elam and was now under the great Cyrus, conquered all four states in twenty-five years.   Babylon and Egypt had now, for all their splendour, no real vitality, for they had each suffered several millennia of priesthood and bureaucracy. Cyrus's conquest of this area offers obvious parallels to the Arabs', twelve hundred years later.   The Medes, as near relations of the Persians, retained a privileged place in the new empire.   Only once, on the death of Cyrus's son, Cambyses, were they to give the

---

[1] In the *Antiquaries' Journal*, 1942, pp. 88 ff.
[2] Clearly too early, this, for Greek architecture!   But there is a close resemblance between the early Greek columns at Neandria and articles of furniture that the experts attribute to Urartu.

Persians trouble.   Darius, who then reconquered the empire for
Persia, enforced his own control, organised the lands in satrapies,
each under a Persian nobleman, and improved trade by building
an impressive system of roads.   The Persian kings soon found
Babylon a more central and convenient town than their native
towns, Susa and Persepolis, near the south-east fringe of their
empire.   However, they returned to these for the summer months,
and held some of their most colourful levées in the pavilions
erected there by foreign or subject craftsmen.   Simple-minded
soldiers, they proved unequal, except in Palestine, to fostering the
cultures of these dying lands.   Even before the next conquest of
Asia, by Alexander the Great (330 B.C.), the irrigation of Sumer
was becoming too difficult, and Ur of the Chaldees, after over
three thousand years of history, was almost as deserted as it is
today.[1]

[1] The latest tablet known from Ur is dated to the twelfth year of
Alexander the Great (Woolley, *Royal Cemetery*, p. 3).

CHAPTER II

EGYPTIAN ARCHITECTURE

Of all these civilisations, Egypt had an architecture the most homogeneous, the most imposing and the longest-lived. Indeed, it survived the conquest by the Persians under Cambyses in 525 B.C., and even that by Alexander two centuries later, to blossom once more under Macedonian Greek kings, the Ptolemies. Even after the suicide of Cleopatra, the last Ptolemy, in 30 B.C., it preserved many of its forms as late as the reign of Diocletian (A.D. 284–305). So strongly had it resisted outside influences that the Ptolemaic temples are indistinguishable, at first sight, from those of a thousand years before. We take it, then, in its entirety before the architectures of all other early peoples.

Egypt consists of two parts, Upper Egypt, the last five hundred miles of the Nile Valley, and Lower Egypt, the delta of the river, a nearly equilateral triangle of alluvium on a side about one hundred miles long, and with the apex at Memphis (Cairo). Its earliest buildings were of reeds and mud, the shapes of which the stone temples fairly faithfully copy. There was little rain to fear over most of the country. Like the Greek, the Egyptian technique of building 'exports' rather badly.

The existing monuments give a rather lopsided view of the Ancient Egyptians. The flimsy booths and bouquets of everyday life, from which they drew the elements of their architecture, are known, of course, only from frescoes.[1] Even royal palaces are now barely known, apart from foundations at el 'Amarna and Memphis and the small apartments and banqueting halls of stone found once or twice attached to stone temples. Moreover, the annual floods and the fellaheen have destroyed all ancient cities, such as Sais and Buto, in the zone of cultivation, while the accumulation of silt, by raising the level of the Nile, has led to the flooding and often the destruction of buildings such as Karnak, once high

---

[1] As at Akhnaton's new mushroom capital, el 'Amarna. See Frankfort, F. G. *Newton Memorial Volume* (London, 1929), a beautiful book.

and dry in the desert.[1]   The temples of the Middle Kingdom at
Deir-el-Bahari, Karnak and Luxor were pillaged or entirely rebuilt in the New Kingdom,[2] few of whose monarchs respected
the work even of their own dynasties.[3]   Rameses II is notorious
for the number of buildings he destroyed, or appropriated by
setting his cartouche upon them.   One may compare conditions
in modern Burma, where it is meritorious to erect but not to
conserve, or in Renaissance Rome.

Nevertheless, the great religious buildings, on which the
Egyptians had set their heart, still show fairly enough the values
they placed highest.   As Champollion said, 'No people, either
ancient or modern, have had a national architecture at once so
sublime in scale, so grand in expression, and so free from littleness
as that of the ancient Egyptians.'   They have left monuments far
surpassing in size and magnificence those of any other race of
monarchs, the Roman Emperors not excepted.   That they achieved
so much is due largely to the brute force that their numbers and
perfect organisation made possible.   But it is their yearning for
personal immortality that alone explains their architecture.

I. THE OLD KINGDOM

The vast monuments of the Old Kingdom, all sepulchral, cover
an area on the west side of the Nile about fifty miles long and over
two miles broad.[4]   They are of two kinds: royal tombs, or
pyramids, and private tombs, or mastabas—an Arabic word,
meaning a platform used as a seat.   Each kind contains a chamber
for the embalmed bodies, or mummies, of the dead, whose cult
required a sumptuous room for their comfort in the future life
and a place for worship and offerings.   The Egyptians generally
preferred to place their tombs in the western desert with its wide

---

[1] The floods penetrate the porous stone and leave salts inside the
columns upon evaporation.   A trench 7 metres deep has now been dug
round the main group of Temples at Karnak.   See Clarke and Engelbach,
pp. 69 ff.

[2] See, e.g., Naville, *Deir-el-Bahari*, VI (1908), p. 18; Jéquier, *Temples
Memphites et Thébains* (Paris, 1920), Pl. 10.

[3] An exception is the Mortuary Temple of Seti I at Abydos, intended
largely for the worship of much older kings and aligned on a landmark
guiding it to their tombs.   See Petrie, in Caulfeild, *The Temple of the
Kings* (London, 1902), p. 14.

[4] 'The pyramid field extends from Abu Rowash in the north to Lahun
in the south, a distance of about fifty miles.'   See M. A. Murray,
Egyptian Temples (London, 1931), p. 4.

A house at Trelleborg, Jutland

Plate 1

Zoser's Colonnade, Sakkara

Granite Temple, Gizeh

Plate 2

Pylons at Edfou

plateau of limestone; and from nearly the beginning we find royal temples, among the most beautiful ever built in Egypt, some for worship and some for embalming, to the east of the pyramids. The passage to the tomb chamber is itself always from the north. In the temples in each case were the famous portrait-statues, intended to house the souls of the dead, should the mummies be destroyed. The pyramids themselves can hardly be said to possess architectural pretensions, but are, after all, the largest and oldest structures of civilised times.

Mastabas, of course, are far more numerous than pyramids, and cluster around them. At Gizeh they form whole streets laid out at right angles by the royal architect.[1] They vary greatly in size—many of the examples published by Reisner exceed 100 feet in length—and present a simple version in stone of the older, larger and more complicated royal mastabas of mud-brick found under the first three dynasties. These private mastabas often have no attached chambers, merely niches for offerings, although in the Fourth Dynasty cemetery at Gizeh, as Reisner shows, the attached chamber was still the rule. Space could be found for an offering-chamber, or 'chapel', in the thickness of the actual mastaba, normally a vestibule containing the 'stele', a pillar set in the wall and the centre of the cult of the dead. The stele is often of a harder stone than the rest, and represents a closed door and an open window above, through which the dead man is often seen feasting with his wife. Corresponding apparently to the dining-room door in an ordinary house, it 'contains in a small space everything indispensable to the dead man. It not only allows him to enter and leave his underground domain, but assures him subsistence by its position over the table of offerings and often by the list of victuals it contains. A sort of picture, an open window on to the interior, shows him feasting in his tomb. In addition, prayers and formulae secure him a place close to the gods of the dead. His name, carved in large characters, recalls the old function of the stele in marking the grave; while the enumeration of his titles perpetuates his career upon earth.'[2]

The other walls of the vestibule are often decorated with

[1] For mastabas see, above all, Reisner, *Giza Necropolis*, I (Cambridge (Mass.), 1942). Their elements and the stages of their construction are given on pp. 29 ff.

[2] Jéquier, *Manuel d'Archéologie Egyptienne* (Paris, 1924), p. 356. He is more plausible than J. Capart (*Egyptian Art* (London, 1923), p. 83), who believes the stele to represent a small shrine or booth.

representations of everyday life, the preparation, according to Maspero, of all that went to the dead man's feast.[1]   These low-relief pictures of oxen ploughing, of men and women crushing grapes, winnowing corn, picking flax, or stacking the crops, are of the greatest interest, and afford absolutely reliable proof of the manners and customs of the people.[2]

Occasionally the vestibule was omitted, when the stele would stand in a recess in the outer wall of the mastaba.   At other times, a second stele, recessed either in the outer wall or in the vestibule, recalled the exterior of the dead man's house.   It seems to show a structure of poles and laths, with decorative trimmings of wood but without the concave 'Egyptian' cornice.   Jéquier[3] even uses it as evidence for the vanished coping of the large, very early royal mastabas, distinguished on plan from these mastabas largely by the complicated projections and re-entrants of their walls which would have made an 'Egyptian'[4] cornice impossible.

The mummy-chamber lies immediately below the vestibule and is excavated in the rock.   It is approached by a vertical shaft, generally 40 feet deep, cut both through the solid rock and the actual mastaba.   The structure above ground contained behind the vestibule and at right angles to it one or more walled-up passages, or serdabs, each with one or more statues, sculptured 'doubles' of the deceased intended to house his soul should his mummy be destroyed.

Mastabas are sometimes square, more often oblong in plan, are flat topped and have sides battered at an angle of about 75 degrees, like the sides of early 'step-pyramids'.   Their construction is very solid.   In fact, the walls generally cover a greater area than all the inner rooms.   The origin of the type in piles of mud brick is obvious, and we can now trace its development in the royal mastabas of the first three dynasties (see Fig. 4). Each of these was a large, oblong, indented building set down inside a precinct wall, between which and their own many-buttressed outer faces are found the bodies of slaves and animals,

[1] *Manual of Egyptian Archaeology* (London, 1895), pp 123-4.
[2] The same may be said of most Egyptian reliefs of such scenes.   The burden of proof certainly rests on Engelbach, when, to fit his theories on the obelisks, he denies that the famous reliefs of Hatshepsut at Deir-el-Bahari (see below, p. 37) give a true picture of their transport.   See Engelbach in *The Legacy of Egypt* (ed. S. R. Glanville, Oxford, 1942).
[3] *Manuel*, p. 86.
[4] For this term see below, p. 52.   Capart, *op. cit.*, Pl. X, shows the Royal Mastaba of Naqada.

sacrificed to serve the king in the next world—in those early days the priests had not discovered the efficacy of pictures. The earliest of all contained a large room for the king, with smaller rooms around it, probably for more victims. The whole was made inaccessible to the mourners above, who had no chapel, only some niches between the buttresses of the mastaba. Only in the Third Dynasty were stairs provided to the burial chambers.[1]

A king of the same dynasty, Zoser, erected the first pyramid, at Sakkara. It consists of a very high and attenuated mastaba core, rectangular on plan, with a series of diminishing accretions on all sides, and so presents the misleading appearance of a series of superimposed mastabas. At Medum, however, some accretions have fallen away, thus revealing the true structure. The cores of later pyramids, even down to the Fifth Dynasty, are built in the same way; for instance, in the Pyramid of Sahure at Abusir (see Fig. 5), where the sloping external faces in the style of Gizeh form, structurally speaking, a mere coating for a building like Sakkara. The exterior was thus transformed from a step pyramid to a true pyramid,

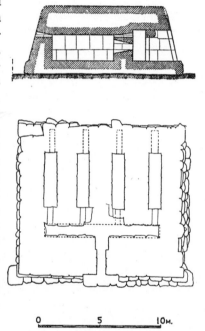

Fig. 4   Egyptian Mastaba.

probably to satisfy the sun-worshippers.[2] The sacred Benben Stone, a meteorite supposed to have fallen from the sun and long worshipped at Heliopolis, must have had the shape of a

[1] As at Tarkhan.   See Fig. 44 of Childe (third edition), from whom I take my account of royal mastabas.   The mastaba of Hor-Aha (Childe, fourth edition, Fig. 43) is generally similar, but with the burial shaft below the small rooms.

[2] Breasted, *Religion and Thought in Ancient Egypt* (London, 1912), pp. 12 ff.   The extraordinary construction of the core was apparently paralleled in at least one Elamite ziggurat—see below, p. 61.

pyramidion and was copied in the divine apex of every obelisk. The continuous sloping sides of the new form of pyramid persuaded the builders to adopt a square ground plan, instead of the rectangle of Sakkara.

We see, then, that the pyramidal shape, at first sight so obvious and primitive, in fact results from a long and tortuous development. We must be careful which architectural forms we take for granted.

The developed pyramid contained a tomb chamber with entrance shaft on the north side, and had on its east side a temple for offerings to the dead, a processional causeway from the Nile for the dead Pharaoh, a landing-stage and, beside this, a temple for the embalming. The pyramid group of Zoser at Sakkara is

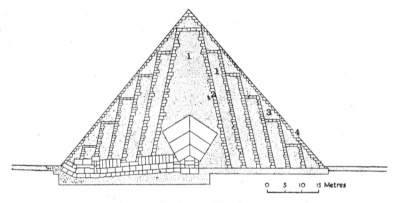

O   5   10   15 Metres

Fig. 5   Pyramid of Sahure, Abusir: cross-section.

still primitive. The limestone he used, which remained the normal building material of the Old and Middle Kingdoms, permitted safe spans no greater than 9 feet.[1]   The arch was, of course, unknown in this stone architecture, an affair of vertical posts and horizontal lintels entirely; and the early dynasties resorted, for their larger beams, only to granite quarries, notably those of Syene (Assuan). Zoser and his famous architect Imhotep[2] were not yet competent to use stone as hard as granite. So we find in their work half-columns engaged to the short ends of remarkable, closely spaced piers crossing the axis of the building (see Pl. 1).

[1] Clarke and Engelbach, p. 9.
[2] For whose career see J. B. Hurry, *Imhotep* (Oxford, 1926).

The visible joints of the masonry are very fine, but the work behind is coarse and rough. The Egyptians never devised a proper bond, and seem seldom to have used a mason's square[1] before Greek times. Zoser's masons apparently fitted each stone to its neighbour by repeatedly lifting and chipping it as they made the wall. Their blocks are small, imitating mud-bricks; but the thin Egyptian mortar, intended chiefly to distribute the load during setting, has already appeared at Sakkara.

The oldest true pyramid on a square base is at Medum. But we hasten to the most famous, the three of the Fourth Dynasty at Gizeh, built for Kings Cheops, Chephren and Mycerinus. Their masonry is immeasurably superior to that of Sakkara. Except for the tomb chamber and the corridors which lead to it, they are solid, and were faced with limestone or granite, the latter being used for the ground-course of the second pyramid and the lower portion of the third. The facing blocks are trapezoids of great size, and were laid with horizontal beds; the face of each block being worked to the required angle and then polished. The accuracy with which the pyramids were set out appears conspicuously in the Great Pyramid of Cheops. Its mean length at the base is 755·8 feet, and the difference between its longest and shortest sides about 8 inches. The height of this pyramid is 481·4 feet, and the angle of the casing to the horizon is 51 degrees 52 minutes, which is about the usual slope, although all the examples vary slightly.[2]

The ruling principles on which the pyramids were erected were everlasting durability and eternal secrecy. The entrance to each was carefully concealed, the body was hidden away, and special care was taken to guard against its discovery and profanation. These precautions have proved vain; and hardly a pyramid exists which has not been entered and rifled. No decoration is to be found inside, although in most instances the mummy chamber and the corridor are lined with carefully finished stone. We know from the contemporary tomb of Queen Hetep-Heres how sumptuously

---

[1] This apparently existed late in the New Kingdom. See Clarke and Engelbach, Fig. 264.

[2] Where possible I have corrected my dimensions from Clarke and Engelbach, who in Chap. 5 have made various suggestions, all resting on inference alone, on the way the Egyptians obtained true right angles (by sighting along the lines of a gnomon and turning it through 180 degrees) and a level site (by temporarily flooding the ground and obtaining equal depths at many scattered points below the surface of the water).

some chambers could be furnished.[1] But the dead king was still, it seems, supposed to take pleasure less in the pictured scenes of his past life than in the megalithic nobility of his surroundings. Even the offering temples of the Fourth Dynasty

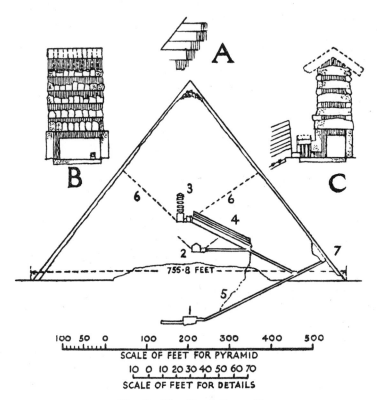

Fig. 6   The Great Pyramid.

1 = First Chamber.
2 = Second Chamber.
3 = Final Chamber.
4 = Great Corridor.
5 = Passage (workmen's escape passage?).
6 = Air-shafts.
7 = Main Entrance to Pyramid.

A = Outer Casing of Pyramid.
B = Final Chamber, longitudinal-section.
C = Final Chamber, cross-section.

[1] The reconstructed furniture is shown in the Cairo Museum.   For illustrations of some pieces see Sir E. D. Ross, *The Art of Egypt through the Ages* (London, 1931), pp. 116–17.   The new discoveries this spring (1954) at Sakkara and Gizeh will presumably throw a flood of new light on this subject.

look severe compared with later works. But as late as the Middle Kingdom the burial chamber of Amenemhet III in his pyramid at Hawara is a monolith with an internal hollow 22 feet long, 8 feet wide and 6 feet high.[1] The sarcophagi too are plain. All this is in great contrast with the pictured corridors and elaborate sarcophagi of Pharaohs of the New Kingdom, of which we possess a noble example in the Soane Museum. We tend to forget that Egyptian religion and burial customs evolved considerably during the centuries.

The corridor and chamber were probably built in one piece before the rest of the core. The chamber has a different position in each pyramid. In the third it is excavated in the rock, some 33 feet beneath the lowest course of stone; whereas in the Great Pyramid the present chamber is placed about one-third of the height of the building above ground level (see Fig. 6). But this pyramid contains two earlier, abortive chambers, the first below ground, the second about halfway between the ground and the final chamber.[2] Such changes of plan are not unusual in pyramids.

Elaborate, though primitive, precautions were taken to protect the corridors and chambers from the heavy mass of masonry above. In the Great Pyramid the final chamber, 17 feet wide and twice as long, has five tiers of lintels over it, with a space between each pair, and above these huge lintel stones slope upwards and butt against one another in order to throw the weight to its sides. The corridor is roofed on the 'corbel' principle; each stone course projects very slightly beyond that immediately below it, thus gradually diminishing the width, until the opening at the top is sufficiently narrow to be spanned by lintels.[3]

Of the offering temple attached to this pyramid little but the floor survives. By contrast, the Second Pyramid, of Chephren, retains much of its original setting, planned, unlike the congeries of courts and passages at Sakkara, by one great architect, the earliest in history whose character still stands out (see Fig. 7). Above the landing-stage stands the Great Sphinx, representing the king himself as the sun on guard over his pyramid. Carved from a

[1] See Petrie, *Kahun, Gurob and Hawara* (London, 1890), p. 16. The roof is a separate block.
[2] The second is often wrongly called the Queen's Chamber. But queens and princesses, we now know, were never buried in the pyramid of the king, but in separate small pyramids on its eastern side (information I owe to Mr. Alan Rowe).
[3] The best picture of this is still probably that in Napoleon's *Egypt* (Vol. V, Pl. XIII).

jutting rock some 66 feet high, it is the mightiest of many similar composite forms executed at all periods of Egyptian art.[1] Mistaken, centuries later, for Harmachis the Sun-God, it was

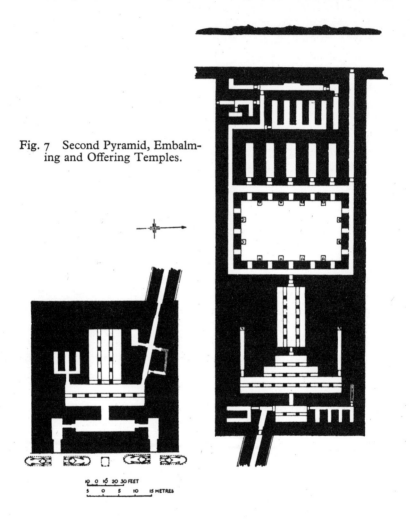

Fig. 7   Second Pyramid, Embalming and Offering Temples.

---

[1] For the benefit of readers unfamiliar with ancient mythologies, one may observe that a sphinx is a human-headed lion, a siren, a human-headed bird, a gryphon, a blend of a lion and an eagle. These are common to the mythology of Greece and the Ancient East. But the Egyptians went further and endued their greater gods with animal forms —a practice which, if prevalent in Early Greece, survives in classical times only in a few literary epithets.

given a small temple between its paws and a second, larger, temple
to the east. Beside the Sphinx is the famous Granite Temple, its
two entrances guarded by sphinxes of their own. Here Chephren
was embalmed on his way to the tomb. The T-shaped plan
comprises a long ante-chapel of two aisles and a main chapel of
three aisles. The pillars, as in the contemporary temple of Osiris
at Abydos, are rectangular monoliths of red granite, and are 15 feet
high, without capitals or bases. They support a plain red granite
architrave of comparable blocks. The enclosing walls are faced
internally with red granite, and the ceiling was entirely of granite
slabs (see Pl. 2). The lighting was originally indirect and subtle,
by vertical wells hollowed in the thickness of the walls and
suddenly turning at right angles into the temple. Colossal green
diorite statues of Chephren, about the severest and noblest work
of the Old Kingdom, stood one between each pair of pillars.
Fragments of nine are known. This contrast of dark green and
dark red resembles little in later classical architecture. The
Treasury of Atreus at Mycenae affords a limited parallel. North-
west of the ante-chapel begins the causeway to the pyramid,[1]
600 yards long and flanked originally by the royal bark and the two
solar barks meant to accompany Chephren on his voyage with the
sun to the realms of the blessed. Before the east front of the
pyramid are remains of the offering temple, where worshippers
collected for the cult of the dead king. Much larger than the
Granite Temple, it contained a long rectangular vestibule, a
square colonnaded court and inner shrines, separated by engaged
pillars with attached statues of the king, of the type known in later
examples as 'Osirid'. In 'Osirid' piers, the statues are invariably
attached to the fronts of pillars and carved from the same blocks.
Under the New Kingdom they represent the Pharaoh as Osiris,
God of the Underworld. In the plan of this temple, we see
already the long approach, the colonnaded vestibule and court
and the inner shrine familiar to us in scores of later Egyptian
temples, but seldom so nobly laid out as here.

But the simple sublimity of this early architecture was to give
way in the next dynasty to art of a more ordinary kind. In the
offering temple of Sahure at Abusir the columns of the court have
dactyliform capitals of palm-leaves (see Fig. 23 (i)), the oldest
known,[2] and the walls are covered with painted reliefs of corpulent

---

[1] Jéquier, *Temples* (Paris, 1920), Pl. 2.
[2] *Ibid.*, Pl. 5, 2; Capart, p. 67 and Pl. XI.

tribute-bearers, so-called 'Niles', in procession. One may admit their ornamental purpose was secondary. But the change is lamentable. The pyramids, too, are now more stunted. Several centuries after Cheops, the exhaustion of the people, the failure of the endowments and the unwise grant of lands to the nobles were to bring down the Old Kingdom in ruin.

2. THE MIDDLE KINGDOM

Power now shifts to Thebes, and under the Eleventh Dynasty we can discern the beginnings of the great national temples in the Theban plain and the royal tombs and temples in the gorges around the Nile.

Some tombs, notably at Abydos, are still pyramidal, but small

and steep and of crude brick (see Fig. 8). Externally, they are only 25 feet high.[1] Square on plan, and sited on the axis of a small rectangular enclosure, they have a small arched porch at ground level, attached to the front of the pyramid; and internally two chambers, one below and one above ground. The

Fig. 8   Brick Pyramid, Abydos.

lower, which had almost straight sides, a segmental tunnel vault running from back to front, and no means of access, is said by Mariette to have contained the mummy. The upper was internally a beehive of circular plan and ogival cross-section, built up of corbelled brick-courses. The resemblance of these chambers to the beehive-tombs of Mycenae[2] is probably accidental. They are a last withered, almost rational remnant of the Age of Pyramids, and are soon supplanted by a very different type of tomb, the 'Grotto', perhaps Asiatic in origin.[3] The most famous are the grottoes at Beni Hasan, excavated in cliffs on the east side of the Nile (see Pl. 3). The fronts are open and resemble porticoes, since portions of the rock are left standing as columns to support the weight

[1] F. Mariette, *Abydos*, II (Paris, 1869–80), Pl. 66.
[2] For which, see below, pp. 82 ff.
[3] One thinks of the Cave of Machpelah, bought by Abraham as the burial-place of his family. See Genesis xxiii.

above. The tombs have in some cases one chamber, in others two or three, their roofs often supported by rock columns different in design from those of the façade. The roofs are in many cases not flat but segmental. Since we have just noticed segmental brick vaults in the brick pyramids, and true brick arches of many shapes are found throughout Egyptian history, there seems no need to follow the ingenious theory of Choisy that the roofs of Beni-Hasan copied ceilings of logs laid longitudinally side by side, partly supporting one another and thus giving a curve.[1] The walls of the chambers are frequently decorated with sculpture and painting of a high order, showing that in the new form of tomb the old ritual of burial and commemoration largely remained.[2]

Of the two kinds of columns, the internal have typical Egyptian forms. The shaft rests on a low circular plinth and resembles a bundle of lotus stalks tied immediately under the buds, which form the 'echinus' of the capital. The other kind, at the entrances, designed to harmonise with their stern setting, are really piers, roughly planed to give eight or sixteen sides, except at the top, where a few inches are left square and so form the simplest of capitals, flush with the smooth portion of rock above that acts as the architrave. The multangular form is almost as strong as the square, but less clumsy, and offers less obstruction to sunlight and visitors.

These rock-cut piers were called by Champollion and other early writers 'Proto-Doric' columns. We shall return to this question.[3] We need only note here that, Deir-el-Bahari excepted, they appear on no buildings of the New Kingdom, and so, it seems, fell out of fashion nearly a thousand years before the beginning of Greek architecture. This argument is not by itself absolutely conclusive, since the towns of the Delta, the most accessible to the Greeks, have now so completely perished.

Jéquier has traced a few remains at Karnak,[4] but only one temple of the Middle Kingdom substantially survives—the mortuary

---

[1] Choisy, *L'Art de Bâtir chez les Égyptiens* (Paris, 1904), pp. 5–6. A similar curve appears in stone on one of the first buildings of the Old Kingdom, at Sakkara. Roman architecture shows that the form is natural both to brick and stone.

[2] These tombs and their decoration have been measured and published by P. E. Newberry, *Beni Hasan*, 2 vols. (Egypt. Expl. Fund, 1893).

[3] See below, p. 84.

[4] *Temples*, I, p. 3.

temple of Mentuhetep II, a king of the Eleventh Dynasty, at Deir-el-Bahari.[1] Standing to the south of the later, famous, temple, it was much more carefully constructed. Like its neighbour, it formed a series of terraced colonnades facing eastwards, the roofs of which were reached from below at right angles, by long ramps on its central axis. The inner court, however, before the shrine, was here quite filled by a small stone pyramid, surrounded by an ambulatory several columns deep, but containing no burial chamber. The king was possibly buried in the cliffs near by. From the westernmost aisle of the ambulatory opened the shrine. The architect still employed the square piers and simple architraves of the Old Kingdom. But he already painted the underside of his roof slabs with gold stars on a sky-blue field, a convention henceforward followed not only in Egypt but on Greek, Roman and Byzantine ceilings.

3. THE NEW KINGDOM

Under the glorious Eighteenth and Nineteenth Dynasties (1580–1200 B.C.), Egyptian architecture proliferates. The sandstone from the quarries of Silsilah, near Thebes, ignored by the Old Kingdom, possibly as too soft, makes practicable the roofing of far larger spans. The hypostyle hall with wider and loftier central aisle makes its first appearance. Large pyramids are no longer built, but their place in the landscape is taken by the gate-towers of the temples, erected by similar means,[2] and almost comparable in size—the pair at Karnak, for instance, are 146 feet high, 50 feet thick at the base, and 376 feet wide, including the central doorway or pylon.[3] New forms of temple, like the small peripteral pavilion, now appear, and display ingenuity in the harmonisation of colonnades with low encircling walls. A king such as Thothmes III (effective reign 1479–1447 B.C.) who had had to fit himself to new conditions of life in Asia, returned to build at Karnak a stone replica of his campaigning tent, or to cover a small chamber of exquisite design with scientific paintings of the plants he had collected.[4]

[1] Published by Naville, *The Eleventh Dynasty Temple of Deir-el-Bahari*, 3 vols. (Egypt. Expl. Fund, 1907–13).
[2] See below, pp. 48 ff.
[3] A name commonly but inaccurately transferred to the towers, and in modern days to much baser things—one of the words like Odeion, that we have brought down to our own level.
[4] See Murray, *op. cit.*, p. 89. Jéquier, *Temples*, I, Pl. 52.

The penalty was paid for all this hurried activity in a certain shortsightedness and a carelessness in the craftsmanship. Fragile and ephemeral frescoes replaced the hard reliefs and unfading colours of the Old Kingdom. The bonding of walls was particularly bad at this time,[1] and the hidden portions of Karnak and Deir-el-Bahari are wretched beyond belief. The so-called foundations, made of random rubble without mortar and extending for less than the width of the wall above (see Fig. 9), have proved more fatal to the buildings than even the Copts or Assyrians. The builders seem to have inserted foundations from long habit,

Fig. 9 Pylon of Rameses I, foundations.

without remembering their purpose. Technique, moreover, stagnated until the period of Greek influence.[2]

The 'hundred-gated city of Thebes', as Achilles calls it in the *Iliad*,[3] lay in a wide plain on the right bank of the Nile, and must

[1] Clarke and Engelbach, pp. 133 ff., are particularly informative on this, and their Fig. 129, showing the interior of a burst gate-tower, is almost horrifying.

[2] One seeming exception is the sudden appearance of stone tunnel vaults during the last independent dynasties. They seem to be pioneer works, the first of their kind in the world—when all contemporary Egyptian work is so decadent. But actually they are tentative and still half-corbelled. See below, p. 50.

[3] *Iliad*, IX, vv. 383–4.

have presented towards the end of the New Kingdom a blaze of architectural splendour, which in scale and magnificence has had no parallel. Every king felt it his duty to add to one or other of the great national shrines, sacred to Amon and known today as Luxor and Karnak; and these contain almost all the features that most distinguish the age. Near them, but small in comparison, were temples for the direct worship of other gods, such as Ptah or Sekhmet. The shrines on the opposite bank were private temples of the kings, where they were to be worshipped alongside the gods as their incarnations. The actual tombs lay farther west still, in the Valley of the Kings. Of the private temples, the Ramesseum is 590 feet long by about 180 feet wide and the temple of Medinet Habu about 500 feet by 160 feet: whereas Luxor is about 850 feet long, and Karnak 1215 feet by 376 feet at its greatest width. Of course, only portions of these vast spaces were roofed.

The leading idea of these temples is still that found in the Old Kingdom. Courtyards, lined in most cases by colonnades, are succeeded by a labyrinth of dark chambers surrounding the sanctuary (see Fig. 11). The colonnades between court and sanctuary are now often thickened into a hypostyle hall. Sometimes encircling the labyrinth one finds double walls with a passage between, as in the great temple of Karnak. The state temples have their sanctuaries to the east, the private to the west.

Most often the temple is approached by an avenue of trees[1] or figures. Luxor and Karnak are connected by a famous avenue of ram-headed sphinxes. Immediately before the towers, on either side of the gate or pylon, are often found obelisks, one pair before each pair of towers. They are monoliths, and the small gilt pyramid at the apex of each was an object of worship. Many have been removed by foreign plunderers. Louis Philippe, for instance, pilfered one of the two great obelisks at Luxor and re-erected it in the Place de la Concorde in 1836—a miserable fate,[2] remembering the marvel of its first erection, its beauty in its original setting and the lost symmetry of the great temple, which all depended on its presence. According to Warburton, 'Those who have seen obelisks at Rome or Paris, can form no conception

---

[1] Hatshepsut's temple at Deir-el-Bahari by trees. See below, p. 37.
[2] 'It was removed from its place of honour, where it had stood for thirty-three centuries, only to decorate, with the help of bronze and gilding, a spot in Paris which has been stained with a thousand crimes' (W. Brockedon in David Roberts' *Holy Land*, IV (London, 1856), opposite Pl. 147).

of their effect where all around is in keeping with them.'[1] But, alas! Senseless 'vertical features' and 'baroque' town planning are now so much the rage, that some modern critics might prefer the Lateran to Luxor.

The gate-towers have walls battered at an angle of 75 degrees. But in most cases certain niches run nearly the full height of the front wall, and their backs are dressed to the vertical. In them stood the flag-staffs, held firm by horizontal clasps through openings set high in the walls. Before the gate-towers and almost attached to them were often colossi; and the walls themselves were covered with large figures in very low relief. All this imparted scale and even lightness to the front of the temples (see Pl. 2).

Beyond the gate, the main court had colonnaded sides and at times some isolated columns or unroofed colonnades down the centre, perhaps serving, like the obelisks, as objects of worship.[2] The architect might, as at Karnak, interpose a second pylon and gate-towers between the court and the roofed portion of the temple. More reasonably, as at Luxor, he might throw open the hypostyle hall in all its glory at the inner end of the court (see Fig. 10). Or, as in the second court at the Ramesseum, he might partly conceal it with Osirid piers.[3]

The enclosing walls of the courts, like the walls of the gate-towers and even, in this period, the shafts of the columns, served as a field for reliefs. Carved with unusual shallowness in intaglio, and at the same time so large as to outrun the scale of the architecture, these suggest and perhaps originated in enormous hangings blanketing the entire temple.[4] They continue throughout the hypostyle hall and the shrines. They can be very successful, avoiding in their shallowness the barbarous luxuriance of the Dravidian and Flamboyant styles, and it is strange that they

[1] Quoted by Brockedon, *op. cit.*, opposite Pl. 200.
[2] See Capart, p. 135. His Pl. 49 illustrates a group of such columns, before the temple of Ptah at Thebes, where they almost form a pavilion of the sort described below (p. 38). They will have originated, thinks Capart, in tapering floral bouquets. Luxor, remarkably, has two courts, their sole connection an avenue of such columns (Jéquier, *Temples*, Pl. 61). According to Jéquier, however, this is the only finished portion of a grand hypostyle hall projected by Amenhotep III and never built, owing partly to its size and partly to Akhnaton. The twisted western or outer court was added rather later.
[3] See above, p. 25.
[4] See R. Demangel, *La Frise Ionique* (Paris, 1932), pp. 29–31.

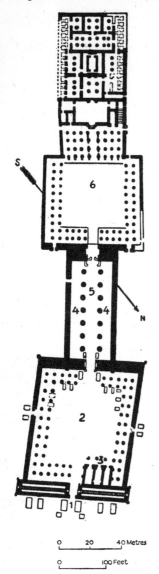

Fig. 10 Plan of Luxor.
1, 2 and 3 = Additions of the
Egyptian Decadence; 4 and
5 = Amenhotep's Approach;
6 = Original Forecourt of
Amenhotep III.

Fig. 11   Great Temple
of Karnak at Thebes.

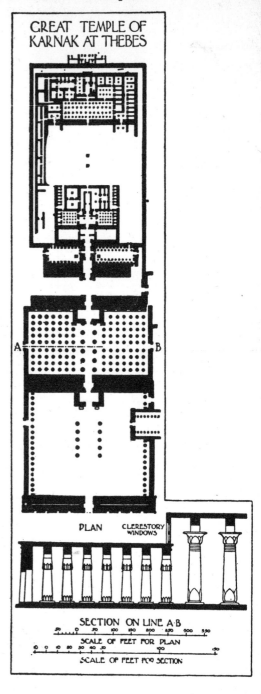

GREAT TEMPLE OF
KARNAK AT THEBES

PLAN   CLERESTORY
WINDOWS

SECTION ON LINE A·B

SCALE OF FEET FOR PLAN

SCALE OF FEET FOR SECTION

Tomb at Beni Hasan: exterior

Tomb at Beni Hasan: interior

Plate 3

The Great Temple, Deir-el-Bahari

Plate 4

should have had so little later influence. They have a lesson, perhaps, even for our century.

The hypostyle halls usually extended the whole width of the temple. The largest, at Karnak, is 340 feet wide. From east to west they measure far less—170 feet, for instance, at Karnak—probably because they began as a mere thickening of the colonnade

Fig. 12 In the Hypostyle Hall, Karnak.

3—1

at the inner end of the court. At Karnak, which may be taken as the type,[1] the higher portion of the hall down the main axis of the temple is 72 feet wide and 76 feet high internally, as opposed to the 50 feet of its flanking aisles. It is divided longitudinally into three aisles by two lines of columns. East and west above these, as above all the other colonnades, run continuous architraves directly supporting the sandstone slabs of the roof. The gap resulting between the central and side roofs permits a clerestory for lighting the three central aisles. This consists of piers, square on plan, and between them vertical slabs of stone, each about 16 feet high and 14 inches thick, pierced with slits about 6 feet long and 10 inches wide. The streaked light falling through such huge gratings must have produced admirable effects (see Fig. 12). With that from the two doors, it was the only light admitted to the hall. In the Ramesseum are similar, but smaller, openings. The columns found over most of the hall at Karnak are 'closed papyri' of the somewhat degenerate smooth type, with which, however, the two central rows, smooth 'open papyri', provide a striking contrast.[2] The same types occupy the same positions in the Ramesseum.

The floor of the hypostyle halls usually rises almost imperceptibly towards the sanctuaries at the farther end. In the mortuary temple of Seti I, at Abydos, the change of level received architectural recognition (see Fig. 13). Here the sanctuary consists of seven chapels, and the columns of the inner hypostyle hall are grouped to provide a broad aisle or lane to the entrance of each. The hall contains three transverse rows of twelve columns each, but the effect on plan becomes one of six longitudinal groups of six each, with the lanes between. The twelve columns nearest the sanctuary stand on a platform higher than the rest of the floor, and this extends over most of each lane as far as a step aligned with the east faces of the columns in the central transverse row. The columns are all of the same height. But the modelling of the floor and the interplay of the axes make this one of the most interesting Egyptian interiors.[3]

The roof at Karnak was surrounded by a high parapet wall, on which the level of the roof slabs was indicated at most by large

---

[1] Luxor is in fact more primitive, as it lacks the three taller central aisles. The Festival Hall of Thothmes III perhaps played a part in developing the type. See below, p. 41.

[2] For these terms, see below, p. 54.

[3] Fully described by Caulfeild (for whom, see above, p. 16, n. 3).

gargoyles.[1] Vertical joints between the roof slabs, where rain might penetrate, were carefully protected with small covering slabs.[2] Here again the Temple at Abydos shows unusually careful building (see Fig. 14).

The sanctuaries beyond the hall were of every variety. The largest often contained a bark sacred to the god, which floated during the Nile flood around the fields. Another might contain

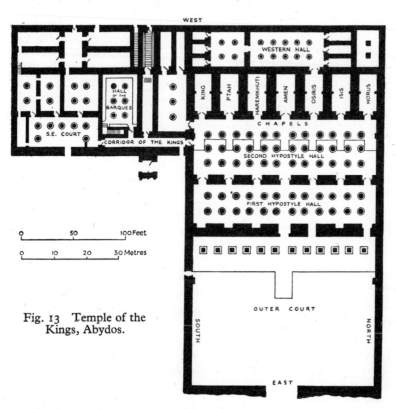

Fig. 13 Temple of the
Kings, Abydos.

the sacred cow of Hathor (Isis), the goddess of the Underworld, necessarily worshipped in all mortuary temples. The seven sanctuaries at Abydos are dedicated to Horus, Isis, Osiris, Amon, Harmachis, Ptah and King Seti I himself, who thus takes his place beside the great Egyptian gods.[3]

[1] The Ptolemaic Temple of Edfou contains perhaps the best-preserved examples. See Capart, Pl. IX.
[2] See the diagrams in Clarke and Engelbach, p. 155.
[3] See Perrot and Chipiez, I, p. 395.

Behind the sanctuaries and sometimes intermingled with them were treasure-houses and rooms for priests: but a neat grouping here was seldom attempted before Ptolemaic times.

The type of temple with hypostyle hall was adopted as far as possible for the famous rock-cut temples of Nubia, the chief of which, at Abu Simbel, had a small forecourt with the normal stone-built pylon (long since destroyed) and a splendid inner 'wall', cut from the cliff and containing the four famous colossi of Rameses II, two on each side of the central door and each about 65 feet high. Inside was a long hall, like the centre of a hypostyle hall, with eight Osirid pillars of the king,[1] and beyond that the sanctuary, reached by the rays of the sun for a few minutes only, at sunrise. We have lost today such art as this, that can raise a building, noble in itself, to a more vivid splendour at great religious moments.

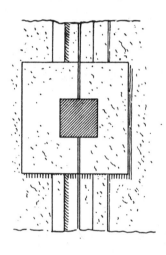

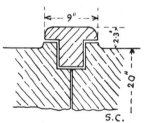

Fig. 14   Roof-joint, Abydos.

Of the rare examples of other types the most famous is the mortuary temple built by Queen Hatshepsut at Deir-el-Bahari (see Pl. 4). It is one of the earliest large buildings of the New Kingdom, and precedes, in fact, the fashion for temples with hypostyle halls. An enlarged copy of its neighbour of the Middle Kingdom, it comprised three terraced colonnaded courts, the upper and middle reached by ramps at right angles across the centre of the middle and lower (see Fig. 15). For the form of their architecture the builders owed everything to their neighbour, which did not prevent their plundering it for the violet sandstone to use on ground-courses in their own white limestone colonnades.[2]

---

[1] Well illustrated by David Roberts, *op. cit*, Pl. 139.
[2] See Clarke in Naville, *Deir-el-Bahari* (London 1908), VI, p. 18.

The building lies close under a semicircle of cliffs, with which its long, horizontal lines provide the perfect contrast. A long, tree-lined avenue approached it from the Nile. The lower and middle courts were each flanked by double colonnades on three sides. Behind the west colonnade of each stood the retaining wall of the court above, covered with large, shallow reliefs, which, at the back

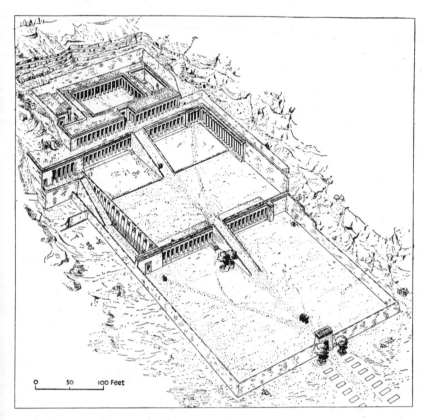

Fig. 15   Temple of Deir-el-Bahari, Isometric.

of the lowest court, contain the famous scenes of the embassy to the land of Punt and the floating of the two great obelisks of Hatshepsut from Syene to Karnak—precious evidence of the ways of the Egyptian builders. The obelisks are laid longitudinally in one line, base to base, on a boat that must have been over 200 feet long, which a thousand men are towing in three lines of five

tow-boats each.[1]   Hatshepsut, dressed as a Pharaoh, presents the
obelisks to Amon.

The architect has given the outer faces of most of the outer
pillars a severe rectangular form, varied only in the north colonnade of the middle court.   The inner faces and inner colonnades
tend to have the angles of the shaft planed away, as at Beni Hasan.
This external severity is in true harmony with the grandeur of the
site.   The greatest moment came for the visitor to Deir-el-Bahari
as he reached the top of the first ramp and entered the middle
court.   For the upper court, unlike the others, had a double
colonnade on all sides, while between its east enclosing wall and
the retaining wall at the back of the middle court extended a
further double-colonnaded walk.   The two tiers of colonnades,
above and before the retaining wall, must have presented a magnificent prospect from the middle court, flanked on either side of their
great length (200 feet) by the vestibules of subsidiary shrines to
Anubis and Hathor.

One dwells on Deir-el-Bahari, because it is the most classical
in feeling of all Egyptian buildings.   Some of its details may not
please.   The Hathor-headed capitals, for instance, almost the
oldest known, inside the vestibule of Hathor, are much less graceful
than those of the next century in the rock-cut chapel of El Kab,[2]
which reflect the culture of Amenhotep III.   The masonry is too
often a veneer of thin 'stretchers' over a poor rubble core.   But
for properly architectural virtues, harmony with the site, repose
and clarity of line, combined with variety and sustained interest
in the approach and a relegation, rare in Egypt, of the decorative
film to the less immediately visible features, it has few equals even
outside Egypt.

Some small temples or stone pavilions, of the type best known
from 'Pharaoh's Bed' at Philae and popular in Ptolemaic times,
also survive from the Eighteenth Dynasty.   They served, it
seems, as resting-places for the sacred barks on their journeys round
the irrigation channels,[3] and generally have a small rectangular

---

[1] Clarke has interpreted the reliefs in this way (Naville, *Deir-el-Bahari*,
VI, pp. 2–5).   Engelbach denies that the Egyptians could have made a
boat of this size, and impugns the good faith of Hatshepsut's artists (see
above, p. 18, n. 2).

[2] Jéquier, *Temples*, I, Pl. 73; Capart, Pl. XXXV.   The head of the
goddess is here treated virtually as a mask attached to one side only of
the column.   The Ptolemaic builders later evolved monstrous forms
with four heads, as at Denderah (Roberts, *op. cit.*, Pl. 194).

[3] See Jéquier, *Temples*, I, p. 7 (on Medinet Habu).

cella, surrounded on all four sides by a colonnade of mixed columns and pillars. They are thus the oldest known example of the peripteral treatment; and, as in the normal Greek Doric peripteral temple, the cella walls and outer columns or pillars are nowhere aligned. Finally, these buildings afford the earliest known example in Egypt of walls across the lower portion of the intercolumnar spaces, a feature very popular later.[1]

The purest example of the type was undoubtedly that formerly existing at Abu Simbel, which was published in Napoleon's *Egypt*.[2] Two lines of square piers down the flanks contrasted with two columns in the centre of the short fronts, and almost anticipated the later Greek treatment of columns between antae. The intercolumnar wall was here kept low, and carefully designed to stop gracefully against the two centre columns of the façade, leaving the centre opening free (see Fig. 16). In most later examples, such as Pharaoh's Bed, the wall is much higher and a broken pylon encumbers the centre opening—an unsatisfactory feature, but popular even in the Eighteenth Dynasty, as Egyptian drawings show.[3] The friezes of hieroglyphs at Abu Simbel were enclosed within a sunk border, as important aesthetically as the slight sinking of the whole frieze in the Siphnian Treasury.[4] The whole building was raised upon a podium some 6 feet high, the proportions of which anticipated those of classical examples.

The brick pyramid of Ahmose I (*c.* 1570 B.C.) was the last royal pyramid to be built for some centuries. The royal tombs were henceforward rock-hewn and situated in the mountains west of Thebes, mostly in the Valley of the Kings, where they were concealed from the river and the mortuary temples. The Pharaohs had seen the advantage of having their tombs at a distance, in more or less inaccessible regions, but they naturally preferred their temples near at hand. Prayers, it was now felt, could be efficacious even for the dead buried many miles away. So we see another change forced by circumstances upon the Egyptian religion.

Each king excavated his tomb in his lifetime and was buried in

[1] As the earliest known, the small temple of Medinet Habu, is certainly a work of Thothmes III, one might guess the type came from Asia. See M. A. Murray, *Egyptian Temples*, p. 154.

[2] Vol. I (Paris, 1809), Pl. 34 ff. The example at Medinet Habu (see p. 38, n. 3 above) was erected by Thothmes III.

[3] See, e.g., Clarke and Engelbach, Fig. 55.

[4] See below, p. 169.

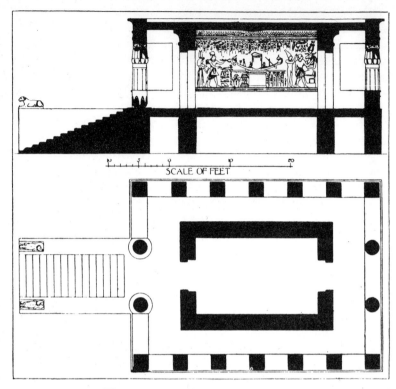

SCALE OF FEET

Fig. 16   Small Temple, Abu-Simbel.

the last chamber reached before his death abruptly stopped work. During a long reign, a king would continue haphazardly adding chambers and vestibules, and it would seem mere chance where he at last stopped. The tombs of Seti I and Rameses III are both over 400 feet long.[1] Trouble seems to have been taken to conceal the immediate approach to the mummy-chamber, as, for instance, in the tomb of Seti I, described by its discoverer Belzoni.[2] The walls of the tombs, profusely decorated with carvings and vivid paintings, were to be seen by the soul of the dead king alone. After the immense labour of their excavation, they had to be decorated by such slight aid as lamps and torches would provide.

[1] For sections through a typical tomb see Fergusson, *History of Architecture*, I, second edition (London, 1874), p. 128.
[2] It is the sarcophagus of this king that may now be seen in the Soane Museum.

Together with the columns and segmental roofs, they show a final elaborate development of the types of Beni-Hasan.

Most surviving Egyptian houses belong to the New Kingdom, including the only stone palace, that of Rameses III at Medinet Habu, the Festival Hall of Thothmes III at Karnak and the large houses built for the courtiers of the heretic Pharaoh, Akhnaton, at his new, model, capital of Tell el 'Amarna.

The Festival Hall is a long rectangular building across the main axis of the temple, resembling the central aisles of a hypostyle hall but running north and south. The remarkable form of its columns has baffled many.[1] Murray has very plainly interpreted them as tent-poles,[2] and thus sees the building as a heavy, stone version of a light pavilion, perhaps the king's campaigning tent.

It gains an additional interest when we remember that it is the first known building to use large slabs of Silsilah sandstone, which alone made hypostyle halls possible, that it is, indeed, the earliest Egyptian example we know of broader and loftier centre aisles with lower side aisles and a clerestory.[3] Moreover, the painted decoration of its ceilings must have been very beautiful.

The palaces proper present no new architectural features. Besides Medinet Habu, a mere annexe to the temple of Rameses III, there survive the foundations of a large rectangular 'coronation hall' at Tell el 'Amarna, which once contained 544 columns, disposed without subtlety.[4]

We are told these days that we should all study the history of houses, preferably of the 'people'. What are we to do with races like the Egyptians and the Greeks, who lacked our interest in the more mundane sides of our subject and preferred to employ real architects on other things? The houses of the nobles at el 'Amarna, however, are not without accomplishment (see Fig. 17). The typical large house here stands detached in its own grounds, with a large columnar central hall reaching probably to the roof.[5] The braziers show the family would sit here in the cool of the evening. The doorways, as in later Persian imitations of Egyptian palaces,

[1] Including, e.g., H. Statham, *Short Critical History of Architecture*, second edition (London, 1927), p. 37.

[2] *Op. cit.*, p. 88.

[3] See above, p. 34. For pictures of the Festival Hall, see Jéquier, *op. cit.*, Pls. 49–52.

[4] See *The City of Akhenaten* (Egypt. Expl. Fund) III (1951), Pls. XIII–XIV.

[5] Examples are published in Vol. II of *The City of Akhenaten*. Those on Pls. XII and XVI are typical.

were of stone set in walls of mud, and, where necessary for the symmetry of the apartment, were shamelessly balanced by stone frames for false doors.   The other rooms, normally including a fair-sized loggia, were wrapped as neatly as possible around this central hall.   In houses of this size, with no more than two or four columns in the largest apartment, the frescoes showed up to great advantage.   But the windows remained stone gratings, impossible to open, as at Karnak.[1]   We first encounter movable casement windows in Syria, though one may suspect that, like so much else, they were invented by the Sumerians.

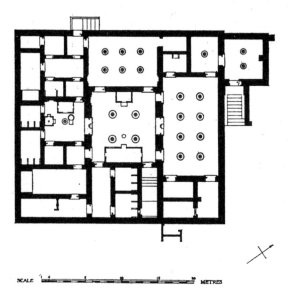

SCALE   METRES

Fig. 17   The House of the Vizier Nekht.

4. THE PTOLEMAIC AGE

During the slow decay of Egypt between 1150 and 660 B.C. few buildings were erected worthy of record.   Both Sheshonk and the Ethiopians added to Karnak.   The Saite kings may have attempted more, and their connection with the early Greeks might have made their work of some interest.   But, being in the Delta, their buildings have vanished.   The architectural remains of Naucratis,

[1] Perhaps in this, as in other things, Solomon's Temple was a miniature copy of Karnak.   'And for the house he made windows of narrow lights' (I Kings vi, 4).

where the Greeks were concentrated by Ahmose II ('Amasis': 569–525 B.C.), though partly of the Saite period, are very fragmentary.

When they finally conquered Egypt, in 332 B.C., the Greeks accepted the vernacular style for their temples. This is not to be wondered at. The Ptolemies had quite enough to do to govern the people without forcing them to change methods of building, the very minutiae of which had existed for nearly a thousand years, and which were suited to the climate and religion. In secular buildings, especially their new city of Alexandria, they probably made far greater changes. But of Greek Alexandria, apart from the recently discovered Serapeum of Ptolemy III, there survive only some cisterns and tombs. Three hundred years later, the Romans followed the lead of the Greeks. This was still more natural. The Romans were ever ready to adapt the architecture of other nations, and, when they succeeded as rulers of Egypt, they can hardly be said to have had an original style of their own.

During these periods Thebes was no longer the great centre, and temples were built in all parts of Egypt. The principal Ptolemaic temples are at Edfou (237–57 B.C.) and Denderah (c. 200 B.C.). The temples at Esneh and Kalabshe are among the best-known Roman examples. At Philae we have an assortment of the work of Ptolemies and Romans.

These buildings all show the customary pylons (see Pl. 2), colonnaded courts, sanctuaries and enclosing walls, with the traditional intaglio reliefs. But they omit the hypostyle hall and revert to a comparatively shrunken portico largely open to the court. Its front colonnade was now, however, blocked at the bottom by the screen wall whose appearance we noted in the small pavilions of the New Kingdom,[1] and entered in the centre through the 'broken pylon' first popular, as we saw, at the same date. The lintel merely extends a few inches inwards from the inner face of each jamb, when its moulding is returned. A beam across the doorway would have interfered with the free passage of banners and effigies.

A colonnade of this sort was more easily built than a hypostyle hall. The upper, open half, of the front, sometimes helped, as at Edfou, by an hypaethral opening above the central bay, afforded ample light and rendered unnecessary the elaborate clerestory of an earlier time (see Fig. 18). But the screen wall was considered

[1] See above, p. 39.

beautiful as well as economical. At any rate, some were added at this time to the upper court of Deir-el-Bahari, to reconcile it to the Ptolemaic eye.[1]

Ptolemaic temples resemble each other more closely than do their predecessors. The architects display their originality consciously and only in a few obvious places, such as the capitals of columns, of which Philae, for instance, can show a profusion of types. The masonry and planning of the pylons and the grouping of the chambers in the sanctuary show a slickness absent from real Egyptian work.

To the Ptolemaic period belong most of those small peripteral

Fig. 18   View of the Inner Court, Edfou.

buildings, whose first appearance under the New Kingdom we described above. The example known as 'Pharaoh's Bed' at Philae consists of columns connected by screen walls and supporting the usual Egyptian entablature. As it lacks cella (sekos), podium and roof, it evidently served as a porch at the river side, where illustrious visitors could be received. The doorway at each end has a broken lintel, and the abaci have a remarkable elongation, hard to explain except by their general 'lateness'. The purpose of the very similar pavilion, 18 feet high and 22 feet square, on the roof of the sanctuary at Denderah, is not at all clear. It would make a bad belvedere.

[1] See Naville, *Deir-el-Bahari*, V, Pl. CXIX.

5. BUILDING SCIENCE AND DECORATION

Mathematics were cumbrous and technical knowledge rudimentary.[1] Certain geometrical formulae were known empirically, without any attempt to demonstrate their mathematical necessity. As Heath points out,[2] two concern right-angled triangles, in which the angles of slope of the hypotenuse are 54 degrees and 76 degrees respectively—very close to those of the Pyramid and the Mastaba. The Egyptian had also measured the value of π as 3·16, possibly by drawing a circle on a finely squared surface and counting off the squares.[3] He certainly ascertained the proportions of the human figure by fitting it into a field of squares,[4] and thus prepared the way for classical theorists. Similarly, when an architect of the Old Kingdom drew a curve to his own taste, he would take its co-ordinates from the side of an enclosing rectangle and so 'scale it off' for the instruction of his workmen.[5]

Arithmetic was very backward. No signs existed for integers between 1 and 10. In consequence, no fraction, except, strangely, two-thirds, existed with any nominator but unity[6]; so that four-sevenths, for instance, had to be expressed as

$$\frac{1}{1+1} + \frac{1}{10+1+1+1+1}$$

Dimensions and units of measurement had to be few and simple. The cubit (forearm), its seventh part, the palm, and its twenty-eighth part, the dactyl (finger), sufficed for all buildings. The cubit was the so-called 'royal cubit', of 20·6 inches. But these units had no clear relation to the scale of feet and inches.

From the Pyramid era onwards buildings were laid out in round numbers of cubits. To take well-attested dimensions, we find that surviving Egyptian measurements of doorways generally give exact numbers of cubits for the length, breadth and height.[7] Again, the Temple of Seti, at Abydos, as measured in Caulfeild's

[1] The interested reader is referred to the detailed study of Clarke and Engelbach, now the standard work.
[2] T. L. Heath, *Manual of Greek Mathematics* (Oxford, 1931), pp. 79–80.
[3] Clarke and Engelbach, Figs. 53 and 54.
[4] Clarke and Engelbach give two examples in Figs. 242 and 243. See also S. Mackay, *Journal of Egyptian Archeology*, No. IV., pp. 74–5.
[5] Clarke and Engelbach, p. 53 and p. 56.
[6] For all this, see Heath, pp. 11–12.
[7] See Clarke and Engelbach, p. 63, and Lethaby, pp. 62 ff., for the general simplicity of Egyptian proportions.

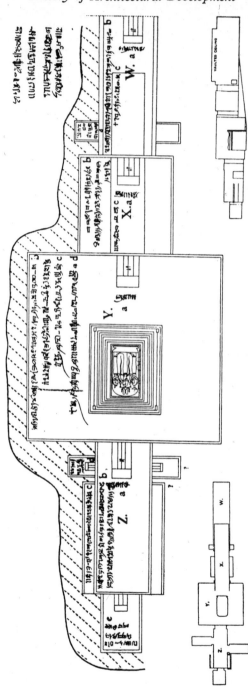

Fig. 19   Tomb of Rameses IV.   Modern plan and section and papyrus plan.

plausible cubits of 20·85 inches, has bold and simple lateral dimensions. Its width totals 110 cubits, 100 internally (see Fig. 13). In the first cross-wall, each door, except for a centre door of 7 cubits, is 5 cubits wide and spaced exactly 10 cubits from its neighbour. Each of the seven chapels[1] is 10 cubits wide, and the separating walls, like the external wall of the temple, each 5 cubits thick, giving a sum of 7×10 plus 6×5 plus 2×5, or 110 cubits, the total external width. These dimensions read like an exercise in Egyptian arithmetic; but they had the merit of giving simple, 'masculine', proportions of a kind favoured by the Athenians themselves.[2] However reached, such ratios have enormous architectural value, seldom though the English have perceived it. One must confess that the longitudinal dimensions of Abydos are less elegantly simple, but this seems due to a change of plan.

Architectural draughtsmanship suffered from the well-known convention of Egyptian art, that every object must be shown in its greatest extension. So, on Egyptian plans, doors, windows and pillars appear as often as not in elevation, as on surviving plans for Twentieth-Dynasty tombs (see Fig. 19), and also on the famous plan of an estate found in the Tomb of Merire at el 'Amarna.[3] It is on the whole wonderful that the Egyptians, from such plans, could ever erect a building of any size. Their architects must have supervised the work from start to finish, including the organisation of the working gangs; and once more a limitation in theoretical knowledge proved beneficial for architecture. For personal supervision on the site perhaps conduces more even than simple proportions to the excellence of a work.

We can only guess how the Egyptians squared and levelled a site.[4] Moreover, as the great days of all three kingdoms lay deep in the Bronze Age, we are even less certain how, from near the beginning, they could quarry the hard granites of Syene or bring them to the admirable finish of the figures in the Granite Temple without the aid of hard cutters or revolving drills, which alone can remedy the softness of a point. Most often they must have pounded and rubbed them with dolerite. Even so, it is hard to see how by such means they could have separated obelisks from the living rock: for, though only a few feet wide, these might be

[1] For which, see above, p. 35.
[2] See below, p. 172.
[3] Clarke and Engelbach, Fig. 55.
[4] See above, p. 21, n. 2.

anything up to a hundred feet long,[1] and the pounders will have needed to tunnel under them.

For carrying stones overland and raising them into position, the Egyptians used sledges, levers and 'rockers'. Pulleys and capstans were unknown. The uses of the rocker, of which an Egyptian model from Deir-el-Bahari[2] is at University College, London, have been exhaustively discussed by Clarke and Engelbach. It resembled the legs of a rocking-chair, connected at intervals by a few cross-bars. The block to be moved was, of course, slid across the top of the tilted rocker. After that, the rocker could be levered backwards or forwards by poles inserted between the cross-bars or held in position by logs placed under the ends. It was obviously easier to swing a large stone round on a rocker than on a sledge, and numbers of rockers were probably used to align the stones for dressing in the order destined for them in one course of a wall. To lift a stone in a small space while building, one could first raise one end of the rocker and insert a log under it. A reverse movement brought the rocker on top of the log, and at the same time allowed another to be put under the other end. By these means, rocker and stone would slowly rise.

Blocks would be dragged overland by sheer force of numbers. An inscription records that a sarcophagus-lid required three thousand men for its transport.[3] The mere moving of a vast mass is not so difficult after all, provided the ground is level. The Egyptians understood leverage, at any rate. So they must have levered one end of the block above the earth, filled up the space beneath it and thus formed an inclined place to give it a start. Once started, it probably never stopped night or day, except at obstacles—when it would be restarted by the same process.

Earth ramps were also indispensable in actual building. As the hypostyle hall rose, ramps and platform will have risen with it. An army of workmen can soon fill even Karnak with earth; and Legrain, who took down and rebuilt the columns of the hypostyle hall in this century, required nothing but this to pile

---

[1] The obelisks of Hatshepsut at Karnak are each $97\frac{1}{2}$ feet high (*Cambridge Ancient History*, II, p. 65).

[2] It is from a foundation deposit, and is illustrated by Naville, *op. cit.*, VI, Pl. CLXVIII.

[3] Clarke and Engelbach, pp. 85–6, quoting from Vol. I, § 448 of Breasted's *Ancient Records*. 'With a few capstans one hundred men could have carried out the work in a month.'

and remove the necessary earth twice over.[1]   It is truly wonderful,
however, that the Egyptians should have been able to slide an
obelisk into position from the brow of the ramp, sometimes one
hundred feet high, up which they must have dragged it base
foremost.[2]   For the Romans, with their ropes and capstans, it was
by comparison child's play to move an obelisk.

Having normally only the plumb-line,[3] and ignorant of internal
bonding, the Egyptian laid his masonry neither in rectangular
blocks nor in parallel courses.[4]   Two types of trapezoidal masonry
were popular.[5]   In either, every stone was specially dressed to fit
its neighbour, and its neighbour alone.   Mortar was used only
to help the blocks settle.   Visible fronts were left rough until
actually in position.   The windows of the palace at Medinet Habu
and the unfinished masonry of 'Pharaoh's Bed' at Philae both
show the process well.   Like the Greeks and unlike the medieval
builders, the Egyptians related the constructional joints as little as
possible to the surface articulation of the building.   In the staircases of pylons, for instance, an individual block might contain
several treads and part of a side wall.   As in Greek work, also,
dowels of metal or sycamore wood were often employed to hold
these large blocks in position.

Fittings were few.   Alabaster was sometimes used as a decorative veneer.   Though the hinge was known very early, most large
doors, as in classical Greece, swung on pivots.   The characteristic
'broken lintel' would make it easier to insert such doors—perhaps
another reason for its popularity.

The Egyptian stone-mason feared lateral thrusts more than
anything.   All his colonnades are trabeated, and even the pointed
tunnel vaults in the sanctuaries at Deir-el-Bahari and the seven

---

[1] Capart, *op. cit.*, pp. 99–100.

[2] Several books have been devoted to this subject: e.g. Engelbach,
The Problem of the Obelisks (London, 1923).

[3] One T-square is known, of the Twentieth Dynasty (Clarke and
Engelbach, Fig. 264).

[4] At the same time, we should notice that the long sagging courses,
sometimes supposed (e.g., by Atkinson and Bagenal, pp. 102–3) to be
typical of Ancient Egypt and to derive from its stacks of mud bricks, are
not attested in surviving buildings earlier than the Ptolemaic; although
the predynastic models of mud houses (e.g., Childe, Pl. X, *b* and *c*) do
seem to show walls that sag in the middle.

[5] Clarke and Engelbach, Figs. 105–6.   The very earliest Egyptian
masonry, that of Zoser at Sakkara, is of much smaller blocks, closer in
shape to unbaked brick, and laid by a much more laborious process, as
Clarke and Engelbach show, than were the later walls.

chapels at Abydos are all corbelled.   Moreover, the pointed form
is the strongest possible for such a roof.   Some semicircular
vaults of stone, probably of Saite date, are found at Medinet
Habu.   But they form no real exception.   Each consists in cross-
section of three blocks, two haunch blocks which rest securely,
without overbalancing, on the supporting piers, and one horizontally elongated keystone, grooved securely into the vault between
the haunch blocks.[1]

Egyptian brick building knows no such restraint.   These
early races were forced by the small size of the brick to experiment
from the very beginning, and evolved daring forms ignored by
stone-masons until the rational, reflective Hellenistic period.   It
is just possible[2] that at the beginning of his civilisation the
Egyptian took his brick forms from Sumer, and then merely
perpetuated them, although his work is never so bold or straightforward as the Sumerian, and his bricks nearly always crude, i.e.,
sun-baked only.   In any case the difference between the forms of
brickwork and masonry warns us against facile attempts to trace
the ancestry of tombs and temples in flimsier and poorer buildings.
Only in the earliest masonry of all, at Sakkara, is there a timid
imitation of unpierced brick walls.

Professor Flinders Petrie describes a vault at Denderah composed of three rings of crude brick of the Fourth and Fifth Dynasty,
and two arches at Rahotep of the same date.   Mariette says he
found a semicircular arch at Abydos of the Sixth Dynasty with
brick voussoirs and a limestone keystone, the mortar joints being
galetted, i.e. having small pebbles embedded.   The Egyptian
arched vault of brick (for which see Fig. 20) is found at its best
behind the Ramesseum,[3] and at el 'Asaseef near Thebes, where
the wall surrounding the tombs is pierced by an arch of nine rings
of brickwork.

Like the Byzantines, the Egyptians dispensed with timber
centering whenever possible.   Their vaults and arches, which are
of all forms, semicircular, pointed, segmental and, above all,
elliptical, generally bear witness to this.   They would build the
bottom courses with horizontal beds as high as the factor of
stability permitted, so forming a haunch which reduced the span

[1] See Clarke and Engelbach, Fig. 220.
[2] See Childe, third edition, pp. 125–6, for some discussion of this.
The fourth edition (see, e.g., pp. 100–1) is noticeably more sceptical.
[3] Clarke and Engelbach, Fig. 215.

and resisted the thrust of the vault. Above this point they employed special tile-shaped bricks, and laid them edgewise, not voussoir fashion.[1] They first traced the outline of the vault on a wall built across the end of the space to be vaulted, and then built the haunches for the entire length, specially stepped to receive

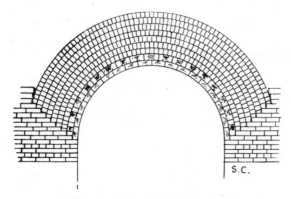

Fig. 20   Egyptian brick arch.

the vault proper.   Next they built a semi-circle of the special bricks flat against the end wall, to form the first slice of vault, and the next slice to adhere to this.   When the face of the end-wall is skew-backed and all the slices therefore slope backwards, the vault of course gains greatly in strength (see Fig. 21).

Fig. 21   Vault constructed without centering.

[1] Clarke and Engelbach, Fig. 216.   The bricks of the Ramesseum vaults are each 14 by 7 by 2½ inches—'royal bricks', as opposed to the ordinary brick of 9 by 4½ by 3.

But sometimes even vaults of brickwork are built of horizontal, corbelled courses throughout. In the remarkable tomb at Drah Abou'l Negah, examined by Piéron and perhaps as early as the Eighteenth Dynasty,[1] pendentives of horizontal brick courses form the transition from a square room to a beehive cupola of horizontal brickwork rings.[2] The Egyptian showed sensibility and some inventiveness, where not controlled by the rigid official tradition; as we may see even if we examine mouldings and ornamental members, where this tradition showed itself perhaps at its strongest.

The mouldings used were very few. The most characteristic is the 'gorge' or 'Egyptian cavetto', which crowned walls, pylons and smaller doorways, and even the rare pedestals for sculptures, as in the Avenue of Sphinxes at Karnak. Examples are known as early as 3000 B.C.; and it was considered the only appropriate finish for a wall long after the Roman Conquest. Corners are generally finished with a roll, which mitres with the lower member of the 'gorge' (see Fig. 22). Virtually no other mouldings are found, although at all times slight sinkings and raised panels might give variety to large plain surfaces, while in very early times complicated surfaces of pilaster strips and recesses broke up the façades of the royal mastabas in a fashion recalling the early Sumerian.[3] Like the Minoans, Syrians and other early races, the Egyptians never troubled to interrupt their walls artistically, where they needed an open colonnade. At Edfou, for instance, it looks as if the builder has merely torn a rectangular gap to make room for the columns. It remained for the Greeks to rid architecture of this brutality.

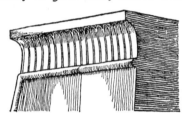

Fig. 22   Egyptian roll and gorge.

In short, all Egyptian forms, unlike those of Greek Doric, seem readily explicable as a literal, though heavy, translation into stone of a few shapes of everyday building. Those who wish may see

[1] See Jéquier, *Manuel*, Pt. V, Chap. 4 and Fig. 208.
[2] We return below (p. 228) to the origin of the pendentive among peoples who practised horizontal corbelling.
[3] See Childe, p. 125.

in the simple mouldings and battered walls the type of the predynastic mud hut, the poles to strengthen it at its four corners, its
smooth, sloping wall-surfaces of mud-brick and its 'framework
of palm-branches, the tops of which, standing out free, are pushed
outwards by the beams which form the roof'.[1]

To contrast with the austerity of their walls and roofs, the
Egyptians developed a wonderful variety of columns, almost all

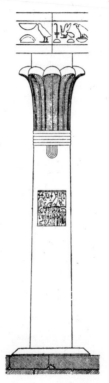 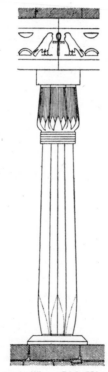

Fig. 23 (i)   Old Kingdom   Fig. 23 (ii)   Old Kingdom
capitals, Abusir. Dactyliform.   capitals, Abusir. Papyriform.

of great beauty, whose luxuriance, before the labours of Bor-
chardt,[2] had defied classification. We now see that almost all
the types, which he first distinguished, have known origins in the
Old Kingdom—in this, as in everything else, the creative age of

[1] Capart, p. 89 (compare the 'architectural hieroglyphs' on his Pl.
XIII). I do not understand Lethaby's explanation on p. 29 of his
Architecture.
[2] *Die Aegyptische Pflanzensaüle*, Berlin, 1897.

Egyptian culture. Besides the so-called 'Proto-Doric' types, wholly lithic in character, described above,[1] one finds three other classes, modelled on the three plants, the palm, the lotus and the papyrus (see Fig. 23). In all three the crown of the plant forms the echinus or bell of the capital, and below this a series of horizontal roll-mouldings represents a cord or thong wound round the neck of the plant[2]—rational enough, where, as often, the shaft represents a bundle of lotus or papyrus stalks. In the earliest and purest examples one finds tiny plants inserted at the level of the thong to tighten the bundle at this vital point.[3] The abacus is in all cases plain and unobtrusive.

The 'dactyliform' column, representing the palm, is found for instance in Sahure's pyramid temple (Fifth Dynasty), Tehuti-Hetep's tomb (Twelfth Dynasty), Akhnaton's Palace (Eighteenth Dynasty) and the Ptolemaic Pronaos of Edfou.

The lotiform and papyriform columns are remarkable for a rapid convex thickening of the shaft for the first few inches above the low, round plinth, showing a close approximation to the stalks of the natural papyrus.[4] The shafts of the lotiform normally represent each a cluster of four stalks; for, the type being seldom used in the degenerate New Kingdom, when too many columns became mere cylinders, there can be few cases where a smooth round shaft replaces the earlier composite modelling.[5]

The capital is composed either of closed lotus buds or of flowers, distinguished at once from the papyrus because the sepals are as high as the petals. Thus no true lotus capital can ever assume the shape of a bell.[6]

It is otherwise with the papyrus. Here one could paint the low sepals encircling the papyriform capital in a distinctive series of dark stripes, while the white, feathery papyrus-flower that they protected one could represent either closed or open. It became, of course, the custom to use the bell-shaped open papyrus[7] on

---

[1] P. 27.

[2] The very early Greek fragment, whether base or capital, just discovered by the British School at Old Smyrna, seems to incorporate this Egyptian thong in its design. See the photograph, *JHS*, 1952, Pl. VI, 3.

[3] Jéquier, *Temples*, Pl. VII.

[4] For which, see Owen Jones, *Grammar of Ornament* (London, 1856), Pl. IV.

[5] The lotiform columns in Rameses II's work at Luxor show careful modelling, but are clearly columns of the Middle Kingdom re-used (Jéquier, *Temples*, Pl. X).

[6] See Capart, Pl. XXXVII.

[7] For a good rendering of one of these, see Capart, Pl. XLIV.

the central colonnades, the closed papyri in the side aisles of the typical hypostyle hall.

Ptolemaic and Roman artists showed much ingenuity in elaborating and contaminating these time-honoured forms to please 'tired eyes',[1] and Capart justly describes the results at Philae or Edfou as a kind of Egyptian 'baroque'. The same artists revelled in hideous Hathor-capitals, nearly equal in height to the shaft they crowned. However grotesque his conceptions may at first sight appear, the true Egyptian of earlier days invested them with a piety and a tranquillity compared with which Ptolemaic rococo seems meaningless and vulgar.

[1] For this stage in a civilisation, see Lethaby, *Architecture*, p. 94.

CHAPTER III

ARCHITECTURE OUTSIDE EGYPT

I. SUMER

DISCOVERIES come thick and fast. The oldest temple known in northern Mesopotamia is perhaps that of Tepe Gawra in Assyria, with many impressive pilasters and responds and a remarkable, almost symmetrical, plan[1] showing an uncanny resemblance to a group of eighteenth-century assembly rooms. It deserves mention here because, while of comparable age, it differs greatly in plan from the earliest temples of Sumer. These form a compact group of closely similar buildings, of which the temples of Uruk, the first to be properly published, may stand as an example.[2]

The 'White Temple' goes back to the beginning of the Uruk period, and so well into the fourth millennium. Resting on a floor of bitumen, and coated with white-wash, the traces of which enabled its German excavators to recover the plan of its mud-brick walls, it crowned the top of an archaic stepped tower of diminishing platforms, of the type known as a ziggurat. This example was sacred, at any rate later, to the goddess Anu. Like its numerous later rivals, it was regarded as an artificial mountain, a stepped platform raised towards Heaven and intended for the descent of the deity. Woolley supposes that at Bethel Jacob dreamt of such a ziggurat, and Herodotus shows us[3] how the god slept on it at night. At Uruk, it was already orientated with its

[1] See E. Speiser in the *American Journal of Archaeology*, 1937, p. 191. For the date of this building, probably later than the Uruk phase in Sumer, see Childe, pp. 208–10.

[2] For Uruk see Jordan, *Abhandlungen der preussischen Akademie Wissenschafts phil. Hist. Kl.* (Berlin, 1932), Nr. 2, pp. 17 ff. For the temples of Eridu, that seem to have set the pattern for the Sumerians as early as the Al 'Ubaid period, see Childe, p. 119. The temple of Uqair is published by Seton Lloyd and Fuad Safar in the *Journal of Near Eastern Studies*, 2 (Chicago, 1943), pp. 131 ff. It resembles the 'Red Temple' at Uruk, but has no proper transepts. The earliest temple at Gawra itself was a small building of Sumerian plan (Childe, p. 119).

[3] Book I, 181–2.

corners to the cardinal points. The crowning temple measured externally 22·3 by 17·5 metres, and comprised two ranges of rooms, each only one room thick, facing each other across a court 4·85 metres wide.

Even more perfectly preserved was the slightly later Red Temple,[1] whose covered rooms occupied three sides of a central court presumed un-roofed from the niches in its walls (in most of this early work it is exteriors only that are buttressed and niched). The whole building is about 100 by 30 metres—as wide as the Parthenon but consider-ably longer. The main room, with special niches, occupies the far end, and before it the central court broadens out into 'alae'[2], or transepts, which thus appear at the very beginning of architecture, and give a cruciform shape enclosed in a rectangle (see Fig. 24). All external faces have the pilas-ter strips and niches so char-acteristic of them in this architecture, and the covered rooms, almost carved out of the thickness of the walls, have the door in the long side, as in all later Sumerian build-ing, and also, surely, the Sumerian tunnel vault.

Of the same age is the 'High Gate' (see Pl. 5), which is the building Loftus

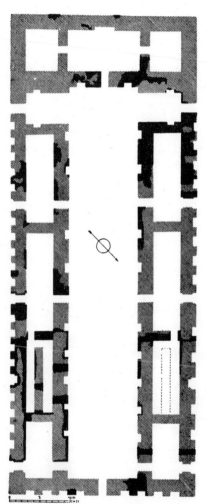

Fig. 24   Red Temple at Uruk, plan.

[1] Illustrated by Jordan, *op. cit.*, Abb. 2, and, in its relation to the other early buildings, Taf. 3.

[2] A term, important, as we shall see (below, p. 255), for the earliest architecture of Italy.

had already partly uncovered a century ago and which Bell
made generally accessible to the student.[1]   The wall of
engaged columns, so interesting to these scholars, is now found
to have enclosed a short stairway, to one side of an entrance
flanked by free-standing columns and even provided with responds
to them—features found rarely enough in later Babylonia.   Small
painted cones of baked clay, deriving, it seems, from bent nails,
were driven into the surfaces in vast numbers, so that, as in Roman
reticulate work,[2] their broad bases alone were visible.   Coloured
red, white or black, they were grouped in geometrical patterns
deriving from the woven hangings of the preceding Al 'Ubaid
period.[3]

These buildings show a perfect mastery of the rectangular
plan, in this at least contrasting favourably with the unusual
temple of the Jemdet Nasr period at Al 'Ubaid, excavated by

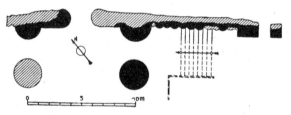

Fig. 25   Plan of High Gate, Uruk.

Woolley.[4]   The architect there attempted but failed to achieve a
rectangle for its platform, because he built the main southern
stair at the same time as a building ramp and failed to align the
south-east face across it.   But it was well drained, and had tanks
for the rainwater.[5]   Moreover, this architect was the first we

[1] See Bell, p. 50.
[2] See below, p. 294.
[3] Wilhelm König in the frontispiece of Jordan, *op. cit.*, gives a faithful
rendering of these columns.
[4] Woolley and Hall, *Al 'Ubaid* (Oxford, 1927).   The reconstructed
fragments can now be studied in the British Museum.   Delougaz has
lately discovered that it was surrounded by an oval precinct-wall, hugged
on the inner face by a set of rooms, for the most part one deep.   A similar
'temple oval', dated about 2500 B.C., has been excavated at Khafajah,
in Akkad.   See P. Delougaz, *The Temple Oval at Khafajah* (Chicago,
1940).
[5] Woolley and Hall, p. 72.   Delougaz, *op. cit.*, pp. 142 ff., is unhappy
about their restorations.

know to develop into splendid decoration the utilitarian protective crust of a building, designed to throw the rain off its mud core. The temple could be almost completely reconstructed from the order in which the fragments had fallen, during a period of neglect, to the foot of the platform. Its decoration included a continuous frieze of copper bulls and another of pastoral subjects in a mixture of coarse limestone and mother-of-pearl, all set in a dark field of bituminous shale and backed by planking. Numerous coloured rosettes of baked clay were also found, perhaps designed to imitate plants. Flanking the temple gate at the top of the grand stair were the foreparts, at least, of two copper lions, and some columns, whose shafts alone have been identified. About 11 feet high and 1 foot wide, they contain the trunk of a palm tree overlaid first with bitumen and then with a mosaic of mother-of-pearl and limestone. This no doubt imitated the palm-bark, and a thin border of bitumen was carefully shown round each piece. Seeing how fashionable it later became to set the shaft on an animal, one is tempted to combine these remains with the lions. Otherwise, both base and capital have vanished —scarcely strange, if they were made of some precious metal, as scholars have reasonably believed. Demangel holds that the column in the tabernacle of Shamash on the relief of Nabu-apal-iddin, King of Babylon some two thousand years later (ninth century B.C.), is similarly a tree-trunk, sheathed in bronze and provided with a volute capital and volute base of metal.[1] At Al 'Ubaid itself other columns and beams survive, of palm-wood overlaid with sheet copper. Finally, one of the friezes shows a rustic byre, of the greatest importance for a knowledge of lighter Sumerian construction.

The Royal Tombs at Ur, also of the Jemdet Nasr period, are equally marvellous.[2] If chapels existed above these death-pits, they have left no trace. Each tomb was a large rectangular excavation, approached by a short stair and partly filled by a stone room or group of rooms. This, as Woolley says, is the period of Sumerian history when stone was commonest. The rooms, where grouped, are set across the axis. The chief corpse, with a few attendants, occupies one room, and the human victims immolated at the funeral, sometimes as many as eighty, the rest

---

[1] *La Frise Ionique*, p. 83.
[2] Fully published by Woolley in his *Royal Cemetery* (2 vols. London and Philadelphia, 1934).

of the pit. The walls are thick and of the roughest unhewn stones set, like the brick voussoirs of the vaults, in coarse clay mortar. 'Coffer-construction' was the rule. Yet the builders could make not only a good corbelled tunnel vault, but were familiar with the arch (arches of burnt bricks survive in Tombs 31B and 32), the apse and even the dome on pendentives over a square chamber.[1] They showed their science equally by their willingness to use centering, which they either removed or retained on completing the work. So this masonry, at first sight so rough, rivals in its inventiveness the metalwork for which the tombs are now so famous.

The plano-convex brick was subsequently introduced—that is a brick whose upper face, for no obvious reason, is given a sharp convex curve like the upper part of a loaf. Henceforward it was used exclusively, down to the time of Sargon of Akkad. The earliest bricks are the smallest and most convex. They must have had some purpose, as they were introduced at the flowering-time of Sumerian inventiveness, *c.* 2800 B.C.

From this period dates the oldest certain example of a real palace, at Mari on the Euphrates, the extreme north-western limit of pure Sumerian civilisation. Comparable in size with the later Assyrian palaces,[2] it displays most of their features, the attached ziggurat, the axial vistas across open courts to the throne-rooms and halls of audience (themselves up to 40 feet wide) and the interiors faced with dadoes, in this case of imitation stone. The doorways of most rooms give on to the centres of the long sides, and windows, if they existed, were rare. While, however, tunnel vaults are found, they spanned normal rooms at Mari far less often than at Khorsabad. The plan also is less closely knit than at Khorsabad, and the two large courts are rather clumsily connected.[3]

The oldest Sumerian buildings, besides their great inherent interest, are also among the best excavated, because most recently discovered. Later temples and ziggurats are larger, but seldom

[1] See Woolley, Pl. 57.
[2] See below, p. 67.
[3] Mari was published by A. Parrot in *Syria*, Nos. 16 to 19 (Paris, 1935–8). For the general plan of the palace, see *Syria*, 19, Pls. III and IV. Parrot discovered no trace of windows or lanterns, and concludes that the lofty doorways sufficed to light the interior (*Syria*, 18, p. 66). Holes for numerous large ceiling-joists still exist on many inner walls (*ibid.*).

display important new features. The Ziggurat of Ur (see Pl. 6) is typical of the series. That of Bur-sin, also at Ur, is perhaps the best preserved.[1] It remained the chief act of piety to build and restore temples, and many famous kings have left their names on the baked facing-bricks with which they repaired the crumbling walls. The pious King Gudea styles himself architect on his famous seated statue in the Louvre, and has across his knees a stilus, a scale and the plan of his temple to Ningishzida (see Fig. 26), all illustrated by King in his *History of Sumer and Akkad*.

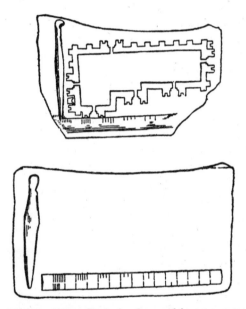

Fig. 26   King Gudea's plan and instruments.

Unhappily, the enormous activity of sixth-century Babylonian restorers has skinned or buried hosts of Sumerian shrines, and we still have not the material, as we have in Egypt, to determine their artistic merit. We do know that the sculpture is superb, and that about the time of Gudea artists carved figured friezes on pedestals,[2] like the pedestals of some Greek cult statues.

[1] The French have now discovered, at Tchoga-Zambil in Elam, a Ziggurat, constructed exactly like the Egyptian step pyramids (see above, p. 19) and noticed in the *Illustrated London News* for 8 Sept. 1956. So the interest of Ziggurats is by no means exhausted.

[2] See King, *History of Sumer and Akkad*, p. 69.

Much later a temple at Uruk built by the Kassite king Kara-Indash (1450 B.C.) introduces a form the Greeks made even more famous, the standing columnar figure.[1] Several examples occupy grooves in the external wall, each representing a deity and holding a vase to spout water. The German restorer assigns them no structural functions; so we cannot yet directly relate them to Telamones or Caryatids.

The Sumerian style represents a very early translation of reed-building. Woolley shows this by comparing the temple of Al 'Ubaid to the rustic byre on its frieze.[2] Like all large Sumerian buildings, its existing platform has a strip of flush brickwork at the bottom, and above this the buttresses and recesses, here narrow and of equal width. Whether of this form, or broad and equal, as on the Ziggurat of Ur, or more complicated, with grooves forming T-shapes on plan, such wall-faces derive from upright standards grooved into a running floor-plate, while the series of continuous horizontal ribbon-like friezes represents the bands of rope that once secured them (see Fig. 27).

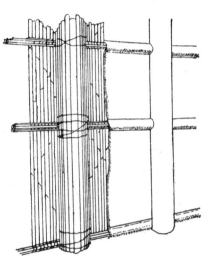

Fig. 27   Reed Wall, Al 'Ubaid.

The plain strips of ground-course are generally low and of ordinary bricks, but suffice to distinguish this technique from the Egyptian of the royal mastabas, where the grooves continue to the ground. The Sumerian way of building lasted into Assyrian times and on page 126 of his *Nineveh* Layard figures a clear example from a tower at Nimrud. Courses of orthostates, the lofty slabs of stone facing or even supporting the wall at the foot, had not been greatly developed in Sumer except for some inner dadoes at Mari. In one settlement of the Jemdet Nasr time at Kish, liable to floods, the house-

---

[1] Published by Noeldeke, *Abhandlungen, etc.*, 1929 (1930).
[2] *Al 'Ubaid*, p. 114. See also *The Development of Sumerian Art* (London, 1935), Fig. 7b.

fronts were protected at the foot by closely-jointed boards and, outside them, by a continuous open drain at the bottom of the wall.[1]   But this received, so far as we can tell, no monumental development later.

Sometimes the Sumerians used colonnades for sheltering not only themselves but their brick walls. Demangel refers to a

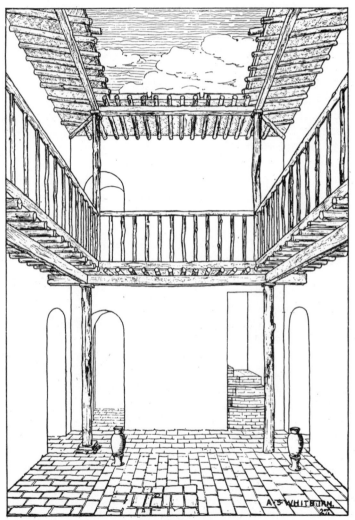

Fig. 28   Courtyard of private house, Ur.

[1] Watelin in Langdon, *Kish*, IV (Paris, 1924), p. 9 and Pl. XI.

small peristylar court, with eight wooden columns on brick plinths, discovered at Lagash.[1] The houses of Ur under the great Third Dynasty were even more sophisticated (see Fig. 28). Here wide eaves supported on wooden posts guided the rain water into a tank in the middle of the square centre court. We have, in fact, already the system of the Roman impluvium, except that the Sumerian houses had an upper storey.[2]

Where they used brick columns, the Sumerians built them of special flat tiles, one completely circular on plan for the centre of each layer, and the surrounding six or eight tiles each shaped as a sector. Asphalt, as usual, served for mortar. The size of the central tile varied in alternate courses. The Hellenistic builders of Babylonia appreciated this technique and transmitted it, without the asphalt, to Pompeii, where it is used, for instance, in the Hellenistic brick columns of the Basilica.[3] Truly, there is no end to the influence of Sumer!

Equally important, as Demangel urges, were the Sumerian protective friezes. At every vulnerable point there ran a frieze of terracotta or some enamelled material. The wall received, in fact, an intelligent articulation anticipating Classical architecture. Moreover, figured friezes already showed the men and animals white against a dark ground, as in the Erechtheum. The Standard of Ur, discovered by Woolley,[4] shows that sometimes, like the Greeks, the Sumerians preferred to silhouette their figures against a blue background, to represent sky. But I know no example of this on a building.

In planning, the Sumerians originated the 'Babylonian' cross-axial room, a long rectangle with a tunnel vault, and with the doors in or near the centre of the long sides. Wachtsmuth supposes[5] there were few or no windows. Indeed, neither the climate nor the heavy vault would have favoured them. So, he thinks, a door in one of the long sides acted as the most efficient source of light. One could add that this plan would give some refuge from the winter draughts to a person at one end of a room. Economical planning would also require the form. It is the best way on a limited site of surrounding a central court with rooms of

---

[1] *La Frise Ionique*, p. 62.

[2] Woolley, *The Sumerians* (Oxford, 1928), Figs. 26 and 27.

[3] For all this, see R. Delbrueck, *Hellenistische Bauten in Latium*, II (Strassburg, 1912), p. 97.

[4] Woolley, *Royal Cemetery*, Pls. 91–2.

[5] F. Wachtsmuth, *Der Raum*, I (Marburg, 1929), p. 13.

Columns of the High Gate, Uruk

General view: restored

(Both reproduced from drawings in *Preussische Akademie der Wissenschaften: Phil. Hist. Klasse, Abhandlungen* 1932, *Nr.* 2.)

Plate 5

Ziggurat at Ur; front view

Pavement at Khorsabad

Plate 6

a decent size; and we find it employed accordingly in houses between 3000 B.C., at Fara (ancient Shuruppak),[1] and 2000 B.C., in Third Dynasty Ur (see Fig. 29).

Even large precincts were often surrounded by buildings only one room deep, appearing almost like tunnels in the thickness of the wall, their ridges running parallel to its outer face. Such, for instance, is the precinct-wall around the Ziggurat of Kish.[2] Even in the vast Assyrian palaces over a thousand years later many courts[3] are still surrounded by ranges of buildings only one room deep, their tunnel vaults identically arranged. The Mesopotamian civilisation could never break out of the Sumerian mould. Indeed, the Sumerians invented all that repertory of constructional forms used in our own building trade until the present century.

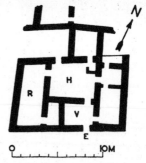

Fig. 29   House at Fara.
E = Entrance; V = Vestibule;
H = Open   Yard; R = Chief Room.

2. ASSYRIA AND LATER BABYLONIA

The first town of Ashur (2700 B.C.), like the gods and mythology of the Assyrians, was entirely Sumerian. Even the distinctive monsters of the gates go back to Al 'Ubaid.[4]   Nevertheless, when, one millennium after the Sumerian collapse, the Assyrian militarists built great palaces for display, in a stonier and rainier country than Sumer they could hardly help twisting the ancient forms.

Theirs is an architecture of enormous palaces. Whereas earlier the palace had stood near the outskirts of the precinct around the ziggurat, the Assyrian palace of Sargon at Khorsabad (722–705 B.C.) entirely enclosed its own private ziggurat. Other great palaces were those of Ashurnazirpal III (884–859 B.C.) at

---

[1] Wachtsmuth, *Der Raum*, I, Abb. 7.   Superstition, it seems, almost forced the Sumerians to give each room a separate door to the Court. 'Rooms opening out of each other are unlucky, but those opening on to the court bring good luck' (Woolley, *Ur of the Chaldees* (London, 1950), p. 168.   So much for Versailles!

[2] S. Langdon, *Kish*, I, Chap. VI, Pl. 44.   At the same time, tunnel vaults, though found at all periods, are rare at first over ordinary rooms.   Cf. p. 1 above and Woolley, *Ur of the Chaldees*, p. 66.

[3] Woolley, *The Sumerians*, p. 47.

[4] See above, p. 59.

Calah, or Nimrud, and of Sennacherib (705–682 B.C.) at Nineveh, or Koyunjik. All stood on platforms approached sometimes by ramps, sometimes by 'Palladian stairs' (flights arranged in symmetrical pairs and running parallel to the wall of the platform). A coping of stepped crenellations generally crowned both the platforms and the palaces. It was indeed universally popular in this age of warfare. It appears on models in the British Museum from Urartu, where it projects beyond the wall-face below, partly, perhaps, to enable defenders to drop objects on the enemy, partly to give the roof-joists and walls a more efficient revetment.[1] On the Ziggurat of Khorsabad, as on the nearly contemporary walls of Ecbatana, the battlements changed colour at every stage.[2] If we can rely on a famous two-handled vase, figured by Andrae[3] and apparently imitating Assyrian revetments, the typical parapet might contain a frieze of bull's heads, each separated from its neighbour by a large rosette, surmounting a bordered strip of smaller rosettes and itself surmounted by crenellations.

We know so much about Assyrian exteriors partly because of the buildings shown in relief on the large stone slabs, or ortho-states, from the courts and halls of the palaces, where they formed a continuous dado along the foot of the walls. The Assyrian reliefs have now been collected by C. J. Gadd.[4] But they are only part of the story. The oldest Assyrian orthostates, from Ashur itself, are of baked clay with scenes in coloured enamels, originally about three feet high,[5] and dated by Andrae, on good grounds, in the reign of Shalmaneser II (1026–1015 B.C.). The later often show a survival of this enamelled dado. At Khorsabad, for instance, a frieze of enamelled bricks, representing a procession, immediately surmounts carved orthostates showing the same subject.[6] Dadoes of any form, let alone double dadoes, are rather a novelty in Mesopotamia; for the planks of the prehistoric houses of Kish left, as we saw,[7] no mark on Sumerian brick-building. The Assyrian examples perhaps derive from the

---

[1] See Demangel, *Frise Ionique*, p. 59.
[2] For the former we have the evidence of the remains (Fergusson, *History of Architecture*, I, p. 155, Fig. 50), for the latter only Herodotus (I, 98), who was long disbelieved.
[3] *Coloured Ceramics from Ashur* (London, 1925).
[4] *The Stones of Assyria* (London, 1936).
[5] See especially Andrae, Pl. 7.
[6] Demangel, *Frise Ionique*, pp. 52–3.
[7] P. 63, above.

protective ground-courses developed by the Hittites to meet
their own more humid climate.[1]

The rooms themselves are of the time-honoured cross-axial
form and must have had most often the long tunnel vault. A
timber roof was reserved for more luxurious rooms and recorded
with more particular boasting. 'On the old platform,' says
Nebuchadnezzar, 'on the breast of the wide earth I made its
foundation stone fast with asphalt and baked bricks. Mighty
cedars from Lebanon, the splendid wood, I fetched for its roofing.
A strong wall of asphalt and baked bricks I cast about it. Royal
commands and decrees I allowed to issue from it.'[2] Yet even
Nebuchadnezzar, as we shall see, had probably to be content with
a vault over his normal throne room; and only a few luxury-
pavilions in Assyria are known to have had the more precious
timber roof.

The palaces are remarkable chiefly for their attempt to force
the rooms into larger and more symmetrical compositions than
most of those known hitherto. In the king's own apartments at
Khorsabad the builders achieved some success (see Fig. 30).
One here had a vista of nearly 400 feet through the great cross-
openings, themselves on a magnificent scale.[3] The famous
winged bulls guarded them in pairs; and great double door-leaves,
swung on pivots, like the famous doors of Balawat, now in the
British Museum, might enhance yet further the splendour of
the court.

But art is now hard and insensitive. The technique can be
brilliant, but the spirit is tired. The winged bulls, in particular,
lack feeling. The Assyrians or their near neighbours had apparently invented the palmette, that fan of elongated leaflets springing
from a small fan-shaped centre, the most pervasive of all their
contributions to art.[4] But they normally arranged tedious strips,
one of rosettes, one of lotus buds and flowers and one of palmettes,
beside or within each other *ad nauseam* on their enamelled brickwork or sculptured stone pavements (see Pl. 6). It remained

[1] See below, p. 92. Tell Halaf is particularly important.
[2] Quoted on Wachtsmuth, *op. cit.*, p. 21.
[3] See especially Bell, pp. 140–1, to whose book I refer the reader for
a good description. But, as G. Loud shows (*Khorsabad*, Chicago, 1936/8),
Khorsabad had few true right angles; and Bell's 'harem' was a chapel.
[4] I am not certain who invented it. Andrae appears to exclude it from
the eleventh-century work at Ashur. It figures on the Nimrud ivories,
which, though found at Calah, are largely north Syrian work of the ninth
century. See below, p. 98.

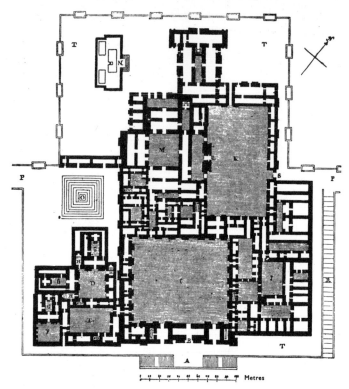

Fig. 30　Plan of Palace, Khorsabad.

for the Greeks to combine the motifs.　Almost the first known alternation of lotus and palmette on a single strip occurs in Cretan bronze breastplates of the seventh century B.C.[1] and heralds an enormous variety of elegant borders and filling-ornaments on the masterpieces of Greek art.　Mouldings in Assyria are equally rare.　One at least, the Assyrian 'gorge' from Calah, repeated from Layard in all the text books, is a mere ungraceful copy of the Egyptian.　One must at present give the Assyrians credit for inventing a simple flat brick hood round the tiled facing voussoirs of their larger arches, as at Khorsabad; and this may or may not have had the influence supposed by Delbrueck[2] on Hellenistic and Early Roman stone arches—one would have

---

[1] W. Lamb figures a good example, *Greek and Roman Bronzes* (London, 1929), p. 63.　Andrae publishes one minor example from Assyria on an enamelled tile from Ashur.

[2] *Hellenistische Bauten*, p. 68.

thought the device sufficiently obvious to be re-invented in any rainy country. For the most part, the Assyrian was asleep.

He may have enjoyed himself more on the small colonnaded pavilions we know from the reliefs; for instance the garden pavilion figured at Khorsabad.[1] The columns show fanciful bases and capitals, probably of metal; and the larger verandahs show what appear to be balconies of Syrian derivation.[2] But even here the responds to the colonnades lack all subtlety. Once again the columns occupy holes in a wall reconstituted immediately above them without any attempt at a frame or entablature. As the Nimrud ivories show, not all the loggias or windows of this time were so brutal as this or as the German restoration of Tell Halaf.[3]

One relief, figured by Fergusson,[4] purports to show the exterior of a palace, with tall columns resting in large bowls or the stylised calyces of lilies, themselves carried on the backs of lions. This is valuable, as it helps us to envisage buildings in Syria, from which many fragments of such columns have been recovered.

The Assyrians seem to have retained the methods of Sumer, for all their heavier and more serious construction. But they depended on north Syria for the forms of their lighter luxury buildings and for a rather ill-ascertained amount of applied decoration.

The revived empire of Babylon has left an enormous mass of remains, nearly all undistinguished except in the capital itself. The administrative and religious centre seems to have been the southern citadel.[5] Here were probably the Hanging Gardens, the substructure of which has perhaps been discovered.[6] Both stone and brick seem, mostly unusually, to have been employed in their construction. But we still know little about them. It is strange that Herodotus never mentions them, though they were later so famous. But his account of Mesopotamia is scrappy. It would be paradoxical to maintain with Delbrueck that this arched construction dates only from Hellenistic times.[7]

The Ishtar Gate, at the N.E. corner of the citadel, exhibits a

[1] See Fergusson, I, p. 182, Fig. 73; from Botta and Flandin, *Monument de Ninive*, II (Paris, 1849), p. 114.
[2] For Syrian balconies, see below, p. 97.
[3] Below, p. 97.
[4] I, p. 183.
[5] See Koldewey, *Das Wieder Erstehende Babylon* (Leipzig, 1925), pp. 65 ff.
[6] Koldewey, *ibid.*, pp. 95 ff.
[7] Delbrueck, p. 102. For the question whether they were built or rebuilt later, see below, p. 245.

new form of enamelled brick decoration.   Instead of dividing the
wall with definite bands or concentrating its decoration, the
architect omits bands and borders and places brick animals in low
relief, the bull and sirrush (the Babylonian dragon), directly
against the blue brick field.   The wall was, however, elaborately
enamelled in the old style at parapet level.   The gate is deeper
than most examples and seems, strangely enough, to have an
open court outside on the north and a barbican inside on the south.
It is badly related to the adjacent buildings.   Once past it, one
sees merely a length of dusty wall.   The entrance to the palace
is comparatively insignificant.

The other object of interest is the enormous throne room (see
Fig. 31 (ii)), 170 feet by 56 feet, according to Koldewey.[1]   Its side
walls are 20 feet thicker than its end walls, pointing to a tunnel
vault, much the largest of its time.   As Babylon remained down
to Greek times a great capital even under foreign domination, a
room of this sort is likely to have impressed the Hellenistic
Greeks.   Its façade on the court displayed enamelled patterns of
palmettes and of architectural capitals with vertical volutes like
those of Cyprus and Neandria.[2]   Their value in history is hard
to assess.   We need not assume with Koldewey that they show
western influence.

The temples have few common features, beyond a maze of
petty rooms, whose disposition varies enormously.   Between the
inner buildings and the thick outer protective walls one often
finds long, thin corridors, as in the temples of Ptolemaic Egypt.
Such features have baffled the later enquirer as seriously as they
must their own builders' attempts at architecture.   'Free planning' walked hand in hand with disintegrating civilisation; and
the Sumerians seemed to have lived in vain.

Mesopotamian building technique resembled Egyptian.   The
wheel was used earlier, but it proved more convenient to transport
colossi by sledge—shown in a relief of Sennacherib's,[3] where
levers and rollers, as in Egypt, also appear.   There is the same
absence of the pulley, except in one relief, and that not a building
scene, but the picture of a well in an enemy city.   The Assyrian
siege engines[4] show only a development of battering-rams and

[1] *Op. cit.*, p. 103.
[2] See below, p. 182.
[3] Layard, *Nineveh* (London, 1853), p. 114.
[4] See, e.g., Layard, *Monuments of Nineveh*, second series (London,
1853), Pl. 21.

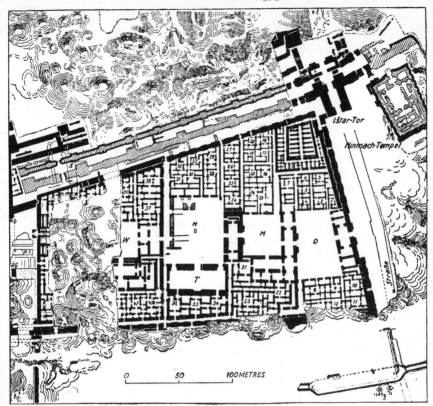

(i)

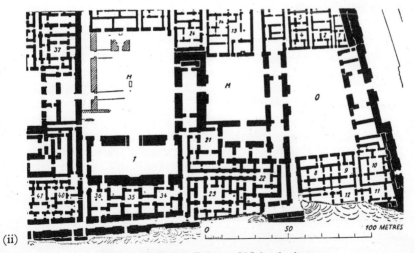

(ii)

Fig. 31 Babylon, Palace of Nebuchadnezzar.
(i) The Ensemble. (ii) The State Apartments.

armour plating. The troops clearly depended on the long bow to win their battles. For Assyrian tents, a forked tree would seem to have sufficed. The number of available slaves and the pleasure of bullying them made mechanical improvement unnecessary.

Babylonian mathematics had progressed much further than Egyptian. Like ourselves, and unlike even the Greeks, the Babylonians used a positional notation 'which by means of columns side by side, one of which contains the units to any number from 1 to 59, and the rest the numbers of each successive power of 60 included in the total, made it possible to express numbers of any size whatever.' So Heath,[1] who adds that the system had the inconvenience of requiring a multiplication table from 1 to 59. On the other hand, the scale of 60 had an advantage in the number of factors of 60. Natural mathematicians, like the inventors of this notation, probably felt less dismay at the length of the multiplication tables, and even the ordinary Babylonian, since it is positional, must have multiplied as quickly as the Greek. In geometry, the Babylonians had propounded by the second millennium problems requiring a knowledge of the Theorem of Pythagoras.[2] Heath hints that they owed their mathematical proficiency, as one might have guessed, to the discoveries of the Sumerians.

3. THE BRONZE AGE IN THE AEGEAN

At the other end of the early world, the peoples of the Aegean, and especially of Crete, though always ignorant of the true arch, were developing a style of remarkable flexibility. Since the discoveries of Woolley at Atchana (Alalakh),[3] Cretan building of the sixteenth and fifteenth centuries is seen to owe much to the eighteenth-century culture of north Syria—for instance, the extensive use of true frescoes, as opposed to the Egyptian tempera, on interior walls, and the free use of cement and of polished stone dadoes. On the other hand, the great Cretan palaces have a plan more subtle than those of Alalakh, where the palace of Yarim Lin is too long and narrow and too heterogeneous. They incorporate light-wells, stepped approaches, entrance halls and external

---

[1] *Op. cit.*, p. 13.
[2] *Op. cit.*, p. 96.
[3] Woolley, *A Forgotten Kingdom* (Harmondsworth, 1953), pp. 72–7.

colonnades of a size and sophistication not found in existing Syrian remains. All things, of course, are still possible in the present fluid state of our knowledge. Syrian conquerors could have flourished architecturally in Crete, as did the Normans in England. But even were this extreme case true, we should still know from Middle Minoan pottery, just as we know from Anglo-Saxon MSS. and sculpture, that the high civilisation of the conquered alone made this possible.

It is harder with Cretan building than with any other to isolate definite elements either in the plan or the construction. For, since roofs were flat outside and in, the designer could combine rooms as he wished and sink light-wells through several storeys where his client might desire them. Moreover, the uneven ground invited him to terrace his palaces both for convenience and effect. One or two large courts, several smaller yards and a series of magazines for storage are the only features everywhere repeated. It is interesting to find the most flexible and least monumental of the early styles arising on Greek ground where, a thousand years later, arose the most unyielding and, in its main shapes, the least variable of all architectures.

As first built, in the Middle Minoan period, Cnossus, the most famous palace,[1] was considerably more solid than it later became, although unfortified[2] even then and no more symmetrical than the present building. However, the Middle Minoan work survives only in patches, as along the west side, where it was re-used as a solid ground-course, or in outbuildings, such as the great viaduct on the south side.[3] The builders generally employed stout upright blocks, or 'orthostates', resting on a spreading stone ground course, or 'toichobate'.[4]

As we see it, the palace is virtually a product of the period 1600–1400 B.C. (Late Minoan I–II). From about 1600 dates the little caravanserai, for the reception of favoured travellers, at the south end of the viaduct.[5] Small though it is, it shows first the

[1] Published, of course, by Sir Arthur Evans in *The Palace of Minos* (4 vols. in 7, London, 1921–36).

[2] A. W. Lawrence argues convincingly in the *Journal of Hellenic Studies*, 1942, pp. 84–5, against the supposed evidence for Middle Minoan fortifications.

[3] Sir Arthur Evans, *PM*, II (London, 1921 ff.), pp. 100 ff. This technique reached its highest level in the second palace of Phaistos (Banti), *Il Palazzo Minoico di Festos*, II (Rome, 1951).

[4] Evans, *PM*, I, suppl. Pl. 1 and p. 208.

[5] Evans, *PM*, II, pp. 103 ff.

Minoan dislike of symmetry and monumental effects—for even the central column in the entrance is placed actually on the stairs and aligned with nothing—second the easy skill of Minoan decoration, with its lightly worn architectural clothing (see Fig. 32). Here, in one of the oldest Cretan buildings we can restore, we find represented in fresco an articulation of pillar and entablature closely resembling that in Athenian fifth-century Ionic. So free, however, is the style, that we can identify from it none of the

Fig. 32   Caravanserai at Cnossus.

materials the Cretans would have used in three-dimensional building. The pillars of this painted architecture are ochreous yellow, with high red 'stockings' and blue bands at the tops. The architrave is also ochreous yellow, and pretends to continue the actual wooden lintel of the door. The frieze above contains a line of birds of many colours, while the cornice above that, though only eight centimetres high, is divided horizontally into three strips, yellow, black and white. When, on the contemporary fresco from the palace,[1] we see a triple shrine, with two red columns in the centre and a black in either wing, each sort with polychrome capitals of quite different coloration, we are forced to hold that the Cretans covered and coloured and probably varied their structural materials as they liked.[2] They veneered many palace walls with thin dadoes of gypsum, and then plastered everything higher.

Cnossus was admirably planned, and fortunately we can recover the design in its main elements. We can ascertain the position of the light-wells and open courts, because they had floors of hard limestone instead of the gypsum used for the rest, which would have disintegrated in heavy rain. Evans has been criticised for re-erecting parts of the palace, but by doing so has at the very least preserved many fragile floors and dadoes.

The palace occupies a hilltop, sloping sharply to east and south, and is roughly a square on a side of over 350 feet, enclosing a large central court running north and south, 190 feet long and 90 feet wide. West of the court were the state apartments, east of it the private apartments.[3] The two main roads, one from the harbour, a little to the north, the other from Phaistos, on the south, converged on the state apartments, along the south front of which ran a colonnaded terrace at least 120 feet from east to west (see Fig. 33). The visitor from the north, after traversing the great parade-ground west of the palace, would usually enter it near its south-west corner and soon find himself at the west end of the south terrace. But the visitor from Phaistos, after refreshment at the caravanserai, would cross the viaduct, climb the great south staircase and find himself at the east end of the same terrace. From the centre of the terrace opened the main entrance of the state apartments, at the south end of an open axis some 130 feet long, continued, with effects that Barry might have envied, directly through light-wells, propylaea, vestibules and further

[1] For a coloured reproduction of this see Evans, *PM.*, III, Pl. XVI.

[2] Dinsmoor says (p. 13) that the capitals of columns on the Great Staircase, crowning as they did wooden shafts, 'must likewise have been of wood'. Why? Sixth-century Greek vases show Doric columns with black shafts, standing on white plinths and crowned by white capitals. Many suppose the plinths are of white limestone. If so, why not the capitals? (In 1948 a possible capital of red sandstone turned up at Mycenne but is still not properly published in 1961.)

[3] I refer the reader for the details of all this to the excellent description of D. S. Robertson, pp. 9 ff.

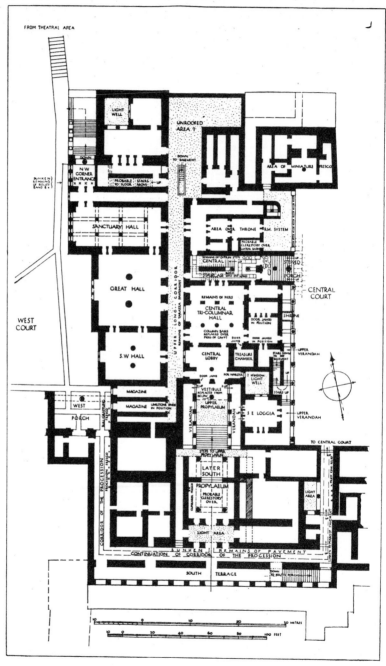

Fig. 33 Plan of State Apartments, Cnossus.

terraces to a central hall.[1] The state rooms to which it led occupied the first floor or piano nobile, above the magazines and corridors of the ground floor. A second grand stair led down from them eastwards to the central court.

The rest of the palace was less impressive. Under the state rooms and opening off the central court is the famous throne room. It is comparatively small and isolated. So, though sumptuously finished and provided with a lustral basin, it was surely not the only throne room.[2] The east side of the central court is irregular, and the private apartments, which occupied most of it, were on a far lower level and turned their back on it. They deliberately faced the south-east and the view, and allowed the prince to relax.

As all have seen, these private apartments form a very interesting architectural group, an example of deliberate asymmetrical planning, for, apart from the grand staircase, a century or two older, they were all built at the same time. They consist of a very open hall, with two distinct suites of rooms, independent of it, cleverly tucked behind it (see Fig. 34). The hall has a south-east verandah, unclassically pivoted on a corner pier, two cross rows of pillars and a light well at the rear. The more northerly suite includes a small hall, another light-well and the grand staircase. The southerly probably comprised the women's quarters. Large windows and open colonnades gave on to the light-wells, and the halls themselves and even the inner walls of the colonnades were decorated with frescoes of fishes and birds.[3] The designs gave even tiny courts an air of enlargement and freedom more whole-hearted than have most similar devices since. The large open hall on the corner closely resembles in plan the verandah-hall of the little Palace and the Grand Entrance of Phaistos,[4] so flexible did the architect find these forms. All alike contain pillars with special recesses, to receive, apparently, the leaves of open doors in the neatest way possible. Their form looks as if it originated in wooden frame and panel construction.

[1] This all seems trustworthy enough. It is based on the plan in Evans (*PM.*, II, Pt. ii, Plan C).

[2] F. Bell, *Prehellenic Architecture in the Aegean* (London, 1926), assumed that the large public throne room was on the piano nobile above. The throne room at Mari (see above, p. 60), without its vestibule, is 90 feet long and 40 feet wide; whereas this lustral throne room at Cnossus occupies, with its vestibule, a mere 45 feet by 22 feet.

[3] See Evans, *PM.*, I, p. 543.

[4] See Bell, *op. cit.*, p. 90.

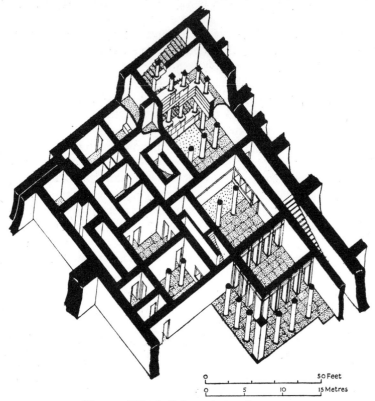

Fig. 34   King's Private Suite, Cnossus.

Phaistos, perhaps slightly later than Cnossus, contains more
small colonnaded yards and also a continuous colonnade around
the large central court.   Like Cnossus, it had a 'theatral area'
attached to its north-west corner, here very well preserved, and
comprising a flat rectangular space, some 40 feet wide, enclosed by
a rectangular auditorium.   We do not know its use.

The Little Palace and Royal Villa at Cnossus and the Palace
of Hagia Triada, near Phaistos, all apparently subsidiary palaces
like the Trianons of Versailles, display the same free plans, the
same open halls and large staircases.   The central apartment of
the Royal Villa, however, deserves some mention.   Its front part
resembles other halls and propyla.   But in the centre of its rear
wall is a recess with a throne and crossing it, a little in front, is a
low wall pierced only in the centre by a passage immediately

before the throne.   This seems to foreshadow the earliest Christian basilicas, with two thousand years intervening![1]   It could have had a religious purpose: for one of the strangest features of this civilisation is the lack of separate temples, certainly of any size. Religious ceremonies regularly took place, it seems, in certain apartments of the palaces or at domestic shrines, one of which faced the central court of Cnossus.   Independent temple-buildings seem to have been almost unknown either to the Cretans or their neighbours on the Greek mainland.

Like the Romans and ourselves, the Cretans had many materials to hand.   No ruthless necessity drove them, as it drove the Sumerians, to make the best use of what they had.   They tried, for instance, many kinds of column, some tapering upwards, some down,[2] some reeded in the Egyptian style,[3] with capitals equally various.   We find some capitals very close to the later north Syrian or the dactyliform Ionic of Early Greece.[4]   Pillars were favoured for basements, stone posts of H-shaped plan, as we saw, for the fronts of halls.   In walls the Cretans kept fairly constant to a very wasteful technique, found as early and as far north as the Second City of Troy (before 2000 B.C.), and ran longitudinal baulks of large scantling for the whole length of their walls at about every fourth course.   The small models of house-fronts, found at Cnossus,[5] show this half-timbering in all its extravagance, and also, like the carved fronts of Mycenean tombs, the flat roofs of unplaned horizontal poles laid to touch one another.   The glut of materials at this time proved fatal to good construction; and, with few exceptions, Minoan talent appears only in planning and applied decoration.

It is not too fanciful to call this the first European style.   The rooms, while often small, have a much more elaborate and less rigid form than the Babylonian.   Colonnades, of inhuman dimensions in Egypt, have been tamed to serve an intimate domestic life.   Hard things have been said about the small house-models.   But at least they escape the standardisation found at Ur.   In disposing his staircases and light-wells, the architect

---

[1] It is described in Bell, pp. 86–7.
[2] Both sorts occur in the fresco mentioned above (p. 75, n. 1), the upward-tapering in pairs, one shaft balanced above the other.   This perhaps accounts for the remarkable, deep abacus-blocks.
[3] See Bell, p. 85.
[4] See below, p. 161.
[5] See Robertson, p. 20, Fig. 8; Evans, *PM.*, I, Fig. 224.

could treat each programme on its merits, unhindered by tradition.

The same seems true of Cretan tombs. They are of many types, and it is dangerous to assign each to any one period. A beehive-tomb at Isopata[1] appears to date from a time when, as was once thought, all beehive-tombs had died out in Crete. Of royal tombs, one at Cnossus, from the end of the Middle Minoan period, has an inner chamber of pure frame and panel construction, a timber technique translated into stone, as in the pillars across the halls of the palaces.[2] A series of halls and passages of ashlar comprise the approach, and the whole was virtually planned in

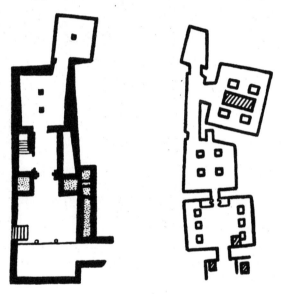

Fig. 35   Temple Tomb at Cnossus and Egyptian tomb compared.

Egypt during the Middle Kingdom.[3] It is known as the 'Temple Tomb' (see Fig. 35). Another royal tomb, one of a pair at Isopata, had a rectangular burial chamber eight metres across internally, sunk, like that of the Temple Tomb, in the ground but lined with coursed ashlar, which, it is alleged, was corbelled

[1] For this tomb, see *Antiquity*, 1948, p. 73. The beehive-tombs of the Bronze Age are generally called 'tholos-tombs'. But there seems no evidence that the Ancients used this term of them. By 'tholos' they seem to mean something shaped like a parasol.

[2] See Evans, *PM.*, IV, pp. 964 ff. and isometric view in folder.

[3] The parallel with some Middle Kingdom tombs is extraordinarily close. See Persson, *New Tombs at Dendra* (Lund, 1943), Fig. 121.

Postern Gate, Mycenae

Plate 7

olumns of the Temple of
Ceres, Paestum

Above and *right*

Blocks of column bases, Senjirli

Plate 8

Nimrud Ivory, showing Temple
Courtesan

to give a roof of pointed cross-section, with an apex about eight metres above the floor.[1] This must have been very unstable, if it existed at all. It is much larger and more deeply sunk than the keel-shaped corbelled tombs of Ugarit, its near contemporaries, whose upper courses, to stay in position, needed heavy counter-weighting.[2] There was an antechamber at Isopata, similarly of ashlar but smaller, approached by a sloping entrance passage, or 'dromos', cut in the rock and not lined—features which put the tomb in the main Minoan tradition, whereas the Temple Tomb is abnormal and much more splendid. At Isopata the bodies were buried under the floor of the chamber. But at Cnossus the gypsum chamber itself held the dead man, for whom rites were presumably performed in a chapel immediately above.

The tombs of the less distinguished began, it seems, early in the Middle Minoan Age as large communal enclosures, rectangular buildings in eastern Crete, at Palaikastro, for instance, or Mallia, circular in the Mesara, the central plain. Some of the latter, the largest some eight metres in diameter, were published by Xanthoudides.[3] Some had very shallow antechambers, like some tombs in Egypt. But perhaps for the plan, and indeed the whole design, we should seek the prototype rather at Arpachiyah.[4] The walls of rough stonework lean inwards at both places, and it would have been possible at both to span the interiors with shallow domes of mud.

But in the Late Minoan and the corresponding Late Helladic Age the favourite form, not only in Crete but over a wide area of the Greek mainland, became the rectangular chamber tomb. This was normally cut in the side of a hill, and possessed a massive entrance with a long approach, or dromos. The richer examples are 'single graves', for at most two or three occasions of burial. The poorer are obviously 'family vaults'. The entrance to the chamber was normally blocked, and the cult of the dead, once the funeral was over, confined to the dromos.

Despite the magnificence of their interiors and their pivoted

[1] Fyfe in Evans, *Archaeologia*, LIX (1905). This tomb was destroyed in the last war.
[2] See below, p. 93. The walls at Isopata certainly sloped inwards. The tomb-chamber could, however, have been spanned with wooden beams above a certain height, giving an effect like that of the Regolini-Galassi Tomb (below, p. 228).
[3] S. Xanthoudides, *The Vaulted Tombs of Mesara* (Liverpool, 1924), Pls. LXI, LXII.
[4] See above, p. 10, n. 2.

6—1

bronze doors, the same seems to have held good of the great
beehive-tombs on the Greek mainland, the noblest monuments of
the Late Helladic, or Mycenaean, Age. At this period, from 1500
to 1200 B.C., we find the Cretan style dominated on the mainland
by more powerful minds; and it is these beehive-tombs, above
all, that show the force of their achievement. Unlike the earlier
Cretan beehives, they served almost certainly as ˙Royal Tombs'.
Like the chamber-tombs, they possess a chamber, here transformed
into a circular beehive, a massive entrance and a long dromos (see
Fig. 36). Of the three most impressive beehive-tombs, the
'Treasuries' of Atreus and Minyas and the Tomb of Clytemnestra,
the two former allow themselves the luxury of a side-chamber. In
the Treasury of Minyas, at Orchomenos, this room has a magnificent ceiling of four carved slabs, which seems to mark it out as the
burial-chamber of the prince. At the beehive-tomb of Dendra,
the only example where the burials have been discovered reasonably intact, the dead were placed in pits below the level of the floor.
But despite this, and despite the evidence that the Treasury of
Minyas was accessible in classical times—for a Hellenistic pedestal
occupies its centre [1]—we should not, it seems, think of the beehive
as meant for a chapel where the relatives and subjects of the dead
prince assembled in later years. In most cases the dromos was
blocked by a wall, probably not long after the funeral. Nor,
perhaps, was the beehive ever to be opened again, even where we
have evidence of several burials. Possibly suttee, practised early
in the third millennium at Ur and under the first Egyptian
Pharaohs, and widespread in the cultures of early Asia, survived at
Mycenae down to these great tombs of Late Helladic II (1400–
1200 B.C.).[2]

The typical beehive has a height equal to its diameter—about
45 feet in the great examples. Ideally it is built of successive
horizontal rings or courses of large sawn conglomerate blocks.
In the Treasury of Atreus the uppermost fifteen rings, the most

[1] See J. G. Frazer, *Pausanias' Description of Greece*, V (London, 1898),
pp. 189–90, where this 'Treasury' is described at length.
[2] A mastery of the literature on Aegean Bronze Age Tombs would
require months of study. I owe to Mr. Sinclair Hood such knowledge
as I may have grasped of the salient facts. The beehive-tombs of
Mycenae are discussed by A. J. B. Wace in his *Mycenae* and in *BSA*,
XXV. That at Dendra, with its intact burials, is published by A.
Persson, *The Royal Tombs at Dendra* (Lund, 1931). The same scholar
has published some chamber tombs, including the unique cenotaph, in
New Tombs at Dendra (Lund, 1943).

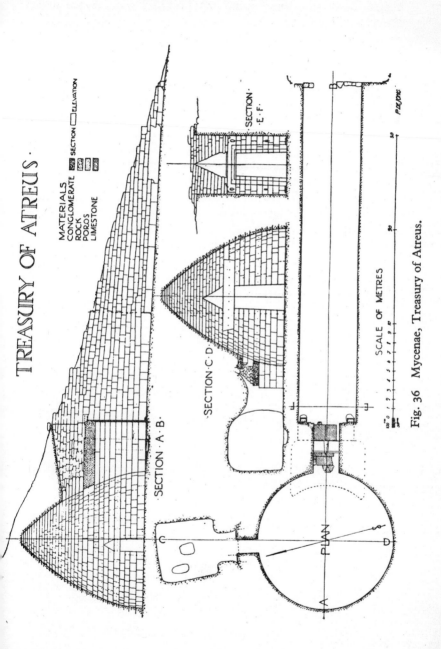

Fig. 36 Mycenae, Treasury of Atreus.

sharply corbelled, are all unbroken, and so quite stable. The principle of the arch, in fact, is here applied horizontally, so that no counterweight is required. The Mycenaeans took many years to discover the principle. Their earliest beehives, faced with random rubble, relied more on the strength of the clay backing for the stones. Even the tomb of Dendra, the contents of which reveal such high skill, was lined with patches rather than courses of stone.[1]

The interior of the Treasury of Atreus was studded with bronze rosettes. But it was the front on the dromos that provided the best field for luxurious decoration. The jambs and lintel were of red conglomerate, the lintel of two colossal blocks, which were yet provided with a triangular relieving space above, as if the builders distrusted even their strength. Their soffit is at the natural ground level, and they were probably quarried nearby and slid down hill into position.[2] The front of jambs and lintel is carved with three fasciae, of which the outermost is the largest, but was largely concealed by engaged columns of green alabaster, and, above the door, by imitations of the circular ends of horizontal ceiling-poles. As it stands today, without these applied ornaments, it seems to foreshadow the architrave on the classical Ionic Doorway with rude ceiling-poles, or dentils, above it. The flanking columns similarly point forward, but this time to classical Doric. They stand on the thinnest of circular plinths, and in the Tomb of Clytemnestra were fluted vertically with simple arrises. In the Treasury of Atreus, where, instead, they are carved with running spirals inside chevrons, the capitals have a low abacus, a cushion or echinus of equal height, and below this a ring of concave leaves, and resemble far more closely than any Egyptian work the resilient Doric form, especially of Magna Graecia (see Fig. 37). It is remarkable to find a Bronze Age tomb anticipating both classical Orders, and with a door opening, the shape of which would do credit to a classical Greek.

The Classicism, it is true, seems greater now that the ornament in green alabaster and red porphyry, once bolted to the front, has

---

[1] Prof. Wace has long made the masonry of the beehives in the Argolid and its evidence for their sequence his especial study. See his accounts in the *British School Annual*, XXV (1923), pp. 283 ff. and Wace, *Mycenae* (Princeton, 1949), pp. 26 ff. The tenacity of clay and its exploitation by the builders of the earlier Mycenaean beehives were discussed by Doerpfeld in *AM*, XXXIV.

[2] Wace, *BSA.*, XXV, p. 362.

fallen away. This façade not only resembled no Greek work in its colours, but had an unclassical upper storey, with columns of its own flanking the relieving triangle—an interesting design, no doubt, but one of which the details remain desperately uncertain.[1]

If we discern a European temperament in Crete, we find at Mycenae one already Greek. For in architecture it is the Greek practice to refine a type of building to its greatest possible perfec-

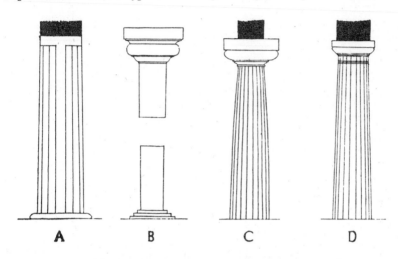

A   B   C   D

Fig. 37   The Doric column and its prototypes.

A = Beni-Hasan (Egyptian Middle Kingdom).
B = Treasury of Atreus (Mycenaean).
C = Basilica, Paestum (6th Cent. Greek).
D = Temple of Zeus, Olympia (5th Cent. Greek).

tion.   Working in this spirit, the builders of the beehive-tombs created the masterpieces of the Aegean Bronze Age.

The best-known mainland palaces show something of the same quality.   When, some time after 1400 B.C., an entirely new palace

[1] The official restoration of the relieving triangle with its flanking and filling ornament is very mean.   For an illustrated account of it, see Wace, *Mycenae*, pp. 29 ff.   Dinsmoor, p. 33, n. 3 (on p. 34) has called for further study.   It is not at all certain which of the more-or-less plausible fragments in the British Museum came from the Treasury of Atreus.   A possible prototype of the engaged columns exists at Phaistos, and is published by L. Banti, *Il Palazzo Minoico di Festos*, II (Rome, 1951), Fig. 277.

was erected over the site of the earlier round house at Tiryns,[1] the builders grounded its walls on large stones, each the full width of a wall. Its central and principal room, with the main hearth, is always called the megaron, for it corresponds closely to the room of that name in the Homeric poems (see Fig. 38). With its two vestibules, it forms a rectangle, externally $12\frac{1}{2}$ by 25 metres, and faces south along the axis of a colonnaded forecourt, entered by a colonnaded propylon large enough to admit chariots, and of a plan already classical. On the west of the forecourt were apparently rooms for guests, with the main bathroom at their north-east corner and equally accessible from the megaron. A long corridor around most of the megaron connected a series of smaller apartments and also admitted one to a smaller megaron and forecourt on the east, long considered the women's megaron but now regarded as a simpler and earlier palace.

The approach to this inner core of buildings, through a small south court and outer propylon, appears to round off the original plan. The massive outer walls, with two fortified main gates on the approach, a small postern on the other side of the hill, and a long low outer bailey on the north of the palace, are perhaps all one later addition.

The Palace of Mycenae is more fragmentary. Its existing megaron faces west, not south. But perhaps another larger megaron once faced south on the crown of the hill, only a few yards away, where a very early Classical temple now stands, with an orientation north and south, very unusual in temples. Nor has the forecourt the beautiful propylon of Tiryns. But the carvings and frescoes were very similar and originally perhaps just as sumptuous.

Before pronouncing on the architectural effect of these buildings, we should doubtless know the pitch of their roofs. In the eighth century B.C., as we know from models and from Homer,[2] a steeply-pitched roof of thatch was the rule. Ancestors of the megaron of Tiryns, with forehall, closed main room and hearth, had often

---

[1] I understand as little as anyone the form of this pre-Mycenaean building at Tiryns. As traced by Mueller (*Tiryns*, III, 1938, and 29 ff.) it had a radius of 14 metres. I can only suppose it had a centre court and a ring of rooms with roofs sloping down to it. Perhaps, then, it had affinities with the famous oval house of the Middle Minoan I Period at Chamaezi (Robertson, p. 8).

[2] E.g., *Iliad* 23, vv. 712–13. Tiles, apparently from flat roofs, have now been found at Lerna, but are still unpublished. They seem, however, to be quite the exception.

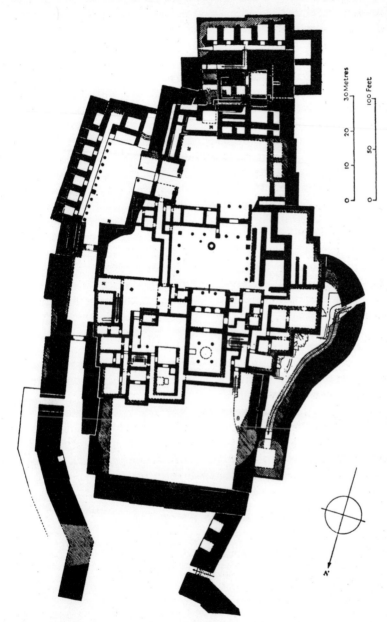

Fig. 38   Plan of Palace, Tiryns.

an apsidal end, as if a central pole once upheld a semicircular tent-like roof. The corridor around the megaron might also derive from an early, open passage to receive the rain from dripping eaves.[1] But Tiryns itself can hardly have had such a roof. Its construction and details are extremely Cretan, and before tiles were invented roofs had to be quite flat, as in Crete, or very steep. Nor can one believe that the corridor, in so sophisticated a building, was open to the elements. Nor, amid the picture of Bronze Age buildings from Orchomenos[2] and elsewhere, does one find any roofs or ceiling-joists other than the horizontal. A miniature Westminster Hall in such surroundings would be outrageous.

The spirit of these palaces is quite new. The chief rooms are arranged on the but and ben principle, that is, are closed at the back and have a short anteroom, quite unlike the apartments in Cretan palaces. Unlike Crete also is the persistence of the same grouping of megaron, vestibule and side passage. Even the unique palace at Gla in Boeotia can perhaps be reduced to two megara, each with attached rooms, backing on to one corner and held together by corridors.[3] Most of the elements are Cretan, the door posts of H-shaped plan, the frescoes that, despite the hearth, enlivened the interior of the megaron and imply an efficient chimney,[4] and the magazines, that now appear, at Tiryns at least, inside the great defensive wall. Some small Cretan buildings, such as the palace-shrines, possessed, we know, a podium carved or painted just above ground level with a very distinctive frieze, with projecting upright oblongs ('triglyphs') and recessed horizontal oblongs ('metopes') each containing two half-rosettes just touching in the centre.[5] The vestibule of the megaron at Tiryns and Mycenae had a nearly identical frieze just above ground level. It is not, then, the elements but the symmetry and simplicity of design that breathe the new spirit.

The Mycenaeans, finally, showed a greater taste for sculpture.

---

[1] The arguments for the steep roof are powerfully marshalled by Baldwin Smith (*AJA*, 1942).

[2] See H. Bulle, *Orchomenos* (Munich, 1907), Taf. XXVIII.

[3] See Bell, *Prehellenic Architecture*, Chap. 21.

[4] Arvid Andren (*Architectural Terracottas from Italic Temples* (Lund, 1940), pp. lxviii–ix, thinks the chimney was a gabled hood, with both ends open, resting on the roof and that the steep roofs of the earliest known Greek buildings were merely an enlargement of this hood.

[5] See Robertson, pp. 30–2. For the restoration by Holland of the forecourt at Mycenae, with this motif forming a low dado, see Dinsmoor, Fig. 8.

We know nothing in Crete to equal the reliefs of bulls from Mycenae, probably from the Treasury of Atreus,[1] let alone the famous lions above the Lion Gate. The sequence of the beehive-tombs[2] shows that the Mycenaeans, at least, learnt to dress hard building stones comparatively late. At the very end, when the last palaces of the mainland were surrounded with Cyclopean walls (see Pl. 7), the piling together of huge stones, dressed or undressed, became a veritable obsession with the Mycenaeans. Nor could the classical Greeks ever forget this particular achievement.

We have now considered the three most distinctive Prehellenic styles. The Egyptian showed the greatest sense of grouping and scale, and paid the least deference to mere utility. The Sumerian could boast an extraordinary skill in the abutment and revetment of masses of fragile material, and decorated the protective shield after a pattern that has survived to some extent in the building of all later ages. Egypt, whose style exports very badly, provided the world with an example, the Sumerians with many necessary skills. The Minoan style, with plans more flexible than either, suffered from a glut of materials, and so remained constructionally amateurish. In its Mycenaean version, however, it not only improved as construction, but evolved forms most precious to us as forerunners of the classical Greek. But before we turn to its brilliant successors, we must survey the intervening styles of Asia Minor and Syria.

4. OTHER PREHELLENIC STYLES

One of the most distinctive is the Hittite, of the later second millennium. Known even today chiefly from the capital, Boghaz-koï, it particularly recalls the Mycenaean style, with which we now know it was contemporary. Over the enceinte of the capital we must not linger. Fortification here, as at Tiryns, had already reached a development seldom surpassed before the discovery of gunpowder.[3] Sally-ports, barbicans, towers to give cross fire

---

[1] See *British Museum Catalogue of Sculpture*, I, Pl. 1 (London, 1928) pp. 28–30.

[2] See above, p. 84.

[3] At only one moment before then did offensive weapons threaten to outrun the science of defence—in early Hellenistic times, when catapults were enormously developed. See A. W. Lawrence, *JHS*, 1946, pp. 99–107.

along stretches of wall and all the other apparatus brought back by Crusaders to Western Europe had existed previously in the East for two or more millennia; and Assyrian reliefs inform us that by 900 B.C. every city-wall had rudimentary galleries, or machicolations, from which to drop boulders upon the enemy.[1]

The gates of Boghazkoï are interesting. Some are deep and narrow, flanked for their whole depth by huge oblong towers and broken near the back and front by pairs of enormous jambs, probably once continued upwards as 'hairpin' arches (see Fig. 39), others are split into a pair of rooms, running across the axis of the gate and both entered towards one side—this class an apparent

Fig. 39   Hairpin arch, Boghazkoï.

adaptation of the Mesopotamian style of room to purposes of siege-warfare. Even in the first class, the hairpin arch reminds us of various buildings on Assyrian reliefs, with entrances of hairpin shape.[2] The truth is that, for reasons we saw when discussing Egypt,[3] the elliptical arch is popular with all early peoples. Lethaby characteristically observes that 'when we become

---

[1] Not, it seems, known to Homer; for Ajax had to throw his boulder out over the battlements—see *Iliad*, 12, vv. 380 ff.

[2] See, for a good example, E. A. Wallis Budge, *Assyrian Sculptures in the British Museum*, London 1914, Plate XVIII.   All arched openings on Assyrian reliefs tend to have the shapes of hairpins—perhaps, however, because the sculptor was too lazy to give them vertical jambs.

[3] See above, pp. 49–52.

accustomed to it, it is seen to be the most beautiful form of arch, for it is the most perfect and scientific.'[1]

Mesopotamian monsters occasionally flank the gates. But, inside the enceinte, it is the Aegean whose influence we feel. As in the West, but not in Babylonia, shrines occupy no separate temples, but probably rooms in the palaces. Puchstein decided rather desperately that the palaces must be temples.[2] But their aspect is domestic, and we have, besides, the analogy of the neighbouring Aegean culture. For, as will appear at once, their arrangement in many ways recalls Tiryns. One must confess that the religious rooms at Boghazkoï are not yet located, not, it seems, being marked with cult signs like some of the rooms at Cnossus. In the main rooms of two palaces (the 'ist and 2nd Temples' of Puchstein) are granite bases, on one of which (placed against a wall) Puchstein sets a throne, on the other a statue. The first could indeed be a throne, the second, if fairly well plastered above, a hearth—both, therefore, secular in intention.

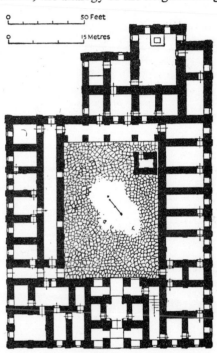

Fig. 40 Plan of Palace I, Boghazkoï.

Magazines, although covering an enormous area, are excluded, as at Tiryns, from the central buildings of each palace. All the four chief palaces have 'megara', with forecourts entered directly from the outside, as at Tiryns, through wide passages at one of the front corners. Palace I (see Fig. 40) has also a magnificent propylon, of a somewhat Aegean type. At the inner end of the courts, a loggia masks the front of the main room. In three

---

[1] *Architecture*, p. 111.
[2] O. Puchstein, *Boghaskoï* (Berlin, 1912). I still (1961) think them palaces.

palaces, II, III and IV, the main room has its walls strictly aligned on the court, but in none is it entered directly through the loggia. Instead, one must turn several times and traverse a small room or two in order to reach it. The bitter cold evidently compelled the Hittites to modify a plan evolved in the milder Aegean world. The ground course, moreover, solidifies into a series of huge 'through' blocks or massive 'orthostates' laid back to back, taking the whole superincumbent wall. Dowel holes near the edges of their upper surface show that this wall was at least faced with wood (see Fig. 41). In the Megaron at Tiryns comparable blocks with similar dowel holes are found only on the southern extremities of the two walls. But the Hittite architect needed them everywhere to protect his upper walls from snowdrifts, and of course left them uncarved. Finally, the palaces are comparable in size

Fig. 41   Door-jamb, Boghazkoï.

and number to the king's house and the surrounding houses of the nobility in a typical Mycenaean 'acropolis'. Experts have long discussed the kinship of Asia Minor and the early Aegean in mythology and ritual; and to these we may perhaps add architecture.

Two other cities of the second millennium, Ugarit and Alalakh, show various links with the Aegean world, especially in innumerable small objects of pottery and metalwork.

The famous tombs of Ugarit are dated securely by the vases they contain to the later phases of the Mycenaean Age (after 1450 B.C.). Like the later graves in Ur, they are private vaults, attached to the richer private houses. The rectangular burial chamber is approached by a dromos with descending stairs, and has a roof of large corbelled blocks in only two or three courses, heavily counterweighted and giving the interior the shape of an inverted keel.

Alalakh, in some of its numerous successive occupations, had a palace approaching the great Minoan buildings in size, though never in beauty of plan,[1] with a large central yard, like the Minoan, between the state apartments and the more ordinary domestic offices. The temple, rebuilt at least four times to widely differing plans during the Hittite overlordship between the fifteenth and twelfth centuries B.C., shows the earliest known stages of the building-type long known to German scholars as the 'Hilani'—a type characteristic of the north Syrian style and employed for the most part as a palace. As understood by most authorities—for instance, Oelmann[2] and Naumann[3]—the developed 'Hilani' is a rectangular building with a loggia, often approached by a wide flight of stairs, in the centre of the long side. To each side of the loggia is a blank front wall, and an almost un-lighted room, while behind it in the centre is a long rectangular central room, its axis parallel to the long axis of the loggia. This, the final plan at Alalakh, which seems to combine Cretan and Sumerian ideals, is found repeatedly in north Syria in the early first millennium and has had a long history in the dry zone of Asia, being traced by Oelmann as far in space and time as modern Tibet (see Fig. 42). However, I must drop the name 'Hilani' in this book, because Woolley has lately argued[4] that the real 'Hilani' was a native of Hittite Asia Minor, not of north Syria, that it had at least two storeys and that the chief room was on the first floor and approached by a corner staircase from one end of the loggia, not on the ground floor or entered by a door on

[1] See Woolley, *A Forgotten Kingdom* (Harmondsworth, 1953).

[2] *Haus und Hof in Altertum*, pp. 80–4. Oelmann agrees with Woolley that a 'Hilani' can have several storeys, as in Tibet, and remain a 'Hilani'. But it must preserve for the whole height of its façade an open centre between massive wings; and Woolley's first Hittite temple is altogether too irregular to conform to the type. For suggestive parallels between the stage-buildings of Greek theatres, Syrian 'loggia-buildings' and possible Egyptian and Sumerian prototypes (none, however, quite like the Syrian), see Margaret Bieber, *The History of the Greek and Roman Theater*, Princeton 1939, pp. 217–19.

[3] In Oppenheim, *Tell Halaf*, II, Pt. III (Berlin, 1943), pp. 369–402. O. R. Gurney, *The Hittites* (Harmondsworth, 1952), p. 210, appears to hold the traditional view, as does H. Frankfort in *Iraq* xiv, pp. 126–8.

[4] *A Forgotten Kingdom*, p. 142. '. . . the Hittite building, the "Hilani" which so took the fancy of the Assyrians, was a religious building and it contained an upper chamber.'

the main axis of the building. He appears to think of it as one of those pavilions on Assyrian reliefs,[1] with a tall massive ground floor and a very open, almost flimsy upper storey. In its early stages, he likens it to the clay model that he unearthed from the Hittite levels of Alalakh, which represents a temple with a first floor over the rear half. The type traditionally known as a 'Hilani' I shall call 'loggia-building'. Neither type seems to share much with the buildings of Boghazköi.

The temple at Alalakh slowly approached the type of the

Fig. 42   Tibetan loggia-buildings.

loggia-building.[2] In its first phase it already contained a large room and an open loggia. But the loggia had an asymmetrical front and was filled with staircases to vanished upper storeys. In the second phase, the stairs and upper floors were removed, and lions and other decorations added to the front of the loggia. In the third, a building of about the thirteenth century B.C., we find

[1] For which see, e.g., Fergusson, *History of Architecture*, I, p. 182, Fig. 73.
[2] Woolley gives the successive plans on pp. 1–22 of the *Antiquaries' Journal* for 1950.

for the first time a symmetrical plan (see Fig. 43), with a tripartite shrine like that of Vitruvius' Etruscan Temple,[1] all panelled internally like Solomon's Temple some centuries later. The development into the full north Syrian style was now virtually complete. But for some unknown reason (perhaps commercial decline) the two side-shrines were moved, in the last phase, into the loggia, while its façade was given a flight of steps.

When, after the great turmoil of 1200–1050 B.C., north Syria and Cappadocia regain some tranquillity, we find a widespread

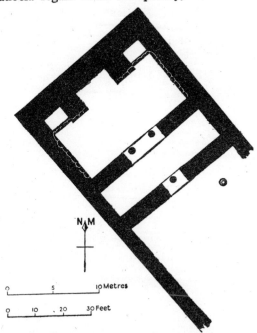

Fig. 43 'Third Temple', Alalakh.

and distinctive group of buildings erected over about three centuries. Their style is best known at present from the remains of Arban, Tell Halaf, Carchemish and Senjirli and from the elegant small ivories found at Nimrud. Although Nimrud is, of course, Calah, the capital of their destructive enemy, Assyria, these ivories have been shown by Barnett[2] to come from the north Syrian states; while the monuments of Arban, thought by Bell[3] to

[1] See below, p. 224.
[2] *Iraq*, 1935, pp. 180 ff.
[3] *Early Architecture in Western Asia*, pp. 128–9.

be early Assyrian work, are now seen to have the north Syrian characteristics, such as the turning of the muscles into geometrical constructions.

On north Syria one can here merely epitomise Naumann's most excellent and exhaustive discussion.[1] The technique of these buildings combines Western and Mesopotamian elements. Like those of Sumer, most lack proper stone foundations. But occasional examples, such as the 'Temple-Palace' of Tell Halaf, have stone orthostates as facings for the lower walls, bound to the crude brick cores by horizontal 'through' beams, the notches for which survive on their upper faces. The orthostates of the palace are carved in relief; but on the adjacent 'Scorpion Gate' they are plain and give an effect purely architectural. The builders seem to be remembering ancient Hittite construction in another land and climate; and their orthostates, from being the socle, have degenerated into a facing for the brick wall. In one of the oldest north Syrian buildings one finds a transitional technique, with a socle of rough stones, a line of 'through' beams resting upon it, and, pushed between these, the lowest bricks of the wall. Assyria appears to have derived her orthostates from this style. None of stone are known in Assyria before the ninth century.

North Syrian buildings flaunt brick arches in important positions. The Fountain Gate of Tell Halaf has a notable pointed vault. The jambs bond into the wall, but the vault itself, three voussoirs deep, does not. The technique is as good as anything of the time in Mesopotamia, from which it must derive. On the other hand, the architects have altogether abandoned the pilaster-buttresses of Mesopotamia and use the Babylonian bitumen-mortar only very sparingly. They have in fact consciously assimilated elements from East and West into their own new style.

The normal palace is a loggia-building. The north Syrians had, indeed, invented another type, the *Iwan* (Wachtsmuth's 'liwan'), with a great future before it. A long, tunnel-vaulted throne-room, entered, unlike the Babylonian, at one end, extending from the front to the rear wall of the building, and flanked by simpler, smaller rooms, it appears certainly at Tell Halaf and perhaps at Senjirli.[2] But it is still rare. It only comes into its own, at Hatra and Ctesiphon, centuries after Alexander the Great.

---

[1] See above, p. 93, n. 3.
[2] Naumann, *op. cit.*, p. 397.

At present it is the loggia-building on which north Syrian art is lavished (see Fig. 44).

The loggia-building of Tell Halaf has an illuminating history. In its first phase the loggia occupied an eccentric position in the long south front. In the second, some attempt was made to give it a symmetrical frame and wings. Long symmetrical compositions were now coming slowly into fashion.

Much thought was expended on the loggias themselves and on the windows of the chief apartments (see Pl. 8). Unlike the Egyptians, whose windows could not open, and the Babylonians,

Fig. 44   Tell Halaf, cross-section of front loggia.

who largely avoided windows, Syrians almost lived at the window. One thinks of the King of Byblos, who gazed out of it instead of answering Wen Amon,[1] of the Mother of Sisera and of Jezebel herself. Their windows are far less crude than known Cretan examples, such as those actually restored at Cnossus, or represented on the Minoan house models[2]; although some basalt models found at Tell Halaf,[3] which show a downward tapering shaft in place of a mullion, suggest Cretan influence. Some Nimrud

[1] See *CAH*, II, p. 193.
[2] See above, p. 79.
[3] *Tell Halaf*, II, iii, Abb. 9.

ivories, plaques with the sacred harlots of Astarte displaying their
attractions at her temple windows, represent a variety of elaborate
balconies.   But reliefs or remains of north Syrian casements or
lattices appear so far to have eluded us.

The entrance of the loggias possessed not only the customary
flanking monsters but others, singly or in pairs, under the free-
standing columns (see Pl. 8).   On the backs of these monsters
stood the stone bowls, stylised lotus-flowers or other fancifully-
shaped members designed to support the actual shaft (see Pl. 8).
Despite their appearances, they are not actually hollowed out to
receive it.   The normal base thus consisted of two stone blocks,
the animal support and the base proper, an elaborate combination
of cup-shaped or cushion-shaped members, with or without
circles of down-turned leaves.[1]   At Senjirli the two parts, it seems,
were merely mortared together.   The famous pedestal of the
sphinxes has a flat upper surface, while the upper member has
apparently a flat underside.   It is interesting to find that this
block tapered downwards, which would necessitate a downward
tapering shaft, as in the windows [2]   Simpler single bases also
exist, one of which shows a horizontal torus between two rope-like
members, and thus dimly anticipates the Erechtheum   Shafts and
capitals have vanished, so were probably of wood.   The mixed
materials, the probable downward taper and the odd number of
columns found in loggias at Senjirli all recall Minoan Crete.

At Tell Halaf in the 'temple-palace', the architect substituted
stone caryatids above the monsters for these wooden columns.
One must call them that, although they are in fact male figures,
for they have the long columnar garment and the tall fez or 'polos'
of so many early Greek female statues, whether caryatids or free-
standing 'dedications'.   For figured piers, the Greeks insisted on
draped female figures, as only so could they achieve an architectural line.

We know more about the caryatids and other ornaments of this
time from the Nimrud Ivories.[3]   Known in some cases to give

[1] In the mid-seventh century Babylon seems to have used such
column-bases, to judge from the relief of Ashurbanipal in the British
Museum. See H. R. Hall, *Babylonian and Assyrian Sculpture in the
British Museum*, Plate XLII.

[2] See Koldewey in Von Luschan, *Ausgrabungen in Sendschirli*, II
(Berlin, 1898), p. 197 and Abb. 88.   I cannot resist his arguments that
the base and the shaft tapered downwards.

[3] Fully and excellently discussed by R. D. Barnett in his paper *The
Nimrud Ivories and the Art of the Phoenicians*, in *Iraq*, 1935, pp. 180–210.

exact copies of features in large buildings—part of an ivory sceptre, for instance, comes very close to the upper member of the bases at Senjirli—they suggest a wider variety of motifs than has survived in stone. Some naked ivory caryatids, instead of wearing the polos, have a crown of downward-curling leaves,[1] for all the world like the column-capitals on that early Greek master-piece, the Massaliot Treasury at Delphi. The naked caryatid, often found on mirror-handles, was sacred to Astarte, goddess of love; and her consort lived in a palm or cedar, trees often used for columns at this time. The symbolism of the type is evidently deep and complicated.

A second type, the servile, carries the load not on the hand but the arms, is usually male, and is called a 'Telamon' or 'Atlas' (Vitruvius' 'Persian') in later, classical days. And there is yet a third type, certainly developed in north Syria, although it perhaps originated in Egypt. This, consisting of figures holding hands around a central pier, on which they turn their backs, developed in Greek hands into the acanthus column, of the early fourth century, at Delphi, with its 'three marble dancing maidens . . . grouped round the central support for the bronze tripod kettle.'[2] The 'Caryatid' and 'Persian' that Vitruvius describes in his introduction go back to periods and religions of which he never dreamt.

It is interesting to see Greek taste, in its purge of architectural crudities, retaining the Caryatid but banishing the monsters from beside the gates and beneath the columns. The Etruscans, too, suppressed them; and they disappear until revived in force in the Italian and some French Romanesque.[3] Although they place the shafts directly on the animals, without the bowl, the Italians surely owe something to their Syrian predecessors of two thousand years before. Occasionally their monsters, their sphinxes, for instances, have a rather Phoenician appearance, as on the candelabrum at Anagni.[4] For a moment the Classical style and its even more severe successor, the Byzantine, lost some of their hold, and

[1] See Barnett, *op. cit.*, Pl. XXVII, 2 and 4.
[2] Dinsmoor, p. 254. For an Egyptian and a Syrian example, see Barnett, *op. cit.*, Pl. XXIII, 1 and 2.
[3] On a window of the twelfth-century church of S. André-le-Bas in Vienne, rigid columnar figures surmount the monsters, as at Tell Halaf.
[4] Hutton, *The Cosmati* (London, 1950), Pl. 43 B. There is even a suggestion of the North Syrian bowl and base in an example at Cori, Hutton, *op. cit.*, Pl. 42 A.

influences from the immemorial orient penetrated by channels, which we can only guess, to the west of Europe.

The north Syrian style in its heyday spread south over Phoenicia and Israel. Solomon's temple, however planned, was at any rate decorated like a north Syrian building. The brazen sea and bases recall the column bases of Senjirli, the decoration of the panelling with golden palms several of the ivories from Nimrud. The Egyptian influence traced by many in the plan is hard to pin down, because the writers of *Kings* and *Chronicles* were no architects.

North Syrian furniture, whose style was shared to a large extent by that of early Greece on the west and Urartu on the east, it is impossible to discuss here. Enough has been said to show the importance of this work for the origin of Greek building, especially of the Ionic Order. The Greeks were not wholly mistaken to ascribe their earliest lessons to the Phoenicians.

5. THE TRANSMISSION OF THE FORMS

Prehellenic architecture seems unequally divided, at first sight, between the ponderous, unalterable, defensive world of Egypt, and a chaos of peoples and schools over the rest of the Levant. Further scrutiny has revealed two great schools, in Sumer and the Aegean. The latter has its connections, indeed, with the Hittites at Boghazkoï and Alalakh, but for the most part goes its own way until cut off in the twelfth century. The Sumerian, by contrast, shows an extraordinary vitality, and reigns in Babylonia for two thousand years. Hittite motifs, such as the lions flanking the gates, are often Sumerian. Even in the north Syrian loggia-building there is something clearly akin to the long Sumerian front as found, for instance, at Uruk.

It is interesting also that the true arch, both in north Syria and in Egypt before Saite times, should be confined to buildings in brick, and should never reach the Aegean at all. It is as if, originating among the Sumerians, innovators of genius, but living far from stone quarries, it was perpetuated in brick by conservative builders, but never properly translated into stone, even in Egypt. For, as we saw,[1] Egyptian stone 'arches', even the tunnels of Saite tombs, are timid, predominantly corbelled affairs. So also,

[1] Above, p. 50.

if they were arched, were the massive stone gates at Boghazkoï.[1]
As, further, we shall find[2] that the alleged early stone arches in
Etruria are now discredited, it seems we must assign to the
Hellenistic Greeks the honour of building the first-known monumental arch of proper stone voussoirs. Conservatism and
'specialisation' are what we should rather expect in Asia after the
third millennium; while abundance of natural building materials
in the Aegean and north Syria probably long delayed the adoption
there of a sound arcuated construction, or, indeed, good clean
construction of any kind. Woolley[3] connects the introduction of
the arch in Greek lands with Alexander's occupation of Syria and
Babylonia. It required the cool intellect of the Greeks, once they
had experienced in Babylon the advantages of large vaulted spaces,
to translate the vaults from brick to stone. When first erected,
the Great Arch of Priene,[4] so ordinary to our eyes, must have given
the Greeks some of the excitement felt last century at the Crystal
Palace.

The ground course of large upright slabs, or orthostates, found
in most Greek buildings but not in Egypt, had, as we have seen, a
long history in Asia. Asiatic conditions generally necessitated a
firm ground course, among the Hittites most of all. Nor can we
doubt from the pictures on Assyrian reliefs of battlemented buildings with corbelled parapets that over much of Asia the dangerous
junction of roof and wall received its own special protection.
Sumerian walls, as in the Temple of Al 'Ubaid,[5] may have had no
special ground courses; but they did possess a protective impervi-
ous film, often treated decoratively as a series of coloured friezes.
As Demangel[6] observes, the Sumerians logically divided a building
into two parts, the structural core of unbaked bricks and this
protective shield of glaze and coloured enamel. They similarly
protected their rare columns with a glazed film around the shaft
and, at the base and capital, stout coils or cushions of metal,
preferably gold. All these systems of protection and revetment
will have their echoes in Greek stone building, the massive Hittite
ground-course in the orthostates, the long enamelled parapet

[1] For a 'suggested reconstruction' by Puchstein, see Bell, *Early
Architecture in Western Asia*, p. 78. (My Fig. 39).

[2] Below, p. 223.

[3] *The Sumerians*, (Oxford, 1928), p. 191.

[4] Below, p. 262.

[5] Above, p. 59.

[6] *Frise Ionique*, pp. 40 ff.

friezes in the carved processions along the roof-gutters of the first
Ionic temples, the other friezes in the surprising number of
sculptured bands encircling at various levels buildings like the
Nereid Monument and the Mausoleum, the metal coils at the ends
of the columns perhaps in the Ionic and Corinthian volute-
capitals.[1]

On the other hand, these Asiatic styles offer little support for a
contention Demangel makes elsewhere,[2] which is true enough
of primitive mud architecture,[3] that window openings, where they
exist, tend to come between the ends of ceiling beams or the short
struts supporting timber roofs and not in the middle of walls.
The Cretans placed their windows where they wished, and north
Syrians and Assyrians regarded not only windows but the fronts
of their largest loggias as holes torn wherever needed in the ex-
panses of their mud-brick walls.   The Greek Doric frieze perhaps
originated as a framework of posts and openings at the bottom of a
heavy timber roof; but, if so, it would seem to owe nothing to
Asiatic or Cretan ancestors.

Among Syrian decorative details, the various types of Caryatid,
the dactyliform capital and the palmette, like the torus-base with
cable mouldings and the use of volutes and canalis on several
capitals all attest the decisive influence of north Syria on the
beginnings of the classical Greek style.

To Egypt the Greeks owe other, less tangible, features;
first, perhaps, the idea of building wholly in stone, and then the
long colonnades and colossal statues of their great shrines.   'The
idea of making life-size colossal statues came to Greece from
Egypt,' observes Beazley.[4]   Probably, also, the idea of a
canon of proportion for the human figure.[5]   The proportions
of columns and entablatures in Egypt cannot have failed to teach
the Greeks much.   Finally, the vast smooth faces of the best
Egyptian masonry served as a model for the Greek temple walls.
Statham[6] reminds us that Deir-el-Bahari was once covered
externally with a fine white plaster; and so, of course, were Greek
temples.

[1] Demangel, *Frise Ionique*, pp. 83 ff.
[2] *Bulletin de Correspondance Hellénique*, 1931, p. 122.
[3] I have seen an oil painting of the gates of Kabul, which shows this
forcibly.
[4] Beazley and Ashmole, *Greek Sculpture and Painting* (Cambridge,
1932), p. 11.
[5] See above, p. 45.
[6] P. 43.   See also Atkinson and Bagenal, p. 117.

One Egyptian detail, the cavetto or 'gorge', was eagerly adopted by the first Greek architects, and for a short time, before they had enlarged the repertory, was liberally used in a great many positions. This, perhaps, as much as anything, will account for the strong Egyptian atmosphere that seems to pervade the early Greek ruins of Paestum. But the Egyptian spirit differs altogether from the Greek in matters of ornament. More than any architects before Gothic times, the Egyptians carried into details the literal imitation of plants and flowers. The Greek, especially in the sixth century, reduced all his plants to geometry. So, at the beginning of his history, he borrowed far more easily from the schematised palms and palmettes of north Syria than from the too literal luxuriance of Egypt.[1] He seems during one century (*c.* 650–550 B.C.), to have taken all he needed from the older civilisations. After that, he felt his own power and went his own way.

In many, perhaps most cases, the point where he should abandon the search for influences and sources and acknowledge the originality of an individual artist would seem for ever to elude the historian. Yet he seems bound in our field to assign the credit again and again to the brilliant inventors of Sumer and the Old Kingdom, where building at its very birth aspired to the glory of architecture. What real progress can he discern between that epoch and classical Greece? The world waited a long time, indeed, for a rationale of proportion, for an architecture of thoughtful understanding rather than mere sensibility. Even Deir-el-Bahari supplies no canon. Nor had the Egyptians, artists though they were, embarked on that methodical exploration of successive worlds in art and thought that has formed the distinctive glory of the Greeks and their European successors.

[1] One exception may, perhaps, prove the general rule. We know the Egyptians sometimes decorated their cavetto with a long geometrical leaf bending slightly forward at the top. See Clarke and Engelbach, Fig. 48. The earliest Greek and Etruscan cavettos are decorated in the same way. See below, p. 128.

PART TWO

GREECE

CHAPTER IV

THE HISTORICAL SETTING

I. SUMMARY OF GREEK HISTORY

THE Greeks appear to have erected their first entirely stone buildings towards the close of the seventh century. The poems of Homer know few wholly of stone, like Priam's palace,[1] and it is only natural that such an innovation should have had to await the great revolution and expansion that is now seen ever more clearly to have marked the turn of the seventh and sixth centuries. For reasons still mysterious, the Greek world round the Aegean then became more wealthy and efficient and politically more unstable. The old order, described in Homer as one of large princely coalitions and shown by the remains as one of commanding palaces and royal roads, had given place at an unknown date to cities without princes and citadels devoted to housing not a king but the statue of a god. Sometimes, as at Therapne, near Sparta, the Heroes depicted by Homer were now worshipped in temples on the very sites of the Mycenaean houses where we may presume their prototypes passed their lives.[2] Only rarely and in outlying cities, like Larisa in Aeolis, do we find a prince sharing the citadel (acropolis) with a god as late as 500 B.C.[3] The road-systems had decayed, and the new cities communicated mostly by sea.

Like the early Sumerian cities, these Greek cities of the seventh century had learnt the art of sending out orderly colonies, but, unlike them, usually required no special subservience from their daughter-towns. In a world less youthful and more crowded than that of 3000 B.C. they won for Hellenism most of Sicily, the south-east shores of Italy, South Provence, Cyrene, the Chersonese

---

[1] *Iliad*, VI, 242.
[2] For Therapne, see Herodotus, VI, 61, and Arnold Toynbee, *JHS*, 1913.
[3] Kjellberg, Schefold and Boehlau, *Larisa am Hermos* (Stockholm, 1940). The identification of this site with the ancient Larisa is now questioned.

and the shores of the Black Sea.   They had evolved a new method
of fighting democratically in a heavily armed phalanx, and used
their military superiority to buttress several kingdoms, such as
Saite Egypt, in the now degenerate older world.   In short, they
throve wherever their way of life is possible, where the sea is near
and the summer long and rainless, and where man depends on corn
and wine and oil, and on exercise and conversation in a central
agora (piazza or corso) in the open air.

Their most efficient rivals are no oriental empires, but the
Phoenicians who, like themselves, have learnt to collect riches in
small impregnable towns and, rather than submit to a permanent
military caste, to fight and contribute in their own way for a state
they have framed themselves.   As an old Greek poet, Phocylides,
observes, 'A small city on a rock, well governed, is better than
stupid Nineveh.'   Ponderous despotism gives place for a few
centuries to the achievements of the intelligent few.

Up to 550 B.C. the Greeks made good their place in the Mediter-
ranean, and between 550 and 480 encountered and defeated the
Persians and Phoenicians, the first serious aggressors upon their
world.   These two periods, from the unknown beginning up to
the Persian Wars, are known as the Archaic Age.   At its opening
Greece and the shores of the Aegean were divided between the
Dorians, the latest comers to the land, and the longer-established
Ionians, with a few groups of uncertain age and origin, such as the
Achaeans and Aeolians, in fairly small regions, but of some
importance before their absorption into the two largest divisions.
One of the most brilliant early centres was the Aeolian island,
Lesbos; and the richest Greek city of the west, Sybaris, with its
famous colony Poseidonia, or Paestum, was Achaean.   The very
attractive sixth-century Doric temples of Paestum show many un-
canonical forms, best explained, perhaps, by some Achaean
influence, which in the fifth century, strictly Doric, Temple of
Poseidon have left mere vestigial remnants.[1]   Among Dorians,
the chief cities were Sparta, Argos, Aegina, Corinth and Thebes;
among Ionians, Athens, Chalcis and Eretria (both in Euboea) and
the twelve cities of Ionia, on the west coast of Asia Minor.   The
Dorians, while extending westwards from the Gulf of Corinth
up to Corcyra (Korfu) and across to Sicily and the especially
large and famous Dorian town of Syracuse, reached Cyrene on

[1] See below, however, p. 113, where I attribute their actual mode of
construction to the nature of the stone available.

the south and, south-eastwards, covered Crete and Rhodes and established several towns on the south-west tip of Asia Minor. The Ionians, especially those of Miletus and Phocaea, turned their attention north-eastwards to the Propontis and the Black Sea, with the steel-smelters (the Chalybes) of its southern and the cornlands of its northern shore, and north-westwards even to such distant coasts as Provence, where the Ionian city of Massalia (Marseilles) already flourished in the sixth century.

This Archaic age is one of expansion, of competition between innumerable cities and of much political experiment; also, however, of increasing approximation of the main cultures. In all the cities similar demands are made of artists and poets, great men are welcomed, as a rule, wherever they go, and the latest of countless fashions, the slightest of a long series of improvements in technique, makes itself felt, in an incredibly short time, over the whole Greek world. One can argue, for instance, at least plausibly that the rise of the great school of Argos affects the whole character and course of Athenian sculpture.[1] Greeks have consciously separated themselves everywhere from the barbarians around them. Every individual who can proceeds to Olympia and the lesser centres of those athletic festivals, in which Greeks alone can take part.

As Lowes Dickinson points out, the Greek was able at once to ask fruitful questions, to give bold, simple answers and then to test, to discard and to modify. At an early stage, he had equated the mysterious forces of nature with the caprices of gods who resembled human beings. During the Archaic period, furthermore, he devised not only the remarkably varied systems of Greek versification, made possible by attention purely to the quantity of syllables, but also a science of geometry probably covering at least the first book of Euclid, including the marvellous propositions 44 and 45. Practical discoveries included the proper use of pulleys, the coining of money, the musical octave and tiled roofs. But the Greeks always paid far more attention to the speculative than to the practical. For instance, as Penrose observes,[2] they brought the science of conics to perfection, because of their love of shapes, but never passed on to calculus, having no use for moving bodies; and failed, with all their mathematical skill, to

[1] E. A. Gardner, *Six Greek Sculptors* (London, 1910), p. 58 (on Ageladas).
[2] *Principles of Athenian Architecture* (London, 1851), p. 89.

invent a sign for zero and the decimal point, although the Babylonian place-system already pointed the way.[1]

Up to 480 B.C., no city had so outdistanced the rest that one can call its work metropolitan, although Athenian work was already as good as any. The western colonies tended to prefer mere size. Of the Ionia of this time, with temples as large and remarkable as the western, we still know too little. It is less accessible, and its great buildings were too thoroughly renewed in the fourth and third centuries B.C.

Between 500 and 490 B.C. Ionia was overrun by the Persians; and in the next ten years Greece was saved only by the tyrants of Syracuse and Akragas (Girgenti),[2] and a coalition of mainland cities, with Athens as the most prominent. The wars thus enhanced the prestige of a few cities, especially of Athens, who, by retaining the fleet built by Themistocles for the crisis, gathered nearly all Greeks round the Aegean into an alliance against Persia and, after 454 B.C., into an empire, which assured a new peace in the Aegean itself and at Athens an accumulation of wealth and a differentiation of trades greater than any Greek city had yet known. So the fifth century, the Classic century, is the age of Athens, more especially of Pericles, her most powerful statesman between 460 and 445, her unchallenged ruler between 445 and 430. It is also the period of the most famous Athenian buildings. For, besides numberless smaller works, the Hall of the Mysteries at Eleusis was slowly rising after 450 B.C. while the Parthenon was built virtually between 447 and 438, and the Propylaea between 437 and 432. Athens retained the initiative for all that her enemies could do, until, shaken by a plague (430 B.C.) and a long war (431–421 B.C.) with her jealous neighbours of the mainland, she forfeited it between 415 and 413 in the disastrous expedition to Syracuse, an outburst of megalomania and greed, and finally succumbed in 404 to a combination of Persia and almost the whole of Greece. The Sicilian Greeks, cursed with their own jealousies, succumbed, all except Syracuse, at nearly the same time to the Phoenicians of Carthage.

Continual discord now prevailed. Persian bribery and Greek parochialism brought the cities to ruin and to defeat by a barbarous

[1] See above, p. 72.
[2] Akragas—Agrigentum—Girgenti. Mussolini replaced the last with the vile hybrid Agrigento, which unhappily bids fair to stick, but which I refuse to employ in this book.

power, Macedon, in 338 B.C. at Chaeronea.   Athens, whose naval and commercial industry had enabled her to recover from 404, still struggled under Demosthenes and Lycurgus to reform her government and finances.   But with the triumphs of the Macedonian conqueror, Alexander (356–323 B.C.), the weight of power passed permanently to the barbarian; and with the collapse of Athens in the Lamian War and the death of Demosthenes (322 B.C.) Ancient History loses much of its attraction.   It is individuals that matter; and henceforward, apart from a few scientists and poets, they are mostly mere kings and their ministers, or academic philosophers.   The miracle of Athens, where the practical man and the politician were also well educated, and where the useful arts were determined, to use Aristotle's phrase, by the architectonic, was not to be repeated in Antiquity.   Its most promising successor, Ciceronian Society at Rome, was to be struck down by the soldiers and the plebs and expire under the 'crafty tyrant' Augustus.

The fifth century, the Classical Age proper, saw the perfection of the Athenian drama and of Greek sculpture and architecture, the writings of the first great historians and a remarkable outburst of philosophical inquiry, in some ways not unlike that of Europe around 1700.   It also saw the invention of solid geometry and perspective.   But practical sciences made little headway, as is shown by the crudity of fifth-century siege tactics.

In the fourth century, oratory and philosophical writing reached the greatest height they have ever known.   The painters of this period were those most admired in Antiquity.   Polite, intimate drama, the so-called New Comedy, from which our own drama springs, flourished towards the end of the century at Athens, the source, from beginning to end, of all the famous Greek plays. Aristotle, in the same city, was comparing and bringing under one system the first principles and guiding hypotheses of all known arts and sciences.   Thus most of the activities that justify and improve human life began very suddenly in Greece between the sixth and fourth centuries B.C.   The Greeks, first of all the men we know, attempted to give a reason for all they did; and we cannot escape from the impression that, by using their minds, they have made upon all later history.

Following the three periods we have marked out, we shall divide Greek architecture also into three phases, the Archaic down to 480 B.C., the Classical down to 400 and the late Classical down to about 330.   There is in fact a notable division between the numerous, lavish buildings of the fifth century and the few, fragile, delicate masterpieces of the fourth.

2. CONDITIONS OF LIFE AND TYPES OF BUILDING

Greece is a country of great mineral wealth. Mountain ranges separate small plains, whose most convenient entrance is by sea. Good fertile land is too rare to support many farmers. Like the Sumerians, then, many Greeks, Athenians especially, became devoted to manufacture and trade. Under the spell of reactionary philosophers, induced by the fall of Athens to consider them evil and banausic, we probably underestimate the prestige of these activities in Greece. Nor is it true that they had passed into the hands of slaves. In the earlier sixth century, most Athenian citizens were called 'craftsmen'; and although in the fifth, successful wars did provide numbers of slaves to be instructed in the crafts, these left the citizens even then no unlimited leisure for that administrative and social life necessary in a great capital. A manufacturer has to use his brains more than the average farmer, especially in markets as civilised and exacting as the Greek; and the typical Greek listener to Socrates was as much interested as any Medieval burgher in the finer points of craftsmanship. In fact, such were the conditions of his life that he could seldom transcend the mentality of a manufacturer.[1]

In marble and other building materials the land is so rich that it has provided three successive civilisations each with a very different range; the Mycenaean with its hard limestone, porphyry and conglomerate; the Hellenic with its white marble, soft and hard limestone and baked clay tiles; the Byzantine with its coloured marbles, limestone mortar and bricks. So far is it from true, in a land like Greece, that materials condition the architect. We can grant at most that the Byzantine had probably less timber than his predecessors and was less able or less willing to transport enormous stones.

Marble was not at first used for stone buildings. Roofs and ceilings of wood, with tiles and revetments of baked clay, would crown temples of limestone. As Paestum shows, the builders would employ the softer limestone, or 'poros', for the most

---

[1] For an amusing statement of this, see R. G. Collingwood, *The Principles of Art* (Oxford, 1938), Chap. II.

delicately moulded courses and a hard white limestone for the plainer. This will partly explain the unusual entablatures there (see Pl. 7). The delicate, carved architrave-crown is naturally of a softer stone than the plain fascia below. But the Greeks could soon carve each section of architrave to its full height out of one hard block. Again, the earliest roof-tiles were of terra-cotta, embedded in unbaked clay. But fairly early in the sixth century Byzes of Naxos[1] first carved marble tiles; and these, where necessary, could repose directly on the rafters.

Marble façades became the fashion about 525 B.C. Famous early examples were the buildings on Siphnos and the contemporary temple of Delphi, both noticed by Herodotus.[2] Buildings entirely of marble, like those on the Acropolis or the Temple of Athena at Tegea, were always rare. Island marble, where possible Parian, was favoured up to 480 B.C. but after that, Pentelic, from a mountain some twelve miles north-east of Athens. Both provided smooth, unveined surfaces, to take paint or polish of any degree of fineness. But whereas Pentelic goes rusty in places, Parian retains its whiteness. Very occasionally, the darker, less evenly textured marble of Mount Hymettus or the dark grey limestone of Eleusis (see Pl. 9) was used on one or two special courses.[3] Ordinary hard and soft limestones continued in use in the vast mass of buildings.

More fortunate than Sumer, Greece has clays of all degrees of fineness. Their colour when baked will vary, of course, according to the length and intensity of the firing. But, to take one instance, the redness of Athenian contrasts strongly with the whiteness of Corinthian clays; and experts can often assign a provenance to the smallest clay object largely from its colour and texture.[4] Colouring earths are, naturally, also common, the most famous being the ruddle of Chios. The most useful dye was that of the purple-fish. Of the precious metals, silver, gold and a natural alloy of the two, called electrum or 'white gold', were all abundant in several regions. Among the baser, the copper of Cyprus sufficed for all demands. For iron the Greeks had to go

---

[1] Pausanias, Bk. V, 10, 3, says he was contemporary with the Lydian king Alyattes and the Median Astyages.

[2] Bks. III, 57, and V, 62.

[3] See L. T. Shoe, 'Dark Stone in Greek Architecture,' *Hesperia*, Suppl. VIII; see also below, p. 176.

[4] See, for instance, the remarkable exercise of this knowledge by R. H. Jenkins in his *Dedalica* (Cambridge, 1936).

only slightly farther afield, to Etruria (Tuscany) and northern Asia Minor. Only tin was lacking, and supplied very uncertainly from mines along the Atlantic coasts. Bronze, an alloy of copper and tin, was the favourite metal of the Greeks, so that the gap was serious. Otherwise their little world, rationally ordered, could support itself. Charcoal from the forests, apparently inexhaustible, played with the Greeks the part that coal plays with us. No one then could foresee the soil-erosion, so terrible to a modern eye in the view from Acrocorinth, caused by the charcoal burners and shipbuilders of antiquity, and by the wasteful timber roof-trusses of the classical Greeks. But are we today using our natural wealth more wisely?

The Greek year consists of a long summer and a short winter, cold, perhaps, but one in which, as Lord Byron observed,[1] snow never lies in the plains, at least in Attica. Athens suffers no frost hard enough to shatter the sharp undercut mouldings of marble so appropriate to the clarity of the air. The sun is glaring, and the surface of the ground a 'reflector' nearly as bright as the limestones of the temple. When these received their normal coat of marble plaster, they were probably as dazzling at mid-day as some famous modern villages on the Cyclades. Surfaces normally in shadow thus become luminous; and the ceiling of a Greek portico has to display a finely chiselled beauty unimaginable in England.[2]

Moreover, like their predecessors, the Greeks needed to foster the slightest breath of air on a summer day. Symmetry, too often a nuisance in the north, is desired in the south for the draughts it creates. But the classical Greek, of the mainland at least, employed it in moderation. For instance, he eschewed axial planning. The Doric temple looks best and was properly seen first from a point on the diagonal, where its precinct was entered (see Fig. 45): and when the Greeks of the fourth century began to develop long, straight, colonnaded stoas, they rightly avoided all symmetrical grouping of them about architectural axes; for this could have led, in an agora like that of Assos,[3] only to effects like those of the painter Martin. These innumerable stoas, or public lounges, like the pastas, the small southward-facing loggia of the Greek private house, afforded shade and circulation of air in

---

[1] Note to *Childe Harold*, Canto II, Stanza 73.
[2] See Atkinson and Bagenal, pp. 24–5.
[3] Dinsmoor, Fig. 125.

summer and some sunlight and protection for the rooms behind them in winter.

But we must not overestimate the Greek love of comfort. As Vitruvius observes,[1] one should take care, when designing a theatre, to avoid a southward-facing auditorium, in which the mid-day sun will shrivel the bodies of the spectators. Yet the theatres at Athens and Syracuse both face south.[2] The landscape and life of Greece seem made for ecstasy rather than comfort—a word, appropriately enough, of Roman origin.

Rainfall in Attica and the Islands has always been scanty. The roofs of any large buildings, not to mention the auditoria of theatres, served to catch rain water, which was then carefully transferred to underground cisterns, very numerous and a real danger to the explorer of ancient sites. The Theatre of Thera and the Temple of Aphaia (see Fig. 45) on Aegina show good examples of these attached cisterns.

The real Greek winter lasts from January to mid-March. It is too short and broken to call for permanent hearths. A short, bright spring follows. Cheese is made and the corn harvested in June. The Greek then found leisure, broken only by the vintage in late September, to resume his festivals, excursions and politics until the time of the olive harvest and November ploughing.

As citizens were at home and roads dry at the end of June, it was usual to hold the annual elections then: and the new year at Athens was dated from mid-July. It virtually opened with the Panathenaia, the special festival of the city goddess, Athena, which included a procession from the north-west gate through the Agora, the secular centre of the city, to the Acropolis and the sacrifice there of a hecatomb (literally 'a hundred oxen') on the old altar south-east of the Erechtheum. Every fourth year was marked by a more splendid procession and an international contest in athletics, chariot-racing and music, which included the public recitation of all Homer. The Acropolis and the buildings below its south side formed the setting—Pericles built a new Odeion or music hall beside the Theatre, for the Homeric recitations—and one should always try to imagine the Parthenon at the moment of its

[1] V, iii, 2.
[2] I think this a strong argument against Dinsmoor's view that the theatre at Athens was given its present site as late as 500 B.C., thirty years after the drama was publicly established (see Dinsmoor, p. 120). Surely, the site was tolerated only because of its ancient religious associations and the festivals long held there.

dedication, the great Panathenaia of 438 B.C.   Other Greek cities
had their chief festivals at the same season, Sparta, for instance,
the Karneia.   But ranking even above these were the festivals at
international sanctuaries, especially the Olympic and Pythian
Games at Olympia and Delphi, both held at four-yearly intervals.
The great sanctuaries, then, occupied the centre of Greek art and
life, and had Stadia, gymnasia and odeia all as so many appurten-
ances.   One can see in the poet Pindar, who wrote odes for the
victors, the thought that the god used the contests there to select
the best of his worshippers and once more assure their cities
and families of the divine favour enjoyed by their heroic
ancestors.

Throughout the public life of Athens, religion and politics
intermingled.   Thus the theatre, organised and maintained by
the state with the money of the few richest citizens, was a temple
of the god Dionysos, with an altar, or thymele, for sacrifice in the
centre of the orchestra.   The Pnyx, or place of political assembly,
had a similar altar.   The gymnasia, the official centres of physical
training, were each under some god or hero.   The public record-
office was a temple of Demeter; and the national banks, as in
Babylonia, were those great temples where alone wealth could
accumulate.   When the Athenians borrowed, in times of strain,
from their national temples, they did so at an interest rate of
$1\frac{1}{5}\%$ and scrupulously recorded their debts.[1]   So, in Greece,
'where'er we tread is haunted, holy ground'.

The familiar peripteral temple, we now see, was only the most
important of innumerable shrines and was developed as a type
about 600 B.C.   It would normally contain a statue, an emblem
or more rarely an oracle of the presiding god.   The statue
possessed the divine qualities, and as such would be escorted with
honour in procession, like the statue of Dionysos Eleuthereus at
Athens.   Thieves might run off with it for the good fortune it
brought, as in the Iphigenia Taurica of Euripides.   At Athens, the
time-honoured standing image of Athena, the Palladium, kept first
in the old sixth-century temple between the Erechtheum and
Parthenon and then in the Erechtheum itself, seems to have
received at each great Panathenaia the present of a new tight-
fitting robe.   The emblem might be a meteorite, as at Ephesus,[2]

---

[1] M. N. Tod, *Greek Historical Inscriptions*, second edition (Oxford,
1946), p. 143.
[2] Acts xix, 35.

or a snake, as in the Old Temple of Athena on the Acropolis.[1] The oracle, where the God pronounced, might assume various forms, a chasm inside a crypt at Delphi, pigeons on an oak at Dodona and a little hut in a laurel grove at Didyma.

The central shrine of the temple almost invariably faced the rising sun, as, probably, did most Greek cult images. Aeschylus at any rate seems to talk of household gods as facing the sun at dawn.[2] So the great altar of offering to meet the eye of the idol usually faced the eastern side of the temple and was joined to it by a causeway (see Fig. 45). The Parthenon is one of the very few peripteral temples without causeway or external altar, because the altar of the old sixth-century temple to the north remained in use for the hecatomb centuries after that building had vanished. Besides, the Parthenon had no time-honoured, mystic cult-image, only Pheidias' gold and ivory statue.

The cella-building and peristyle, as we shall see, were chiefly to protect the growing wealth stored round the image. But why they took the familiar Greek form, at first sight so simple, is by no means understood; and we must consider the history of the Greek temple a little more closely. Several elements, at first sight disconnected, went to its making.

Greek religion, as Dinsmoor has well said,[3] combined 'the worship of personified natural phenomena with that of deified heroes or ancestors.' Demeter is an instance of the former, Herakles of the latter. The nature gods were worshipped of course in places where they still acted or had once shown themselves, the deified ancestors, or heroes, on the sites of the palaces where their actual prototypes had lived, as, for instance, Helen at Therapne.[4] Something of the arrangement of the Bronze Age palaces perhaps survived in the Greek shrines on their sites. The earliest known temples of the classical Greeks, in Crete, seem to have had altars and offering-tables inside the cella in positions where the Bronze Age megaron would have had a hearth and serving-table.[5] Sacrifices were soon, for the most part, moved to the great altar outside the temple. Yet even for this there apparently existed a precedent in the Mycenaean House: for at

[1] Plutarch, *Themistocles*, 10, 1.
[2] *Agamemnon*, v. 519.
[3] Dinsmoor, p. 38.
[4] See above, p. 107.
[5] For these temples, see Marinatos in *BCH*, 1936. See also below, p. 182.

Tiryns, at least, an altar apparently faced the front of the megaron across the forecourt.   So the forms of temples appear to have a partly domestic origin.   But they are soon modified by the cult-statue and the peristyle.   Indeed, between the Bronze Age and classical Greece there came into existence the cult of life-size or colossal statues.   None are known from the Bronze Age.   One of the oldest known, of which a colossal limestone head survives, is apparently that of Hera (*c.* 600 B.C.) in the famous early temple, the Heraion, at Olympia.   There seems no need to suppose, with Seltman,[1] that the art and function of the most famous cult-statues, such as the Zeus by Pheidias at Olympia, have come down over the centuries from the little portable gods, which he presumes were of gold and ivory, worshipped in the house-shrines of the Mycenaeans.

At Ephesus and Samos respectively, where the sequence of buildings in the great sanctuaries is well known, the cults of Artemis (Diana) and Hera began, each with an altar and one or more small images on bases, all set on a small platform in the open air.[2]   This seems to be the stage represented by a story in Herodotus,[3] in which Athenian sailors bring ropes and attempt to drag two statues at Aegina down to the boats, but are deterred by thunder and lightning.

By 600 B.C. it was becoming the fashion in large shrines to enclose the statues and the offerings made to them inside a protective room, or cella, and, less explicably, to surround the whole with a colonnade on all four sides.   The two processes and the first employment of stone, another novelty, are almost simultaneous.[4]   In fact, there are few temples anywhere before 600; while after that date almost every temple of even moderate size is of stone and peripteral.   Here again we see the mushroom growth of Greek culture at that time.   Rudimentary encircling colonnades or ptera had occurred, somewhat rarely, in the light pavilions of Egypt and Assyria.   In Greece they became immediately the distinguishing mark of the larger temples and, apart from a few Ionian tombs, were never employed on any other buildings.   On

---

[1] C. Seltman, *Approach to Greek Art* (London, 1948), p. 16.   For arguments that the head of Hera in Olympia is indeed from the first cult-statue in the Heraeum, see Searls and Dinsmoor, *AJA*, 1945, p. 74.
[2] See the careful descriptions on pp. 39–40 of Dinsmoor.
[3] V, 85.
[4] At Thermon indeed, as most have noticed, the earliest peripteral temple seems to precede stone building by a century.

Doric temples they were nearly all hexastyle, that is, with six
columns on the front.

They were not needed, as some have thought, to protect the
archaic Greek walls of mud brick, for these, when whitewashed,
were perfectly durable. Nor can one think colonnades along the
sides of the cella of much practical use, although one must always
remember that it is only peripteral temples that have a false porch

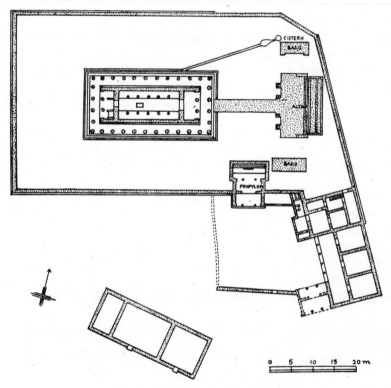

Fig. 45   Site plan of Temple of Aphaia, Aegina.

at the back. This was presumably used for something, and could
be reached from the front of the temple only along the side ptera.
Yet one suspects the peripteral plan was chosen mostly for aesthetic
reasons.

In the developed peripteral temple the long, rectangular cella-
building would normally fall into three divisions. The cella
proper held the image and occupied most of the length. Its porch,

or pronaos, had a façade on to the peristyle resembling the vestibule
of the Mycenean Megaron and containing two columns 'in antis',
that is, between the ends of the two side walls. The false porch
at the rear of the cella roughly balances the pronaos in the front,
but usually has no door into the cella. The eccentric door in the
Temple of Aphaia on Aegina remains an unexplained exception.
None of the names for the false porch is very satisfactory.
'Posticum', sometimes used for it, means in Vitruvius simply the
rear façade of the temple.[1] The Greek word 'opisthodomos',
assigned to it by most architectural histories, was used in Athens
of a famous treasury, imagined by some scholars as the vestibule of
the west cella of the Parthenon, by others as the patched-up
western room of a complex of chambers in the cella building of the
archaic temple,[2] by others as a free-standing secular treasury west
of the Parthenon, but never as a false porch of the kind we have
described.

In early Doric temples, particularly in the west, the false porch
was less common than an inner room, or adyton, a 'holy of holies'
entered only from the cella and terminating the cella buildings
externally with a blank wall. Its presence requires no explanation,
so long as men understand the nature of religious ritual. It is the
false porch that needs explaining. Why, for instance, should it
appear in the first true Doric temple at Thermon and not its
predecessor on the site, 'Megaron B'?[3] Nor do we seem to have,
on any site, records or existing remains of its furniture and uses.
So far are we from understanding Greek temples.

One or two peripteral temples, such as the Parthenon and the
sixth-century Temple of Apollo at Corinth, contained neither false
porch nor adyton, but two cellas back to back, each with its
pronaos.

It will come, perhaps, as a shock to learn that grilles closed the
whole façade of the pronaos. They were needed to protect the
accumulation of wealth. There is no reason to believe they
appeared so bleak and tasteless as those restored by Fiechter in

---

[1] Compare Vitruvius, III, 2, iv, and III, 5, iv.

[2] See, e.g., Dinsmoor, Fig. 70. Much of the endless argument is
retailed by W. S. Ferguson, *The Treasurers of Athena* (Cambridge (Mass.),
1932).

[3] See Robertson, Fig. 20. In fourth-century Delphi 'opisthodomos'
perhaps meant the false porch. See the account of the Naopoioi for
342 B.C., Col. III, v. 35. Pausanias (V, 16) certainly calls the false porch
an 'opisthodomos'.

the Temple of Aphaia,[1] or that they ever inflicted themselves on the external colonnades.

Every temple possessed a surrounding precinct or 'temenos' (the latin 'templum'), usually entered at one point only, through a propylon. The plans of propyla seldom varied, and recalled Mycenaean days. Each contained a cross-wall, continuous with the wall round the precinct and pierced by an odd number of doors, and two porticoes behind and before it. The two short side walls of each portico enclosed on its façade a pair of columns in antis; and a common roof covered both porticoes on an axis at right angles to the cross wall, giving pediments on the two façades.

Apart from the propylon, sited to give a diagonal view of the temple, the precinct was dotted with altars, votive offerings and houses for the priests. Whereas in Egypt, the propylon, main temple, adyton and priests' houses were all incorporated in one vast edifice on a great level site, in Greece they were kept separate and only loosely related, chiefly by their scale and the aid of contours. Where possible, the main temple was set on the crown of a hill; and, of course, the most revered sanctuaries normally occupied the acropolis, the ancient citadel of a town. Vitruvius advises[2] that the temple of Jupiter, Juno and Minerva and those of the other tutelary gods should occupy the highest ground, to command the longest stretches of the city wall. Our twentieth-century towns are so horrible because the rightful hierarchy of buildings has been set aside, and electrical power-stations have at present usurped the chief place.

The secular centre of the city was the Agora, a large open space intended for market-stalls, the hearing of legal and commercial disputes, political gatherings and discussion of all kinds. Near it, if we are to believe Thucydides,[3] there existed from the earliest times a council-chamber (bouleuterion) and some sort of residence

---

[1] In A. Furtwaengler, *Aigina* (Munich, 1906). Cockerell's, of course, are much better. See his *Aegina and Bassae* (London, 1860), Pl. 6, which confines them to the pronaos. But Fiechter (Furtwaengler, p. 34) holds that the three central bays of the East Peristyle were also enclosed by grilles at Aegina. He can find, however, no evidence for the grilles that would be necessary between the antae of the pronaos and the second and fifth columns of the façade. Nor does he produce any photographs of holes or sockets. I cannot think the temple had grilles here in the fifth century.

[2] I, 7.

[3] II, 15.

for councillors (prytaneion). Solon, a statesman of the early
sixth century, is credited with lodging all nine chief executive
officials, or archons, in a building called the Thesmotheteion.[1]
There were also temples and altars, constantly on the increase.
At Athens, for instance, the younger Pisistratus in 522–521 B.C.,
dedicated in the Agora the Altar of the Twelve Gods,[2] henceforward reckoned the centre of the Attic road-system.   Statues,
shrines of the founders in colonies[3] and, on the fringe of the Greek
world, even the tombs of eminent men[4] all made constant en-
croachments on the space in the Agora.   Town planners com-
pensated for this by increasing all the time the number of long
covered colonnades, or stoas, for quiet, unofficial discussion and
rest in the hot part of the day, and in the Hellenistic Age by
relegating the less savoury trades to separate enclosures.

Stoas were few and small in the fifth century; and gymnasia and
palaestrae, or wrestling grounds, were equally popular with talkers.
But early examples of these athletic buildings have not survived.
Situated on the fringes of towns—at Athens mostly outside the
walls, at Priene just inside them—they were administered for men
and boys by the state or one of its local divisions (given limited
power in such matters) and always under the protection of some
deity.   Combined in Roman times with suites of baths, they
must have been far simpler in classical Greece, where it was the
rule to oil and scrape oneself clean.

Musical competitions fell into two classes, for choirs and for
soloists.   For the latter, Pericles provided at Athens his roofed
Odeion, or music-hall, about 200 feet square.   Choirs, it seems,
drew an even larger audience, both for the dithyrambs, or hymns
to the god Dionysos, and the drama, which began life as a special
kind of musical performance.   So the Theatre of Dionysos at
Athens, employed for most choric performances, contained an
earth orchestra, or dancing-place some 85 feet across for the choir,
and an auditorium for about 17,000 people.[5]

Apart from military buildings, such as arsenals and frontier
forts, we have now exhausted the short list of building-types
recognised as properly architectural.   Schools for children, unlike

[1] The Aristotelian *Constitution of Athens*, III, 5.
[2] Thucydides, VI, 54, vi.
[3] Thucydides, V, 11.
[4] As at Xanthos in Lycia.   See Tritsch, 'The Harpy Tomb', *JHS*
1942, p. 40.
[5] See Dinsmoor, pp. 120 and 247.

the gymnasia, were private and held in ordinary private houses of mud brick. In towns, at least, stone was rarely used on houses; and almost our only evidence for it is the mockery in Aristophanes of Megakles' columns.[1] Attic farmhouses, it seems, were rebuilt fairly sumptuously by Greek standards after the Persian Wars, but of what materials we cannot tell.[2] Professional masons found private clients for little but tombstones outside the city gates and private dedications in the temple precincts, and for the occasional drain built piecemeal, like parts of the 'Drain of Pisistratus' across the commercial quarter of Athens, by the owners of properties it happened to traverse.

[1] *Clouds*, v. 815.
[2] The Oxyrhynchus Historian, just as he is telling us, is interrupted by a lamentable lacuna. See *Hellenica Oxyrhynchia* (Oxford 1909), § 12.

CHAPTER V

THE GREEK ORDERS

I. INTRODUCTORY

IT will be clear from the previous chapter that temples and their subsidiary buildings engrossed Greek architectural thought. It is for them that the Orders were devised and modified. But before we see how, we should try to recall the spirit in which their creators went to work.

If we are to believe Pliny, by far the most voluminous critic surviving,[1] the greatest Greek artists aimed quite shamelessly at realistic representation. Of course, the Greeks further insisted on a scale of value in the subjects they painted, so that Zeuxis reproached himself when, in his painting of the boy and the grapes, the grapes allured the birds while the boy failed to frighten them. By the fifth century the sculptor and painter were mastering the art of dramatic psychology; and the contemporaries of Polygnotus (c. 460 B.C.) already preferred to show not the moment of a great deed, but rather the suspense between 'the acting and the first motion'. The great classical Greeks could represent the smallest flicker of a mood by the tiniest subtleties of outward gesture. If Turner painted light, the Greek painted the soul: and Pheidias surpassed Polyclitus because he could reveal the souls of gods rather than men.

This humanist art the Renaissance did its best to revive—with what success it is difficult to judge. In general, one is inclined to consider Renaissance Art more artificial, less principled and more erratic: while the greater coarseness and obviousness of Renaissance work is at once apparent in the single field—that of coins and gems—where the condition of surviving Greek examples permits a fair comparison.

In the fifth century, when the musician, poet and sculptor moulded the tastes of society,[2] the architect was expected to provide above all the setting for festivals and sculptured groups.

[1] *Natural History*, Bks. 34–6.
[2] See Pericles' education and friends, as described by Plutarch in his invaluable *Life of Pericles*.

Plutarch, as everyone knows, credits the sculptor Pheidias with generally supervising the architects at work on the Parthenon[1]: and it is not fanciful to see in some of its features (see Pl. 10) the programme he must have laid down. Thus the wide cella with the return, the earliest known, of its colonnades across the west end will have resulted from the needs of his great statue: and the octostyle façades, almost unique in a Greek Doric temple, make the wide cella aesthetically possible—for it was by now the custom to align the cella walls with points only slightly inside the penultimate columns of the end façades. They also ensure, compared with the normal hexastyle, a relatively larger pediment, relatively nearer the eye, for the display of large sculptured masses. Finally, present evidence suggests that the great chryselephantine statue cost perhaps 700 silver talents—far more than the 400 or 500 talents probably expended on the building.[2]

Few important Greek buildings, even the secular, can have lacked large displays of fine sculpture, of an extent we can hardly imagine. In Athens the only stoa of the fifth century we have recovered, the Royal Stoa, has life-size standing figures for its akroteria. The sculptor was always expected to design compositions of a few definite shapes for a few definite places—akroteria, metopes and the tympana of pediments. Both sculptor and architect, given the overall dimensions of a Greek temple, could grasp at once the scale of the details, and could collaborate as easily as artists ever can.

The force of tradition, particularly in the Doric Order, controlled from a very early period the forms not only of the main features but even the lesser mouldings. If we take the classical Doric temple and describe it in detail, noting and dating the variations that are found in each part, we shall find that nearly all important discrepancies have disappeared by 500 B.C.

It will be convenient to end this introduction with the chief Greek mouldings, before describing in the next section the members of the Doric Temple and the methods of constructing it. In the third section we shall follow an analogous course with

---

[1] Plutarch, *Pericles*, 13, § 6. The architects, he says, were Ictinus and Callicrates.

[2] The cost of the statue is fairly well established. Thucydides (II, 13, v) says it contained 40 talents of gold, alone worth more than 500 silver talents. In the year 444–443 B.C., when the actual temple was in the middle of building, its board of works seems to have received little more than 38 silver talents (Tod, p. 114) and it was virtually completed in ten years, between 447 and 438. It may well, then, have cost less than the statue.

Ionic. The Greek artists (although by nature as original and as daring—in the right place—as any people in history) followed their rules of construction as religiously as their tradition of architectural shapes.

Compared with earlier styles, the Greek exhibits a wealth of thoughtful detailing. The Egyptians had devised the roll for angles, the cavetto for cornices. In their earlier days they had planed or even fluted their columns. The other early peoples had achieved rather less, so that without the Greeks building might have relapsed into bleakness and baldness. Thanks to them, that dreary fate was postponed to our own day. They devised not only new types of moulding, such as the ovolo and the hawks-beak, but also new combinations, and fitted each with seeming inevitability to the most suitable parts of the building.

I take my brief account from the indispensable book by Miss Shoe.[1] This, with its full-size sections of mouldings of every type, makes it quite clear that the Greek craftsman worked by eye, that his curves are too subtle for mathematical instruments and that a single stretch of moulding varies too much in profile to have been carved mechanically.

He employed the cavetto by itself only rarely. After the very earliest cornices and roof-gutters, where he seems to be aping the Egyptian form, he set it on some early anta-capitals, Doric at Paestum, Ionic in the Peloponnese.[2] In the Doric world he proceeded to continue outwards and downwards its upper and outer end, there forming the profile of a drooping leaf, the so-called 'hawksbeak'. In the Ionic, he soon added a convex quarter circle above or below the simple cavetto, forming respectively the cyma reversa and cyma recta.

The roll he either enlarged into a torus, the distinctive moulding of the Ionic base and repeated in the Attic variety above and below a concave semicircular moulding (the scotia) or reduced to a mere subsidiary bead, usually carved as a line of bead and reel ornament (the so-called 'astragalos'[3]).

[1] *Profiles of Greek Mouldings* (Cambridge (Mass.), 1936). Another admirable book, now slightly dated, but still a treasure-house of Greek forms, is Allan Marquand, *Greek Architecture* (London and New York, 1909).
[2] The so-called 'sofa capitals'. For the Doric, see Dinsmoor, Fig. 32, and pp. 86 and 94; for the Ionic, E. Fiechter in *Jahrbuch*, 1918, pp. 209–18.
[3] The word originally meant a knuckle-bone or a vertebra. Its transference to the bead and reel is unexpected, but well attested for the fifth century by the Erechtheum accounts. See Shoe, *op. cit.*, p. 7.

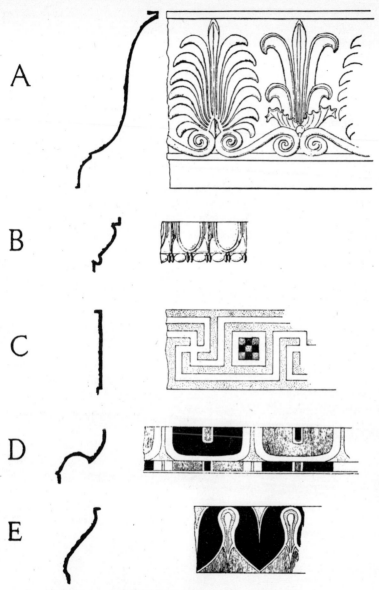

Fig. 46   Profile and decoration of Greek mouldings.

A = Cyma recta and cavetto.
B = Ovolo and astragal.
C = Plain taenia.
D = Hawksbeak.
E = Cyma reversa.

Generally speaking, each form of moulding had its appropriate decoration, normally carved in Ionic and painted in Doric, but in any case related as closely as possible to the profile (see Fig. 46). Thus the cyma reversa, an Ionic moulding with a convex curve above a concave scotia, has carved Lesbian Leaf of ogee-shaped outline, the ovolo, a moulding common to both orders, a carved or painted egg and dart and the flat fascia, fillet or taenia one or other of the rectangular Greek frets. The cyma recta, concave above and convex below, and favoured in the later Ionic for roof-gutters and hoods, as on the north door of the Erechtheum, may have an alternation of palmettes and lotus-flowers, the so-called 'anthemion' ornament, which fits the profile gracefully, if somewhat more loosely than usual. The large half-round, or torus, on the Ionic base was at first fluted horizontally in Ionia, but came later, under Attic influence, to be left plain. The hawksbeak alone consistently broke the rule. As a deep, undercut, fragile moulding, it permitted no carved pattern on its face. So it is the distinctive Doric moulding. It would have been hard, indeed, to decorate its face with shapes taken from its profile. Instead, its painted surface imitates a line of closely-packed, forward curling leaves with very strong median ribs and rectangular outlines. As we saw,[1] the curled leaf was used on the Egyptian cornice, and it appears on a good many cavettos along the terra-cotta cornices of sixth-century Asia Minor and Etruria, at Larisa, for instance, or Caere.[2] There seems little doubt that the Doric craftsman, taking it in this loose, sprawling form, disciplined it, strengthened it and made it into the hawksbeak, his favourite moulding for cornices. The cornice of Temple C at Selinus[3] apparently shows him half way through the process. Small details of this sort will show how he hellenised the whole of art.

2. THE DORIC TEMPLE

The foundation of the Doric Temple is a solid platform, resting where possible on bed rock, the four uppermost courses of which

[1] P. 52 and n. 103.

[2] For Larisa (as late, perhaps, as 530?) see Schefold, *Larisa am Hermos*, I, p. 193. For Caere, Palestrina, etc., see Giglioli, *L'Arte Etrusca* (Milan, 1935), Pls. 19 and 100.

[3] See Robertson, Fig. 28. Dinsmoor, on p. 92, supposes that the cornice on the Temple of Kardaki derives from the Doric hawksbeak. More probably it is on the way there. I consider Kardaki early. See below, p. 153.

are nearly always raised above ground level, to form the euthynteria and three large steps below the colonnade. The euthynteria
appears to the eye as a single low-level platform on which the whole

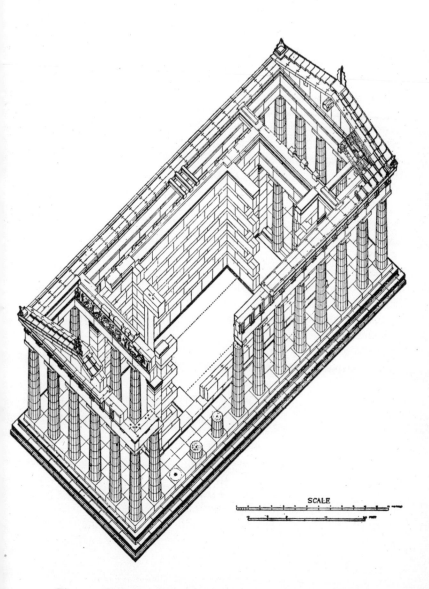

Fig. 47 Temple of Poseidon, Cape Sunium: Axonometric.

building rests. At Sunium it averages 8 inches in height for a temple totalling 40 feet. Modern 'classical' buildings, by accepting a sloping site, often lose half their effect. The three steps often have a total height about equal to the lower diameter of the columns, thus offering to the eye a support for the peristyle at once measurable and adequate. Proportionately lower in the Temple of Zeus at Olympia, they far exceed the required height in the Treasury of the Athenians at Delphi. Most Periclean buildings strike the happy mean. In some examples, such as Bassae and Sunium, the lower part of the face of each step was slightly recessed, to produce a band of thin shadow. Variations from these steps are rare and found usually in propyla, not viewed in the same way as temples. Yet even in the Athenian Propylaea (see Pl. 9), the four marble steps of the main front and the three of them which return along the flanking halls add up, in each case, to a total giving the normal proportion.

Doric steps, besides being very steep (almost two sides of a square), need often to be very large. Demands of access will then lead in the central bay of the main façade either to small intermediate steps, as on the Parthenon, or ramps, as in nearly all large temples.

The Greeks were conscious of the uppermost step, or stylobate,[1] as the plinth of a continuous colonnade. It is sometimes raised, like those of the Parthenon (see Pl. 9), slightly above the level of the floor, and corresponds to the toichobate, the continuous spreading course partly visible below the cella walls. The specification for Philo's Arsenal at Piraeus, dated about 340 B.C.,[2] describes each row of columns as a 'tonos', literally a 'line stretched taut'. Such was the importance to the Greek of the continuous plinth. Thus the Doric column has no base, and in lower diameter nearly equals the width of the stylobate.

In classical Doric, the height of the column totals some $5\frac{1}{2}$ lower diameters, of which the shaft accounts for over 5. The upper diameter is about four-fifths, the side of the abacus about eleven-tenths. In earlier examples the shaft tapers and the abacus spreads rather more, especially in Greek Italy. Abacus and echinus are normally of nearly equal height. The echinus, circular on plan, has in the best Greek work a singularly subtle hyperbolic profile

---

[1] In this definition, as in most others, I follow Dinsmoor's excellent glossary.

[2] *Inscriptiones Graecae*, II, second edition (Berlin, 1927), No. 1668.

and a maximum diameter a little distance below the abacus. The beautiful shadow that results is missing from Roman work, where the profile has become a flat chamfer. At the bottom of the echinus come three annulets, raised rings encircling its junction with the shaft and forming a neat transition. Penrose[1] divides the profile of the column from the top of the echinus to the foot of the shaft into three distinct curves. A few inches below the annulets the shaft is marked by one or more necking grooves at a point where, in the construction, the capital-block meets the first drum.[2] Buildings of about 500 B.C., notably the temples of Corinth and Aegina, often show the affectation of as many as three grooves. The chief divergence from these forms appears in the sixth century in Greek Italy. Here, at Paestum and Selinus, a ring of the curling leaves (see Pl. 7) displaces the central annulet, and the top of the shaft is strangely pinched. A similar capital has appeared at Kardaki in Korfu, on the Italian route.[3]

The surface of the Doric shaft is broken into twenty vertical hollows, or flutes, separated by sharp ridges or arrises and each following in plan, at any point, a curve struck from three centres.[4] Though narrowing towards the top of the shaft, they keep the same depth throughout. Early examples, small shafts used internally (even as late as the Parthenon) and shafts of soft marble in exposed positions (as on Cape Sunium), might have only sixteen, rather shallower flutes. This is almost the opposite of the rule of Vitruvius that columns in the pronaos, in fact slightly smaller than the outer columns, should have more flutes to disguise their thinness; nor does one find such columns in an existing pronaos. In the Temple of Poseidon at Paestum twenty-four flutes were unaccountably preferred on each outer column. Using twenty, one naturally obtains the desired result of a central hollow on each front of the column and an arris nearest the corner of the abacus.

The columns are usually spaced at an axial distance approximating to half their height. This proportion, however, was hardly reached very easily or very exactly. In two famous temples, indeed, as shown in Dinsmoor's very valuable table,[5] it

[1] *Principles of Athenian Architecture*, p. 50.
[2] See below, p. 148.
[3] Society of Dilettanti, Supplementary Volume (Vol. IV) to Stuart and Revett (London, 1830); *Temple of Cadachio*, Pl. 5.
[4] See Penrose, p. 52 and Pl. 21.
[5] Inserted between pp. 340 and 341.

exactly obtains—Zeus at Olympia and Aphaia at Aegina.   But in Periclean buildings the columns are too high, 34·65 feet in the Parthenon to a normal interval of 14·1 feet, giving a proportion of nearly 2·5 to 1.   So Periclean architects must have designed their works on another system altogether than that of their older contemporaries.   One significant proportion sometimes observed where columns are higher is that of 1 to 3 between the interaxial distance and the height of the whole order; as, for instance, in the Argive Heraion, where the height of the column by itself amounts to 2·3 times the interaxial distance.

As the table in Dinsmoor makes clear, no easy ratio existed in Greek Doric or Ionic between the interaxial distance and the lower diameter.   Vitruvius in the third chapter of his fourth book divides the stylobate of a hexastyle Doric temple into forty-four modules, allots twelve to the six columns and thus leaves six each for four of the spaces and eight for the centre.   Not only his numbering but his actual system here lacks all classical Greek precedent, and we had better omit all reference to modules in Greek Doric.   The most we can admit is Dinsmoor's Law, enumerated not in his book but in an article in *Hesperia*,[1] that in all Periclean buildings, except the small side wings of the Propylaea, the clear space between two columns, no matter what their size, is about half a metre (and thus an ancient cubit) greater than a lower diameter. One knows no reason for this undoubted fact.

The height of the entablature normally totals something over a third that of the columns—even more in early examples.   The architrave, its lowest member, has in the fifth century a height somewhere between the upper and lower diameter—usually about four-fifths of the latter—and a thickness of one lower diameter. Its outer face consists of one smooth fascia and a continuous taenia, a ribbon-like crown less than one-seventh of its total height.   In some other buildings, such as Temple C at Selinus, the taenia was higher in proportion.   Below it, and centred at points over the centres of the columns and the intervals, are stretches of generally narrower fillet of slightly less projection, the regula.   Each stretch is in length about half one lower diameter.   From its soffit project six stone pegs or 'water-drops' (guttae).

In two archaic treasuries at Delphi, the Athenian and that

[1] *Hesperia*, IX, p. 22.

generally known as the Sicyonian,[1] there are only five guttae to each regula, and on a circular colonnaded building there, the archaic 'tholos', one finds none at all. The sixth-century buildings of Paestum have, instead of taenia and regula, a continuous carved architrave crown of cyma reversa profile. This corresponds with the cornices there, also designed to dispense with guttae. Above the sixth-century architrave at Kardaki, on Korfu, is a continuous ovolo, on which, it seems, the cornice rested directly. We are not concerned in this section to explain these freakish buildings, only to give as exhaustive a list as we can of the known exceptions to Doric rules.

The next member, the frieze, is about the same height as the architrave, and comprises projecting triglyphs and recessed metopes. A triglyph contains three vertical upright fillets, the glyphs, with flat front faces and side faces chamfered at 45 degrees. The two vertical hollows between them are 'stopped', or arched over, in a very delicate curve, whose careful undercutting distinguishes most classical Greek work from even the best Roman copy. On the whole, the earlier the triglyph, the steeper and more undercut the curve.[2] Over the two outer corners are two half-curves, forming delicate drip-stops, very similar to those on some buttresses of the late twelfth century A.D., notably those on the Chapter Library at York, built by Archbishop Roger. The earliest Gothic is full of half-conscious Classical feeling.

The front face of the triglyph never projects beyond the plane of the architrave fascia, and is thus always set back from the guttae. An imaginary timber prototype, in which visible pegs were thus used to fasten, most indirectly, the posts or beam-ends represented by the triglyphs to continuous balks, the supposed original architrave, and in which these beam-ends were never allowed to project even as far as the plane of the pegs, would all be something of an absurdity.

A taenia, a plain fillet of about the same height as its fellow on the architrave, crowns the triglyph and brings its total height to one and a half times its width. But the metopes between the

---

[1] Dinsmoor (p. 116) would assign it to Syracuse rather than Sicyon on evidence, e.g., its carved metopes, not, perhaps, adequate. See below, p. 185, n. 2.

[2] I am not satisfied, despite Dinsmoor, p. 183, that some of the triglyph-blocks at present lying round the fifth-century Temple of Rhamnous are Roman replacements. The little arches on the Hephaisteion and at Bassae are as flat, and the workmanship of the blocks at Rhamnous pretty good.

triglyphs are nearly square. This in fact follows from the normal width of the Doric triglyph, about half one lower diameter, from the normal position of triglyphs in the frieze, one centred over each column, one over each interval, and from the customary spacing of the columns. The very early Temple of Apollo at Syracuse, where the columns were most thickly spaced, had metopes hardly wider than the triglyphs and spaced without relation to the columns. Temple C at Selinus, in the same tradition, has reinstated triglyphs over the axes; but with its close, thick colonnades it has no place for real square metopes. By 500 B.C., however, square metopes everywhere prevailed, and only one difficulty remained, how to shape and dispose the awkward metopes at the corners. For while one rule enjoined a triglyph centred over each column, another, kept with equal strictness, prescribed two complete triglyphs on each corner of the building. With columns evenly spaced, a rectangular peripteral temple cannot easily obey both requirements. Robertson has clearly shown why.[1] To adjust it, so that it appears to do so, fifth-century architects either slightly lengthened the last and the penultimate metope, as on the temple of Poseidon at Paestum, moved the corner column inwards, as on the same temple,[2] or shared this 'angle contraction' between the corner columns and their neighbours, as in the later Doric temples of Sicily, by the process known to Dinsmoor as 'duplex angle contraction'.[3]

The Doric frieze, even more than the columns themselves, is the most constant and distinctive feature of the order; and its square metopes greatly enhance the serenity of the Doric Temple. Only one known example omits the frieze entirely, the temple at Kardaki. Only one has triglyphs spaced without regard for the columns, the sixth-century tholos at Delphi. A few western temples experiment with triglyphs of strange shape, notably a building at Locri and the 'Church of Samson' at Metapontum.[4] It is rare to find a Greek temple like the Parthenon, with carved figure subjects on all its metopes. Smaller Athenian temples, like

---

[1] Pp. 106–12.

[2] It was moved two feet inwards in the Parthenon, to offset, as Dinsmoor rightly says (p. 161), the abnormal proportions of an octostyle façade.

[3] *Hesperia*, IX (1940), p. 15.

[4] Locri is illustrated in the textbooks (e.g., Dinsmoor, Fig. 39), which tend to consider its 'pentaglyphs' Ionic (e.g., Robertson, p. 105). In themselves they have nothing obviously Ionic. I know no adequate illustration of the 'Church of Samson'.

the Hephaisteion, may have them on the main eastern façade and on the adjacent corners of the long sides. But at Olympia even the great temple of Zeus, as large as the Parthenon, had no external carved metopes. Its twelve famous metopes of the labours of Herakles adorned instead the façades of the pronaòs and false porch. Nearly all metopes, except those from Foce del Sele, near Paestum, and the 'Sicyonian' Treasury at Delphi, have a crowning taenia,[1] but it need not equal in width the taenia over the triglyph. Both taeniae are usually left plain, but are given a crowning bead on the Parthenon and Propylaea.[2]

The Geison, or Cornice, the uppermost member of the entablature, has a height about half that of the frieze, but projects from the front plane of the triglyphs for a distance nearly five-eighths of their height. It has a strong bed, usually flat and vertical in front and projecting only slightly beyond the taenia of the triglyphs, and above this a heavy and complicated corona, whose soffit slopes downwards and outwards at an angle rather less than that of the roof. From this soffit hang mutules, shallow rectangular slabs as long as the triglyphs are wide and wide enough from front to back to accommodate three rows of six guttae each. As one mutule is centred over each triglyph and each metope, only small spaces, known as the 'viae' (or passages), are left free over the ends of the metopes. The close spacing of the mutules and their refusal, like that of the soffit, to follow the pitch of the roof make it difficult for those who, like Vitruvius,[3] would trace their descent from timber principals.

A very short way outside the fronts of the mutules the soffit is itself cut short to form a vertical fascia about as high as the front of the bed. Projecting beyond this, and separated by a concave curve sloping downward and outward, is a second, higher fascia, the corona proper of the cornice, itself capped with a small, continuous hawksbeak.

[1] See H. Kaehler, *Das Griechische Metopenbild* (Munich, 1949), Pls. 36 and 38 ff. The 'Sicyonian' metopes are very oblong already, and a taenia would have made their field for carving even worse. In the Temple of Zeus, Olympia, the carved marble metopes were crowned each by a taenia of the local coarse stone.

[2] According to J. Bousquet, the crowning moulding of the taenia has a subtle purpose on the mid-fourth-century Treasury of Cyrene at Delphi. Its addition creates a subtle mathematical proportion between the frieze and neighbouring courses. See J. Bousquet, *Le Trésor des Cyréneens* (Paris, 1952).

[3] IV, 2, iii.

At Olympia, owing to the coarse stone, some buildings omitted a few sharp mouldings. Thus, as officially restored, the cornices under the pediments have no hawksbeak crowns in the Temple of Zeus.[1] The Athenians, by contrast, elaborated the bed, giving it, in the main hall of the Propylaea, a crown of its own, a cyma reversa in profile. In a few archaic western examples coffering replaces the mutules, while the bed may acquire a most complicated series of mouldings. The Temple of Ceres at Paestum provides, of course, the most famous example. The architect wisely refused here to carry his coffering across the foot of the pediment, but applied it to its sloping (or raking) cornices only.[2] The bed parts company with it, continues horizontally and is sufficiently heavy to separate frieze and tympanum. On the long sides of the temple the coffered soffit has a downward and outward slope analogous to that of ordinary mutules and gentler than the pitch of the roof. But the pitch of the pediment continued to the corners and the adjustment to this shallower slope was made as deftly as possible on the soffit of the large corner coffer-block.[3] In a temple at Kalydon, nearly a century earlier, the cornice had similar coffering, quite flat, however, on the long sides of the building, so that the pediment ended at each corner in a stretch of horizontal cornice. The evidence for this 'Chinese roof' is published by Dyggve.[4] The corner block survives with the two outer faces both horizontal.

In Kardaki, alone of all early Temples, is the pronounced overhanging cornice replaced on all four sides with a combination of roll and cyma reversa not resembling even the Ionic cornices of the time, merely the bed that is continued in isolation across the façade of Ceres at Paestum. Yet the school behind these two western examples, in a way no one has yet unravelled, contrived to exert a powerful influence on western barbarians long after the fall of classical Greece; for the favourite Roman Doric of the first century B.C. had a normal architrave and frieze, but a cornice like that of Kardaki.[5]

[1] See, e.g., Robertson, Fig. 17. Dinsmoor prints on Pl. XXXIV a restoration by J. K. Smith showing a hawksbeak. His text seems unconscious of the discrepancy.

[2] I shall explain these terms immediately.

[3] See F. Krauss in *Roemische Mittheilungen* (1931), pp. 1 ff. The block survives.

[4] *Das Laphrion* (Copenhagen, 1948), Taf. XXII and XXIII.

[5] Whereas normal Hellenistic work of the second century B.C. combined a Doric architrave and frieze with an Ionic cornice. See below, p. 259.

Above the cornice, then, on the two shorter façades of a normal temple came the gable, or pediment, consisting of a frame, the 'raking cornice', forming with the horizontal cornice a very flat isosceles triangle, and a deeply recessed tympanum of large flat slabs, usually in the plane of the architrave. As the raking cornice has a pitch of no more than 15 degrees and, in the extreme example, the Temple of Poseidon on Cape Sunium, only $12\frac{1}{2}$ degrees, it will be found that the tympanum and the sculpture in front of it have, in hexastyle temples, a height in the centre very nearly equal to that of frieze and architrave combined, or twice that of the carved metopes.

The corona of the raking cornice repeats that of the horizontal, and in the best examples merges with it on the corners to form a 'feather-edge'. But its soffit is very different, comprising as it does a small, very elegant hawksbeak bed-mould and, stretching downwards and outwards from this, a long, graceful soffit curve, unbroken by mutules and cut short only by the plain, single fascia of the corona. The long curve closely resembles that of early Ionic cornices, horizontal and raking. One Order probably borrowed it from the other. Which invented it, we cannot tell. But the connection may one day prove important. Mutules are never found in pediments, except one inexplicably barbarous example at Crimisa, on the south Italian coast,[1] and Graeco-Latin works of the Roman Republic, as, for example, the Doric Temple of Cori.

The edges of the tiled roof, which rested immediately upon the blocks of the geison, prompted many ingenious treatments. After slight variations at the very beginning, and before the adoption or copying of scale-tiles for some small buildings, like the Monument of Lysicrates, a little before 300 B.C., virtually all Greek roofs employed one system of tiling. Their cover-tiles, of semicircular or polygonal cross-section and about 6 inches wide, protected the joints between the sloping sides of flat pantiles, which had visible upper surfaces between 2 and 3 feet square. The foot of each, whether pan-tile or cover-tile, rested, usually with the help of grooves and flanges, on the top few inches of the tile below it. The sizes vary surprisingly little on buildings of very different magnitude.

It was possible to prolong the cover-tiles to the roof-edge and

---

[1] See Dinsmoor, Fig. 31. Three fasciae replace the soffit-curve on the raking cornice of Temple D at Selinus.

protect their ends with antefixes, ornamental plaques of clay or
marble, moulded, carved or painted.   These might hang slightly
over the geison, as in some temples at Kalydon,[1] or rest upon it,
their fronts flush with its hawksbeak crown, as in a large number of
examples.   On the Parthenon, because the building is too large,
aesthetically, even for the widest possible pan-tiles, only a third
of the cover-tiles are given the width the scale requires.   Each
third row is prolonged to a real antefix on the eaves.   The other
two are smaller, and are stopped some way back.   Then on the
eaves is set a false antefix midway between the two true antefixes.
This nice example of pictorial architecture was recovered and well
described by Orlandos.[2]

As the cover-tiles ran only one way, up the slope of the roof,
antefixes on the pediments were unthinkable.   So in all cases,
except the barbarous building of Crimisa, the pan-tiles were given
a continuous up-turned edge, the raking sima, externally of a constant height and strictly parallel to the raking geison and internally
nicely adapted, by very careful jointing, to the stepped overlap of
the normal pantiles.   Where antefixes appeared on the long sides
of the temple, it was usual to return the raking sima a few inches
and then stop it, as on the Parthenon, with a false lion's head
spout.   The roof of the Parthenon thus formed a very artistic
arrangement of several members, mostly useless.   Alternatively,
one might continue the sima as a horizontal gutter along the sides,
piercing it, where necessary, with spouts, at first trumpet-shaped,
later nearly always lion-headed.   On archaic buildings in the
west, where clay revetments were very popular, a sima was often
carried even across the floor of the pediment.   In true Greek
buildings the variation amounted to no more than that.   But in
Italic examples, such as the famous model from Nemi,[3] we find a
tiled roof sloping forwards and downwards inside the pediment.
No one has satisfactorily explained them.

One cannot list here all the varieties of moulding and decoration
on the sima.   They form an attractive field of Greek art.   The
earliest builders, doubtless under Egyptian influence, favoured a
tall flat fascia, separated by a roll from a crowning cavetto.
Examples appear in the east at Larisa in Aeolis, and in great

[1] See the illustration on Dyggve, *op. cit.*, p. 226.
[2] A. K. Orlandos, Notes on the Roof Tiles of the Parthenon, *Hesperia,
Suppl. VIII*, pp. 259–67.
[3] Robertson, Fig. 87.

numbers in Sicily. In Etruria they linger long after the archaic period. But about the middle of the sixth century the Corinthians introduced another type, with a large crowning ovolo, which prevailed for over a century in old Greece.[1] Its painted decoration at first suited its profile less than in most Greek work. But in the fifth century the ovolo increased as the fascia shrank, and the palmettes on the former dominated the fret that covered the latter. In the fourth century a single dull and decadent form supplanted all others. A flat-faced sima, adorned with endless scrollwork, known to Dinsmoor as 'rinceau' ornament and anticipating the Roman scroll, now everywhere supported antefixes placed at a rather absurd height but aligned with every second cover-tile. Midway between the antefixes and so aligned with the other cover tiles, stopped some way behind them, very large lion-headed spouts projected from the sima (see Pl. 11).

Where a horizontal sima obtained, the builders in all periods usually made some attempt to align its spouts on features below—at Rhamnous, for instance, on the centres of the metopes[2]—even though few temples would satisfy Vitruvius, who recommends at the end of his third book the piercing of no spouts except above the centres of the columns. Antefixes keep step more rarely. Neither on the Parthenon nor on the Temple of Aphaia do they take the slightest notice of the triglyphs.

Each line of cover-tiles, where it crossed the ridge, rose into a flat, ornamental crest-tile, parallel to the antefix and of about the same size, but often, as it was less easily seen, of inferior workmanship and material. On the Temple of Aphaia, for instance, only the antefixes and lower roof-tiles were of marble. Over the centres and lower corners of the pediments stood the akroteria, large pieces of sculpture, variously men, monsters, tripods, floral designs and even carved groups. The precept of Vitruvius,[3] that the corner akroteria should equal the height of the tympanum, while the central should even exceed it, seems to apply well enough to the examples we know; and it will be evident that the Doric designers reserved their most original external features for the roof.

We now walk under the peristyle. The inner face of the architrave is plain, except for a crowning taenia, omitted in some

[1] Shoe, *Mouldings*, I, pp. 32–3.
[2] See J. P. Gandy in *The Unedited Antiquities of Attica* (London, 1817), 'The Temple of Nemesis', Pl. 11.
[3] III, 5, xii.

temples and always of very slight projection, but sometimes as high as the outer taenia, regula and guttae together.   It is occasionally replaced, in temples under Ionic influence, by a moulding like the Ionic architrave-crown, for instance in the Hephaisteion by a cyma reversa and astragal.   The back of the frieze is plain, and only once, perhaps, before 400 B.C., the East Hall of the Athenian Propylaea, do the ceiling beams meet the entablature at this level, perhaps to gain height for the open relieving space over the central door concealed between the ceilings and the roof.[1]   At Oropus and sometimes Olympia, it seems the plain backers rose to less than the full height of the outer frieze, so that the simple inner cornice, or epikranitis, can occupy the upper few inches of this course and bring the soffit of the ceiling beams to the soffit of the geison blocks. But in the ordinary temple of the fifth century, the same block contains stretches of the outer cornice and the epikranitis.   The latter comprises a painted fascia and a small crown, in profile a hawksbeak, on which the ceiling beam freely rests.

In earlier examples, wooden ceiling-beams had been notched into the back of the entablature.   Holes for them remain in that of the Temple of Poseidon at Paestum.   But the Athenian builders preferred, it seems, to leave their more brittle and valuable beams of marble all the free play possible in the event of an earthquake; so that at Sunium, for instance, nothing existed to fasten them to the geison.   The cella walls, of course, had an epikranitis of the same form and at the same height as that on the peristyle.   In themselves the ceiling-beams were a shade taller than the epikranitis and had the distinction of a crowning ovolo, a detail rare in Doric.   Their breadth, in section, is always greater than their height, presumably to give them stability.   The gaps between them over the epikranitis were closed by vertical slabs, on which their profile was returned.   They were often spaced at intervals of rather less than twice their own width.   Above them, the moulded and painted coffers might occupy the thickness of a single slab, as in the Propylaea, or might have separate removable lids, as in the Hephaisteion.

In some small early buildings, ceiling-beams and coffer-slabs seem together to have supported the outer roof.   This became impossible with temples of any size, where the ceiling is hard put to it to carry its own weight, and simply rests, without attachment, on the cornices.   So timid were some architects that at Bassae,

[1] For this relieving space, see below, p. 178.

for instance, the beams are largely hollowed out from above. Nor is the ceiling very often aligned with the rafters and purlins. Coming in Doric as high as it does, and having itself a height less than one-third of the frieze alone, the ceiling-beam is by no means tied in its placing to the columns below. It is exceptional in Doric to find it directly over a column or observing with its neighbours any interval found on the entablature. The large, low ceiling-beam, with the respond attached to the cella wall and directly aligned on an outer column, are signs not of Doric but of Ionic and later, Renaissance work. So the Doric, for all its seeming heaviness, escapes the deadness of overdone Classicism and clogging responds.

On the front of the pronaos stand two columns between the thickened wall-ends or antae, and their stylobate continues along the foot of the walls as the toichobate. The anta, like the column, has in pure Doric no base. Its sides are vertical, or at least as vertical as the wall, to the bottom of the capital. This comprises a very thin abacus, a series of mouldings, always including a prominent hawksbeak, below it, and below these again a rectangular block projecting only very slightly from the rest of the anta. Although in form so different, in height the capital about equals those of the columns, and the single block of which it forms the upper part similarly equals the capital-blocks. Exceptions to the normal type are rare and early, centred, so far as we know, on sixth-century Paestum. Here, in the Basilica, the sides of the antae have an entasis, or convex curvature, as pronounced as that of the columns; while the capitals, as at Foce del Sele nearby, have the profile of the Egyptian gorge.

The entablature of the pronaos-front normally repeats that of the exterior. Some fifth-century temples in the Peloponnese preferred to exhibit in this position such carved metopes as they possessed, while leaving those outside uncarved. More remarkably, one sometimes encounters here horizontal oblong metopes. Perrot and Chipiez, who cite the Temple of Poseidon at Paestum,[1] actually claim that these show the traditional shape and position of the metopes, before the aesthetic of the Doric Order reduced them to squares and transferred them to the colonnades outside. As, after the corner triglyph, the frieze is not returned along the sides of the pronaos and cella, Perrot and Chipiez further see in it an imitation of the ends of ceiling-beams that once spanned the

[1] *Histoire de l'Art dans l'Antiquité*, VII (Paris, 1898), pp. 378 ff.

pronaos (see Fig. 48). At least two difficulties strike us here. Most known ceilings, even in the pronaos, come one course higher; and the triglyph, an upright oblong, resembles the shape of no extant ceiling-beams. Finally the Temple of Poseidon has under each of these triglyphs a remarkable regula of nearly twice its length. This would promise by itself triglyphs of normal size, normally spaced. It would seem that the architect, on completing the architrave, had suddenly changed the design and resorted to a lower frieze, with triglyphs of normal shape, but too small for the existing regula.

An epikranitis in normal Doric crowns all four sides of the cella buildings.

The single door to the cella, from the pronaos, often has a lintel

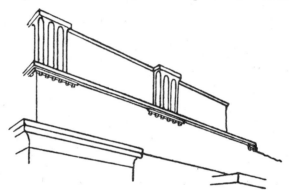

Fig. 48   Temple of Poseidon, Paestum: Metopes of Pronaos.

level with the architrave of the pronaos or one course below it, and made of orthostates, slender upright blocks twice the height of ordinary wall-blocks.[1] These giant lintels brought forcibly home to the Greeks, however little they applied it to their rafters, the principle that strength in a beam depends on depth. The facing of the jambs and lintel has in most cases disappeared. Scholars seem disinclined to agree on whether it was of wood or of marble.[2]

As we approach the heart of the temple, we become alas! far less certain of the arrangements. The cella was normally roofed.

[1] The Parthenon had five such orthostates over the door of either cella (Penrose, Pl. 16), the Hephaisteion, according to Mr. B. H. Hill, had two over its single main door.

[2] Compare Dinsmoor, p. 201, n. 2, and Miss Lorimer, *Homer and the Monuments* (Oxford, 1950), p. 416.

The Chronicle of Lindos, for instance, the famous temple record written in 99 B.C., makes it quite clear that a roof protected the cult-statue.[1] Inner colonnades are often found, partly, one supposes, to support the roof, but in some cases so near the side walls that they serve a mainly decorative purpose. In some examples, like Bassae, they are actually engaged. In early temples they run the full length of the cella (see Pl. 12), but after the Parthenon are normally returned across its western end. For obvious reasons, they are always much smaller than the columns outside, and even in the fifth century had normally a mere sixteen flutes. To reach the roof, therefore, two tiers were needed—the only instance of Greek superimposed columns. There was no question of a clerestory or even, in most cases, of galleries. Only an architrave was allowed to separate the two tiers, and the line of diminution of the lower columns is continued through this to give the lower diameter of the upper. So at Paestum the upper tier is less than three-fifths the height of the lower.[2]

One may therefore wonder about the roof and roof-supports intended for the famous giant temple G at Selinus. It is 361 feet long by 164 feet wide, and even its cella, though comparatively small, had a width of some 60 feet, with 25 clear feet between the colonnades. Dinsmoor alleges that it was not open to the sky, or 'hypaethral', but had a roof supported on three tiers of columns,[3] certainly Doric, for the only remains are Doric.[4] Yet the lower diameter in the lowest tier, as Dinsmoor admits, is only 3 feet 9½ inches, compared with 10 feet on the outer peristyle. The difference is enormous when compared with that in the Temple of Poseidon at Paestum. There the inner columns are two-thirds the diameter of the outer. But with three tiers, Temple G should have had internal columns proportionately larger.

Now suppose we allow the ascertained columns, 3 feet 9½ inches in lower diameter, proportions fairly slender for the Doric of that time (c. 480 B.C.), namely a shaft five diameters high, an upper diameter three-quarters of the lower, and a consequent diminution

[1] Delphi orders the Lindians to open the cella to the air for three days 'and to strip that part of the roof that is above the image'. (Col. D, line 60, of the Chronicle, edited by C. Blinkenberg—*Kleine Texte*, No. 131 (Bonn, 1915)).
[2] See Perrot and Chipiez, p. 451, Pl. XXIX.
[3] Pp. 99–100.
[4] I may add that I found no remains on this site of any column-drums sufficiently small for Dinsmoor's third tier.

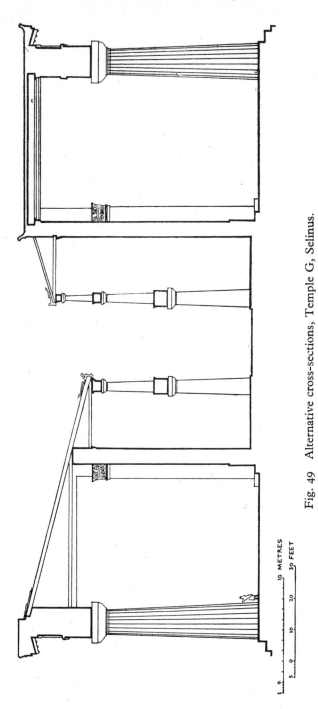

Fig. 49   Alternative cross-sections, Temple G, Selinus.

of one-twentieth in a height of shaft equal to the lower diameter. Calculation will give an absurdly small upper diameter for the uppermost columns—no more than 16 inches—and a total height of only thirteen and a half times 3 feet 9½ inches, or 51 feet. But Dinsmoor, although he gives the giant external columns a height of only 48 feet 2½ inches, cannot with decency reach a height to the top of the geison-blocks of less than 67 feet.[1] So, even with a third tier of inner columns, the roof could only have sloped downwards from all sides towards the cella, treated, one presumes, rather in the manner of an Italian 'impluvium',[2] with a central hypaethral space in front of the shrine. But a third colonnade would be so flimsy, so monstrous aesthetically and so very squat that it is at once desirable and possible to remove it.

The large, open pronaos and the wide space between the peristyle and the cella walls are both more understandable with such a sheltered 'compluviate' roof, not required to ride the winds; and we are entitled to a sound restoration of Temple G, which was a great and noble work, whatever some scholars have tried to make of it. One would like to believe other large temples were similarly roofed. For one feels instinctively of this style that in external views the whole roof should be either invisible or visible and complete. Fergusson himself was unable to make his hypaethral openings torn through a normal Greek roof look beautiful from outside.[3] The Temple of Didyma, near Miletus, certainly had a cella entirely hypaethral and perhaps was intended to have a roof of the type we have assumed for Temple G. But we run into difficulties at Ephesus, where the size of the sanctuary and the 'image which fell from Jupiter' would both suggest that part at least of the Temple of Artemis (Diana) was hypaethral, but where, according to ancient coins, pediments certainly existed on the façades.[4] The fifth-century Temple of the Giants at Akragas, the roof of which, according to the historian Diodorus,[5] had not been added when, in 406 B.C., disaster overtook the city, might seem a likely candidate for our compluviate scheme. Unhappily, there exists in the Girgenti Museum an enormous lion-headed false

[1] For the proportion of entablature to columns in Temple G, see Robertson, Fig. 38.
[2] See below, p. 254.
[3] See his illustration opposite p. 83 of the *R.I.B.A. Transactions for 1876–7*.
[4] See *B.M. Catalogue of Greek Coins, Ionia* (London, 1892), Pl. XIII, 7.
[5] XIII, 82.

spout, fitted by its size[1] for this temple alone.   The natural place
for it is the strip of false sima along the akroterion-holder on the
lower corner of the pediment, where, for instance, we find it in
the Parthenon.[2]   It seems to show that pediments were at least
projected for the Temple of the Giants.   The cella, only 40 feet
wide from pier to pier, might have made an ordinary pedimental
roof just possible.

Having failed to restore these larger buildings, we shall find
the smaller no easier.   The Greeks give no evidence before the
later fourth century of employing any principle but the trabeated.
Everywhere they rested ridge-poles and purlins of very square
cross section on walls or wooden blocks or bearer-beams; and we
know, from the surviving holes for rafters and longitudinal beams,
as well as from specifications for fairly narrow roofs preserved in
fourth-century inscriptions, the enormous, expensive scantling
that this simple, restful construction required.   Scholars none the
less try to roof in this way all the Greek buildings they can.   Thus
B. H. Hill takes it for granted[3] that over the central aisle of the
cella in the Hephaisteion, a space of about 14 by 33 feet, the cross-
beams of the ceilings held up the ridge-pole and central roof-tiles;
and the treasuries of Delphi and Olympia are generally restored
with the outer roof resting on the beams and even the coffers of
the ceiling.

This was not, as we saw,[4] possible in the peristyles of temples
even fairly large; and there are many cella-buildings on which it
would equally strain our credibility.   That of the Parthenon itself
has a span of over 60 feet from wall to wall and over 30 feet
between the inner colonnades, themselves of no great strength;
and Dinsmoor cites a number of fifth-century Sicilian examples,
each with a wide uncolonnaded cella, such as E at Selinus (40 feet),
Athena at Syracuse (38 feet) and Herakles at Girgenti (38 feet
10 inches).   Mere bearer-beams are surely inadequate for such
spans.   We know that at one point inside the Erechtheum, where
the wall was weak, the builders inserted a diagonal brace below
the horizontal ceiling-beam in the angle it made with the wall.[5]

[1] The front of the lion's face is some 2 feet 2 inches across.   The
similar false spouts on the Parthenon are only half as wide.

[2] See Penrose, Pl. 17.

[3] In *Hesperia*, Suppl. VIII, p. 208.

[4] Above, p. 140.

[5] See B. H. Hill, 'Structural Notes on the Erechtheum', *AJA*, 1910,
pp. 296–7.

But one cannot believe Greeks would use so unsightly a method except in a building so makeshift as the Erechtheum. It would interfere hopelessly with the restfulness of a normal cella and the effect of a horizontal ceiling.

An attractive suggestion is that of Jeffery,[1] that pairs of un-trussed, straddling beams, resting in the normal temple on the cella walls, supported the large central ridge-pole, on which rested the rafters. One might be tempted to connect the adoption of the first peristyles with the invention of such a device, which facilitates a wide cella and outer rafters of Classical pitch. Could one believe the Greeks ever used triangular tie-beam trusses, it would, further, have been easy to use the ceiling-beams over the cella to prevent the spread of the straddlers.[2] We know one fourth-century building, the Philippeum at Olympia, that had perhaps outgrown the use of mere bearer-beams. At the apex of its circular roof stood a 'bronze poppy that tied the beams together,'[3] perhaps holding them in position like the key of a stone vault. The principle of straddlers and ridge-pole would be the same. But we must admit all is speculative. We have no evidence of straddlers inside the line of the rafters and more steeply pitched, even on the inner faces of the tympana of the Temple of Concord, Girgenti. Despite Jeffery, the evidence there seems to amount to holes for purlins in a roof, presumably substituted in the Middle Ages,[4] of steeper pitch than the classical Greek.

Daylight must have reached the Greek cella through its main door only. The classical Greeks, like the modern, preferred a very subdued light in the sanctuary, where the images and treasures could glitter more richly and mysteriously. The flickering of artificial lights was carefully envisaged by the designers; and the lamp in the Erechtheum, that burnt, it was said, one whole year without attention, was further memorable for its elaborate hood, a

[1] *Archaeologia*, 1928, pp. 45–9.
[2] I owe these speculations, and much else in this passage on Greek roofs, to conversations with Prof. Sir John Myres and Mr. W. A. Eden. The faults and errors are mine. Actually, we cannot be sure when the tie-beam truss first appeared even in Rome. See below, p. 302.
[3] Pausanias, V, xx, 10.
[4] At the same time, one must protest vigorously against the Italian Archaeological Service, that has lately filled up all the beam-holes it could with some sort of reconstituted stone. This is not the way to treat historical evidence. At Girgenti, too, the authorities have embedded genuine Greek Doric drums at regular intervals in walls flanking the new arterial road!

palm tree of bronze openwork reaching to the roof.[1]   Of course, darkness brings its dangers to such buildings, and in 423 B.C. the priestess of Hera at Argos seems to have left a sanctuary-lamp in the wrong place, too near the garlanded image, and so burnt down the whole temple.[2]   The evidence for dark interiors and lamps was collected as early as 1821, in the sensible introduction to the re-published first volume of the *Antiquities of Ionia*.

Inconclusive as my scrutiny has proved to be, I make no apology for considering the roof and the cella at such great length in this account of the Doric Order.   The latter in particular was the crowning glory of the temple, and it is tragic that we should know so little of it.   Its detail-ing and the great refinement and inventiveness of its architects in the later fifth century will occupy us further below.[3]

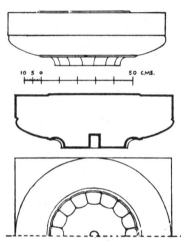

Fig. 50   Doric capital, Tiryns.

The construction of the Doric Temple changes as little as the details of its profile.   Unlike the Gothic builders, the Greeks made as few constructional joints as possible along the lines of architectural division. Few antae, for instance, contain any blocks cut off by vertical joints from those of the wall behind them—the Temple of Poseidon on Cape Sunium is here quite exceptional—and it is rare indeed, from the very earliest times, for the block that includes a Doric capital not to include also the few uppermost inches of the shaft.   In one or two very early buildings, the first Temple of Athena Pronaia at Delphi and the Heraion at Olympia, existing remains seem to indicate a joint at the echinus;[4] but they

---

[1] Pausanias, I, xxvi, 7.
[2] Thucydides, IV, 133.
[3] See below, pp. 188 ff.
[4] See the illustrations, *Fouilles de Delphes*, Planches II (Paris, 1925), Pl. XIII, and *Olympia*, Tafelband I (Berlin, 1892), Taf. XXII, No. 5. The stone is coarse and soft and the amount of weathering (crucial for our theories) uncertain.   Schliemann, *Tiryns* (London, 1886), p. 293, shows a joint at the echinus of a similar column (see Fig. 50).   But contem-porary examples at the Argive Heraion all had joints well down the shaft.

probably deceive us, and have been generally restored with normal jointing.

Each wall or colonnade possessed a firm foundation wall, usually about twice its own width and built of carefully squared stones. The uppermost course was always at least partly visible. The intervals between these foundation-walls were often packed with polygonal masonry of large blocks, the whole forming a solid platform, the krepis, carried down in good construction to a foundation-raft, as at Ephesus,[1] or to solid rock, as in the

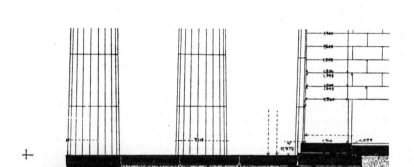

Fig. 51   Foundations of the Temple of Athena Alea, Tegea.

Parthenon. The stylobate and its supporting steps of course enclose the whole structure (see Fig. 51).

Each column simply rests, unfastened, in the slightest of hollows on the surface of the stylobate. This is a construction natural with upright monoliths, and early Greek stone columns were monolithic. Once raised vertically on the stylobate, each could be coaxed, without actual lifting, into its final position, where it would afterwards remain of its own weight. How much easier,

[1] Diogenes Laertius, II, 103. A layer of ashes was first shovelled on to the marsh.

this, than lifting it and lowering it precisely on to a dowel! But even the later marble columns, each of several drums, still observed the tradition. Pl. 15 illustrates a base drum and an intermediate drum at Sunium.

The jointing of these drums without mortar provides the most elaborate example of the method called 'anathyrosis', employed, *mutatis mutandis*, throughout the building. In rolling and hauling his stones, the Greek might fear chipping and other damage. So he never completely dressed them until they were in position. Having finished and polished the final sharp edges and corners, he left a rough, raised, protective surface over most of the faces he intended to be seen on the finished building, a surface carried close enough to the edges to shield them from any accidental hit. Some new ceiling beams intended for 'restorations' on the Acropolis and lying about there in the winter of 1947–8 had lost a good deal from their sharper edges for want of such protection. But on faces intended to close joints the classical craftsman, instead of leaving a raised surface, rough-picked the whole of the centre to sink it to the slightest degree behind the plane of the edges. So in Greek masonry the edges of the blocks meet in a hair-joint and the rest fails to touch. A fine joint is obtained, of course, far more easily and cheaply in this way than by any attempt to polish the whole surface in one plane.

In the fifth century, the curved faces of the drums were left rough during the actual erection, with projecting handles, or 'ancones', for ropes. Only at the top and bottom of the shaft were tiny stretches of fluting already completed. But the horizontal faces had received the elaborate finished pattern illustrated by Penrose.[1] The outer rims only were made to fit. Nearer the centre was a large, more roughly picked area, imperceptibly recessed. Nearer it again, a deeper hollow encircled the final raised centre, with its square sinking for the olive-wood box or 'empolion', from either end of which protruded the dowel to fasten the drums. Dinsmoor seems to imply that the sharp corners of this cubical box, once it rested in the drum below, compelled the builders to place the next drum in its exact position and hindered accidental shifting once it was laid.[2] This seems the easiest explanation.

[1] *Principles of Athenian Architecture*, p. 22. Reproduced by Dinsmoor, Fig. 61. Penrose does not allow the dowel to project from the box. But what is the use of so short a dowel?
[2] See Dinsmoor, p. 172.

When the whole structure was finished, the craftsmen would proceed to flute the shafts from top to bottom. There survive, of course, several examples where this was never done, notably the temples of Segesta and Rhamnous. Where it was, and the columns had later to be repaired after some earthquake or other disaster, the drums could be lifted in only one way, by sinking a large hole and inserting a lewis. Dinsmoor has tried, with considerable optimism, to trace from lewis holes in drums the exact amount of rebuilding necessary at Olympia after a later earthquake,[1] but he fails, as in some of his other work, to reduce the unknown factors to a manageable number.

The construction of the entablature depends chiefly on the size of the temple. On examining the metric measurements of Doric hexastyle temples, conveniently set out in Dinsmoor's appendix, one finds most examples between 13 and 18 metres broad and 28 and 38 metres long, giving columns a little over 1 metre (or nearly 3½ feet) in lower diameter. The methods of construction, one can hardly doubt, were devised to suit buildings on this scale, of which the Hephaisteion at Athens is typical. We know that even the seventh-century temple of Thermon had an entablature comparable in size, although of wood, to that of the Hephaisteion. On a front about 12 metres wide it had metopes nearly 1 metre square, the Hephaisteion, on a front of nearly 14 metres, metopes of 83 by 78 centimetres.[2]

On this scale, one naturally assigns one course of blocks to the architrave, one to the frieze and one to the cornice; and while architrave and frieze are commonly made two blocks deep, the cornice, greatly projecting but less than half the height of either, consists of single 'through' slabs or geison blocks, roughly square on plan and containing at the back stretches of the epikranitis that supports the ceiling. Its bed, below the mutules, is firmly horizontal.

The architrave-blocks and their backers can extend only from centre to centre of the columns. For visible masonic tricks like that in the latest forum at Pompeii[3] would be out of place in this serene style. But the frieze is carefully designed to break joint as much as it can. Normally, its front blocks contain each one

[1] W. B. Dinsmoor, 'An Archaeological Earthquake at Olympia', *AJA*, 1941.
[2] H. Kaehler, *Das Griechische Metopenbild*, pp. 96 and 106.
[3] See below, p. 290.

triglyph and one metope; while its backers, often of the same length, are aligned neither with them nor the architrave-blocks.[1] One often finds a gap between frieze-blocks and backers, which lightens the load on the architrave. Above the cornice the sima might consist simply of upward-curving tiles dowelled to a sloping surface, or of thick blocks, each in section a long right-angled triangle, resting firmly on the level top of the geison-blocks. Much might depend on the arrangement of rafters and battens under the tiles. Extant inscriptions, notably the building accounts of the Erechtheum,[2] describe an elaborate system of laths, battens and even, it seems, coffers. But the normal fifth-century temple seems from its remains to have room for nothing but rafters; and it would have been possible, given tiles as large and carefully fitted together as the Greek, to rest them directly on rafters normally less than two thicknesses apart.[3] The corner-blocks of the cornice, each destined to receive the sima, raking-cornice, raking-sima, ceiling-beams and akroterion, were given elaborate upper surfaces to ensure as interlocking a structure as possible.[4] Here we find a complete contrast with the simple trabeated architrave.

The larger temples show a modified construction. The builders of the Parthenon made an architrave three courses thick from front to back and each triglyph of a single, separate block. Those of Nemea and the Temple of Zeus, Olympia, saved themselves trouble by cutting several steps in the back of the frieze-blocks and resting on each a course of small backers. At Olympia, also, the cornice was sliced horizontally, so that the hawksbeak on the corona became in section the small visible apex of a massive triangular block supporting the sima.

Differences of construction not explained by mere size appear for the most part in Greek Italy alone. We have noticed the unusual architraves at Paestum. On the Temple of Ceres there the architect combined sound construction and high finish at frieze level by poising large beams of the hard limestone, as long as the architrave blocks, over the centres of the columns, and then

---

[1] The illustration (Fig. 47) of Sunium shows no joints between the backers, because I never discovered their length.

[2] For instance, the account, *Inscriptiones Graecae*, second edition, Vol. I, No. 374.

[3] At Rhamnous and on the Hephaisteion the cornice-blocks and ceilings barely leave room at some points even for rafters.

[4] See, e.g., the corner-blocks at Sunium (Orlandos, *Archaiologikon Deltion*, 1915).

grooving into the front face triglyphs of the softer stone. The rest of the front remained visible as metopes.

The cella-building rested always on a toichobate, a continuous ground-course of large spreading slabs, sometimes protruding less than an inch above the floor of the peristyle, but always visible and comforting. It might be doubled, as in the Parthenon. It might, as in the Hephaisteion or, partly, at Sunium, support a low, moulded course showing Ionic influence. It might even in late temples, like that of Apollo at Delphi, be given an Ionic moulding on its own outer face and a plain, secondary toichobate above. In some buildings, such as the Athenian Treasury at Delphi, it might be concealed on the inside. But it is never absent. It represents the stone 'oudos' of Homeric days, the unbroken footing, continued even under the door-opening, of the primeval mud hut. So in classical temples the toichobate continued under the great door as an enormous threshold-block, over 12 feet long. On this the heavy pivot-hung leaves could rest without fear of sinking.

The course above consisted of orthostates, large slabs set on end, two deep. In the Hephaisteion they are about 3 feet high, rather less than twice the height of the average wall-course. Projecting very slightly beyond the line of wall above, they represent the second stage in the petrifaction of mud hut into temple. In the Heraion at Olympia, one of the earliest temples, the orthostates were the highest stone course. All above was of mud or wood. Here also they are a mere facing, towards the peristyle, of a low wall four courses high. The similar construction at Kardaki attests the very early date of that most interesting temple.[1]

Above the orthostates the wall was usually one block thick and consisted of 'plinths', originally mud bricks but in classical times stone blocks wider than they were high and about two widths long. The construction of the anta sometimes masks that of the wall behind it. Never, except at Rhamnous,[2] does it show a vertical joint down its face, even at orthostate level. This treatment, like its slight projection, recalls its origin as a timber sheath on the end of a mud wall.

As many examples show, the door frame long remained of wood, perhaps with bronze sheathing. The Mycenaean technique

---

[1] See further below, p. 185.
[2] *Unedited Antiquities of Attica*, Chap. VI, Pl. 3.

had disappeared. Instead of being pivoted in the front of the aperture and fitting, when opened, into the reveals, the leaves were placed in its rear and swung back over the floor of the room behind. From examples like the Athenian Treasury at Delphi, where the blocks of jambs and lintel are planed back, it would seem that the whole aperture, not merely the face next to the leaves, was given a special clothing, probably of timber; as would, indeed, have been necessary in the days of the mud hut. The clothing spread laterally for some distance on the lowest course, giving the door frame a neat artistic footing.

We have stated above what little we know of the cella.

In lifting his stones, the Doric craftsman preferred where he could to tie his ropes round projecting bosses, or ancones, later chiselled off. Not only column-drums but the plinths of ordinary wall-courses were hoisted in this way. Blocks which he preferred to carve completely before setting them in position, such as frieze and geison blocks, he would normally lift by rope-holes (at as Paestum) or claw-holes (as at Sunium) in the concealed sides. At Sunium, having laid all the blocks of the architrave precisely in their place, he evidently lifted the backers over the top by claw-holes in their upper surface.

Every block of a Greek wall was normally clamped to its neighbour with a horizontal tie on its upper face, and fastened with a pair of vertical dowels to the course below. These attachments were often embedded at the moment of building in a small pool of molten lead. The traces of dowels, which always came at one end of the upper block, enable us to restore with fair certainty a good many vanished wall-courses. The forms of clamps used may help to date a temple. The double-dovetail clamp, for instance, shaped like a diabolo, Dinsmoor calls 'archaic'. It is found afterwards, in the later fifth century, for instance, at Rhamnous; but it is apparently rare then. Another form, a long straight rod with the two ends bent opposite ways, is also favoured in the sixth century, as at some treasuries in Delphi. But the H-shaped clamp is that most used in classical times.

An excellent discussion in Dinsmoor[1] will remind the reader of many constructional topics we cannot raise here. The subject is enthralling, since the Greeks themselves took special pride in their masonry. It seems certain that when Pausanias, the ancient writer, praises the 'harmonia' of the temple of Bassae or the

[1] Dinsmoor, pp. 169 ff.

Theatre of Epidaurus,[1] he meant by it the beauty and fineness of their actual jointing.

It seems unprofitable, in the present state of our knowledge, to ask which parts of the building were completed first. The accounts of the 'temple-builders' (naopoioi) at Delphi for the year 342 B.C. suggest that peristyle and cella-buildings were being constructed at the same time, and had both reached triglyph level nearly together.[2] At any rate, triglyphs for the inner buildings and corner-blocks for the geison of the peristyle, called 'carding-combs' from their general shape, were both purchased in that year. On the first marble Parthenon, cella and peristyle had reached nearly the same height when the Persians destroyed them. At the Temple of Aphaia on Aegina all the columns are monoliths except three on the north side. Obviously, as Dinsmoor justly infers,[3] a gap in the peristyle was left until the last moment 'to facilitate the erection of the interior, after which the limited space demanded the use of smaller units for the remaining columns'. At Sunium the central column of the south peristyle was made of nine blocks only, one less than its neighbours.[4] It seems possible that one or two columns here were similarly omitted until the last moment. But the evidence is much less certain than at Aegina. If today we find incomplete temples, as at Segesta, with perfect, though half-dressed peristyles and no trace of cella-buildings, we must remember how much more useful than column-drums were squared blocks to the plunderers of any age.[5]

No Doric temple was complete without its colouring, chiefly in red and blue. The rectangular leaves painted on the favourite hawksbeak moulding were always alternately red and blue. Other mouldings had their traditional colours. The small

[1] See, e.g., Pausanias, II, 27, and VIII, 41, viii, as interpreted by Penrose, *Athenian Architecture*, p. 22. J. Bousquet (*Revue Archéologique*, 1953, pp. 41 ff.) supposes that the former passage, on the 'harmony' of the Theatre of Epidaurus, means what we mean by harmony. He has not perhaps sufficiently considered the second passage nor the etymology of the word, which both make against him; as also does Pausanias, II, 25, viii.

[2] The curious can see the text in Dittenberger, *Sylloge Inscriptionum Graecarum*, third edition (Leipzig, 1915), No. 342, Col. III.

[3] Dinsmoor, p. 106.

[4] See my article on 'Three Attic Temples', *British School Annual*, 1950, p. 82. There were other columns like it, but I do not know where to place them.

[5] I must admit, however, that neither in the photographs nor in Koldewey's plan (*KP*, Taf. 19) can I find a trace of cella-buildings, and that the site is remote from later towns.

astragaloi, like the guttae, stood out pearly white against a dark background. The large fascia of the epikranitis often received a polychrome fret, as did the external taenia of the architrave and the bed of the cornice on the exterior of the Parthenon. But more often both these external strings became continuous bands of scarlet. For traditionally the artist saw strings and the necking-grooves of columns as red and the tympana and similar flat back-grounds of sculpture as blue, silhouetting the figures like the sky. More exotic colours, such as gold, purple, and apple-green, he reserved for more broken mouldings like the regula and for the roof. However, in the Doric frieze blue was impossible on the field of the metopes. For an unexplained but well-attested tradition prescribed it as the colour for the triglyphs[1]; and the earliest metopes, we now know, were thin plaques of warm red terracotta. Later, in some archaic buildings on the Acropolis, they were of Parian marble between triglyphs of poros limestone; and we may now be fairly certain that, where they used a choice marble, the Greeks were too sensible to paint its whole surface.[2] Not only have we no sure traces of colouring on the shafts or abaci of the columns or on the main fascia of the architrave, but we know from Corinth and elsewhere that the coarser stone was generally coated with a fine whitewash of powdered marble, the only covering to survive and the only one really needed on large stretches of the masonry.

But it was on the sculptures, the revetments and the roof that the painter felt really free. The archaic poros pediments in the Acropolis Museum preserve even today the original gaiety of their coloured sculpture; while on every Greek site appear the almost indestructible remains of coloured roofs (see Fig. 52), full of fancy and invention except in late archaic Sicily. Besides red, white and blue, the colours most favoured were straw, black, purple and chestnut. On early classical roofs and revetments we find more often lemon-coloured palmettes and lilies against a black or darkened background.[3]

Internally, each ceiling coffer—in this recalling Egypt—was painted to imitate a large sun or star, flaming in an azure sky but

---

[1] Vitruvius, IV, 2, ii, alleges that they were originally daubed with blue wax.

[2] These triglyphs and metopes, built into the north wall of the Acropolis after 480, are described and illustrated by Penrose, p. 73 and Pl. 40.

[3] See E. Buschor, *Die Tondaecher der Akropolis, I, Simen* (Berlin, 1929).

rendered geometrically with all the vigour of Greek convention. Frescoes abounded on Greek walls; but we hear of the most famous in stoas, not temples. Perhaps some existed in the pronaos; for in that of the Temple of Zeus, Olympia, we find a floor of coloured pebble mosaic inserted not long after 400 B.C. But inside the dark sanctuary glitter must have maintained itself against the more ordinary attractions of colour, as it always has, from the palaces of the Homeric Heroes to the Iconostaseis of the seventeenth and eighteenth centuries.

Having studied the details of the Greek Doric Temple and the deviations, so surprisingly few, from its overruling canon, we can only say that it is a creation more wonderful than any of its extant examples. It is a kind of Platonic Form, that dominates

Fig. 52   Athens, Sima of Old Temple of Athena.

all the particular instances.   More constant in its shape than a succession of the most stereotyped Hypostyle Halls, it can be derived, unlike them, in only the smallest degree from the ordinary building of the times.   Its entablature remains inexplicable and obdurate.[1]   Lucid innovators in all else, the Greeks created it, so far as we can see, by an inspiration not at all logical, and

[1] Signora P. Zancani-Montuoro argues from her discoveries at Foce del Sele that the earliest triglyphs tapered considerably and also that the earliest known roofs and ceilings of Greek Italy are an evident attempt to fit a traditional circular covering to newly invented rectangular buildings of stone.   It is doubtful whether these discoveries, highly interesting in themselves, will throw much light on the origin of the Order.   In Greece, even earlier metopes and triglyphs at Thermon and Kalydon had an apparently negligible taper; and the ignorant shifts of the Italiote carpenter seem to show he was fitting his roof to an importation he did not understand—the Doric entablature.

maintained it, down to its smallest member, with a conservatism more rigid than the Babylonian. It is wonderful that it should ever have arisen; yet more wonderful that a people so independent should have submitted for so long to a discipline so exacting. But, granted its history in Greece, one can begin to see why it has ruled ever since the educated intelligence of Europe.

3. THE IONIC TEMPLE

At first, in Greek Asia, Ionic was developing a discipline of its own. It had no feature so strong or insistent as the Doric triglyph; indeed, it omitted the frieze from its entablature. On the other hand, it aligned its columns with its cella walls and depended, except in the centres of certain large temple façades, on a spacing that gave exactly square compartments of ceilings to each bay.[1] For in this order ceiling beams were large and low, with a soffit midway down the architrave, and aligned on the axes of the columns. Even the Athenians, who later modified this rule, aligned at least the alternate beams on the columns (as in the Erechtheum and Propylaea) and rested their soffits at the highest on the top of the architrave. Thus, in the early sixth century, when the stone peristylar temple first appears, it assumes two widely different forms in Europe and in Asia. But the comparative hesitancy of the Ionic, even in its homeland, will appear if we describe its details and their variations, beginning with the Ionic of Asia.

The Ionic Krepis had no set form. Its builders, unlike the Doric, generally attempted to make its steps usable, and so in most cases numerous and shallow. Sometimes they would even set their column-bases several feet behind the face of the stylobate. On the front they might dispose the steps in an elaborate way, which never, however, approached the more intricate Roman, far less the 'Palladian' examples. In early temples, steps were few and low; but in the latest of the archaic temples at Samos and the fourth-century temple at Ephesus a lofty series was planned for all sides. As, however, this was never finished at Samos, the columns appeared to stand on a straight-sided platform, or podium.[2] Intentional podia, with moulded crowns, appear in

---

[1] For illustrations, see, e.g., the convenient restoration by Lethaby of the Order of the Mausoleum (*Greek Buildings*, Fig. 33).

[2] See Robertson, Fig. 43.

Asia fairly early as supports for tombs; for instance, the Nereid
Monument of about 400 B.C. at Xanthos in Lycia, where the
colonnade rests directly on the podium, with no intervening step.
Temples on podia, with steps on the façade only, are apparently
rare before Roman times, but did exist. Miletus has an example
of the fifth century. In the Ionic buildings of Athens, and a few
works in Asia probably influenced by Athens, such as the Temple
of Athena Polias at Priene, one finds three steps of an almost Doric
size and strength.

But normally the artist would use the bases of his columns
to achieve the necessary firmness of foundation. Every Ionic
column had a base; but the forms are legion. Although they
hinder circulation, plinths appear early and late, at sixth-century
Ephesus and fourth-century Priene, and generally equal in area the
square gaps between them.[1] The base above the plinth is usually
of about twice its height. In archaic Asia we find two types, the
Ephesian, destined to develop into the normal Asiatic base of the
fourth century, and the Samian. The former comprises two
members like highly compressed reels and a torus or cushion
surmounting them, fluted horizontally in about ten concave
channels. It has a height, without the plinth, about half its
greatest diameter—a proportion Vitruvius recommends for base
and plinth together.[2] The Samian, which has no late successors
and seems but distantly related to the Attic,[3] consists from top to
bottom of a small unfluted torus, a large fluted cushion, as at
Ephesus, and finally, to replace the reels and plinth, an even larger
member of circular plan and concave profile, divided into two
borders and six horizontal concavities.

One could add subsidiary ornamental members to the bases or
the capitals. Thus on the façades of Ephesus a band of life-size
figures in relief surmounted each base and received its own crown
of leaf and dart. Lethaby suggests with reason[4] that the cella

[1] For instance, in most of the large fourth-century temples, such as
Priene, Ephesus and Didyma.
[2] Vitruvius, III, 5, ii.
[3] See Robertson, Fig. 44. The large 'flaring' member on the bases
at Bassae (see below, p. 171) perhaps comes closer. But perhaps we
can consider the earliest Attic bases (as in the Temple of Athena Nike)
Samian, with a very low torus added at the foot to improve their appearance.
[4] *JHS*, 1917, p. 1. Possible remains of such a dado, with a winged
lion, exist even from a Roman building at Vienne, where they at present
stand just outside the main entrance to the Musée Lapidaire.

walls were faced in the oriental manner with a dado of carved slabs, and that these carved drums were designed to complete the effect.

The earliest shafts had very numerous flutes, separated by sharp arrises, as at Ephesus. The canonical form, with twenty-four flutes only and fillets between them, found everywhere after the early fifth century, is taken for granted by the great Ionian architects of the fourth. But strangely enough, its earliest examples and even those of the transition all appear outside Asia. Whatever the form of the shaft, it swelled slightly to meet base and capital in an 'apophyge'.

The Ionic capital, like the Doric entablature, is one of those Greek designs that seem at first sight to imitate some simpler structure of more perishable material, but on closer inspection are revealed as inspired creations leaving far behind them the world of primitive construction. It comprises three members, the squat echinus of ovolo profile, carved with an egg-and-dart moulding, the volute-member, rectangular on plan, and the small abacus, square on plan, with a cyma reversa profile. All three had a total height about equal to half the lower diameter of the shaft. Robertson has given a clear[1] description of the volute-member as resembling 'a bolster laid on the echinus, with its loose ends wound up in dropping spirals on each side of the shaft. On the front and back faces there is a wide shallow concave channel (canalis), edged by small mouldings between the echinus and the abacus; this channel curls round into the spirals of the volutes, which usually have button-like eyes (oculi) at their centres. At the sides the echinus is usually covered and partly absorbed by the under surface of the volute-member' (where it meets this under surface, on each side, it is usually masked by a half-palmette). 'The sides of the volute-member, which are called the pulvinus or "cushion", resemble reels pinched up below, and are decorated in various ways.' Clearly the capital was to be seen chiefly from front and rear, and was designed, one would suppose, for columns between antae or responds.

Almost all examples, in Asia and Europe, have the abacus, difficult as it is to see the structural or aesthetic need for it—for one sees little force in the reasoning of Statham[2] that, without it, the architrave would appear to crush the volute. About 500 B.C. a transient fashion set in of omitting it. But this appears mostly

---

[1] Robertson, p. 46.
[2] *Critical History*, p. 110.

Propylaea and Pinakotheke,
Athens

outh Peristyle of Parthenon

Plate 9

West elevation of Parthenon, restored

Plate 10

outside Ionia, at Neapolis in Macedonia and Locri in Italy[1]; and
one can think of only one example in Asia, the small, though fairly
early capital seen by Mr. John Cook by the quayside of Budrun
(Halicarnassus). Even in these, the abacus has left a 'vestigial
remnant'. Indubitably, then, serious architects regarded the
capital as neither a bracket nor a socketed 'fork', like those of
Achaemenid Persia.[2] Yet in some early examples like Ephesus
the abacus is oblong and so half way to a bracket, not the square
on plan that it later became.

The origin of the volute-member is still quite unknown.

In some very early capitals like that under the Naxian Sphinx
at Delphi, to be reckoned as Asiatic because dedicated by a very
Ionic island, the echinus below the volute-member is still a ring of
curling leaves[3] like those on the Nimrud Ivories, not the later
cushion of ovolo profile. The 'dactyliform' capitals of sixth-
century Ionic treasuries at Delphi, described below,[4] have points
in common with it, but have a broad square abacus and no volute-
member. At Naucratis, the Greek emporium in Egypt, was
found an echinus yet stranger, generally made by restorers,
Dinsmoor, for instance,[5] to recede rapidly from the top of the
shaft. As, further, the neck of the shaft is ornamented with a
band of lotus buds and flowers, without the Assyrian palmette,
and as volutes were never shown to have existed, this echinus
perhaps crowned the whole column and completed a profile not
unlike those of Thothmes' tent poles.[6] In any case, the canonical
Ionic echinus appears to represent a leaf-crown drastically
remodelled.[7]

[1] For Neapolis (Kavalla), see Balalakis, *EA*, 1936, and for Locri
Dinsmoor, p. 137, Fig. 49 (from Durm). On the column of the Naxian
Sphinx (see immediately below) the abacus naturally becomes a plinth
for the statue.
[2] See, for the Persian 'fork' below, p. 218.
[3] See the photograph, Dinsmoor, Pl. XXXIII. The rendering in
Perrot and Chipiez, VII, p. 633, Pl. LIV, is very incorrect. The monument is now published by P. Amandry in *FD*, Tome II, Paris, 1953.
Puchstein published many examples with a Lesbian Leaf ornament on
the echinus. See below, n. 7.
[4] See below, p. 169.
[5] P. 126, Fig. 47.
[6] See above, p. 41.
[7] Here I agree with Puchstein, who figures a series of early Ionic
capitals where the Lesbian Leaf replaces the Egg and Dart. He even
refuses to call this member the echinus, but compares it with the ring of
leaves below the echinus on Mycenaean and Paestan capitals. See *Das
Ionische Capitell* (Berlin, 1887), especially Figs. 4, etc.

II—I

One other problem faces the student of early Ionic. Its abaci were oblong. But it had full peristyles, turning the corners in the normal way. How, then, was the corner capital, the meeting place of two oblong abaci at right angles, to acquire a presentable outline? With an abacus of square plan, one can turn the corner by juxtaposing two 'fronts' on the external faces and two 'sides' on the internal, with a two-sided volute turned through 45 degrees at the angle of the former and two shortened pulvini along the latter, merely touching one another near the line of the shaft on the inside corner. Dinsmoor, following Lethaby, supposes that with the early oblong abaci the volutes must have crossed one

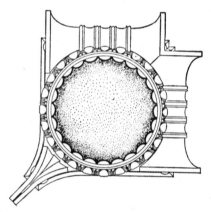

Fig. 53   Ionic corner-capital: mirror-plan.

another, as on some capitals at Persepolis.[1] I am inclined to believe merely that the corner-volute was aligned on the diagonal of the rectangle, giving a shallower angle on the front and a sharper on the side façade.[2] Or was there sometimes a corner pier, given the mouldings of an anta?[3]

The volute-member developed steadily. In the sixth century,

[1] See Dinsmoor, pp. 64 and 131. Lethaby, of whom Dinsmoor may or may not be conscious here, made the suggestion in *JHS*, 1917, p. 10.

[2] A mysterious, unpublished fragment of a small Ionic capital now lying beside the Temple of Ceres at Paestum, does not alas! seem to come from a corner capital of this temple. The Ionic capital from the Pronaos, published by Krauss (*Mitteilungen des Institutes*, 1950), is larger and of a different design. The fragment I am considering comprises two parallel volute-faces, each about 1 foot in diameter, on a block about 5 inches thick!

[3] As in the Sarcophagus of the Weeping Women, anticipated in some ways by a sixth-century Sarcophagus from Samos (*AM* 1900, p. 209), brought to my notice by Mr. Robert Cook.

most are wide-spreading, with eyes well outside the line of the shaft. The canalis sags heavily in the centre and in cross-section is convex, not concave. The pulvinus at the sides is cylindrical, not pinched, and partly separated by a deep undercutting from the half-covered echinus. Apart from several encircling rolls, it has a plain surface.

By the fourth century the eyes have moved inwards to the line of the shaft, the canalis is concave in section, but with less of a sag in the centre on elevation, and the pulvinus pinched and often decorated with such features as laurel leaves (first known to appear on the fifth-century temple at Locri). The echinus after about 300 B.C. is no longer visible under the pulvinus, so that the degenerate craftsman saves himself much careful labour : and whereas in the best period the mouldings bordering the canalis show a most beautiful contraction as they approach the eyes, in Hellenistic and Roman work they maintain a constant width.

Up to the mid-fourth century at earliest the Ionic builders of Asia continued to use a distinctive entablature, without a frieze.[1] In this the architrave was crowned with a large, carved ovolo and was divided into three small fasciae, subtly increasing from the lowest, the smallest and most recessed, to the uppermost, the largest and most projecting. The whole architrave had a height of over one lower diameter. Where covered with reliefs, as on the Nereid Monument at Xanthos, it had, of course, only one fascia.

The cornice comprised first a row of horizontal projecting dentils, rectangular stone blocks about as high as one fascia of the architrave, and set less than their own width apart. An astragal and ovolo projected above them, immediately beneath the concave soffit of the corona, the face of which below the crowning ovolo equalled in height an average fascia of the architrave. The whole cornice projected a distance at least equal to its height.

The sima was nearly always heavy and continuous. One finds moulded examples of terracotta, as at Larisa, and even, at Ephesus, one of heavy marble carved with processions of chariots and worshippers. On the Sarcophagus of the Mourning Women we find a line of figures, half reminiscent of this sima, half realistic, in front of the attic and above a small sima of later type. As

---

[1] I am not persuaded by Dinsmoor (pp. 259–60) that the Mausoleum had a frieze. It had a very low ceiling, so that a frieze would necessitate a heavy additional course everywhere. Without a frieze the entablature would have proportions found on the Sarcophagus of the Mourning Women from Sidon, its near contemporary.

Demangel shrewdly observes,[1] some early Ionians attempted to establish the carved frieze as a parapet above the cornice and the flat ceiling, whose joists formed the first dentils, because it was here that the early Asiatics had placed their most elaborate revetments. He assumes with justice that they were copying the Asiatics, not their own earlier buildings, with steep, thatched roofs. By the fourth century their attempt had failed, and the archaic

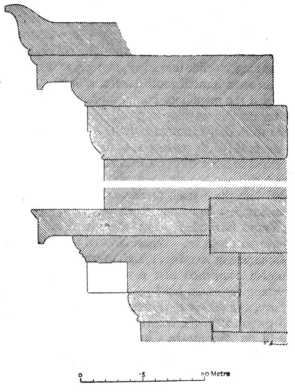

Fig. 54   Priene, Temple of Athena Polias: section through tympanum.

figured parapet of Ephesus gave place to a monotonous cyma recta with lion-headed spouts.

The pediment tended to shallowness. The plane of the tympanum at Priene heavily overhung that of the architrave, and was set back a mere 2 feet from the corona[2] in a building over

[1] *La Frise Ionique*, in several places, especially p. 275.
[2] Wiegand-Schrader, *Priene*, Abb. 75 and 76.

60 feet wide (see Fig. 54). Moreover, the roof had a slope even flatter than the Doric. Its restorers conclude[1] that in Ionic it was general to leave such pediments without sculpture, an omission which would certainly relieve the weight at very important points in temples like Ephesus. The tympanum-frame, we gather from Priene, was carefully moulded. There is little

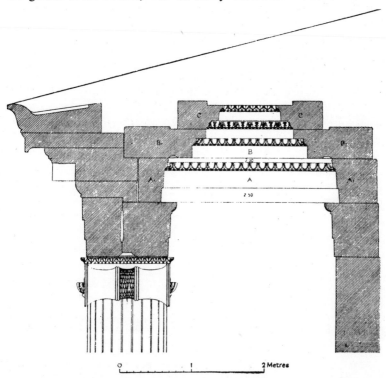

Fig. 55   Priene, Temple of Athena Polias: section through ceiling.

A = Ceiling-Beam; B = Lower part of Coffer-Frame;
C = Upper part of Coffer-Frame.

evidence for sculpture in Asiatic pediments, except in the tiny Nereid Monument at Xanthos, designed in any case under Athenian inspiration.[2] The second-century temple of the White-Browed Artemis at Magnesia certainly had no sculpture in the tympana, but instead three openings, copied, thinks Dinsmoor,

[1] *Priene*, p. 106 and note.
[2] Dinsmoor, p. 257.

from the great fourth-century temple of Ephesus.[1]   At Ephesus, he thinks, sculpture was presumably to conceal them.   But Mrs. Bluma L. Trell has recently collected the coins that show this temple, and that provide the only direct ancient evidence surviving for most of its upper parts: and although, following them, she restores four sculptured figures inside the pediment, she also follows them in providing three large and visible doors in the tympanum and aligning these, reasonably enough, with the three central intercolumniations.   But I am not wholly convinced that she is right to place even four figures in the pediment, in front of the remaining stretches of tympanum wall.[2]

Internally, the large ceiling beams, aligned on the columns, rest in the architrave at a point only slightly, sometimes only one fascia above its soffit.   This was the distance in the Mausoleum, and offers good evidence, as Lethaby saw,[3] that there was no frieze outside; for the ceiling was obviously set so far down to keep it from rising above the low entablature.   Asiatic coffers were large, square and lofty, and the several courses of which they were made, for instance at Priene (see Fig. 55), reveal the Ionians as past masters of the cantilever and the counterpoise.[4]

Of the cella walls, too little is known.   At Ephesus, as we saw, they perhaps had a dado of carved slabs,[5] and later temples in Asia, like early Ionic work in Europe, have a continuous carved Ionic moulding along the toichobate.   This was perhaps balanced,

---

[1] Dinsmoor, p. 276.

[2] Her invaluable paper, to which my attention was drawn by Professor Michael Grant, is printed as *Numismatic Notes and Monographs*, No. 107, New York, 1945.   I am not sure, despite her arguments, that coins always show features of this temple in positions where they in fact appeared.   For instance, some coins have persuaded her that antefixes appeared up the pediment—a barbarism hard to credit at Ephesus.   So I wonder about the four figures shown inside it.   Her interpretation of the supposed sculptural scene—four Amazons waiting outside a propylon— I find hard to accept.   Why, if they are akin, as she thinks (*op. cit.*, pp. 26/7) to the Polyclitan and Pheidian Amazons, does no coin show them with spears?   And what Greek propylon could be made to look like the three bare doors of this Ephesian pediment?   So I am still attracted to the view of Lethaby (*JHS*, 1914, p. 87) that there was no sculpture here. No surviving sculpture from classical Greek pediments is quite so colossal (over fifteen feet high) as Mrs. Trell's Amazon would have to be.

[3] Lethaby restores the order of the Mausoleum in his *Greek Buildings*, Figs. 33 and 40.   The ceiling, he says, was low to make room for the coffers below the pyramidal 'attic' above the entablature. See *JHS*, 1916, p. 35.

[4] See *Priene*, Abb. 68.

[5] Above, p. 159.

as in Athenian fifth-century Ionic, by a continuous carved mould-ing, the epikranitis, along the top of the wall immediately below the architrave. But whereas in Athens the moulding continued the profile of the anta-capitals, a device easily managed owing to their thinness and lightness, the early Asiatic anta sometimes had three tiers of thick, carved ovolo for a capital, aesthetically incapable of being carried round the building.[1] But we are still ignorant even whether the normal anta projected.

Asiatic Ionic proportions are far less certain than Doric. The columns, between eight and nine lower diameters high, were spaced less than three interaxial diameters apart on bases (and often plinths) exactly equal in diameter to the gaps between them, above a krepis that had no definite relation to the dimensions of the columns. The whole entablature had a height perhaps one-fifth of theirs.[2] As in Doric, smaller buildings tend to show lighter construction; and the more closely spaced the columns, the greater, perhaps, their slenderness, a tendency later reduced to a system in Vitruvius. This earliest Ionic differed from Doric not in the column-spacing but in the height of the shaft and the depression of the entablature.

So the European Greeks, when designing light, flimsy buildings, seem at first, as the vases show, not to have borrowed from Ionic but to have taken liberties with Doric. Architraves were perhaps lower—though the vase painters, like almost every layman, probably tended to depress them[3]—triglyphs much smaller and more numerous. In some cases, however, they did decorate with Ionic capitals the posts or columns of these flimsy pseudo-Doric buildings; and about 500 B.C. we find, in the Athenian Stoa at Delphi, a complete though small Ionic colonnade of stone with intercolumniations of six or seven diameters that supported a wooden entablature perhaps as gay as theirs.

[1] I am not convinced that the famous sixth-century 'anta-capital' from Didyma (Dinsmoor, Pl. XXXIA) is from the temple at all. An identical member is shown on an altar on the famous Busiris Vase, an Ionic work of the same date. See J. D. Beazley and B. Ashmole, *Greek Sculpture and Painting* (Cambridge, 1932), Fig. 46. However, the temple at Locri did have such an anta (Dinsmoor, Fig. 49), and Lethaby notes others, *JHS*, 1917, p. 11.

[2] Despite the disagreements of its excavators, the Temple of Priene still offers the best evidence. It seems to have had an entablature 2·13 metres high, and columns of 11 metres by 1·15 metres. For a good, responsible discussion, see Lethaby, *Greek Buildings*, p. 186.

[3] But possibly, as in the first Forum at Pompeii, single planks served as the architrave (see below, p. 251).

Nearly all evidence for these structures has perished, so we cannot tell whether they pre-existed or derived from the stone orders. We have, however, a long series of small Ionic stone capitals, painted rather than carved, found in Athens and Attica, some of which may come from them rather than from votive offerings in temple precincts. None appears to precede 550 B.C. and most are far later. I am not in general inclined to consider the influence of these vanished, minor buildings very important; and their Ionic capitals, although their only stone feature, will tell us little more about true Ionic than Elizabethan fireplaces about the true Renaissance.[1]

In stone, it took the European Greeks over a century to remodel the order and produce an alternative version of it, which holds an equal place with the Asiatic in the third book of Vitruvius and now, thanks to the accessibility of Athens, has almost supplanted it as 'true' Ionic in the eyes of the student. Their first stone buildings were all tiny. No temple of any size is known, even in Magna Graecia, earlier than that at Locri, a solitary fifth-century example of the standard Doric size,[2] but of a design imported from Asia, with the close Asiatic spacing of the columns. In European Greece, if we omit the 'Parthenon' at the remote Neapolis, probably designed under influence from Miletus in Ionia,[3] and the small abnormal Temple of Athena at Sunium, the Erechtheum (*c.* 410 B.C.) is the first Ionic shrine of any size, and even the Erechtheum is not peripteral. The earlier buildings are mostly small treasuries at Delphi.

So, while retaining the Asiatic proportions for the columns themselves, the builders space them more widely, a feature noticed in 'The Antiquities of Ionia'[4]; over four diameters from axis to axis in the Massaliot Treasury (530 B.C.) and nearly four in the North Porch of the Erechtheum. The entablature, too, is heavier, totalling on the same porch 5 feet 3 inches in height, or nearly one-quarter of the columns. It was modelled on the Doric, without dentils and with architrave, frieze and cornice. The frieze equalled the architrave, and the latter had, until late in the

---

[1] For information on these buildings see B. Dunkley, 'Greek Fountain Buildings', *BSA*, 1935–6.

[2] See above, p. 151.

[3] We know Miletus at this very time was most interested in this part of Macedonia. See Herodotus, V, 23.

[4] Vol. III, p. 31. 'The Ionian Temples have their columns less distant than is observed in those of Greece.'

fifth century, only one fascia, like the Doric.[1] Having a proper frieze, the Europeans could dispense almost at once with the carved procession on the sima. Only on the Siphnian Treasury do we see a small vestige of it in the lions promenading at the angles. Pediments, as on neighbouring Doric buildings, receive full sculptured scenes. Ceiling-beams, while set higher than in Asia, never appear above the level of the outer frieze; at which level, however, the architect deemed it aesthetically possible to set the alternate beams midway between the columns. Once the Europeans had adopted the Asiatic architrave, with its three fasciae, they found a continuous carved epikranitis necessary to set it off from the walls below. With an architrave of one fascia, as in the Delphic Treasuries, this had not often been employed.

The column was altered most. Little was constant except the proportions, the volutes and the abacus. At Delphi, even the last two were threatened. For in the Treasuries of Massalia and Clazomenae (mid sixth century), the builders eliminated the volutes, turned the abacus into a square plinth resembling the Doric and enlarged the ring of leaves, from which we saw the echinus develop, until they assumed the curled form, drooping over at the top, so common in the Syrian and Phoenician work of the time.[2] In two other treasuries, the Cnidian and Siphnian, the whole column was replaced by a draped female figure, or caryatid, another Ionic feature recalling Syria. Such caryatids were always possible, though rare, in the European Ionic order; but none seems to be known from Ionia.

However, nearly all columns soon came to have a recognisable Ionic form. Variations in the capital might assume the shape of an elaborate floral band below the echinus, as on the Erechtheum. Here, with good taste, the designer suppressed the two palmettes in the angles of the volutes. Or the sides of the pulvinus in the fifth century might have carved or painted lilies in some of their compartments—Möbius plausibly assigns some such ornament to the capitals in the Propylaea, the purest ever designed.[3] Or, finally, the wide sagging centre of the pulvinus might in the early

[1] See Dinsmoor, pp. 139, 185–7. The Siphnian frieze is carved, and is much higher than the plain architrave. A raised frame encloses its reliefs, with excellent effect.
[2] See above, p. 99. There is no need to call these capitals, with Dinsmoor (p. 140), Aeolic. But he is surely right to restore a single ring of leaves, not the monstrous double ring of Pomtow.
[3] Möbius, *AM*, 1927, pp. 165 ff.

fifth century invite the patterning with scroll and palmette found, for instance, on Inwood's famous capital[1] and seized with delight by minor craftsmen in jewellery and on graves (see Fig. 56). It seems clear from finds of their work at Taras[2] that they played with it for some fifty years, and possible that they gave it back to building as the Corinthian Capital. The position and size of the large palmette on the earliest known Corinthian Capital, at Bassae, remind us strongly of Inwood's capital.

Some early bases at Delphi, such as the Massaliot, observe the

Fig. 56   Early Corinthian capitals.

A = 'Ionic' Capital from Taras; B, C, E = 'Corinthian' Capitals from Taras; D = Capital in Cella, Bassae.

Ephesian form. But one completely different, the Attic, makes its appearance in the Athenian Stoa, and becomes universal, until it conquers Ionia itself in the second century B.C. It comprises an upper torus roll, a scotia and a more spreading lower torus, at first very pinched, as in the Stoa, and reaching its canonical

[1] *The Erechtheum* (London, 1831), Pl. 23.
[2] See H. Klumbach, *Tarentiner Grabkunst* (Reutlingen, 1937). I owe my knowledge of these pieces to Paul Jacobsthal.

dimensions only much later, in the Erechtheum. But all Athenian examples and even the unique flaring bases at Bassae remain faithful to the tripartite form.

The profile of the anta-capital develops, on the whole, in harmony with the columns. On some Delphic Treasuries the three ovolos are reduced to one, obviously because of the small scale. In Attic work the triple division is retained, but the profiles and carved patterns are most carefully varied, as on the Erechtheum. Yet another type, the 'sofa-type', seems to originate in the Peloponnese or Sicily. It comprises a carved relief, usually floral, framed between two outward-curling vertical volutes at either end of a long, horizontal fillet. The early examples, though not rare, have nowhere been traced to a definite building; and formally the type is as mysterious as the column-capital. Its volute member seems to represent the same original, crushed by a heavier load. But again the abacus is present, balanced with even more precariousness on the tips of the volutes; so that the sofa-capital obscures, if anything, the already obscure derivation of its fellow.

For all that, it conquers Ionia, where it figures on nearly all the fourth- and third-century temples; and thereby gives us an epitome of the European achievement. The early Ionian temples had been large, harmoniously constructed and famous for their structural ingenuity. The Europeans designed a smattering of petty buildings. Yet such were the keenness of their criticism and the intensity of their vision that even on an Order not their own they imposed forms the cogency of which no one, not even its inventors, could resist.

So, within the limits of their two Orders, the Greeks found exercise enough even for their remarkable originality, in devising proportions, perfecting craftsmanship and defining with ever greater strictness the areas of decoration—all matters on which, whatever our century may think,[1] agreement is necessary before a common language is evolved. If in fifteenth-century Florence, according to Mr. Geoffrey Scott,[2] the inventor of a new moulding

[1] 'After all,' writes a critic in *The Times Literary Supplement* for June 5th, 1953, 'it is a most notable fact that for the first time since the end of the Gothic style an age is with us which has evolved its own independent language of architecture.' Boastful words! Is our critic sure that this modern 'language' is more than the babbles and screams of a baby, or a lunatic?

[2] *The Architecture of Humanism* (London, 1924), p. 203.

risked persecution, in Dorian Greece, through most of her history, he was nearly unthinkable.

4. THE DESIGNING OF INDIVIDUAL BUILDINGS

We have already discussed the fairly rigid proportions of the Orders, which will largely, but not wholly determine those of the buildings. The architect using them could begin either with his whole building or a single bay. In the Arsenal of Piraeus (*c.* 340 B.C.) we know from the surviving specifications[1] that the architect Philo began with the whole building. A modern architect would surely have taken the single bay, for it was a shed to house the standard equipment of sixty-eight ships (the doors at each end, extending to the first of the thirty-five columns down either side, left sixty-eight clear compartments for their tackle). But Philo subordinated the size of the compartments to the general dimensions, a total inner width of 50 feet, of which the central hall took a clear 20 and the side compartments 15, and an inner length of probably 400 feet. The Greek is a little ambiguous: 'To be four plethra' (*sc.* 400 feet) 'in length, in breadth fifty feet and five with the walls.' But with Doerpfeld and Fabricius I presume the external length was 405 feet and that the draughtsman, starting from internal dimensions, meant: 'Four plethra by fifty feet, or fifty-five if one includes the walls.' Choisy translates: 'In length four plethra, in breadth fifty-five feet, including the walls in each case.' But this, besides giving unusual Greek for fifty-five, results in a building whose length and breadth have no clear relation externally or internally, which is contrary to the spirit of this document.[2] For Choisy goes on to show that the main dimensions of the façades are all as close as possible, working in exact numbers of feet, to simple fractions of their width, 55 feet (see Fig. 57). Their height totalled 36 feet, two-thirds of it, the height to the bed of the geison (an interesting point of division, not often taken by modern surveyors of Greek temples) 27, that to the top of the door-hoods probably 18 and the width

---

[1] See above, p. 130.

[2] Compare Doerpfeld and Fabricius *AM*, 1883, p. 148, and Choisy, *Études Épigraphiques sur l'Architecture Grecque* (Paris, 1884), Pt. III. Le Corbusier, in his untrustworthy way, shows a simplified elevation, derived perhaps from Choisy, with the caption 'From the marble slab found in 1882', as if the drawing were on the stone! See his book, *Towards a New Architecture* (London, 1931), p. 75.

of each door 9. The actual stones used, Greek construction being what it was, have less simple measurements than the Roman. But the main dimensions are bold and 'masculine'.

For temples we have little explicit ancient evidence, and where we do not know the scale observed by the builder, we can only guess where to begin. The attempt of Dinsmoor to establish two standard feet, the Doric and the Ionic for which little literary evidence exists, has led him into many discrepancies, besides causing him to abandon the obvious dimensions of 100 by 225 feet for the stylobate of the Parthenon.[1] Every city, as the coins

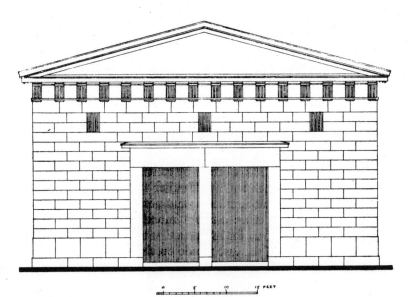

Fig. 57   The Arsenal, Piraeus: after Choisy.

also prove, could have its own standard weights and measures, and we know that Athens altered hers at least once in the sixth century. So we can infer the scale of each building only from itself; but this is not always impossible.

In Ionic it was easy to take as one's governing dimensions the distances between the axes of the four corner columns, as, for instance, with the six end and eleven side columns on the Temple of Athena Polias at Priene. In fact, as Dinsmoor convincingly

[1] See, for his doubts and difficulties, his notes p. 161, n. 1, p. 222, n. 2, and p. 229, n.2.

shows,[1] its architect could amuse himself with an interaxial length
of 120 feet and breadth of 60 feet, with 100 feet for the length and
40 feet for the width of the cella-building, 50 feet for the length
of the cella and 6 feet for the width of each plinth.

Doric, with its angle contraction and its unrelated cella-buildings,
was far less tractable, and here Dinsmoor, who is specially well-
versed in this topic, considers the efforts to use simple dimensions
'rare', even on individual columns and axial spacing—though we
have found one or two in his table.[2] Another instance is provided
by the most beautiful surviving building at Akragas, the mid-fifth-
century temple of 'Juno Lacinia'. Using a foot apparently
identical with the modern English, it has an axial inter-columnia-
tion of 10 feet, stylobate blocks 5 feet square, and floor blocks of
6 feet 8 inches from the stylobate to the cella-wall. The cella
internally was exactly 25 feet wide. Moreover, the frieze had a
height of 3 feet 4 inches, and was harmoniously divided between
metopes 3 feet and triglyphs 2 feet in width.[3] Not all the
dimensions will fit the scale so exactly, although the architect had
a fondness for exact numbers—for instance, the cella-wall at
orthostate level is exactly 3 feet thick. But the stone of Akragas
is very rough, so rough that errors of column spacing, it seems,
can be as much as an inch and a half either way and I had to take
the averages of many measurements; and possibly an investigation
with more time, in a more clement month than August, may
confirm other proportions, for instance that the door-opening was
a fifth of the breadth of the east façade on the stylobate.

The Parthenon, according to Dinsmoor, was laid out to give
as many instances as possible of the relation 9:4. But his
description on pp. 161 ff. leaves little room for dimensions in
simple units; and surely its architect began with two, 225 feet
by 100 feet on the stylobate. It is surely no accident that the
stadium at Athens, which should represent 600 Athenian feet, has
a length of 606 feet 10 inches, almost exactly six times the 101 feet
3½ inches of the Parthenon's east front.[4]

[1] See Dinsmoor, p. 222.
[2] Above, p. 131.
[3] All according to measurements I took myself in August 1952. An
entirely different system, whereby each part of the façade is given a
geometrical rather than an arithmetical relation to the whole, has been
propounded by Bousquet for the Treasury of Cyrene (see above, p. 135).
H. Koch has now argued that the East Front of the Hephaisteion was
divided on the Golden Section (*Studien zum Theseustempel*, Berlin,
1955, pp. 70 ff.).

We cannot consider here the early archaic fashion of spacing smaller columns less widely on the flanks than on the fronts, or the slightly later habit, perverse functionally, of enlarging the columns on the fronts.[1] But we must remember that no classical Greek architect appears to use the module of Vitruvius, to break up each façade into an arbitrary total of lengths, or to assign one whole number of these to each column shaft, another to each clear inter-columnar space. Vitruvius thus divides his hexastyle Doric temple-façade into forty-two modules, of which he assigns twelve to the shafts, thirty to the spaces.[2] The Greek was less mechanical, and used rather the interaxial distances. The best Attic work is known to observe only one strange proportion, namely that the clear intercolumniation, no matter how large the building, exceeds the lower diameter by about 50 centimetres, or probably an ancient cubit.[3] The large Parthenon gains its massiveness, the much smaller Hephaisteion its attenuation from observing this strange rule.

We turn next to the methods and skill of the Greek designer, which appear nowhere more impressively than in the Athenian Propylaea, a work of the high Classical age (437–432 B.C.), well known, thanks to the brilliant studies of Doerpfeld and Dinsmoor,[4] and interesting for its unusual complexity. The completed portions comprise a 'gate-wall' with five doors, a shallow inner hall to its east and a larger outer hall, at a lower level, to its west, both hexastyle prostyle and of equal width, and two much smaller halls, with colonnaded fronts in antis, flanking the western approach (see Fig. 58). The southern interfered with the Temple of Athena Nike and was left incomplete. The northern, used as a picture gallery, had no pediment, only hips: but the architect, Mnesikles, was still so careful to give its important west wall a deceptive symmetry, that he balanced the return of the south-west anta, a few inches wide, with a spurious anta-return on the north-west corner. Its southern colonnade set him a nice problem. How was he to join it to the main building? At stylobate level, his solution was masterly (see Pl. 9). Because it was a Propylon, not a temple, and pierced between the central

---

[1] Dinsmoor discusses the first with several early temples, for instance the Syracusan (Dinsmoor, pp. 77–8), the second, for instance, on p. 152.
[2] Vitruvius, IV, 3, iii : four spaces of $5\frac{1}{2}$ modules, and one of 8 modules.
[3] Dinsmoor discovered the fact, and records it in *Hesperia*, IX, pp. 20–2, but for some reason suppresses it in his book.
[4] Especially in *AM*, 1885, and *AJA*, 1910.

columns by the Sacred Way, the main building could be given a krepis of four smaller steps equal to the three of normal Doric proportion.   But the order of the side halls required at most a krepis three-quarters that of the central.   So he had merely to return the lowest step around the sides in a different material, the dark limestone from Eleusis, to give them a krepis of apparently three steps, adequate to the eye and yet inseparably tied to the main building.[1]   Wisely, he omitted pediments from the side halls; and he apparently covered the recesses formed between their

Fig. 58   Athens; Propylaea from south-west.

fronts and the central portico with great hoods, each of one marble block.

The two main halls enclosing the gate-wall were proportioned, as Dinsmoor sees, to give the more easterly the largest possible clearance.   Its internal span, about 20 feet from east to west, just permitted a ceiling of Pentelic marble.   But the western, internally some 60 feet across by 45 deep, required two inner colonnades flanking the Sacred Way up to the central door, each of three Ionic columns.   Only that order could give shafts of the requisite height and thinness and an architrave immediately below the ceiling-level required by the outer geison.   The krepis, though

[1] See Miss Shoe, 'Dark Stone in Greek Architecture', *Hesperia*, Suppl. VIII, p. 345.

Sanctuary of Marmaria, Delphi

Plate 11

Plate 12
Temple of Poseidon, Paestum; two interior views

not stepped, was treated as a return of that outside, and died into the slope of the Sacred Way, left rough and 'natural', some distance from the actual gate-wall. Its low blocks, suitable for Ionic, of course equal in height the Doric outer steps. All this, with the gap made by the Sacred Way, left it impossible to give the great west stylobate the normal convex curvature, which thus began only with the architrave—clear evidence that this Greek 'refinement' was deliberate.[1]

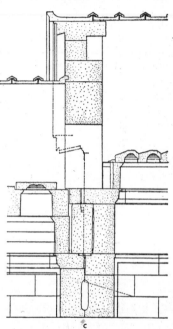

The Doric columns of this façade are nearly 29 feet high, 1 foot higher than those of the eastern, probably to reduce the difference in height of the two halls. To obtain a wide passage for the Sacred Way, the central columns of both are spaced not two but three metopes apart. Too few propylaea of the time survive for us to know whether Mnesikles here broke the rules. To lighten the load on this large opening, he formed the frieze substantially of long blocks, balanced them over the axes of the columns and grooved the thin triglyph-blocks into their fronts. This recalls, of course, the Temple of Ceres at Paestum; and other features remind us of early western temples, for instance the elaborate bed-mould of the

Fig. 59   Propylaea: section through central gable.

cornice, as in the Temple of Ceres, and the pattern on the ovolo of the sima, pierced for rainwater, 'somewhat as in Temple C at Selinus' (Dinsmoor). The tympana of the pediments, again to lighten the load, had in the centre a thickness of only one orthostate, carefully grooved into its neighbours.[2]

Mnesikles had elsewhere the task of relieving heavy loads. The long marble ceiling-beams inside the west hall rested alternately

---

[1] Dinsmoor, p. 201.
[2] Dinsmoor, *AJA*, 1910, p. 149.

over the columns and midway between them, and he apparently used iron rods to transmit the weight of the second series, hollowing out below them a cavity sufficiently deep to allow a certain 'play'.[1]   The upper courses of the gate-wall were likely to bear very heavily on the doors: for, as it marked a change in the roof-level, it had not only to support some of the timbers but also at least an apology for a pediment.   Its thickness was reduced above cornice level, and it was given a relieving space three courses high (see Fig. 59), hidden from below by the ceiling on either side. Partly, one supposes, to enlarge this space as far as possible, the eastern ceiling was placed one course too low, at frieze level. This is, perhaps, unique in classical Doric.   Finally, the western-most triglyphs of the east hall stopped short by 18 inches of the west side of the cross-wall, a distance that just allowed it to be cleared by the cornice projecting from their own west sides (see Fig. 60).   Thus between them it had only an apparent cornice, and above this a truncated sima in harmony.   There was no fear that in rough weather it would overbalance.[2]

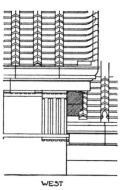

WEST

Fig. 60 Propylaea: central gable.   North elevation.

Two large side halls were originally meant to enclose the main building on the north and the south.   It is difficult to envisage them, because quite clearly, as shown by Dinsmoor's plan,[3] the ridges of their roofs were to meet it not at its gate-wall, where the level changed, but at a point half way between the main east and west façades.   The main evidence for them consists of two stumps of wall, just behind the eastern antae.   I think these were themselves intended for small antae to terminate long eastern colonnades as envisaged by Doerpfeld.   Dinsmoor considers they were meant for door-jambs, apparently because they would have had to come below metopes, and this was unthinkable for antae.   We shall need to await his promised book on the Propylaea, to see whether metopes must come here.   But is this building not sufficiently

[1] Dinsmoor, p. 203 and Fig. 66.
[2] For clear descriptions and illustrations of all this see Dinsmoor, *AJA*, 1910, pp. 162 and 168, especially Fig. 7.
[3] Dinsmoor, Fig. 75.

heterodox to make an anta under a metope of little moment? Moreover, the jambs, as Dinsmoor feels bound to restore them, have no space for a veneer, and thus seem unique for the Periclean Age; while his east façades, each with its two doors balancing across a blank central space, convey an effect of meanness improbable even if, as he thinks, they were to serve 'primarily utilitarian purposes.'

The details are beautifully designed. The orthostate course consists in the West Hall of dark Eleusinian limestone, in the East Hall on each side of one enormous block of Pentelic marble, that also embraces the anta. Beneath the gate-wall, and broken only by the Sacred Way, is a large threshold of Eleusinian stone, its surface aligned, very decoratively, with the top of the western orthostates. But its primary purpose, as seen by Miss Shoe,[1] is to warn the visitor leaving the Acropolis of the steps he could hardly notice otherwise amid the glare of the marble. On the side walls of the western hall, below the Ionic architrave, down the face a short distance from each corner and above the orthostates there ran a very small, shallow sinking, designed to frame a large central space, perhaps for frescoes. But enough has been said to show the thoughtfulness of the design; and we pass on to the refinements that such workmanship made possible.

No Renaissance architect could make very much of the rules for minute increases and gradual curvatures in buildings laid down in the third and fourth books of Vitruvius. Indeed, the materials and workmanship of most later styles would make it absurd, for instance, to aim at an effect by sloping one's columns inwards so that their inner faces are parallel to the vertical walls of the cella they enclose.[2] Vitruvius is, of course, a Roman deliberately Hellenising, four centuries after the Parthenon and a century after the final collapse of Greece; and, as he himself says, few of his contemporaries were prepared to take the pains he recommended. But the definite rules he does give show a subtlety infinitely less than that of true Greeks.

Only his rule for making the corner columns thicker by one-fiftieth than the rest appears to correspond to classical Greek practice. His Doric and Ionic columns are slender, diminish slowly and are to have axes with sufficient inward inclination to give inner faces parallel to the perpendicular cella walls. The

[1] *Hesperia*, Suppl. VIII, p. 347.
[2] Vitruvius, III, V, 4.

centre columns on the façades are to be vertical.[1] But in the Parthenon the cella walls themselves lean inwards, the columns diminish rapidly and the axes, if prolonged, would form an imaginary hipped roof, its ridge-pole 5,856 feet above the ground.[2] He also recommends that each member of the entablature lean outwards a distance one-twelfth (or, as corrected by Penrose, one-fortieth) of its height. But the architrave of the Parthenon, for instance, in fact recedes by one in eighty.[3]

Vitruvius alludes to curvatures, another class of refinements. He gives two examples, the upward curve of stylobate and entablature, at their highest in the centre of each façade, and the swelling, or entasis, in the centre of each column-shaft. The former is achieved, he says, by 'unequal steps' (*scamilli impares*), and Dinsmoor shows what this may mean—a series of points on a parabola, each vertically distant from the level of the central point by a number of units forming the square of the number of the horizontal units from the centre.[4]

Vitruvius gives no amounts for his curves. Those on the Parthenon, here measured in English feet and inches, are very slight. The entasis amounts to 0·68 inches, one twenty-fourth of the difference between the upper and lower diameter and one 1/550 of the height of the shaft. The eastern stylobate rises 0·228 feet in its length of 101·34 feet, the northern 0·355 feet in 228·14 feet. The eastern architrave rises 0·171 feet. The orthostates of the cella walls have a slighter curve, rising in the centre by 0·11 feet in 170 feet. These measurements, all taken by Penrose,[5] are very reliable. With the Greek system of jointing, accidental displacements can at once be detected and allowed for.

Vitruvius obviously envisaged very slight curves, their sole purpose, he thought, to correct optical illusions. But while, in Periclean buildings, the entasis is almost too subtle to be seen—I could never detect it on the North Porch of the Erechtheum—it is often, in sixth-century western examples, pronounced; and,

---

[1] III, v, 4. He prescribes vertical columns for the pronaos and posticum. But he clearly means by these the centre of the front and rear façades. See above, p. 120.

[2] Penrose, p. 35.

[3] Penrose, p. 36.

[4] Dinsmoor, p. 168, Fig. 59.

[5] Chap. III, Sect. III, of Penrose for the horizontal curvatures; Chap. V for the entasis.

although far rarer and more moderate in old Greece,[1] will not have remained wholly unnoticed by the classical eye. Small curvatures give life to a design; and Lutyens, the last architect to practise them in a truly Greek spirit,[2] used them with precisely this intention. Humfry Payne writes of an early and slightly asymmetrical Attic statue[3]: 'It would, of course, be foolish to insist that asymmetry is always intentional, but that it is often so no one will doubt who remembers the analogous subtleties in classical architecture.'

Another series of refinements in Vitruvius, intended more evidently to obviate optical illusion, comprises the enlargement of upper diameters and entablatures in very high buildings. Pierce found the head and shoulders of a giant from the famous Doric temple at Akragas to be on a considerably larger scale than the rest; and while this would have seemed crude enough, were the giants on the exterior and caged between the columns, it might have exactly corrected the figure as seen facing down upon a narrow cella or the hypaethral court restored by Pierce.[4] But we know too little of the larger Greek entablatures to decide on this class of refinements: and in this age of economical building we have little practical knowledge of any refinements whatever.

It only remains to trace very briefly the history of architectural fashions in temples and lesser buildings, Greek and barbarian, around the Mediterrranean between 600 and 300 B.C.

[1] Dinsmoor has lately verified entasis at Bassae (Dinsmoor, p. 156). It is pronounced on some of the columns of the Olympian Heraion (nearly one hundred and thirtieth of the height—*Olympia*, Tafeln, XXI).
[2] Hussey, *The Life of Sir Edwin Lutyens* (London, 1950), p. 376.
[3] Payne and Young, *Archaic Marble Sculpture from the Acropolis*, first edition, p. 20.
[4] Pace and Pierce in *Monumenti Antichi*, 1922.

CHAPTER VI

ARCHITECTURAL DEVELOPMENT, 600–300 B.C.

I. GREEK BUILDINGS: TEMPLES

IN Crete and Aeolian Asia, two of the first regions to reawaken just before 600 B.C., we find temples of curiously similar plan,[1] carelessly orientated and neither Doric nor Ionic in character. In both, stone rectangular 'megara', without peristyles, enclose two or more posts on the central axis. The decoration is essentially an ornamental trimming added to primitive buildings; and one undifferentiated style seems to prevail over lands soon to be divided between the Doric and Ionic. At Neandria in Aeolis, in a megaron externally some 30 feet by 70, seven unfluted stone columns occupy the long axis. Their capitals had split, vertical volutes and no proper abacus. As, however, the bearing surface of each capital was square, we can reasonably suppose they supported a beam, perhaps even the ridge-pole itself, as in later stoas, down the long axis; and the temple seems to have had a roof of the normal Greek pitch, one of the earliest known, for some primitive tiles have survived. Neandria is not only the largest but the most advanced of the group.

The Cretan temples still had a hearth in the centre and a roof at least partly flat. The two posts at each end of the hearth in Temple A at Prinia are thought to have supported a gabled hood or lantern, a slice of steep roof like the centre of a card-house for the escape of the smoke. In the rather earlier model of a house or temple from the Argive Heraion, most clearly illustrated by Dinsmoor,[2] a very steep roof seems to rest uneasily on a flat roof of horizontal joists; and some scholars would see in this a chimney-hood like that restored for Prinia but extended to cover the whole building except its vestibule.[3] Yet there also survives from Prinia

---

[1] A full, methodical description of these early temples is found on pp. 56 ff. of Robertson.

[2] Dinsmoor, Fig. 15.

[3] Marinatos devised the theory of the central hood at Prinia—see *BCH*, 60, p. 246—and Andren seized upon it and developed it to explain the Argive Model in his *Architectural Terracottas from Etrusco-Italic Temples* (Lund, 1939), p. lxviii.

a long frieze with horsemen in relief, the form of which, like that of
the closest analogies elsewhere, suggests that it came from the
parapet of a flat roof. We think also of the marble parapet of
Ephesus (*c.* 550–540 B.C.), reduced there to form the sima of a
normal Greek roof; but our frieze is about a century older.[1] One
feature of Prinia is unique, its façade with three massive square
piers, one on the central axis, and two seated goddesses facing one
another, probably on the flat roof. Jenkins considers these
figures replacements. Without influence on the future, this
design probably owes much to the Minoan past. Comparable
but less ambitious temples exist at Dreros and Palaikastro.

In some cities under Corinthian influence Doric peristyles of
timber apparently existed in the seventh century, contemporary
with the buildings just described. Such are the remarkable
implications of the Doric terracotta metopes and other revetments
dating from this century at Thermon and Kalydon. The finds
entail a Doric timber order, for which the Cretan buildings
provided no evidence[2]: and at Kalydon stone makes its appearance
in the cornice.

The plans of all these temples except, perhaps, Kalydon (not
recovered) included posts or columns down the centre. The
earliest known to dispense with this clumsy feature is the Heraion
at Olympia, now found to date from almost exactly 600 B.C.
Remarkably, it is a work not of the Corinthian but of the Laconian
(Spartan) school, as is shown by its akroteria, its Laconian roof-
tiles and other evidence.[3] It contained originally some timber
columns, as we know from Pausanias (V, 16, i), and had throughout
its history a timber entablature. So we can form no idea of its
original elevation. It is very important for its stone toichobate
and for the orthostates outside, though not inside, its cella walls,
and even more as the first known hexastyle temple. The architect
had at last abolished the central row of posts under the ridge and
in harmony with this substituted the more convenient and beautiful
front with five openings for that with five posts. He flanked his
cella with a series of deep bays or side chapels, partly masked by
the alternate inner columns—a design with a long later history;
and he had sufficiently refined his outer colonnades to give them

[1] Jenkins, *Dedalica*, p. 82.
[2] See especially E. Dyggve, *Das Laphrion* (Copenhagen, 1948), Abb.
222 and 223 (pp. 218–19).
[3] Searls and Dinsmoor, *AJA*, 1945, pp. 62 ff.

angle contraction, a feature not found in many sixth-century temples and seeming to show he had triglyphs of the normal size and pattern, the difficulties of placing which he had already solved in the orthodox way.[1]

A very primitive stone colonnade is that of the palace at Larisa, in Aeolis. The circular akroterion and semicircular cover-tiles found here are similar to those of the Olympian Heraion. But the plan of the building, the form of the colonnade, a loggia between two blank wings, and even the design of the columns with their vertical volutes remind us of north Syria. They show the source and direction of influences in this critical period, before Doric or Ionic were settled. Details seem to show that this palace is later than it looks, perhaps not before 550 B.C. But I believe it reproduces the houses of the preceding generation in larger towns.[2]

Stone Doric columns appear about 600 B.C. at Tiryns[3] and the first temple of Athena Pronaia at Delphi.[4] They are slim, with very spreading capitals, a form perhaps only half way from a timber prototype and very different in all its proportions and shapes from the canonical stone Doric, a timber ancestry for which Viollet-le-Duc could not conceive. Existing stone Doric has little resemblance to timber scantlings and proportions, but we can begin dimly to see how the one grew from the other. The columns of Athena Pronaia have a height of $6\frac{1}{3}$ lower diameters and an abacus $2\frac{2}{3}$ upper diameters in width.[5]

At this early time, stone Doric has not decided its entablature. We now know that the coffered cornice of the Temple of Ceres, Paestum, goes back to the seventh-century temple of Kalydon. At Paestum it sloped downwards at the angle of normal mutules, but at Kalydon it was horizontal, giving the effect of a Chinese roof at the corners of the pediments. It must have existed in many

---

[1] Dinsmoor, p. 55.

[2] Of these we may know more when the houses of Old Smyrna, excavated between 1948 and 1951, are definitively published.

[3] See Schliemann, *Tiryns* (London, 1886), pp. 293-4: also above, p. 148.

[4] Robertson, Fig. 25.

[5] Viollet-le-Duc, in his *Lectures* (London, 1877), pp. 37 ff. insists that real timber capitals must have been oblong brackets. But perhaps an oblong bracket did crown the abacus in the most ancient Doric, and was omitted in stone-work. Some of the timber buildings mentioned above (p. 167) had this bracket, and may so far help us on origins: and just conceivably, as we saw (above, p. 148) the oldest stone Doric columns, at Delphi and elsewhere, had capital blocks quite free of the shaft, resembling wooden building and not classical Doric.

places. Kardaki, which I consider a temple of the earlier sixth century, this tentative period, had no frieze and a series of rolls for the cornice.[1] But soon the unexplained mutular system, found from the beginning in central Greece, prevailed, and hesitancy was over.

At all periods the Greeks of the homeland excelled in the quality of their buildings, as in sculpture, painting and the minor crafts. Between 550 and 500 B.C. the buildings of the west were much larger and grander, but had slight influence on old Greece. So backward is Sicilian sculpture that one must doubt, on this ground alone, the theory of Dinsmoor that the western Greeks invented carved metopes.[2] Critics can bring against their buildings the absence of angle contraction, achieved by setting the architrave back from the front faces of the abaci and thus disproportionately enlarging the latter until they almost touch. Another displeasing feature is the elastic metope of the west. In Sicily one finds upright oblong metopes at first unrelated to the columns, then spaced two to each intercolumniation. The mutules vary in size. It is true that in the oldest peripteral temple on the Athenian Acropolis the metopes are only apparently square and their crowning mutules short, though less obviously than the Sicilian, compared with those above the triglyphs.[3] But the mainland Greek, unlike the Sicilian, very seldom compromised on the main shapes he regarded as essential. He could not tolerate in his main order that amiable compromise with the floating repertory of ivory workers and goldsmiths that gives a delicate charm to the temples of Selinus and Paestum. He knew that Doric was really a rhythmical architecture of simple shapes.

Several early western temples have a second colonnade, two column-spaces behind the façade, across the front peristyle, reminding us on the one hand of sixth-century Ephesus, with its additional colonnade across the front, and on the other of Etruscan and Roman temples with their enlarged front peristyles. In Temple G at Selinus and its probable copy, that of Ceres at Paestum, we find, instead of the inner cross-colonnade, that the

---

[1] For the date, see above, p. 153. For the restored entablature, see F. P. Johnson, in *AJA*, 1936, pp. 46 ff.

[2] See, for instance, Dinsmoor, p. 117.

[3] Robertson illustrates them (p. 83, Fig. 35). Dinsmoor attributes to Syracuse the beautiful early carved metopes of the 'Sicyonian' Treasury at Delphi. They are admittedly horizontal oblongs, but this does not show they are western.

cella-building ends in a tetrastyle prostyle portico two column spaces deep. There is no false porch at Paestum. Such cella-buildings, taken by themselves, closely foreshadow the Roman temple plan. In the temple of Ceres the inner portico was Ionic, presumably to admit more light to the narrow cella.

For, in sympathy with his enlarged front peristyle, the architect would often widen the sides as much as possible, at the expense of the cella. G at Selinus was pseudodipteral, a word used in Vitruvius of temples with only one encircling colonnade, but with space for two. For the cella the western Greek designed no inner columns if he could avoid them, unlike the Greeks of the home-land, who used them for aesthetic effect even where they could do the structure little good.[1] The sixth-century temples at Selinus and the Temple of Aphaia on Aegina well show the respective tendencies. The immediate future, even in the west, lay with the form closer to the Olympian Heraion, with the wide, diversified cella; and the fifth-century temple of Poseidon at Paestum is, in its main lines, an import from Old Greece.

The decorators of archaic Doric temples employed little but the fret, the oriental coil, the tongue-pattern,[2] the wave-tendril (rinceau) and combinations of the lotus, papyrus and palmette.[3] The forms are bold, strong and rather fat.

We were forced, when describing the Ionic order, to trace its history in the archaic age and even some of its blends with Doric. This is not the place to ask whether the Temple at Kardaki is very early Doric, and not a self-conscious mixture of Doric and Ionic of about 500 B.C. We might decide this by closely comparing it with the Throne of Apollo at Amyclae, near Sparta, late archaic and an obvious mixture of two already established orders. But we must pass to the Periclean Age, to consider a far subtler attempt to unite them, and one of its consequences, the Corinthian capital.

With refinements, ornament engrossed the fifth-century archi-tect. As on the vases, light patterns on dark backgrounds had come into fashion for the painting of eaves and cornice. Boldness of form was here needed more than ever. But artists now added considerably to the sixth-century repertory. About 450 B.C. the lily appears, growing from the axils between the wave-tendril and

---

[1] See an acute discussion of this by R. L. Scranton in *AJA*, 1946
[2] For which, see, e.g., Dinsmoor, Fig. 45.
[3] See, for illustrations of these patterns, E. Buschor, *Die Tondaecher der Akropolis* (Leipzig, 1929).

the lotus or palmette.[1]   About the same time the acanthus first
appears, not in painted ornament but carved on gravestones, antefixes and ridge-tiles, and usually shown rather depressed at the
bottom of a palmette.   Normally, it resembles a soft acanthus-
plant growing.   Only rarely, as on the ridge-tiles of Rhamnous,
does the artist dispose two or three of its leaves in a formal pattern.
So it would be out of place on the very formal painted sima,
although the Athenians, who had long supplemented carving with
painting (as on their early Ionic capitals), were prepared for certain
tricks of decoration.   If they painted lilies on the Ionic pulvini of
the Propylaea, they carved them but painted their stems on the
gravestone from Salamis.[2]

The Parthenon (see Pl. 10) is the first known building to employ
the acanthus and the cabbage stalk, or cauliculus, on its akroteria.
The two were to become almost inseparable on the Corinthian
capital.   The Parthenon also splits into two the palmette,
hitherto unbroken, except on the Ionic echinus, but generally
in pieces in the fourth century.   The ceiling-coffers of the
Parthenon show the 'honeysuckle palmette', with reversed leaves
of compound curvature, and its akroteria, if Praschniker is right,[3]
palmettes with similar leaves but completely split down the centre.
As in the late thirteenth century A.D., a breath of nature, but far
gentler and more controlled than the Gothic, passes over the old
stiff world of archaic forms.   But we are still far from the autumn
that follows, the rank convolvuli, the hanging seed-pods and the
palmettes with dry, uneven, straggly leaves that mark the plastic
antefixes of the fourth and succeeding centuries.

This growth of ornament and the pre-eminence of the fifth-
century sculptors partly explain each other.   The other feature
of the fifth century, its mixture of Doric and Ionic, arises partly
from the Athenian mastery of both orders.   Up to about 440 B.C.
artists often tried to incorporate features of the one in the other;
after that date, while using both in one building, they would try
to isolate each.   Examples will make this plain.

The older Parthenon, of about 485 B.C., possessed a moulded
Ionic wall-base between toichobate and orthostates.   This was
repeated soon after 450 B.C. in the Hephaisteion and, in a curtailed

---

[1] Buschor, *Die Tondaecher der Akropolis*, Simen, Taf. XIX–XXI.
The text, p. 41, would date its appearance to the 'thirties.

[2] Buschor, *Die Plastik der Griechen* (Berlin, 1936), p. 66.

[3] 'Die Akroterien des Parthenon', *JOeI*, 1910.

and very shrunken form, at Sunium, but not again in Athenian work. The Periclean Parthenon employed an Ionic frieze along the outside of the cella wall just below the Doric epikranitis. So, at either end of the cella-buildings, did the Hephaisteion and Sunium. In later buildings it is not found. Nor is the Ionic inner taenia of the architrave, associated with it on the eastern peristyle of the Hephaisteion. Of Ionic buildings, the temples on the Ilissus and of Athena at Sunium (both not much later than 450) are the last to use the simple architrave of one fascia, apparently derived from Doric. From the Propylaea onwards three fasciae are always found. Henceforward the orders only remotely affect each other in points of proportion and planning. Thus frieze and architrave are equal on Periclean Ionic, as on Doric buildings; while the Temple of Nemesis at Rhamnous, severely Doric externally, shows an Ionic alignment of the peristyle and cella.

The earlier fifth-century temples had broad Doric cellas divided longitudinally from end to end by two rows of Doric columns in two tiers. The Parthenon is the first building known to return them across the west end, behind the cult-statue: and here, too, in the western room, Ionic columns first appear, to solve the problem of the high roof and the small area of floor.

The main chamber was copied in the Hephaisteion[1] but the western room had more influence in the long run. Bassae, Tegea, Nemea and the fourth-century temple of Delphi, to say nothing of the circular tholoi, all have slender internal columns, engaged or free standing, but never Doric; and even the cella of Rhamnous, too small for columns, was given a thoroughly Ionic character.

We saw that the Greek cella had a dim light and glittering ornaments. In the Parthenon, for instance, the column under the right hand of the goddess, necessary to her whole posture, will have had a metallic shaft of open foliage.[2] So we are not surprised to hear from Vitruvius[3] that the Corinthian capital was invented by the bronze worker Callimachus, who, according to Pausanias, made the famous lamp of open foliage for the cella of

---

[1] For its colonnades, see now B. H. Hill, *Hesperia*, Suppl. VIII, p. 207.
[2] For its necessity, see Lethaby, *JHS*, 1917, p. 148. For its possible form, see P. Jacobsthal, *Ornamente Griechischer Vasen* (Berlin, 1927), Textband, p. 98, where, however, only indirect evidence is collected.
[3] Vitruvius, IV, i, ix.

the Erechtheum[1] : nor that the oldest full-scale examples are all from interiors of temples. The closest fifth-century analogy to the capital of Bassae, the earliest stone example we know, is a wonderful gold pin said to come from the region of Patras. The fifth-century capital of the Tholos at Delphi, like its much smaller but perhaps earlier cousins from Taras,[2] is also fairly metallic, with its coiled, wiry volutes. An example in Herculaneum, centuries later, shows how well the form, with its lower rings and leaves, its large angle and smaller intermediate volutes and its imitation flowers, at any rate translated into metal[3] : and the old oriental capitals that partly prefigured it went back themselves, we argued,[4] to the metalwork of the Sumerians.

We are less certain than ever on the roofing and lighting of the first Corinthian interiors. At Bassae, the solitary Corinthian column[5] occupied a central space between the cella and the adyton. The temple, unexpectedly, faces north and south, and the adyton has a large east door, one presumes to welcome the rising sun. Ictinus, the probable architect,[6] was much concerned with the lighting of buildings at dawn—a problem he had to face when designing the Hall of the Mysteries at Eleusis.[7] But we cannot recover his arrangement of Bassae. Dinsmoor has probably discredited the positive evidence Cockerell adduced for a framed hypaethral opening.[8] But the continuous frieze above the columns of the cella cannot have remained in total darkness.

---

[1] Pausanias, I, 26, vii. This lamp, however, probably resembled not the Corinthian capital but the Etruscan lampstands, Giglioli, *Arte Etrusca* (Milan, 1935), tav. ccx–ccxii.

[2] See above, p. 170. For the gold pin, see P. Jacobsthal, *Greek Pins* (Oxford, 1956), pp. 65 ff. and Figs. 274–9. A four-sided Ionic capital, with a palmette in the centre of each face, supports a flower surrounded by small acanthus leaves and four vertical corner-volutes.

[3] This capital is in the garden of the Casa dei Cervi, and can just be discerned in the general view given by A. Maiuri on p. 73 of his *Herculaneum* (Paris, N.D.). The decoration of the house is post-Augustan.

[4] See above, p. 101.

[5] Dinsmoor believes all three southernmost columns were Corinthian. But only the central column was more slender than the rest or had a base of distinctive design. See Dinsmoor, *Metropolitan Museum Studies*, IV (1933), pp. 211–12.

[6] So Pausanias, VIII, 47, ix.

[7] Vitruvius, VII, Preface section 16. The existing hall seems not to be his.

[8] So much I gathered while in Athens. But I have seen no publication of the evidence. Dinsmoor considers the fragment one of the tiles bordering an ordinary akroterion. It is shown by Cockerell on *Bassae*, Pl. VII, Fig. 2 of his *Aegina and Bassae*.

Still less certain are the interiors of the tholoi at Delphi and Epidaurus and the Temple of Athena Alea at Tegea, all erected some time between 400 and 350 B.C. It is now the fashion to restore the tholoi, buildings with circular walls and colonnades inside and out, with raised drums over the walls and interrupted roofs. At Delphi, it is alleged, evidence exists for a change in the roof-level over the cella, as in the Temple of Heaven at Pekin. But the French have published no fragment of roof-gutter on a radius sufficiently small to crown the cella-walls; and all surviving reliefs and frescoes to show such buildings unanimously exhibit them with unbroken roofs from the cornice to the apex. In the Temple of Tegea the engaged Corinthian columns of the cella reach a height barely two-thirds that of the external order. The probabilities are all against an hypaethral opening. So again restoration seems at present impossible. The surviving details are most beautiful, especially the exquisite unbroken moulding continued around the foot of the cella-wall inside.[1] In fact, like the other buildings, Tegea proves the paradox that the Corinthian capital, now the most hackneyed of all classic forms, was first designed as the precious ornament of sumptuous interiors.

We pass over some famous buildings of the later fifth century, the Erechtheum at Athens, sufficiently described by Robertson and Dinsmoor,[2] the Hall of the Mysteries at Eleusis, the architectural quality of which we cannot gauge from the existing remains, which show too many internal columns and which are probably not from the hand of Ictinus at all, and the Temple of the Giants at Akragas. Of the last, there seems to be evidence for the external walls and engaged half-columns up to the abacus. But I saw no trace on the site of the Doric entablature usually restored. The only carved moulding obviously visible, and in fact the only moulded piece to be figured by Marconi,[3] is a stretch of egg-and-dart supposed to come from a door in the centre of the south front. I do not feel qualified on the evidence I have seen to know where the great figures of the giants originally stood.[4]

---

[1] See Dugas, Berchmans and Clemmensen, *Tégée* (Paris, 1924).
[2] Robertson, pp. 127 ff., and Dinsmoor, pp. 187 ff.
[3] P. Marconi, *Agrigento* (Florence, 1929), Fig. 35.
[4] See above, p. 181. Marconi claims to have discovered some giants between the columns on the south side. His photographs (*Agrigento*, Figs. 33 and 34) offer inadequate evidence; and, characteristically, in August 1952 they had all apparently been moved away (where?) from the place where they were allegedly discovered.

For the fourth century we move to Asia Minor, where the native Ionic had renewed its strength, though destined to fall so strangely, in the third and second, under the influence of Athens. How early and how insidious was this Attic penetration? We saw the Nereid Monument to be partly Attic.[1] But it has a lofty podium, Asiatic bases to the columns and a carved architrave instead of a frieze, to show it is no mere import. Large buildings follow the indigenous Ionic canons, except, it is suggested, the Mausoleum, where Dinsmoor would see a European version of the order.[2]

This was the tomb, made by his widow, Artemisia, for Mausolus, Satrap of Caria, in the years around 350 B.C. According to Pliny the Elder, our chief authority for its appearance, the work of four famous sculptors, Scopas, Bryaxis, Leochares and Timotheos, who each carved one of its four sides, raised it to the rank of a world's wonder. It had a peristyle of thirty-six columns, called the pteron. Before the sculptors had finished their work, the queen died. But they stayed to complete it, 'considering it now the monument of their own glory and skill: and to this day their hands still vie on it. A fifth craftsman joined them. For above the pteron a pyramid equals that below in height' (or perhaps 'equals in height the building below it') 'contracting itself to a top like a turning-post, on which stands the marble quadriga that Pythis made. This addition brings the total height to 140 feet.' Pliny says that its north and south sides were each 63 feet long, its 'fronts' less, but that it had a total circuit of 440 feet.[3] Of these self-contradictory figures, the last is favoured by the cutting, 108 feet by 127, discovered in the nineteenth-century excavation.[4] Its size and the word 'pteron' in Pliny compel us, it seems, to insert a cella and abandon the restorations of Cockerell and Stevenson, the only modern versions, as Law observes, with any pretensions to beauty.[5] The student can judge the merits of the numerous attempts most easily from the careful and convenient collection in J. van Breen,[6] whose own conclusions are marred by fantastic, quasi-mathematical manipulations.

[1] Above, p. 165.
[2] Dinsmoor, pp. 257 ff.
[3] For Pliny's account, see his *Natural History*, Bk. XXXVI, 5.
[4] C. T. Newton, *Halicarnassus, Cnidus and Branchidae* (London, 1862), p. 94.
[5] See H. Law, 'The Mausoleum', *JHS*, 1939.
[6] J. van Breen, *Het Reconstructieplan voor het Mausoleum* (Amsterdam, 1942).

Thirty-six columns on a building of 108 by 127 feet give a peristyle of eleven columns by nine. Scholars, tempted by Pliny's word 'frontes' for the short sides, have sometimes wished to give them pediments: and one could compare the effect of these, with the pyramidal roof behind, to that of the pediments and attic on the Sarcophagus of the Mourning Women.[1] But the odd numbers of columns make pediments unlikely.

Besides the cutting, great lengths of carved frieze were recovered by the nineteenth-century excavators. Even more important, the size and form of the order, internally and externally, has now been virtually settled, and can be studied in Lethaby.[2] As I indicated above, I do not think Dinsmoor has established a case for any frieze in the entablature.[3] We are left with an order totalling 34 feet in height, with columns some 28 feet high spaced 9 feet 9 inches (2⅔ lower diameters) apart and an entablature of two upper diameters.

What is European in all this? Certainly not the column-spacing. Nor the entablature, if we deny it a frieze. Nor the ceiling-beams, as low and Asiatic as any known. Nor the details of the columns; for the bases are thoroughly Asiatic, and the capitals show their ignorance of Attic neatness in the inner corners of the angle-capitals, where the volutes intersect most untidily.[4] Nor has the sima the running anthemion or 'rinceau' decoration, so popular in the fourth century both in Greece and Asia and found a little later in the Temple at Priene (dedicated in 334 B.C.).[5] It has instead the old-fashioned upright lotus and palmette. If, as is generally held, the 'Pythis' of Pliny is the famous Ionian Pythios, and he the designer of Priene, we should finally prove the Asiatic character of the Mausoleum; and we could talk, with Lethaby, of the development of its architect between 350 and 334.[6] But we pause as we remember that Pliny called him 'Pythis' and find Vitruvius mentions only 'Phileos', who wrote on Priene, and Phiteus, the joint author of a book on the Mausoleum. It has been safer and probably sufficient to refute Dinsmoor from the surviving fragments of the building.

[1] Dinsmoor, Pl. LXIII.
[2] *Greek Buildings*, Figs. 33 and 51 and pp. 43 and 60.
[3] Above, p. 166.
[4] Lethaby, p. 59, Fig. 46.
[5] It was dedicated by Alexander the Great on his march through Asia. The dedicatory inscription is in the British Museum, and is illustrated in *The Antiquities of Ionia*, IV, p. 23.
[6] Lethaby, *JHS*, 1913, p. 95.

Of Ionian originality at this time we have another, faint impression from the plan of the Didymaion, the Temple of Apollo at Didyma, near Miletus, designed to house an oracle and its consultants. Like Ephesus, it faces west. As ingenious as Bassae and much larger, it is the first Ionian temple we know to employ the Corinthian capital, to embellish one end of the cella, as at Bassae. Three sides have antae, treated almost like Roman pilasters, at intervals in the wall. But the west wall has, instead, two engaged Corinthian columns—the first instance in a large building of undoubted influence from Europe. The vast space of the cella was necessarily hypaethral, and contained a shrine at the inner end with a grove of laurels in front. Fourteen feet below the floor of the outer pteron, it was reached by two small descending tunnels under an intermediate room, which occupied the position of a normal pronaos but had in this temple a floor 5 feet above the pteron. The room was approached from the cella by a high and wide flight of stairs and three large doors. But the threshold of its single western door stood a sheer 5 feet above the west floor, and apparently served as a platform for the delivery of oracles to the crowds in the entrance hall. Ceremonies and circulation are beginning to influence more obviously the interiors of Greek buildings.

Old Greece in the fourth century produced only a few small temples, two of the most important, at Delphi and Tegea, necessary replacements. The rebuilding at Delphi took forty years,[1] at Tegea perhaps as long, if the old temple was burnt in 395 and the new complete only about 350.[2] Enthusiasm and contributions were running low. Another famous hexastyle temple, that of Asklepios at Epidaurus, lacked the rear false-porch and had only eleven columns on the long sides. The backs of its akroteria show unusual roughness. Moreover, other buildings, besides temples, began to engage the attention of architects. Even the tholoi were not, it seems, shrines for cult-images.[3].

The best temples are at Tegea and Nemea, the former wholly of marble, the latter, its twin, of ordinary limestone but with a full range of refinements. The cella of the former has engaged, the latter free standing columns, both Corinthian. At Tegea, in

[1] Dittenberger, *Sylloge Inscriptionum Graecarum*, I (Leipzig, 1915), pp. 321–2, gives the evidence for the dates (370–330 B.C.).
[2] Dinsmoor, pp. 218–20.
[3] The record of expenses at Epidaurus calls the tholos a 'thymele' (round dancing-floor?).

13—I

addition, a large carved Ionic base moulding encircled the inside of the cella, broken only by the main east door and a door in the centre of the north side, which served, one presumes, to cast an equable light on the cult-statue. So again we find a cross-axis as at Bassae; and plans and decoration are developing towards the sort found three centuries later in the 'Basilical Hall' of Praeneste. Moreover, the engaged columns are so short that perhaps the mural ornament even had a second storey.

Characteristically, floors now receive more florid treatment. The Tholos of Epidaurus, a building with an outer peristyle of twenty-six Doric, and an inner of fourteen Corinthian columns, had a labyrinthine crypt and above it a very handsome pavement. The pattern of intersecting arcs, all of one size, allowed dark and light marble slabs, in the form of lozenges with curved sides, to fill completely the whole circle of the floor. Here we can foresee the later Opus Alexandrinum.[1] To about the same time we must attribute the figure mosaic of coloured pebbles in the Temple of Zeus at Olympia. It resembles some in the houses of Olynthus (destroyed 347 B.C.).[2] Again we look forward to a new art.

In two of the last classical buildings, both of the 'thirties, the Philippeum at Olympia and the Choregic Monument of Lysicrates, we find other innovations. Both combine the European frieze and the Asiatic dentils in a single entablature. The Philippeum is the first known Ionic tholos, the Monument of Lysicrates the first building to employ Corinthian columns outside—justifiably, however, for it is scarcely a building so much as a small, precious dedication (see Pl. 14). Unlike the impoverished Philippeum, whose most fanciful features were given it by its German restorers, it shows a rich imagination, whose charm even familiarity can never destroy.[3] It was meant to support the tripod won by a cyclic chorus in 334 B.C., and stands, half shrine and half table, upon its sober, square, well-drafted pedestal. Its columns, on bases recalling those in the North Porch of the Erechtheum, have

[1] For a similar example from St. Mark's Venice, see the Architectural Publication Society's *Dictionary* (London, 1852–92), Plates, 'Marble Pavements'.

[2] See *Olympia*, Tafelband I, Taf. IX; Tafelband II, Taf. CV. For the Olynthiac pavements, see *AJA*, 1934, Pls. 27–30.

[3] The restorers of the Philippeum have given its interior an upper order of engaged columns with lanceolate capitals, and much else for which there seems no evidence. See *Olympia*, Tafelband II, Taf. LXXIX. The Choregic Monument is beautifully illustrated in the first volume of Stuart and Revett.

fantastic Corinthian capitals, sharply bisected horizontally and vertically and too weak for a building of any size, but not for this dainty piece of furniture. A wall fills the space between each pair of columns—to what advantage, the student can see who compares the Choregic Monument with its imitation, that of Dugald Stewart at Edinburgh—and at the level of the capitals has a frieze of tripods in low relief, natural on a table but the first instance in architecture of that second frieze below the architrave employed to such effect by the school of Vignola. The roof and finial unexpectedly inserted between the 'table' and the tripod are as fantastic in form as in position. The roof, actually made of one block, has a playful wave-crest behind its mock-antefixes and a texture of small scales, imitating a roof of bronze.

Yet, for all its exuberance, the building is true to classicism. Note the restful equality its architect has given to the three divisions of its entablature and the discipline he has imposed on everything except the column-capitals and the roof, so that the balance of the columns responds to that of the whole.

So the Corinthian capital never appears in true Greek art on a single commonplace colonnade. All examples display high originality and deviate far more from the imaginary 'pattern' than any of a later age. The Greeks had now invented the bell, the rings of acanthus-leaves, the cauliculi, the Corinthian volutes and the concave abacus. But it took nearly three centuries to combine them in their canonical form, perhaps achieved for the first time in Greece and Syria under Antiochus Epiphanes (*c.* 170 B.C.).[1] The pattern capital—which we may take to be that of the Temple of Mars Ultor in Rome[2]—contains a lower ring of sixteen spiny acanthus leaves, the lower outside the taller. One of the taller occupies the centre of each face, and flanking it on each side are two cauliculi. From each of these spring two vertical volutes, their lower parts sheathed each in an acanthus leaf. The larger turns outwards and supports a corner of the abacus, the other inwards to touch either the abacus, or a small flower pinned to the centre of its face (cf. the Augustan Capital Pl. 15).

The capitals of Nemea and Tegea dispense with the central volutes and flowers. The central volutes at Didyma are very

[1] See R. Delbrueck, *Hellenistische Bauten in Latium*, II (Strassburg, 1912), p. 163.
[2] Built under Augustus, before 2 B.C. Most beautifully illustrated by H. D'Espouy, *Fragments d'Architecture Antique* (Paris, 1896), Pls. 52–61.

small, to allow room for a whole palmette under the abacus. At Epidaurus the cauliculi are omitted, giving very slender, undercut

volutes, and a flower inserted below the abacus. The capitals of Lysicrates are remarkably luxuriant. While out of favour later, these capitals (see Fig. 61) nearly all display a beauty and fitness that subsequent examples have only doubtfully surpassed. Greece died of physical exhaustion, not of mental or artistic decay: and she showed to the very end of this last, sad generation her unique resourcefulness and her unique restraint.

Fig. 61   Corinthian capital, Epidaurus.

2. OTHER GREEK BUILDINGS

Greek life being what it was, no city was complete without its agora and its walls. Sparta is no exception. For, having no walls, her citizens could not live in even the moderate tranquillity needed for Greek life. Athens, in the fortunate possession of impregnable walls, was less disturbed than most towns.

Complete fortified enceintes are still fairly numerous. The best, perhaps, are at Aigosthena, Herakleia on Latmos, and Messene.[1] The builders have taken care to include in them the highest ground in the neighbourhood, so that in every case stretches of wall run impressively up steep hills. The methods of attackers were still primitive, so that we find the devices familiar from our English castles, the choice of a rocky subsoil to prevent mining, the towers, square or semicircular, at short intervals to enfilade attackers in the 'dead ground' under the wall, and 'barbicans', small enclosed yards inside gatehouses, where hostile storming parties could be trapped. The Arcadian Gate at Messene (369 B.C.) is as well designed for this last purpose as the approach to Beaumaris Castle.

[1] Herakleia is thoroughly published by T. Wiegand in *Milet*, III, 2; Messene by Blouet, *Expédition de Morée*, I (Paris, 1831).

The towers had roofs of large clay tiles of the pitch (see Pl. 17) of a normal pediment.[1] Unbonded into the curtain, so as to reduce the harm of possible breaches, they had walls of large, coursed rectangular blocks. Apart from its drafted edges, each block was left forbiddingly rough, to give that effect of military strength so discouraging, Aristotle observes,[2] to the intending aggressor. The angles of the towers display the most beautiful drafting of all, with a vertical groove on either face to represent, it would seem, the line of the taut rope to which it was set out.

The curtain might have rougher coursing, of blocks less regular but equally large and equally well fitted. One can generally follow individual courses, as at Aigosthena, through all the irregularities of this 'coursed polygonal' masonry.

Archaic retaining walls, such as the superb wall of Delphi,[3] dispensed altogether with coursing. In Asia they have more often the rounded blocks of the 'Lesbian' style, shaped to fit, according to Aristotle,[4] by a curving lead line. Europe favoured the sharper stones of true polygonal masonry.

By 400 B.C. both types were falling out of favour, the Lesbian before the polygonal, and builders tended to employ for curtains and retaining walls (such as the fortifications of Sunium and the retaining wall of the precinct at Rhamnous, both dated about 412 B.C.),[5] a coursed trapezoidal or purely rectangular masonry. The curtains on Athenian border-fortresses (late fifth century?), as at Messene and Herakleia, are all of coursed rectangular masonry, two headers thick at Messene, one and a half, with alternate courses of headers and stretchers on the faces, at Herakleia.

At all periods, the more careful walls have generally at the foot a

[1] See the building inscription, 'The Walls of Athens', *IG*, II², No. 463, and the restoration of the walls by Caskey in *AJA*, 1910, pp. 298 ff. See also the great south tower of Aigosthena, much better evidence but nowhere adequately published.

[2] *Politics*, 1331A.

[3] See Wycherley, *How the Greeks built Cities* (London, 1949), Pl. IX. It must antedate the early-fifth-century Athenian Stoa that leans against it.

[4] *Nicomachaean Ethics*, p. 1137B.

[5] See Orlandos, *BCH*, 1924, Pl. XI. For the sequence and its datings I broadly follow R. L. Scranton, *Greek Walls* (Cambridge (Mass.), 1941), though not without misgivings at his excessive optimism. Fashions are not so tidy chronologically as he makes out. For instance, a true polygonal wall just west of Daphne in Attica, on the main road to Eleusis, has a socket-course of conglomerate, a stone not much used even in the concealed foundations of Greek buildings before about 400 B.C. (cf. Dinsmoor, p. 184).

spreading toichobate or socket course (omitted, however, at Herakleia), and often, as well, something that corresponds to the orthostates of the temples. They are crowned with a coping of flat 'through' stones. As Wycherley rightly observes,[1] Greek craftsmanship and sense of fitness appear even in the shaping of a single block.

The undifferentiated agora of the earliest cities, simply a large open space, served, as we saw, for markets, trials, political meetings, entertainments, and religious rites. Only in Hellenistic times were the less savoury trades relegated, as at Priene, to a well-concealed enclave. But permanent government buildings had begun at Athens to form a compact group towards the Pnyx along the west side of the Agora as early as the Persian Wars. Chief among these were the Council House (Bouleuterion) and the Prytaneion, a kind of residence for the executive. In the Athenian polity, as it was after 510 B.C., the Assembly of the whole People made the laws and determined all important acts, but employed a board of elected generals to carry out its measures, a council of five hundred to prepare the business of its meetings and a sub-division of the council, changed monthly, to receive the generals and others, including foreign ambassadors, and carry on unforeseen daily business. The Pnyx, where the Assembly met, occupied the most convenient site south-west of the Agora, and was an open semicircular space traditionally laid out by Themistocles around a stone platform, or bema, for speakers.[2]

The Council-Chamber was a building 25 metres square, including a continuous south vestibule.[3] The main hall had seats rising on three sides from a rectangular well in the centre of its south side and reached directly from the vestibule. The seats were probably arranged like a small rectangular Greek theatre, and the five posts supporting the roof interfered as little as possible with the view. Such a building would have been much neater than its fifth-century successor, where we already find a semicircular 'theatre' crowded in the clumsiest fashion into a nondescript rectangle.[4] This perverse plan grew very popular in Greece. It damns from the start the Hellenistic Council House of Miletus, a building of about 170 B.C. that commits almost every

[1] *How the Greeks built Cities*, p. 49.
[2] See Plutarch, *Themistocles*, XIX, 3.
[3] See Wycherley, p. 58, Fig. 12.
[4] Wycherley, p. 128, Fig. 36.

possible error.[1] The Greek artist, so wonderfully awake when building a temple, falls impenitently asleep at the humdrum problem of a Council House. Nor had the Prytaneion, although a very varied building-type, any greater attraction for him. The Athenian Record Office, for its part, occupied the Temple of the Great Mother, merely, it would seem, because this happened to offer the nearest consecrated space for the archives. So one can take no architectural interest in the normal government building. The law-courts were apparently no better—mere enclosures which have vanished without trace.[2] The splendour of the agora resided in its temples and its stoas.

The stoa originated as a long shed, open on its sunny side, a sun-trap in winter, shady in summer, and at all times a lounge

Fig. 62   Athenian Stoa, Delphi.

for loiterers. So Hesiod warns his brother to avoid in winter the smithy with its sunny lounge.[3] It might lean, pent-house fashion, against a building or a retaining-wall, or stand on its own, with a long back wall, a blank wall at either end, a colonnaded front and a central row of supports. The fifth-century builders kept their stoas short and tried to diversify them. One of the oldest (see Fig. 62) is a small ornamental lean-to, the Athenian Stoa at Delphi (*c.* 500 B.C.), with a beautiful inscribed stylobate, widely spaced Ionic columns and a wooden entablature.[4] The most famous

[1] For an analysis of the errors, see Dinsmoor, pp. 296–7.
[2] I infer so much from the Aristotelian *Constitution of Athens*, III, 5.
[3] *Works and Days*, line 493.
[4] For a good picture of it, see Wycherley, Pl. IX. P. Amandry has now plausibly assigned to it a date soon after 480, in 'La Colonne des Naxiens et le Portique des Athéniens', *Fouilles de Delphes* II, Paris, 1953.

Athenian example, the Painted Stoa or Stoa Poecile, has not been found, and we have to rely on a stoa west of the Agora, apparently the 'Royal' Stoa, for our knowledge of the mid-fifth-century type. According to the *Constitution of Athens*, the laws of Solon stood here for public inspection[1]; and scholars have recovered from the court in front of it remains of a wall inscribed with the rewritten constitution of about 400 B.C. With a more solemn purpose than the common stoa, it had a nobler form. Its two wings with hexastyle prostyle façades enclosed a recessed centre with columns more widely spaced. For the sake of the roof, the width of each wing had to equal the depth of the centre. Each was pedimented, with terracotta akroteria, while the two rear corners of the stoa had hipped roofs.[2] The external order was Doric, the internal Ionic. The different proportions of the two orders allowed the inner columns to support the ridge-pole directly, without a full entablature or ceiling[3]: and both utility and harmony invited a wider spacing for them, one opposite each external column. This outer Doric and internal Ionic became the rule for Hellenistic stoas.

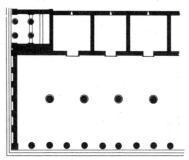

Fig. 63 Plan of double Stoa, Magnesia.

Vitruvius mysteriously describes the fifth-century Odeion as a kind of stoa—one of the many disposed around the theatre in case of rain—but we know too little of it to understand him. If it were in fact a large enclosed hall, we may consider it an ancestor of the Hypostyle Hall at Delos, itself called a 'stoa' in ancient times.[4] In the fourth century the Greeks have abandoned all thought of wings, and stretch the simple stoa as far as they will. The Altis of Olympia, in some sense an agora for all Hellas, now acquired a magnificent stoa, the Echo Stoa, along the whole of its east side.[5] With its front of forty-four Doric columns between the two end walls, this had a length of 300 feet, a depth of only 30. The Ionic

[1] Chap. 7, Sect. 1.
[2] The stoa is fully published in *Hesperia*, VI (1937).
[3] For the effect of this, see Wycherley, Pl. II.
[4] See below, p. 249.
[5] A mid-fourth-century date for this stoa has been vindicated by Kunze and Weber in *AJA*, 1948, p. 492.

columns under the ridge-pole fell as usual opposite alternate columns of the façade. Not so unlike this Echo Stoa was the even larger South Stoa at Corinth, except that here behind the double walk stretched a parallel line of shops, each with its private well-shaft down to the subterranean canal of Peirene. Stoas of these proportions remained the rule during the following centuries, and came to enclose all four sides of an agora, leaving only two small gaps for entrances, usually opposite one another but never on the central axis of the open space. They pro-

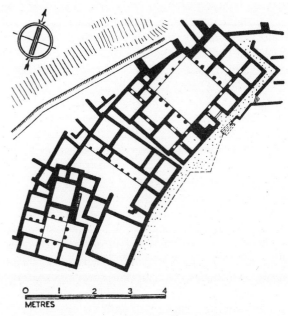

Fig. 64 Grouped megara, Larisa.

vided, if only because they had no easily visible terminations, no dangerous rival to the loftier and more subtle religious buildings. The roofs, too, even of the larger stoas remained of terracotta and less finished than those on temples. That of the South Stoa at Corinth is easily restored,[1] and, with its black and scarlet colouring, must have been handsome in its way. One admires the simplicity of the colonnades and the spirit in which their

[1] See *Ancient Corinth* (American School Guide; Athens, 1947), Figs. 10 and 11. (Oscar Broneer, who has just published this stoa, in *Corinth* 1, Part IV (Princeton, 1954), shows that the roof is more complicated than I had supposed.)

builders, while pitching the key of secular architecture lower than that of the temples, used the stoa to bring a dignified, unregimented harmony to ordinary streets. For all their simplicity, these groups of stoas achieved an effect found in only one modern town, Bologna.

The exteriors of ordinary houses still received slight treatment. Walls remained of unbaked mud bricks, through which burglars might dig at night. Otherwise, mud afforded little inconvenience —indeed even fortifications above a certain height might consist of it—and we can rest assured that such houses, if humble and scantily furnished, were by no means ugly.

From the sixth century there survive several princely houses on the acropolis of Larisa, in the Aeolian border land. The oldest is simply a Syrian 'loggia-building'. A little later, about 500 B.C., the prince erected to one side of it a detached, southward-facing megaron with a vestibule and two columns in antis, strikingly like that of Tiryns. During the next two centuries the palace grew into four megara, each with vestibule, clustering round a centre court, itself entered through a propylon from the east (see Fig. 64). One presumes those with different aspects were used at different seasons, like the halls of Persepolis.[1] But the form of each goes back to the Bronze Age.[2]

We need feel no surprise, then, if the larger houses of Priene, an Ionian city refounded about 350 B.C., retain Homeric features, a central court with one or two verandahs but no complete peristyle, an antechamber like a loggia distyle in antis, opening off its northern side, and behind this, in the position of the old megaron, a room approximately square and still the chief apartment (see Fig. 65). The façade of its antechamber received, furthermore, a Doric frieze and probably a pediment.[3] The passage to one side of it served in the normal house for storage. So Greek intellectual progress had altered the material framework of life very little, although it had made the Homeric conveniences, in a somewhat slighter form and, of course, without the bathroom, available to a larger proportion of mankind. These moderate houses, each normally on a rectangle of some 60 by 40 feet, mark the consolida-

---

[1] See below, pp. 214 ff.

[2] For the plans of Larisa at various stages see *Larisa*, I, Abb. 3–7. I am describing the last palace, that of *c.* 350 B.C.

[3] See the reconstruction by von Gerkan in Robertson (Figs. 124 and 125).

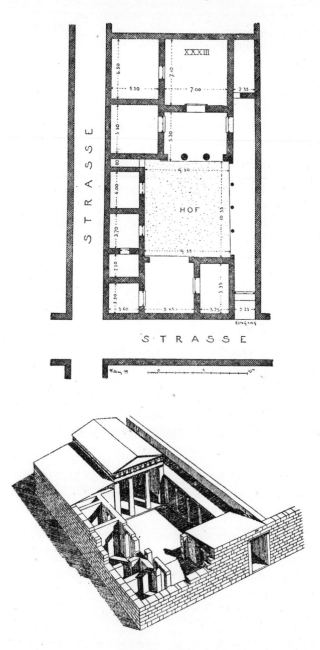

Fig. 65 (i) and (ii)   House at Priene.

tion of a self-governing middle class. They have survived because they were largely of stone. But as a type they had little influence on the luxurious houses of later antiquity.

In the tenth chapter of his sixth book Vitruvius prescribes for the women's quarter of his Greek house a centre court with a continuous peristyle around three sides and on the north a 'prostas' or loggia enclosed by two antae and two-thirds as deep as it is wide. Behind it, apparently, was the great chamber or 'oecus' ('house') and on each side of it the bedrooms. The Vitruvian house has some points in common with that of Priene, but differs from it in the peristyles; and outside Vitruvius the influence of Priene counts for nothing, the peristylar house for everything.

The peristyle appears at Olynthus, a town existing between 435 and 347 B.C. Whereas at Priene the rectangular sites were longer from north to south, at Olynthus each is nearly square and almost bisected by a corridor from east to west. To the south of this is a yard, occupying about a third of the available space, and to the north a set of the more important rooms, none dominating the rest (see Fig. 66). The plot of average size, about 60 feet square, permitted only the yard and single corridor. But it was easy, as a few larger, isolated houses show, to extend the corridor as a peristyle on all four sides of the yard. The large type developed naturally into the stone peristylar houses of Delos. At Olynthus all is still mud and wood.[1]

To which type the normal Athenian house belonged no ancient writer, not even Xenophon, has informed us.[2] That it had some architectural form, as opposed, for instance, to the large but chaotic contemporary house at Dystus, in Euboea, may be inferred from the Athenian character. But the orators of the fourth century are often pleased to recall that in their great days the Athenians gave all to the state and lived in houses of mud. If they are right, we have little cause to linger over Athenian domestic architecture.

With our knowledge of houses stands or falls that of schools,

---

[1] Wycherley, Pl. XV.

[2] See Xenophon, *Memorabilia*, III, 8, viii–x. Xenophon's 'Socrates' merely preaches functionalism, which he proves in this case by saying that a large, southward-facing pastas (loggia) makes a house both beautiful and useful; and adds that paintings and decorations are more trouble than they're worth! It is amusing to read Demangel's praise of 'Socrates' as the forerunner of Le Corbusier. See *La Frise Ionique*, pp. 7–8.

which, for the younger children, were no more than the houses of
schoolmasters; while sophists administered the 'higher' education
either in public places, such as the gymnasia and stoas, or in the
houses of rich patrons or in squalid thinking-dens with inflammable roofs. Even the gymnasia, the forerunners of the great
Roman thermae, maintained as they were by the state or a local
authority and frequented by all the men, not merely for exercise
but the daily oiling and scraping, had throughout this period no
architectural pretensions.

Town-planning, too, it is to be feared, was still in its infancy.

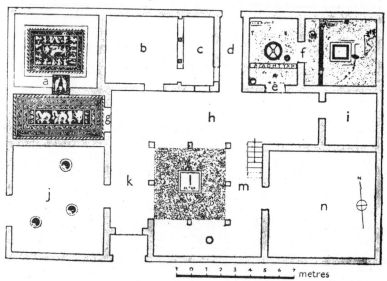

Fig. 66   Villa of Good Fortune, Olynthus.

A few classical writers show conscious appreciation of the forms
of actual or ideal cities. For instance, the Delphic Oracle speaks
of Athens in 480 B.C. as 'wheel-shaped'.[1] Plato in the *Laws*[2]
considers the pleasure to the eye of a city so designed that all the
houses, along the streets and the perimeter, form one continuous
enceinte. He may here have in mind a special type of city, laid
out from a central agora in a series of concentric rings or rectangles
of continuous housing, with more or less labyrinthine streets
around their edges from the gates to the agora. This plan, of

[1] Herodotus, VII, 140.
[2] 779B.

great defensive value, could have obtained, for instance, at Plataea in 431 B.C.[1] It would explain why, even after laying out all their early colonies, the Greeks had to wait until the fifth century before Hippodamus laid out the first rectangular street-grids[2]; and why Aristotle recommends for cities[3] a judicious mixture, for defensive reasons, of the Hippodamian and the 'old' ways of planning. Olynthus, of the late fifth century, is the earliest city we have recovered to show long, straight, parallel streets. The planners, one feels, applied the scheme awkwardly and without imagination, although the absence of public buildings on the plan in the official publication[4] makes a final judgment hard to reach. A few time-honoured tracks are allowed to disregard the network. So tyrannical a system, indeed, requires some relief. A century later the Greeks provided it by arranging rectangular agorai and other spaces and enclosures with conscious asymmetry and yet within the lines of the grid.[5]

As we study the Greeks, we see always the nice distinction they made between secular, utilitarian objects, to whose design they gave at most a perfunctory attention, and those works of art and religion whose creation and contemplation can alone satisfy the energies of mankind. A woman, relegated for most of her life to the inner rooms of a mud-brick house, might possess jewellery of an excellence unrivalled before or since, and might, like Hegeso,[6] be given at her death a tombstone still admired by the educated. Most Greek tombs are alas! too small to be treated as architecture: so we will end this section with another Greek gift to posterity—the Theatre (see Fig. 67).

Our knowledge of classical theatres is hampered by the fact that the Athenian, far and away the most important, was radically altered in Roman times, and the experts can restore it in its earlier phases from mere scraps of foundation, of doubtful antiquity and extent. The Theatre of Syracuse, where comedy enjoyed some

---

[1] Thucydides, II, 2–6.
[2] Aristotle, *Politics*, 1330B.
[3] Aristotle, *ibid.*
[4] Reproduced as Fig. 4 in Wycherley.
[5] On early Greek town-plans I am heavily indebted to Mr. W. A. Eden, whose theory of the first Greek towns I find very attractive. See *British School Annual*, XLV, pp. 16 ff.
[6] A. W. Lawrence, *Classical Sculpture* (London, 1929), Pl. 75. Beazley (*Cambridge Ancient History*, V, p. 442) shows a juster appreciation of Greek tombstones than does Lawrence, who attacks even the Giustiniani Stele.

renown in the earlier fifth century, supplies us, similarly, with evidence that is Romanised and doubtful; and the stage of the small Theatre of Oropus in Attica, once thought to provide good evidence for early rustic drama in the villages round Athens, is

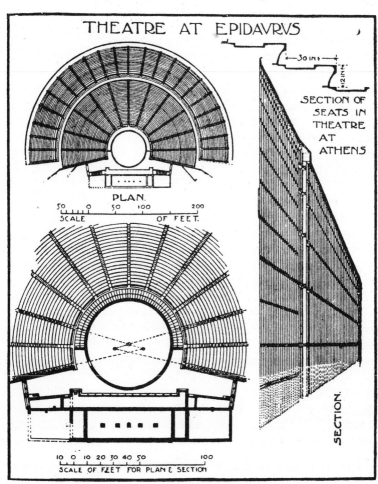

Fig. 67 Theatre at Epidaurus.

now known from inscriptions to date from the second century B.C.[1]

Nor do Hellenistic theatres offer safe evidence for their classical forerunners. For whereas fifth-century tragedy required a chorus of twelve or fifteen men, and comedy one of twenty-four,

[1] Dinsmoor, p. 305.

the Hellenistic drama dispensed with the chorus altogether, except, perhaps, during intervals. The Hellenistic theatre is apparently the 'Greek' theatre of Vitruvius,[1] who distinguishes performers of two sorts, the 'scenici' on the stage and the 'thymelici' in the circular dancing-place, or 'orchestra', in front of it. The stage, he tells us, is raised some 10 to 12 feet above the orchestra. In the classical drama it was possible to pass fairly quickly[2] from the one to the other. Again, the word 'thymelici' seems to signify not a proper chorus but musical contestants. There is nothing, even in Vitruvius, to show that they performed even on the same occasions as the 'scenici'. His information merely helps us to understand why, after the decline of the classical drama, the Greeks, with their love of music, retained for centuries an open orchestra.[3]

The only other classical writer to say much on theatres as buildings is Julius Pollux, a grammarian of the second century A.D. Many fashions had waxed and waned before he wrote, and he seldom makes clear to which phase of theatrical history he refers.

Where nearly everything is in dispute, it seems best to refer the serious student to the indispensable works of Margaret Bieber, and of Haigh and Pickard-Cambridge,[4] and the general reader to the brief but sensible account by Allardyce Nicoll,[5] and to attempt here merely a picture of the classical theatre as it may have looked.

When introduced to Athens in the sixth century B.C., Dionysos, the god of drink, the drunken dance and hence of tragedy, comedy and the dithyrambic hymn,[6] was assigned a sanctuary to the south of the Acropolis—his most ancient temple, according to Pausanias.[7] His theatre was then the gathering-place for a festival of dancing and miming in his honour[8] held in early spring

---

[1] Vitruvius, V, 7.

[2] See the instances collected in A. E. Haigh, *The Attic Theatre*, third edition (Oxford, 1907), pp. 168 ff.

[3] See Haigh, *op. cit.*, p. 146, n. 1.

[4] A. E. Haigh, *The Attic Theatre*, revised by A. W. Pickard-Cambridge (Oxford, 1907); Margaret Bieber, *History of the Greek and Roman Theatre* (Princeton, 1939).

[5] *The Development of the Theatre*, first edition (London, 1927).

[6] The seventh-century poet Archilochus knew how to 'raise the dithyramb when struck in his wits by the lightning of wine'.

[7] Pausanias, I, 20, iii.

[8] *Pace* Nietzsche, he came to patronise miming perhaps by accident. At Delos it was Apollo who enjoyed the acting of the girls (*Homeric Hymn to Apollo*, lines 157 ff.), and at Sicyon Adrastos who was honoured by tragic choruses (Herodotus, V, 67).

North Porch of Erechtheum, Athens

Plate 13

Monument of Lysicrates

(Reproduced from Stuart and Revett, *Antiquities of Athens*, 1761.)

Plate 14

ridge-pole to the tip of the eaves.   The pediment clearly overhangs the front at least as far as the mutuli.   Vitruvius advocates a tympanum on their front plane.   But actual tympana were much farther back, and ridge-pole and purlins perhaps rested, in some examples, on posts supported from the architrave; posts that appear to survive in petrified form encased in the hellenised tympanum on the later, 'Italic', temple of Cori.[1]

The remains supplement Vitruvius for the pediment.   Actual roof-tiles and models of pediments, such as the famous example from Lake Nemi, show that its interior was filled by a roof of normal classical pitch, running down to the front from the tympanum, with its smoke-hole, inside the main roof.[2]   This design, which has some connection with the sima on the pediment floor in some archaic temples of the western Greeks, must surely be explained as a religious survival.   One plausible theory[3] points out that the earliest known Italian hut, reproduced in the hut-urns of about the eighth century B.C., had an oval plan with a steep roof over its nearly rectangular central stretch.   Both its front and rear were curved, and here were lower, lean-to roofs, leaving the necessary hole for smoke at either end or 'gable' of the loftier main roof.   The Etruscans, it is alleged, adapted the type to a rectangular plan.   But, be that as it may, the genuine Etruscan temple offered no scope for large sculptured groups inside the pediments.

Instead, the whole exterior was designed, as Vitruvius, I think, implies,[4] to show as prominently as possible the curious craftsmanship of the roof-covering (see Fig. 73), that so greatly impressed even Roman imperial writers and is still represented in force in so many museums of Tuscany and Rome.   The Temple of Jupiter Capitolinus, with a width of 200 Roman feet,[5] had altogether exceptional dimensions.   That near Orvieto, about 16 metres broad and 22 long, and that of Civita Castellana, $8\frac{1}{2}$ by $10\frac{1}{2}$ metres, give an idea of the range in normal examples.[6]   The

[1] See below, p. 272.
[2] See Robertson, Fig. 87.   The interior is closed behind by a tympanum wall.
[3] See A. K. Lake in *AJA*, 1941, p. 71.
[4] Vitruvius, III, iii, 5.   A fifth-century relief from Chiusi, showing a sepulchral building of some sort, provides notable corroboration: see Ducati, II, Tav. 24.
[5] Dionysius of Halicarnassus, IV, 61.
[6] Those of Veii and Marzabotto are 18 and 19 metres in width.   For Veii, see E. Stefani, *NS*, 1946, p. 37 (plan).

tip of the projecting eaves, probably as low as the tops of the columns, will come in the first case under 20, in the second under 10 feet from the stylobate. This compares with carved metopes 20 feet above it on the Hephaisteion at Athens. In fact, the moderately large Tuscan temple was designed to give a column equal in height to the normal Greek Doric and at the same time to move the roof nearer the eye. Everything, moreover, except the roof and the ground course was of wood or mud-brick until the fourth century at the earliest, when stone columns appear[1]; and, as the pediment could hold no figured groups, the artist disposed these above the ridge-pole, as, for instance, on the

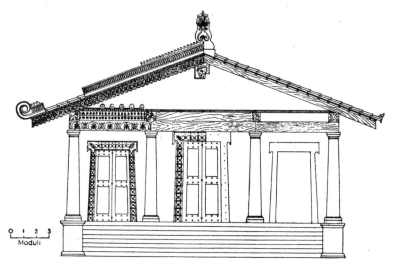

Fig. 73 Tuscan temple, conjectural elevation.

celebrated temple of Apollo at Veii, of the earlier fifth century. Sheaths of moulded terracotta on the fronts of purlins and ridge-pole, fictile akroteria and intricate revetments along the sides completed an elaborate ensemble.

The technique of the tiling is thoroughly Greek. So were the subjects,[2] satyrs wrestling with maenads, the suicide of Ajax, and even Jupiter (Zeus) brandishing in his right hand a thunderbolt

[1] Ducati appears to know no stone columns from temples even in the fourth century (I, pp. 393 ff.). Alatri, which had them, is of the third century (p. 393).

[2] See, for good pictures of these, G. Q. Giglioli, *L'Arte Etrusca* (Milan, 1935).

of baked clay.[1]   The first impulse seems to have reached Etruria
from Ionia, where the gutter was already accentuated with a frieze
of figures.   Despite literary evidence, collected by Blakeway,[2]
which would point to Corinth as the source, the actual sima
copies not the Corinthian type but the parapets of Ionia: and in
Etruria the moulded parapet was balanced by a large overhang
from the revetment of the cornice.   The series of Etruscan roofs
begins about 570 and temporarily ends, for reasons not understood,
about 450 B.C.[3]   An interesting feature of the Tuscan column, the
Hypotrachelium, or raised necking band around the shaft, derives
from a Greek source rather more provincial, Paestum.   Ducati
figures an example from Vulci, apparently of the fifth century,[4]
that exaggerates the Paestan concavity and necking-roll below the
echinus.

The Tuscan Order has obviously suffered more than any other
from later misinterpretation.   Nothing, for instance, could be
further from genuine Tuscan than the bottom storey of the
Colosseum.   Even if it has no future—and this would seem hard
to believe, now that new materials urge us to lighten somewhat
the time-honoured lithic Orders—Tuscan deserves, for the beauty
of its genuine buildings, to be rescued from its distortion by
Renaissance theorists.

The blank rear wall of the Tuscan temple forced its builders to
place it at the back of the precinct, often on a podium.   Moreover,
unlike the Greek temple, it was best seen from a point dead
opposite the façade.   It became the custom to place the propylon
here, where only a few Greeks, and those western,[5] had sited it:
so that we have already, in such Etruscan precincts as Orvieto, an
anticipation of the Roman ensemble at Baalbek.[6]

Etruscan tombs are all either rock-hewn or corbelled.   The
Regolini-Galassi Tomb at Caere (seventh century B.C.), the most
sumptuously appointed of all, reminds us in its chamber of the
galleries at Tiryns.   It differs in having smaller stones more neatly
planed and triangular corbelled openings not brought to an apex

[1] Ovid, *Fasti*, II, vv. 201 ff.
[2] A. Blakeway, 'Demaratus', *JRS*, 1935, p. 147.
[3] See T. Ashby, *The Architecture of Ancient Rome* (London, 1927),
p. 12: compare Ducati, I, p. 97.
[4] Ducati, II, Tav. 177.   Compare the Paestan capital, Robertson,
Fig. 33.
[5] For instance, at Temple A, Selinus (where, however, the crowded
site almost compels it).
[6] See Andren, *op. cit.*, Introduction, p. xlix.

but closed several feet below by neat stone slabs. An exact contemporary parallel, with the same shapes crossing in a similar way, is the rock-hewn Grotto of the Sibyl at the western Greek city of Cumae.[1]   Later rock-hewn tombs are less Mycenaean and more Greek in appearance, and represent with no startling aberrations the interiors of small trabeated buildings with the rafters and ridge-pole showing.

The Tomba della Pietrera at Vetulonia, of the seventh century, shows an important new feature, pendentives, here perhaps used for the first time in stone (see Pl. 16).   Their convenience is obvious.   The vault, as usual, is corbelled, and with corbelling a circular plan, as we saw,[2] is most stable.   But a square chamber below roof-level is obviously more convenient.[3]   So the pendentive originates in a milieu of corbelled roofs as a device for getting the best of both plans.   It appears some time afterwards, probably in the fourth century B.C.,[4] in the half-Greek corbelled tomb chambers of Panticapaeum in the Crimea, which are also square on plan and roofed like beehives.[5]

Although, however, the Etruscans had made this great advance, and although, later, the Romans could have benefited many times from a knowledge of the pendentive, no Roman building contains an example approaching these of the Tomba della Pietrera or even approximating to the form of a spherical triangle, the correct form for a pendentive.[6]   When the pendentive reappears, it is in the eastern Greek world.   So great is the gap between Etruria and Rome.   The Tuscan Temple had a longer influence, and a new example appeared, according to Vitruvius,[7] as late as the time of Pompey the Great (after 75 B.C.).   We cannot tell whether this was mere antiquarian revivalism, under the influence of Varro. But we know both from Strabo and the existing remains that early in the second century B.C. Republican Rome had already entered the full stream of Hellenism.   Her buildings owed the arch and other new features to a world less agreeably rustic than Etruria.

[1] A. Maiuri, *I Campi Flegrei* (Rome, 1949), Fig. 71.
[2] Above, p. 84.
[3] Some of the beehive huts on the Dingle Peninsula, Ireland, are given square interiors, even at the cost of some floor space.
[4] Rostovtzeff, *Iranians and Greeks* (Oxford, 1922), p. 78.
[5] See Sir Ellis Minns, *Scythians and Greeks* (Cambridge, 1913), Figs. 86–9.
[6] See below, p. 296.
[7] Vitruvius, III, iii, 5.

PART THREE

ARCHITECTURE AFTER GREECE

CHAPTER VII

THE HELLENISTIC AGE 322–31 B.C.

I. GENERAL HISTORY

BY conquering the Persian Empire, Alexander the Great ensured the supremacy in some form of his efficient Macedonian Kingdom over the decrepit cities of Greece; and this supremacy remained although, after his premature death in 323 B.C., no single one of his generals had the strength to grasp the whole of his new empire.[1] Antigonus the One-eyed and his son Demetrius the Besieger failed in their great attempt to reunite it—one result of this war being the emergence of Rhodes as the most successful city of the period—and after their defeat at Ipsus in 302 B.C. Egypt, the richest dominion, with its famous Greek capital, Alexandria, remained in the hands of Ptolemy, while the Fertile Crescent and the lands to the east passed definitely to Seleucus. Asia Minor and Macedon remained in confusion for another generation until in 279 B.C. Gauls from the north broke into both regions and were beaten off from Greece only by the Aetolian League of the north-west. In Asia they were subdued as late as 230 B.C. by the seemingly unimportant Kingdom of Pergamum, north of Ionia. Soon after the Gallic invasion, Antigonus Gonatas, grandson of Antigonus the One-eyed, seized Macedon and restored her military strength.

Greece might at this moment have thrown off the Macedonian rule. But Athens played an unskilful game and was finally ruined in the Chremonidean War of 262 B.C. However, one league of cities had shown its efficiency in Aetolia and another, the Achaean, began to grow in the Peloponnese. But King Cleomenes of Sparta, by giving land and power to thousands of serfs, started there a social revolution, the attractiveness of which, together with the military efficiency of its promoters, proved altogether too much for the Achaeans and could be crushed only with Macedonian aid, given, of course, on conditions (222 B.C.). Henceforward only the Egyptian fleet could avert the total subjugation of Greece.

[1] For my account of the Hellenistic political scene I rely chiefly on W. W. Tarn, *Hellenistic Civilisation* (London, 1930).

A survey of the Greek world just before 200 thus shows three great dynasties, the Antigonid in Macedon, the Seleucid in the Fertile Crescent and the Ptolemaic in Egypt, with secondary powers on the fringes, such as the Aetolian League and the Kingdom of Bactria, or in the interstices between great empires, such as the Achaean League in southern Greece, the Pergamene Kings in northern Asia Minor and the island of Rhodes, with its famous fleet, at the meeting-point of almost all the large states.

West of Greece one barbarism succeeded another. Syracuse and Taras alone survived as efficient cities. About 300 B.C. the Carthaginian conquest of all Sicily was averted only by the Syracusan Agathocles. In south Italy the fourth century was the age of the Samnites, who long masked the aggressive power of Rome. She was, however, growing everywhere, thanks largely to the political rewards she had learnt to give her supporters, chiefly an extension of her own citizenship, with its duties and privileges. On the Samnite collapse, soon after 300, she suddenly appeared more powerful in Italy than even Carthage in Sicily. Both powers were now expanding, as it seems efficient powers always must. Pyrrhus, King of Epirus, failed to knit the western Greeks against them (282–275 B.C.). The First and Second Punic Wars, which occupied most of the rest of the century down to 202 B.C. and count among the longest and most destructive in history, ensured that Rome and not Carthage should rule the western world and that in Rome herself the aristocratic senate should wield unquestioned control. After this, it took Rome a mere fifty-five years to absorb Macedon, Greece and the Islands, to ruin the Seleucids and to destroy Carthage—a process completed in 146 B.C.

The unprecedented wealth and power of Rome are evident even from her subordinate cities, such as Pompeii, which now enjoyed, in the so-called 'Tufa Period', a culture of great refinement. They soon demoralised the Roman aristocracy. For eighty years after 146 B.C. Rome made few conquests. Her only new acquisition was by a legacy from the last king of Pergamum (133 B.C.). The Seleucids and Ptolemies survived and, corrupt as they were, might shine by comparison with Roman rapacity and with the Roman slave market on the island of Delos itself. Mithridates, a mushroom king of Pontus, in northern Asia Minor, might even aspire in 88 B.C. to lead a crusade against the Roman officials and traders, and spread disastrous war and massacre, during which much of Athens was burnt, over the Aegean and even over Greece.

Delos, the most important Roman emporium after about 160 B.C., was now sacked, and never fully recovered—an event most useful to the historian in dating certain types of Hellenistic building.

Rome was saved from her eastern subjects, fresh northern barbarians and discontented classes in Italy only by a series of great generals, Marius, Sulla, Pompey and Caesar, appointed over the heads of the politicians and naturally jealous of each other. The struggle between Marius and Sulla temporarily sickened the Italians of civil war, and the victory of Sulla marks an important epoch. He checked, first of all, the attempt to bestow privileges too widely, on the Samnites, for instance, and the Campanians, whose bid resulted at Pompeii in political collapse, the abrupt end of the opulent Tufa Period and the planting of a Roman military colony about 80 B.C. He also did his best to reunite the Roman Senate and restore its effective control over the executive, the tax-gatherers and distant army-commanders. He thereby set the tone of the ensuing Ciceronian Age (70–50 B.C.). Architecturally, he is even more important, as his rule marks the beginning of the new, imperial Roman style.

It now seemed that the more reasonable senators and the Italian middle classes might combine to purify the government. A fair number of the ruling Romans showed a taste for civilised life. But Cicero, the leader of the movement, was without those modern vehicles for eloquence that might serve, at least in our western democracy, to uphold a liberal and reasonable régime. In Rome it was the soldier who had been admired for seven centuries, and Cicero lacked the soldierly virtues. Second to these came pride of pedigree, an asset all too obviously denied to most of the Italian party and to Cicero himself.

Julius Caesar, by contrast, had all the obvious Roman virtues, and, in the Roman way, could oppose a devoted soldiery and a concrete achievement, the conquest of Gaul (58–52 B.C.), to the dreams of moderate republicans. One has reluctantly to agree with Christopher Dawson[1] that this conquest changed the course of history. Gaul was the first and greatest of those new acquisitions, all won before A.D. 14, which included Spain, Illyricum, the Rhineland, most of Asia Minor and large parts of North Africa, and which only an army under a strong, central government could retain and civilise. If it was necessary, as most historians believe, to drill these districts into civilisation, then a military empire

[1] *The Making of Europe* (London, 1932), p. 6,

became a necessity. At the same time, such an empire soon proved the worst possible foe of the only cultured class. Scholars who praise the stout defence of Rome centuries later by Illyricum or Asia Minor forget that these were originally romanised at some expense to Italy and Italian freedom: while those who dilate on the feebleness of the Senate in this age of great captains forget not only that the Empire itself was culturally prostrate, and at the mercy of even worse captains, three centuries later but that, as Thucydides observes, it is not always the best or even the wisest that survive a period of civil war and redoubled proscription. As it was, Caesar made himself sole ruler after 49 B.C., and even his murder in 44 and the ugly quarrels of his military heirs postponed only for a decade the establishment of a regular empire (31 B.C.) by his adopted son Augustus.

In the last years of the Roman Republic, the East begins to recover lost ground from the Greco-Roman world. The Roman defeat of the Seleucids early in the second century so weakened them that soon their Iranian territories broke away under a native Parthian dynasty, the Arsacid. It is marvellous that so maritime a race as the Greek should have held power there for so long, and, as Tarn observes, the history of the cities planted so carefully by the early Seleucids in the heart of Asia is an epic that one longs to recover. In the first century B.C. the Parthians were installed in Babylonia, and the first Roman attempt to dislodge them failed disastrously at Carrhae (53 B.C.). Pompey formally abolished the Seleucids in 63 B.C., and the final campaign of Augustus against his rival Mark Antony involved the ruin of the last Ptolemaic Queen, Cleopatra.

So in 30 B.C. the Greek world is everywhere in chains, under Parthia or Rome; and—what is very important for us—ways of planning and building appear for the first time over our world which show few obvious links with classical Greek architecture. Under Augustus the new Sullan 'baroque', first developed about 80 B.C. in the neighbourhood of Rome, becomes the fashion as far afield as Baalbek; so that, architecturally speaking, his seizure of sole rule marks very conveniently the end of the Hellenistic Age. Vitruvius, the conservative theorist who wrote on architecture in his reign, provided the swan-song of true Hellenism.

Throughout this period war absorbed the energies of too many, including architects; for we must remember that the ancients held military engineering to be a branch of architecture. It is also a difficult period to assess. Its greatest figures were scientists, whose works were garbled or lost in the dark ages that followed. Its buildings have also largely vanished. Some of its cities, like the Ptolemaic capital, Alexandria, have been in continuous and latterly very squalid occupation, that most fatal enemy of all good architecture. Those who cannot understand the virulence of this foe may ask themselves how much the Sultans have left of Byzantine Constantinople, or how much we have preserved of eighteenth-century London. Other cities, like Seleucia and Antioch, the two Seleucid capitals, suffered the almost equally disastrous process of slow decay. Others again, later included in the Byzantine Empire, were too often sacked during Norman invasions or Church Councils and always squalidly rebuilt. Many are too remote to excavate, and it is ironic that modern scholars should have had easy access, for a time, to Taxila in Punjab, which to the ancient Greek was the most distant of all.

2. EARLIER HELLENISTIC ARCHITECTURE, DOWN TO 200 B.C.

In this age the Greek has largely turned from the attempt to improve on his fathers to the easier task of imposing his developed civilisation on others and reaping the profits from his inherited efficiency. Hence in architecture he is less interested in single exquisite buildings than in large plans for new towns and in projects of applied engineering. Where, during the fifth century, Athenians had added to their town two small but exquisite stoas, the third century saw stoas erected by the stade in scores of new or modernised cities. Easy short cuts to good proportion, of the sort Vitruvius gives in Books III and IV, began to tempt the builder, and the client began to ask less for subtlety than for obvious novelties—new combinations of familiar elements, or features, such as the arch or the Corinthian capital, rare or unknown before. Yet even the novelties were too scattered and too inaccessible for the nineteenth-century historians of architecture; who, with their overpowering interest in ornament, would ignore the Hellenistic age and resume the story, after a gap of three centuries, at Augustan Rome. Today we are compelled to look at this central period; and we begin with works of the third century, earlier than even the political supremacy of Rome.

The countless new cities of Alexander and his immediate successors observed very conscientiously the rules of earlier

Greek technique. Inevitably the column grew slimmer, the echinus straighter, the mouldings shallower, the hollows of the triglyph more mechanical and less undercut at the top. But it was only after 200 B.C. at Pergamum that craftsmen substituted a mere continuous chamfer for the ovolo or cyma reversa of classical Greece; and Greek dry-jointing continued in all its excellence at Priene into Roman times, and survived for centuries in the arches and cut stone vaults of Asia Minor, north Syria and even Provence.

The plans of Priene and Miletus, as Wycherley has now made very clear,[1] show equal obedience to classical Greek principles (see Fig. 74). The hallmark of Greek life was the stoa, already of architectural importance in the fourth century. The Echo Stoa at Olympia, for instance, had already a length of forty-four columns between end walls. Doric pilasters had not been invented; nor did a colonnaded first floor seem tolerable before the Pergamene buildings of the second century.[2] Asymmetry and informality of arrangement could alone make such stretches of rigid Doric supportable. So the largest stoas are each given a plan shaped like a modern arrangement of goalposts, and open in bays off the main street, the other side of which, in each case, is given a long stoa perfectly straight from end to end. The effect is closer to Bloomsbury than to George Street, Edinburgh. The most important sanctuaries, while occupying a position that will tell in views of the town from outside or in chance views inside it, are related as loosely as possible to the rectangular grid of streets and stoas. Significantly, Vitruvius lays down that the agora should be central, the chief temple on the highest point inside the walls, but ignores the architectural relation between agora and temple.[3] Shops are segregated from the better middle-class houses, and often included in the rear of the long stoas round the agora—at Corinth, for instance, in the long and famous South

---

[1] Better, I think, in his article 'The Ionian Agora', in *JHS*, 1942, than in his book: because in his article he has to contrast the Greek and Roman practice of town-planning.

[2] I know only one earlier example, the North Stoa at Corinth, apparently of Alexander's time. Its details are very pure. Its ground floor contained half-columns attached to piers, its upper storey rectangular posts of great depth. A plain architrave with epikranitis separated the two storeys, as in classical temple-interiors, and a Doric entablature, with delicate mutules, crowned the whole building. For this seemingly unique experiment, see *Corinth*, I, Pt. III (Princeton, 1951), pp. 163–74 (which I follow for the date).

[3] Vitruvius I, Chap. 7.

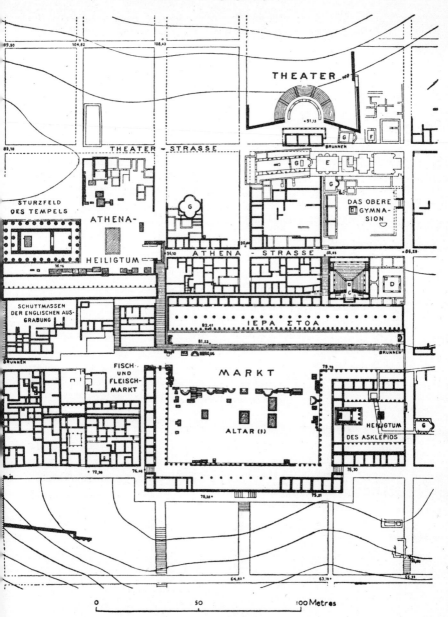

Fig. 74   Centre of Priene, plan.

Stoa. The better houses fill blocks, or 'insulae', in residential districts—four houses to an insula in Priene[1]—and at this time have blank façades of beautiful masonry.

New cities, then, absorbed much creative energy. The design of the better private houses perhaps absorbed even more. This was the first great age of the Greek private house. Douris of Samos tells us that Demetrius of Phalerum, in the sumptuous Athenian house he occupied before his fall in 307 B.C., had made for him many floors with patterns of flowers, elaborately worked.[2] Such sumptuous mosaic floors, now of cut stones, remained up to 100 B.C. the only place in a private house for large realistic pictures.[3] Furniture was still slight and elegant, devoted chiefly to the evening meal; and in dining-rooms the three couches, each for two reclining guests, were arranged touching one another, one at the end and one down each side of a square central space. Naturally, then, most of the floor was designed as a frame of relatively coarse mosaic round a central picture (or 'emblema') designed to fill this space, of exquisite technique and often with an equally beautiful border of scrollwork. Figured emblemata are known from about 200 B.C. onwards at Pergamum, Delos and Pompeii. The most famous is the Alexander Mosaic in the House of the Faun at Pompeii, probably a close copy of a famous painting by Philoxenos.[4]

For the planning and style of third-century houses we have the evidence not only of Priene but of tombs in Macedonia and Alexandria.[5] Unlike the true Greek, the noble Macedonian was buried in an imitation house, with entrance-vestibule, forecourt, loggia (or pastas)[6] and main room (or oecus),[6] treated in these tombs as a dining-room, with a stone couch and a false door in front of the burial-chamber. The detailing, even in the Alexandrian tombs, is at first mainly Greek, and its development the work of consciously Greek artists. As such, it is highly significant.

---

[1] See the plans, *Priene*, Taf. XXI ff.

[2] In Athenaeus, p. 542D.

[3] On all these early mosaics I draw most of my information from the paper by Miss M. E. Blake, *Memoirs of the American Academy in Rome*, VIII (1930)—henceforward cited as *Pavements*.

[4] See Blake, *Pavements*, p. 134; cf. A. Rumpf, *JHS*, 1947, pp. 15–16.

[5] The Alexandrian tombs have been studied by Ibrahim Noshy, *The Arts in Ptolemaic Egypt* (Oxford, 1937), to whom I owe most of my information. I am indebted to Mr. Tomlinson, of the British School at Athens, for some corrections.

[6] For these terms, see above, p. 204. I use 'prostas' and 'pastas' interchangeably.

To understand it, we must anticipate a little and turn to the small south Italian town of Pompeii as it was between the years 200 and 50 B.C. Only here and at Herculaneum have ancient frescoes survived in any quantity.[1] Consequently, although they were fairly ordinary provincial towns, we have to arrange our knowledge of ancient interior decoration around the four Pompeian styles of decoration, as elucidated by Mau.[2] Painted decoration begins at Pompeii about 200 B.C.; and in the First Style, down to 80 B.C., colours are used in inner wall-surfaces of moulded plaster imitating masonry, with a dado, several courses of drafted and variegated blocks, an Ionic cornice, a course of smooth blocks, an upper cornice and a plain unpainted area below the roof (see Fig. 75). The blocks are given many different colours—which indicates the derivation of the style from a technique of polychrome marble veneering. The architraves of doors and other pieces of real architecture are worked naturally into the design. Actual pictures have not yet appeared; but in some examples the small columns and piers that are later to frame them are already found above the lower cornice. With their sober interiors, their exquisite floors, their generous and purely classical proportions and their simple fronts of beautiful masonry, these harmonious houses of the Tufa Period, so well represented by the House of the Faun (see Fig. 83), are the most civilised ever built in Pompeii. It was then in spirit a Greek city, and it would have been well for its artistic reputation had it remained so.

But in 80 B.C. the Roman punitive colony arrived. Building

---

[1] The chief examples elsewhere are from the 'House of Livia' on the Palatine, superb specimens of the 'Second Pompeian Style'. Very recently a beehive tomb of a type still structurally Mycenaean but decorated with Hellenistic frescoes has come to light at Kasanlik in the Balkans. See *AJA*, 1945, pp. 402 ff. See also below, p. 242.

[2] Mau-Kelsey, *Pompeii* (New York, 1899), Chap. 53. The latest, sumptuous publication in colour by A. Maiuri of some of these paintings (*Roman Painting* (Skira, 1953)) shows as never before the real merit they possess. Unhappily, the selection and the critique in the text are both disappointing, while the colours are not always correct. Maiuri dislikes even masterpieces, such as the 'Discovery of the Infant Telephus' (*Cambridge Ancient History*, Pls. III, p. 172), when they are too 'classical' and 'academic', praises more incoherent passages of the illogical Third Style as anticipating cubism and even supposes (p. 42) that it is the Second and not this Third Style that Vitruvius attacks in VII, 5. A good short account in English of the Pompeian styles is given by R. C. Carrington, *Pompeii* (Oxford, 1936), pp. 136–46. Each style, of course, tends to overlap its predecessor, and several paintings are 'transitional' in character.

itself grew nondescript, but the interior decoration became elaborately architectural (see Pl. 18). Inside a room of this Second Style (*c.* 80–50 B.C.) one seems to stand in an open pavilion of somewhat Egyptian type, with an open colonnade reaching to its full height, but placed against a lower wall, allowing views of the country and buildings beyond. Alternatively, columns and half-columns can stand on a podium and punctuate a wall further divided with niches and windows, again giving distant views. In short, this style presents receding planes of walls and columns. Generally, too, it makes use of triads. Two side niches or windows flank the chief window in the centre, while horizontally the scheme

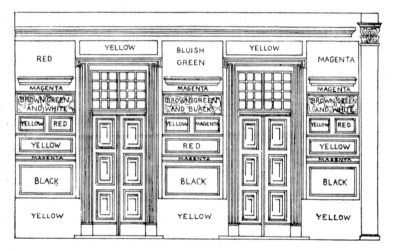

Fig. 75   First Pompeian Style.

is always divided into low wall or podium, the central more open stretch and the entablature of the framing colonnade. No painter now attempts to model the wall-face, but relies on paint alone.

In the Third Style, which begins under Augustus and incurs the censure of Vitruvius, and which takes many of its minor motifs from Egypt, the architecture of the representations itself grows improbable.[1]   But our business is with the two earlier styles.

Much as it harmonises with the façades of tufa, the First

[1] See Mau-Kelsey, *op. cit.*, Fig. 263. As Prof. Toynbee points out to me, the Egyptian element in this Third Style may perhaps be explained by the Augustan conquest of Egypt. Compare the origins of the French First Empire Style.

Column drums from
Temple of Poseidon,
Sunium

Corinthian capital,
Orange

Plate 15

Theatre of Epidaurus

Tomba della Pietrera, Vetulonia

Plate 16

Style was not invented in Pompeii. Its 'encrusted' walls were meant for coloured marbles, not their painted plaster imitations. Still less can we attribute the elegant and convincing architecture of the Second Style to southern Italy or even to Rome, great as was the progress Rome had made by 80 B.C. We have here a refined Hellenistic decoration, intended to give people in a closed room the illusion of gardens and space; and the sort of open and varied building they imitate, with its low walls between columns, surely carries us back to the vanished houses of Alexandria, and beyond them to the pavilions of the Pharaohs.

Noshy has established a convincing sequence for the Alexandrian tombs, based on the changes in their decoration, the gradual curtailment of the portions necessary only in the houses they imitated and the substitution of communal for individual burial as Alexandria grew and tomb-space became more precious. The earliest tombs, at Suk-el-Wardian and Anfushy (300–280 B.C.), have drafted masonry walls with cornices above and orthostates below, in a manner still Greek but anticipating the plaster walls of the First Pompeian Style. The tomb at Shatby, of about 260 B.C., has walls with Doric and Ionic engaged columns, and between them false doors and windows.[1] Significantly a string course, cut by the columns, runs immediately below the windows; and below this level, too, the flutes of the columns are blocked out, as so often at Pompeii.[2] In general design the House of the Centaur at Pompeii, apparently of the Tufa Period, provides the most striking analogy to this Egyptian work, with its blind order of engaged columns against an encrustation of drafted blocks and its cornice halfway up the wall-face. Once before in the west a low wall, modelled in much the same way, had appeared between columns, at Temple F at Selinus,[3] where even the decoration of panel and pilaster anticipates the House of the Centaur. But this likeness is probably mere chance; and it is Alexandria that more immediately anticipates Pompeian building and still more the Second Pompeian Style of decoration, and even the Sullan

[1] See Breccia, *La Necropoli di Sciatbi* (Cairo, 1912), especially Pls. II and III. This is almost exactly the style of a Hellenistic external wall of the Palace of Ptolemais, in Cyrenaica, for which see Fig. 76.

[2] Ashby in the *Encyclopaedia Britannica* (1911, *s.v.* Pompeii, p. 55) maintains that these blocked out Pompeian columns are an unpleasing early imperial innovation. This is not true, as the older colonnade in the Forum (Mau-Kelsey, *op. cit.*, Fig. 14), of the second century B.C., already has the lower third of the columns blocked out.

[3] Robertson, Fig. 29.

16—1

architecture of Praeneste. A little later than Shatby, the Alexandrian tomb at Sidi Gaber (*c.* 200 B.C.) has already translated its architecture into painting. Above a low wall with a cornice we see the sky, and at each corner of the room is a column, giving the effect of an open pavilion.

Thus that immemorial Egyptian building, the pavilion, is having its inevitable influence on the Hellenistic decorator. But elsewhere other artists are developing the new ideas almost as rapidly.

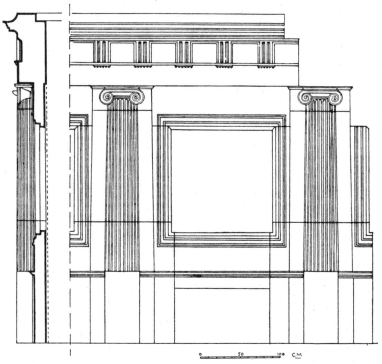

Fig. 76   Hellenistic engaged order at Ptolemais, Cyrenaica.

In Macedonia, in the vestibule of a tomb at Pydna (*c.* 280 B.C.), we again find the encrustation style[1]; and in a tomb of the mid-third century at Canosa in the heel of Italy the stuccoed walls have engaged columns and painted false windows.[2]

[1] L. Heuzey, *Mission Archéologique en Macedoine* (Paris, 1876), Pl. 18. The painted tomb of Kasanlik (see above, p. 239, n. 1) has no 'Pompeian' features, so should be early in the Hellenistic Age.

[2] Nachod in *Roemische Mittheilungen*, 1914, Abb. 15–18. For the presence of this style at Ptolemais in Cyrenaica, see above, p. 241, n. 1.

Larger buildings show the same natural attempt to bind the refractory Greek orders into solid walls. For some time experimenters concentrated on the engaged column and the anta, for which precedents existed. The altar of Athena Polias at Priene, facing the temple, is a most interesting early example, of solid construction but with statues of women standing on a podium and projecting slightly in advance of its front plane, the whole being placed behind large engaged Ionic columns reaching to the ground (see Fig. 77). These columns have Attic bases, but support an Asiatic entablature, with dentils and no frieze. The figures are not Caryatids, but seem close in posture to the 'Mourning Women' of the famous fourth-century sarcophagus, in style to the Demeter of Cnidus. The details are good, and hardly later than 300 B.C., and the design, while recalling fashionable restorations of the Temple of the Giants at Akragas, was managed more adroitly.[1]

The Arsinoeion at Samothrace, a large circular building of 288–280 B.C., dispensed with the classical peristyle and had a continuous outer wall treated as a podium with Ionic crowning mould supporting a ring of square piers treated as antae. Between their lower portions were parapet walls with ox-skulls or bucrania, here used for about the first time in architecture. The building must have looked correct but rather jejune—like most early Hellenistic work. These architects saw the difficulty of combining walls with half-columns, would have hated several tiers of orders and were still guiltless of the pilaster.[2]

The Bouleuterion (Council-House) at Miletus, built a century later, shows a degenerate version of the same treatment. Here externally we find a false podium of similar proportions. But Doric half-columns, engaged in a wall with windows, have replaced the simple square piers. The external entablature, too, shows the altered Doric form found all over the Hellenistic world in the second century and described below.[3] In general effect the building is richer than the Arsinoeion, suggesting a complete peristyle in front of a pierced and modelled wall.

Another innovation made it even more necessary to cultivate this illusion of various walls and colonnades laid against each

[1] See Wiegand-Schrader, *Priene*, pp. 120–6. I am convinced neither by the pseudo-Pergamene design nor the second-century date bestowed upon this monument by A. von Gerkan (*Bonner Jahrbücher*, Heft 129, 1924, pp. 15–35). The 'Mourning Women' Sarcophagus has Attic bases.

[2] For the Arsinoeion see A. Conze and others, *Samothrake*, I (Vienna, 1875), Taf. LIII ff.

[3] See p. 259.

Fig. 77　Altar of Athena, Priene: detail (dimensions in metres).

other in receding planes. This was the Arch. There existed a
strong prejudice, as we shall soon see, against using it on trabeated
buildings, but the division of planes at least enabled one to prevent
it, where it was used, from contaminating the main order.

For the early history of the Arch the researches of Delbrueck
are still indispensable. The topic cries out for a fresh study, as
some of his dates one can no longer accept. Nor can one rely for

ever for so many important examples on the old work of Lancko-ronski, published in 1890.[1]   But here, in the dearth of modern research, I can merely summarise the conclusions of fifty years ago.

Before Hellenistic times the only stone arches or tunnels of any size were found in tombs, the oldest and largest, it seems, in Egyptian Saite tombs of the seventh and sixth centuries.   Even these were timidly constructed; for the builder would corbel out their haunches horizontally as far as he dared, and close the opening at the top of each arched ring with no more than three true voussoirs at the most.[2]   Neither Mesopotamia nor Persia had ever ventured on an arch of stone.   In describing the Hanging Gardens of Babylon, Diodorus[3] gives the impression of a wonderful brick structure, with horizontal stone lintels, 4 feet by 16, over some of the passages.   Diodorus seems to be quoting an Early Hellenistic writer, describing the Gardens as the Greek conquerors found them,[4] and so provides an interesting glimpse of two crafts, masonry and brick-building, each going their own way on one monument.   For properly constructed stone tunnels, let alone large arches used in important elevations, one has to wait every-where until the third, perhaps even the second century.   On the evidence of a good authority,[5] the fifth-century Greek philosopher Democritus had discovered 'how a curve of stones inclining inwards little by little could be tied together at the top by a keystone'. But just as they never used on their rafters the principle they assuredly knew, that the strength of a beam depends on its depth, so the later classical architects, although occasionally tolerating small arches in brick buildings, as in the fourth-century tombs at Rhegium,[6] refused for aesthetic reasons to experiment with the new discovery in stone buildings.

Nevertheless, eastern brick vaults, above all in Babylonia, must have greatly impressed the Greek conquerors.   Seleucia, the new

---

[1] *Staedte Pamphyliens und Pisidiens*, 2 vols. (Vienna, 1890–2).

[2] See above, p. 50.

[3] Diodorus, II, 10.

[4] So Delbrueck, II, pp. 108–9.   Strabo, by contrast, describes its substructure as vaulted, and Delbrueck concludes that he refers to a later, Hellenistic phase.   This is unlikely.   Arches of brick and lintels of a more precious material can be found together on a single Babylonian building.

[5] Posidonius, a scholar of the Ciceronian Age, quoted in Seneca's 90th Letter, §32.

[6] See, e.g., Blake, *Ancient Roman Construction in Italy* (Washington, 1947), p. 285.   The bricks are moulded into the shapes of voussoirs, a labour that suggests the hand of classical Greeks.

Hellenistic capital of Babylonia, was built largely of Babylonian material[1]: and some of the first Greek arches of which we hear are actually vaults. The Roman word 'camera', a chamber, comes from the Greek word for a vault; and Pliny dates for us a Greek project for one of these 'camarationes', the famous unfinished magnetic vault over the tomb of Queen Arsinoe of Egypt, designed before 247 B.C. to hold her metal statue suspended in mid-air.[2] One may add that pictures from Herculaneum of Egyptian scenes show various uses of cupolas over cylindrical and cubical buildings, apparently Hellenistic and of stone.[3] It is natural to see their beginnings in third-century Egypt.

Very few actual buildings survive to recall this phase. Four or five centuries later, as the Oriental Reaction gets under way, we find in Syria, in the Hauran, houses completely Babylonian in plan and form, completely Greek in their dry stone construction.[4] Similar compounds may have appeared earlier in the Seleucid Empire. In Egypt, Alexandria has a famous series of large vaulted cisterns, laid down, one would think, in the prosperous times of the third century and certainly existing in the middle of the first, when Hirtius, the historian of Julius Caesar, said that all the buildings of the city dispensed with timber and were held together by vaults of concrete and dressed stone.[5] These cisterns, as published by Napoleon on Plates 36 and 37 of his *Egypt*, are rectangular buildings of several aisles, and fall into two types, one of longitudinal arches and transverse arches at different levels and resting on piers of cruciform plan, one with both sets of arches at the same level, supported on rough 'Corinthianesque' columns. The structures have a scientific, Hellenistic look, although one must admit some of the carved capitals have a debased, Christian appearance.[6]

Vaults on a small scale cover some third-century tomb-chambers, which are far more rationally built than the Saite Egyptian. One example at Pydna is dated about 280 B.C.[7] The famous tomb at

[1] So Strabo, p. 738 (XVI, 1, §5), quoted, like so much else, by J. Baldwin Brown in an article still valuable and stimulating (*JRIBA*, 1889, pp. 137 ff.).
[2] Pliny, *Natural History*, XXXIV, §148.
[3] *Ercolano*, I (Baiardo, 1755), Tav. XLVIII, illustrates a splendid example.
[4] Robertson, pp. 313–4 and Fig. 133.
[5] *Alexandrian War*, Chap. I.
[6] Napoleon, Pl. 36, nos. 5–8.
[7] Heuzey, Pls. 17–21.

Pergamum, assigned to the early second century, has already a 'groined' vault, that is, two tunnels of the same size and at the same level intersecting over a square compartment, the whole constructed of large squared stones without mortar.[1] Plain undated tunnel vaults, probably of the third century, include the passages into the stadia of Epidaurus and Olympia and the two descending tunnels at Didyma.[2] Moreover, Vitruvius, referring to the 'Greek' type of palaestra, which might well go back to this age, recommends an oblong sweating-room with a tunnel vault and a circular Laconicum (dry sweating-room), the height of which to the springing of the dome should equal the diameter.[3]

Simple datable arches of an early period are rare. The stoas at Alinda and Aegae, both in Asia Minor and on very sloping sites, had lofty substructures of most beautiful masonry. Aegae, though not Alinda, is very near Pergamum, and uses the slope in a very Pergamene way.[4] As Pergamene architecture flourished most some years after 200 B.C., Aegae also is probably of the second century. Its details, on the other hand, are pure compared with much of the Pergamene. Although on its outer side Aegae had three storeys, only the uppermost was colonnaded, corresponding to the low colonnaded façade which it turned to the agora. It avoided, in fact, the two tiers of colonnades fashionable about 150 B.C. in Pergamum and Athens.[5] Inside, a row of large cut stone arches divides the substructure longitudinally—the only place in the building where arches are used. Alinda apparently lacked the arches inside, replaced by piers lengthened on the longitudinal axis, but had large undecorated windows, alternately arched and rectangular, in the back wall of the middle storey. Logically, the arched window had the wider span, and the massive, beautifully rusticated wall provided more than sufficient buttressing. So the Arch had still not infected the Greek Orders; nor was it, perhaps, to do so until nearly 100 B.C.[6]

[1] Illustrations of this tomb seem rather inaccessible. A diagram of the vault is given in Choisy, *Histoire de l'Architecture*, I (Paris, 1899), p. 518.

[2] See above, p. 193. Miss Shoe tentatively suggests that the part of the building, a central part, where they occur is perhaps as early as 300 B.C. (*Greek Mouldings*, pp. 83 and 123). But far later the Roman architects were avoiding such sloping tunnels.

[3] Vitruvius, V, xi, 2.

[4] Wycherley, in the *Town Planning Review*, 1951–2, p. 199.

[5] See below, p. 249.

[6] See below, p. 260.

In the third century Italian arches are no more advanced than
Greek.   Indeed, the Latin for 'vault', though not for 'arch', was
borrowed, as we saw, from Greek.   The early dates of Etruscan
arches are unproven.   The older tombs are trabeated or corbelled,
and the famous 'Tunnel of Pythagoras', near Cortona, a tomb-
chamber with a true tunnel vault, is placed by Riis in the second
century.[1]   The urn from Chiusi, figured by Robertson and
modelled, it seems, on a stately house, shows a big arched entrance
on the short sides, but is no earlier and probably much later than
300 B.C.   Canosa in Apulia has chamber tombs of two kinds and
periods, the earlier without stucco and with unscientific tunnel
vaults, the later with properly built tunnels, engaged columns and
painted false windows—Hellenistic elements all arriving together.
Nachod suggests that this second type dates from the mid-third
century; and certainly it recalls the tomb at Pydna.[2]

In Rome arches were used to support (?) a road of 216 B.C. and
an aqueduct of 179 B.C.[3]   Much more remarkably, their ornamental use went back, according to Livy, to 196 B.C., when
Stertinius, instead of triumphing, erected two in the Forum and
one in the Circus Maximus, and on them set up gilded statues
of himself.[4]   One must reserve one's views on the existence
and importance of these first triumphal arches.   Delphi can show
Greek examples of statues on pairs of columns, forerunners of the
Roman triumphal arch.[5]   The first Roman examples perhaps
resembled the Delphic, but would be called 'arches' on the
analogy of their descendents.   Certainly, the result of our inquiry
has suggested that in civilised towns the architect who attempted
to use the arch on serious buildings would need all his skill with
podia and receding planes to make it tolerable to the classical eye.

3. LATER HELLENISTIC ARCHITECTURE, 200–80 B.C.

We have now arrived at that intermediate period (*c.* 200–80 B.C.),
when Rome was already the political mistress of the Mediterranean, but not yet the cultural leader that she became in the time
of Sulla.   This period is known to us best from Pergamum,
Delos and Pompeii.   It is marked by a new type of stoa and

[1] See M. E. Blake, *Ancient Roman Construction in Italy* (Washington,
1947), p. 192.
[2] See above, pp. 242 and 246.
[3] Livy, 22, xxxvi, and 40, li.
[4] Livy, 33, ii.
[5] See Dinsmoor, p. 327.

covered market, several new forms of house and a certain contamin-
ation of the Greek Orders, provoking a reaction by the School of
Hermogenes.   Towards its end, Rome suddenly surpassed all her
rivals in engineering.

The new stoas were an invention of Pergamum, and are found
not only there but as gifts of Pergamene kings (196–133 B.C.) in
Athens and Delphi.   They are of two storeys, the lower Doric,
the upper Ionic, each with a complete and almost purely Doric
entablature.   The Ionic columns are oval on plan, the better to
incorporate the intervening stretches of balcony.   The intermediate entablature replacing the simple architrave anticipates
Roman work.   But the whole effect is uglier and cruder than the
Roman; for Roman builders equalised the two floors and usually
freed their upper order from the balcony.   The Pergamenes still
mistakenly observed the proportions of a Doric temple cella
between the two colonnades.[1]   The back walls of these stoas
might have a long series of blank arched niches.   So even in
Pergamene work the arch was used in the least obtrusive place,
where it was allowed to appear at all.[2]

This is an age of large secular halls, such as the Hypostyle Hall
at Delos and the Basilica of Pompeii, almost classifiable as covered
markets and made of new materials to suit the needs of new
crowds.[3]   We know the date of the earliest at Rome, the Basilica
Porcia, built appropriately beside the Forum in 184 B.C.[4]   Why the
type is called Basilica (perhaps meaning 'Royal Stoa') no one
knows, except that in Italy it always included a magistrate's
tribunal, as did the normal forum in the open air.   The king,
perhaps a mere magistrate so called, could in some Hellenistic
city have pronounced judgment in some similar building, just as at
Athens the King Archon and the wall containing the Constitution
occupied the Royal Stoa west of the Agora.[5]   The Hypostyle Hall
at Delos is probably called a Stoa in the Delian building accounts,
yet is rightly considered an early basilica.[6]   It seems of about

---

[1] See above, p. 143.

[2] In the stoa of Eumenes at Athens the niches were masked by a flat
marble wall.   See V. Koehler, *AM*, 1878, Taf. 7.

[3] In the present state of our knowledge, D. S. Robertson has said the
last word on their purpose.   See his p. 268.

[4] Livy, XXXIX, 44, vii.

[5] See above, p. 200.

[6] For its ancient name of 'The Stoa by the precinct of Poseidon', see
the extracts made by the French from these accounts and printed as an
appendix to *Delos, La Salle Hypostyle* (1914).   For its comparison with
a basilica, see Robertson, pp. 180 ff.

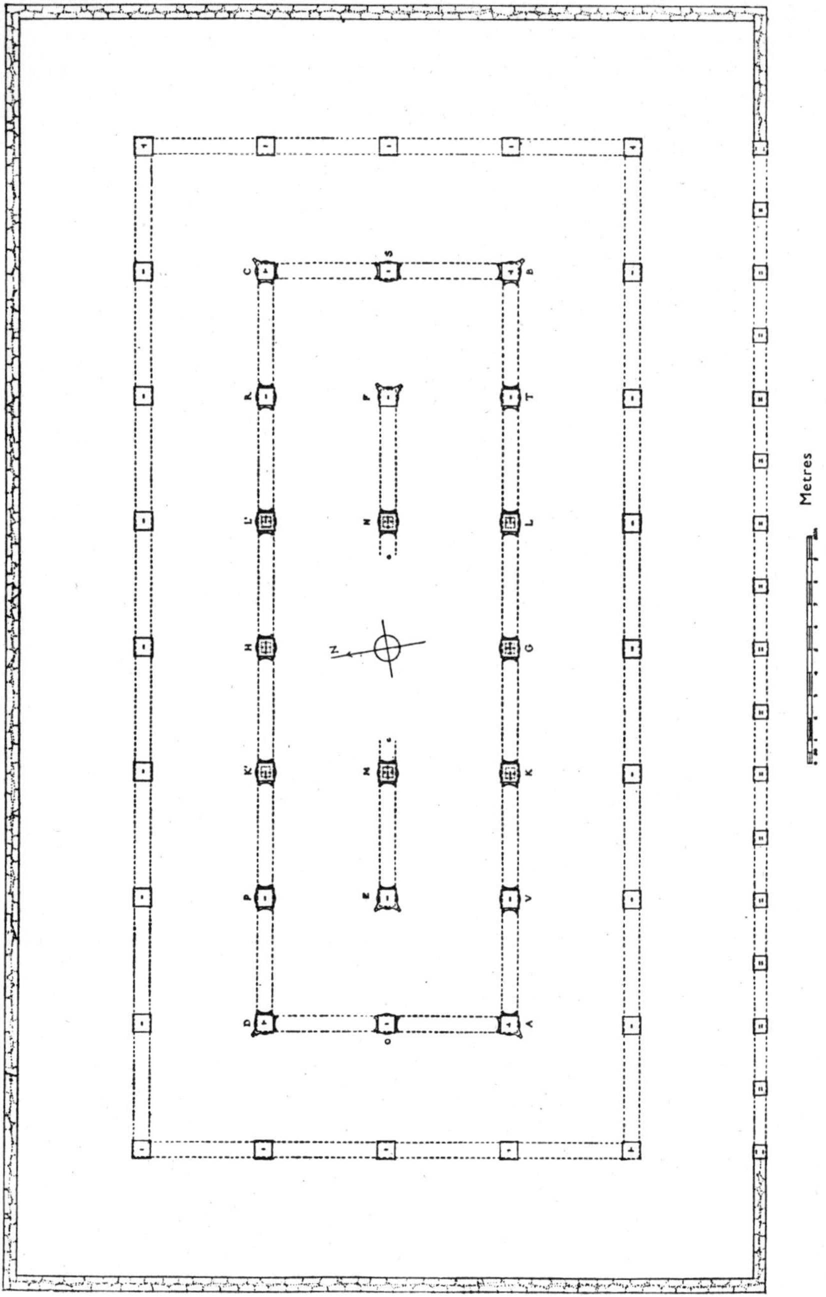
C
S
B
R
F
T
L'
N
L
H
N
G
K'
N
K
P
E
V
D
O
A
Metres

200 B.C., and, in its inner details at least, very pure.[1]   Though
rectangular, it was still centrally planned in the Greek manner,
with a sloping hipped roof supported on five rows of internal
columns and broken by a lantern over a central space two aisles
wide (see Fig. 78).   The extraordinary capitals with two juxtaposed diagonal volutes probably supported the central ridge where
the lantern interrupted it.   Even more remarkably, the piers
forming a frame for the lantern appear to have rested directly in
these capitals which makes it hard to restore any architrave at
all.[2] Vitruvius' Basilica at Fano,[3] with its great timber uprights,
was in the same tradition, which continued into the early Middle
Ages.

The Basilica at Pompeii, the oldest to survive in Italy, was a
brick building, thoroughly eastern in technique.   A comparison
of its columns with the Hellenistic columns of Nippur in Babylonia
will show that the thin bricks used for both were cut into sectors
of alternating shapes for alternate courses.[4]   An apse to hold the
tribunal appears neither here nor on the first extant basilicas in
Rome.

The Italian Forum assumes in the second century a definite
architectural shape.   Surrounded like the Greek Agora by
colonnades masking shops, it has grown, unlike the Agora, into
a long and fairly narrow enclosure with gates in the entrances, and
is not intended to take wheeled traffic.   According to Vitruvius,
gladiatorial fights are staged in it,[5] which explains why at Pompeii
the colonnades are already two storeys high.   Even more important, its plan, even in second-century Pompeii, is to some
degree axial, with the chief temple facing the original civic building
down the long axis.[6]   Buildings are symmetrically disposed and
lead the eye to a focus.   The technique of all buildings and the
plans of most are still wholly Greek.   But Italy is already asserting
her love of symmetry; as will become even clearer from the private
houses of the time.

[1] This makes one suspect that Leroux was wrong to restore for the
exterior triglyphs projecting beyond the architrave (*Salle Hypostyle*,
1909, Fig. 29).
[2] So Poulsen and Vallois, *Delos*, Fasc. II (1914), 'Nouvelles Recherches',
Fig. 24.
[3] Vitruvius, V, 1, vi.
[4] Delbrueck, II, p. 97, who gives diagrams.
[5] Vitruvius, V, 1, i–ii.
[6] See for a good plan R. C. Carrington, *Pompeii* (Oxford, 1936), Fig. 20
—after Mau-Kelsey, Plan II.   The columns are widely spaced, but the
knowledge of construction so primitive that the architrave is of wood.

The new type of Greek house, found at Delos (see Fig. 79) from about 150 B.C., is really a more sumptuous version of the Olynthian.[1] The yard of Olynthus has now become a small, square, colonnaded court, sometimes of two storeys and in all cases with very lofty columns, usually Doric, but of Ionic proportions. The north walk of the colonnade is usually wider and longer, and sometimes higher than the others, and masks the fronts of the principal rooms, in these houses wider than their depth. A sunny colonnade has thus replaced the 'prostas'.[2] But this rational plan reached Delos only about 150 B.C. Previously the houses had been as higgledy-piggledy as the town. In most the peristyle is

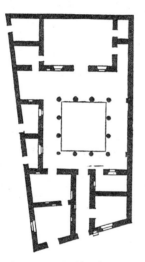

an awkward addition, for instance in the House of Cleopatra, where it dates from 138 B.C.[3] The houses first built at that time, such as the House of the Trident and the House of Dionysos, were really planned round their peristyles: but the older merely adopted the new fashion. Is it too much to consider the monumental peristyle an importation from Hellenistic Athens, whose property Delos became in 166 B.C.? The details, at any rate, are exquisite when compared with the Pergamene.

Fig. 79   Delian house, plan.

In southern Italy about 200 B.C. a native type of house, whose antecedents are still unknown,[4] reached perfection in the earliest houses of Pompeii. We know from the famous marble plan of Rome, the 'Forma Urbis', last engraved about A.D. 200,[5] that it had a long life and was still common then. But

[1] See above, p. 204. One very sumptuous house, probably of the second century but with a large Imperial Roman insertion, has now been published by G. Pesce, *Il Palazzo delle Colonne in Tolemaide di Cirenaica* (Rome, 1951). It is noteworthy for a large columnar hall on the axis of the main peristyle and barely separated from it—standing to it, in fact, almost as the Pompeian 'tablinum' to the 'atrium'.

[2] For which, see above, p. 204.

[3] See J. Chamonard in *Delos, Le Quartier du Théâtre* (Paris, 1922), p.70.

[4] Earlier house-types are known only from models, few and disputable and altogether unlike the Pompeian House.

[5] For some account of this official city plan, see Lanciani, *Ruins and Excavations of Ancient Rome*, pp. 95 ff.

in Pompeii at any rate it was never altered later, except for the worse. For in the second century B.C. Pompeii still revolved round the richer landowners.

The first Pompeian houses, when we meet them, are already strongly Hellenised. The more sumptuous already have at the rear a Greek peristylar court and Greek rooms sometimes covering more than half the site. Only one house, that of the Surgeon, appears to precede 200 B.C.[1] and happens to lack these Greek features; but this is no clear proof that they had then not reached Pompeii. Their importance in the second century would argue that they are as old here as stone houses; and this agrees with Vitruvius, who seems to consider the peristyle, of greater width than depth and apparently surrounded by the more private rooms, an essential feature of his 'Italian House'.[2] Evidence that many houses once stopped short with the 'tablinum', the last room with a Latin name, can be gathered only from Varro, who says that 'at one time during summer men dined in the country in the garden, in town in the tablinum', as if the tablinum were a pleasant room overlooking a small back garden.[3]

Decoration, as we saw during the second century, was Greek. So also were the blank façades on the streets. In the first century A.D., when Pompeii had gone down in the world, small shops were carved out of the frontages of the houses, as they were in parts of Rome. But in our period, the Tufa Period, the better houses had nothing to do with shops. The streets of the rich had a truly Hellenistic tranquillity (see Fig. 80); and one may assume that commerce was relegated to the quarter round the Forum.[4]

Nevertheless, the chief feature of the Pompeian House, the long and lofty atrium, half court and half front room, entered immediately from the short entrance vestibule (fauces) on the street, owes the Greeks nothing in its original form. At Pompeii it has always its longer axis from back to front, and its centre open

[1] Mau-Kelsey, p. 280.

[2] Vitruvius, VI, 3. The Italian peristyle, unlike the Greek, had often a garden, protected in some cases by a low wall between the columns. This is probably in consequence of its different position.

[3] Quoted by the grammarian Nonius, p. 83.

[4] To this day the shops of a Greek town are concentrated in a bazaar, with no tenements above them. I owe my awareness of this Greek aspect of early Pompeii to Axel Boethius (*Roman and Greek Town Architecture*, Göteborg, 1948). Wycherley, on the contrary, supposes in his seventh chapter that the normal Greek house would readily have shops attached, but has to admit (p. 187) that the evidence of Olynthus is against him.

to the sky. The roof is compluviate, that is, slopes inwards, conveying the rain into a tank or impluvium under the central opening. Such atria are the rule, too, among the comparatively few houses so far known at Herculaneum. But one, the 'Samnite House', has an atrium that was lit, like certain types of basilica, by an open colonnade filling the space between its own roof and those of the lower surrounding rooms. It could therefore have had a

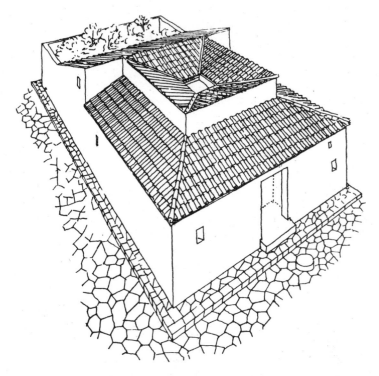

Fig. 80   Pompeian House, exterior.

hipped roof with no central opening—which would make it unique among known examples.[1]

The typical Pompeian house is symmetrical about a long axis, so that through the front door one has a glimpse of the atrium and even more of the building (see Fig. 81). On either side of the

[1] I saw it only during repairs and reconstruction, and did not fully understand it. A publication of it seems hard to find. I am now informed that it had an impluvium.

fauces are rooms originally opening on to the atrium, and on either side of the atrium other small rooms, perhaps offices, as we are still in the semi-public part of the house. They are interrupted by the alae, or 'wings', two rectangular recesses opening generally off the far end, sometimes off the middle of the atrium. In most cases these alae reach to the side walls of the house. Their use is still obscure. Vitruvius alleges that they held ancestral busts.[1] They may also have accommodated clients waiting their turn to

Fig. 81   Pompeian House, interior.

enter the tablinum, or reception room. In ancient Italy the rich noble possessed, besides his slaves, a large number of poor, free dependents, or 'clients', whom his largesse was supposed to help and who in their turn were expected to fight and vote for their patron. The train of humiliated clients awaiting their turn at the levée is familiar to every reader of the Roman poets.[2] Mau also

[1] Vitruvius, VI, 3, vi.
[2] Juvenal gives a very lively description in his First Satire.

sees in the alae a device for letting in light to the atrium from out-side, especially useful if atria were ever completely roofed.[1] Facing the fauces across the atrium is the open front of the tablinum, a large square reception-room, originally protected against winter draughts by curtains or timber 'hall-screens', opened or closed to taste, as we see from one screen preserved at Herculaneum. Its back is as open as its front, and in richer houses gives directly on to the peristyle, the wholly Greek and private portion of the house (see Figs. 82, 83). The rooms or passages flanking the tablinum between atrium and peristyle have no regular form. Vitruvius complains that the passage found here is miscalled the 'andron', or men's room.[2] The bedrooms and dining-rooms round the peristyle are Greek, and often culminate at the rear of the house in a large room, the oecus, closing the main axis.

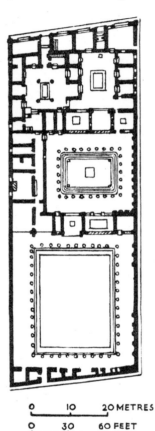

o   10   20 METRES

o   30   60 FEET

Fig. 82   Pompeii, House of
the Faun, plan.

At Pompeii we find all three forms of compluviate atrium named by Vitruvius,[3] the Tuscan, without intermediate supports, the tetrastyle, with four columns at the corners of the impluvium, and the Corinthian, with a regular peristyle —names that seem to show that columns in atria are a Greek importation. The largest atrium at Pompeii, that in the House of the Silver Wedding, is 54 feet long by 40 feet wide (excluding the alae) and had four Corinthian columns, each $22\frac{3}{4}$ feet high (as against $18\frac{3}{4}$ on the Hephaisteion at Athens). The most impressive, in the House of the Faun, is

[1] Mau-Kelsey, p. 253.
[2] Vitruvius, VI, 7, v.
[3] Vitruvius, VI, 3, i.

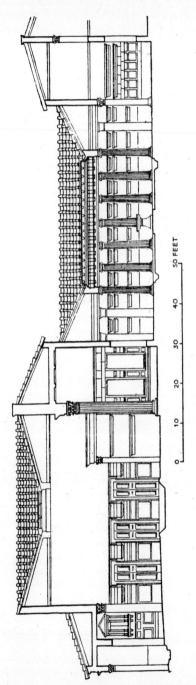

Fig. 83   Pompeii, House of the Faun, longitudinal section.

nearly as large (51 feet long) and 'Tuscan'. In their ruined state
(see Pl. 17) they convey no impression of their former soaring
proportions—sometimes they were twice as high as the peristyle
behind them.[1]   Originally a great wall, supported across the alae
by large wooden 'lintels', enclosed their compluviate roof on all
four sides.   The lateral rooms, the alae and even the tablinum
had far lower roofs, for the most part sloping downwards to the
outside of the house or to the peristyle.   In 'Tuscan' examples
the roof of the atrium itself rested in the first instance on two
enormous horizontal cross-beams running from high in its side
walls and forming in the centre the front and rear edges of the
central opening.   Tiles and revetments were of Greek type, with
lion spouts.   But the height and openness of the atrium and the
independence of its roof suggest, when taken with the description
in Vitruvius[2] of other atria, the 'tortoise-shaped' and the 'displuviate', and the actual model in Florence of a 'displuviate'
atrium,[3] that the Pompeian examples derive at no long interval
from lofty and completely covered astylar halls.

These houses are the first great architectural achievement of
Italy.   It has been the fashion lately to belittle Pompeii.   But
where in our own civilisation can we find small provincial towns as
elegant as the Pompeii of the Tufa Period?

Although in A.D. 200 many rich Roman houses were still
'Pompeian',[4] the Romans were beginning even under the Republic
to develop dwellings of very different design.   At Pompeii, as
space became more valuable, an upper floor was occasionally
added to the rooms just behind the atrium.[5]   Some scholars,
following Varro,[6] believe that the tablinum in very early times had
been a dining-room.   The first upper-room it became the custom
to add was called the 'cenaculum' or supper-room—which would
suit equally well this view of the tablinum and the position of the
oldest upper-rooms, sometimes supplanting it, sometimes appended
to it, but in any case directly above it at Pompeii.   But very soon
'cenaculum' was used of every upper-room, and very soon, too,

[1] The reader can test the details of my description from the series of
careful restorations of these houses figured in Mau-Kelsey.   Vitruvius
prescribes for some atria twice as long as the largest at Pompeii (VI, 3, iv).
[2] Vitruvius, VI, 3, ii.
[3] Robertson, Fig. 127.
[4] See above, p. 252.
[5] See Mau-Kelsey, pp. 267 ff, to which I owe my argument about
'cenacula'.
[6] See above, p. 253.

Rome became a city of 'cenacula', as Cicero tells us it was in the mid-first century.[1] As he also tells us in the same passage, the Campanians, from Pompeii and elsewhere, had then little admiration for Roman houses. Nevertheless, the upper floor and the built-up block, when brought by the Imperial architects—one would rather call them engineers—to the pitch of excellence found in Hadrianic and Severan Ostia, were to provide a lesson in good-mannered urbanism more immediately relevant to our own age than is the refinement of early Pompeii.

At this time, the Orders underwent various modifications. This book must omit local and sterile corruptions of them, such as the 'Corinthian-Doric' Temple at Paestum.[2] But by the second century it was everywhere the custom to give a colonnade, whether of Ionic or Doric columns, a Doric architrave and frieze and an Ionic cornice, usually with dentils. Pompeian peristyles, Pergamene stoas, the Bouleuterion at Miletus and the Roman sarcophagus of Scipio Barbatus, apparently of the third century B.C.,[3] all show this form of entablature. It was made easier by the increasing approximation of Doric and Ionic columns. In Delian houses the Doric columns can be over eight lower diameters high—almost the proportions of classical Ionic. We are here in the milieu of Vitruvius, for whom Doric columns, whether of temples or stoas, are always to be at least seven lower diameters high and spaced at least two triglyphs apart.[4] Ionic capitals, whether in Syracuse, Tarentum, the stage building at Epidaurus or the Capitol of Pompeii, each have four diagonal volutes. Less comprehensibly, the palmettes in the axils of their volutes, instead of lying flat across the echinus, grow vertically upwards across the whole width of the canalis. This fashion is useful for dating many Ionic capitals to about the second century B.C.[5]

At this time, too, Corinthian capitals, especially in Italy, were very free. Egyptian work followed the capital at Epidaurus, with no cauliculi for the central volutes and with slim, graceful leaves failing

---

[1] *De Lege Agraria*, II, 96.

[2] Robertson, Figs. 90-1.

[3] See *Cambridge Ancient History*, Pls. IV, 9, 98; Lanciani, *Ruins*, pp. 321, ff. Scipio was consul in 298 B.C. Such a sarcophagus in the third century is remarkable. Delbrueck (II, p. 154) puts similar Sicilian sarcophagi in the second. Italian Doric often shows a cornice not with dentils but with rolls like those of Kardaki (above, p. 136).

[4] Vitruvius, IV, 3, and V, 9.

[5] See Delbrueck II, p. 155: *Notizie degli Scavi*, 1943, pp. 119-24. The dates are uncertain; but at least none are Imperial.

to cover, even at the bottom, the surface of the elongated bell. In Asia Minor and Greece, though the proportions were sometimes strange and the top of the bell sometimes unduly bare (as in the Propylon to the Bouleuterion at Miletus), capitals kept closest to the canonical form. In Italy, omitting the figured capitals with heads in the centre of each face, used in barbarous work of the fourth and third and in frivolous work (as at Pompeii) of the second century, we find a type with large kale-like leaves enclosing the two inner volutes on each face and, above and outside them, a very large six-petalled lily (see Fig. 84). This type, most

Fig. 84   Corinthian capital, Praeneste.

popular just after 100 B.C., had disappeared entirely by the time of Augustus.[1]

The use of the Orders, too, was now changing.   Builders were at last combining them with the Arch.   It was still rare in Delian houses.   But at Priene, on the south side of the Assembly Hall, it perhaps formed the only feature of the blank astylar south wall, an opening $14\frac{1}{2}$ feet across and 11 feet high.   Outside it was a small enclosure, apparently for officials, who thus faced through

---

[1] Robertson is full and admirable on these Italian capitals.   Delbrueck (II, pp. 157 ff.) gives much information, as does Weigand, in *Jahrbuch des Instituts*, 1914, pp. 37 ff.

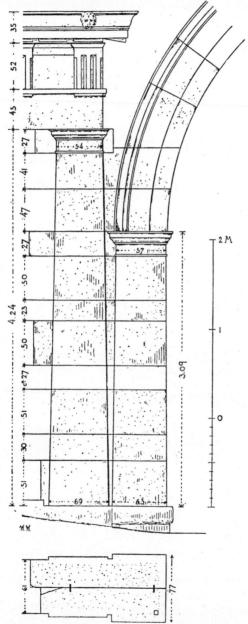

Fig. 85 Arched entrance to Agora, Priene.

it the crowd inside the main building.   Although still plain,[1] it
thus occupies a more important position than ever before; and
prepares us for the extension made to the Agora just about 150
B.C.,[2] which includes the whole eastern approach to the central
space and a great arched gate to the east.   Here we find the oldest
known specimen of exhibition architecture.   The architect has
dragged the arch out of its obscurity in tombs and basements, set
it upon two piers and given it a span of 20 feet.   More boldly yet,
he has omitted to buttress it at the haunches.   He has decorated
it like an Ionic architrave with only two fasciae and a crowning
mould—a form, however, quite undatable in this period and
milieu (see Fig. 85).   So a designer of 'exhibition building' can
still shock the conservatives with a simple arch, and incidentally
give it one of its classical forms, an 'archivolt', not long before
100 B.C.[3]

Priene can boast yet another transitional example, again of
about 100 B.C., in the Lower Gymnasium (see Fig. 86).   One
room exhibits a big blind order of half-columns standing on a
podium in front of a series of niches, and broken in the centre by
a large arched niche.[4]   At Pompeii, besides the fairly common
vaulted bedrooms, one comes across a little masterpiece like the
dining-room in the House of the Silver Wedding.   It is later than
80 B.C., as its decoration shows, but marks a culmination of the
type.[5]   The end next to the door has a shallow segmental vault.
The rest, where the couches stood, has two narrow flat-roofed
'aisles' and a large central nave with a semicircular vault.   Slim
Corinthian columns and a complete entablature mark off the aisles
and seem to support the tunnel.

At Pompeii, finally, one encounters the most striking invention
of all, the pilaster, which seems to make its architectural début
here, at the entrances of the tablinum and alae (see Pl. 17).   Here,
of course, it has to be a corner pilaster, with one front towards
the ala or tablinum, one towards the atrium; the wider towards

[1] Robertson's text seems to have confused this arch with the arched
gate.   The photographs (including his own Pl. VII) show a plain arch,
included also in the elevation *Priene*, Abb. 223.
[2] *Priene*, p. 229, argues that it was planned about 200 B.C., before the
agora was enlarged.
[3] *Priene*, Abb. 199 and 200.   The piers are almost pilasters, which
gives them a late appearance.
[4] *Priene*, Abb. 273.
[5] Carrington, *Pompeii*, Pl. XVI.   Modillions (see below, p. 278)
appear on the cornice, in place of dentils.

the smaller room, because it seems to derive from the Greek door-jamb, in form an anta. But it is a true pilaster, with base and capital of the same profile as on the corresponding column of its order (usually Corinthian) and at the same time no diminution in the flattened shaft.[1] Northern and central Italy took at least a century to adopt the pilaster. The Temple at Cori, of about 80 B.C., seems to have had flat engaged piers round the cella, with the profile of Greek antae; and the Republican Theatre at Ferento

Fig. 86   Lower Gymnasium, Priene.

had strange mixed pilasters, with Attic base, fluted, diminishing shaft and half-Greek anta-capital. When, however, the Temple

[1] For these pilasters, see Mau-Kelsey, Figs. 135, 147, etc. The alternative treatment, with a three-quarter column at the corners, is much rarer at Pompeii. It is amusing to find R. Wittkower, on p. 39 of his *Architectural Principles in the Age of Humanism* (London, 1949), calling this use of the pilaster 'singular' on the openings in the Pantheon. It is for such a position that the pilaster was apparently invented. Most of the pilasters in the Palace of Ptolemais (see above, p. 241) seem no earlier and are probably far later than the Pompeian. Only those on Pesce's small 'pavilion' or 'frontispiece' (Pesce, Tav. V) could be as old: but he gives no evidence for them.

of Fortuna at Praeneste (*c.* 80 B.C.) employed the pilaster, it marked out, as in so much else, the future methods of Roman Imperial building.

All this impurity provoked a reaction, led by the architects of the Temple of Olympian Zeus at Athens and by Hermogenes of Magnesia. It is true that the Temple of Zeus, planned before 164 B.C., is the first large building we know to employ the Corinthian Order externally: but it had probably many predecessors. Its capitals are stiffly orthodox, while the remains of its cornice show some resemblance to the more famous Ionic specimens of the fourth century.[1] By contrast with the broken-backed striations of most contemporary moulding, not to mention the endless Pergamene chamfers, Hermogenes returned to the careful sections of his classical predecessors.[2] In his temples of Teos and Magnesia, of the later second century, he rejected the Ionic diagonal capital, and he formulated a series of proportions closer to the classical Greek than to the work of his contemporaries.

He could not stem the current of the age. His doors are attenuated. He combined frieze and dentils in one entablature. On the other hand, the Attic Base, on which, as Dinsmoor shows, he at last decided as the best form for use in an Ionic column, became the rule from this time onwards. The movement he represents may soon have reached Rome itself, where some early temples show an almost Hermogenean purity. The most famous is the Round Temple by the Tiber. It is entirely of Pentelic marble, and built with anathyrosis and clamps. Greek also are its stylobate, slightly raised above the floor, and its beautiful pseudo-isodomic cella wall. Its Corinthian columns have capitals close in form to those of Olympian Zeus at Athens. Experts cannot tell whether it is of this age or the Augustan, a century later.[3] In any case, Hermogenes maintained classical standards of design in the Greek east, standards embraced by Vitruvius in Rome, and the movement that under Augustus at last

---

[1] I still hold that the block in Athens figured by Penrose (Fig. 15) is from its cornice. G. P. Stevens, followed, one infers reluctantly, by Miss Shoe (Text, p. 19), would date it in the fifth century B.C. and assign it to the pedestal of the bronze statue to Athena Promachos. In profile, however, it is quite unlike any fifth-century moulding in any position. The slight scamillus on its upper surface (Stevens, *Hesperia*, XV, p. 108) is quite consistent with a position in the cornice. Compare the bedmould on the Mausoleum, figured by Lethaby (*Greek Buildings*, Fig. 51).

[2] Shoe, *Greek Mouldings*, I, pp. 21, 24–5, etc.

[3] See Delbrueck, *Hellenistische Bauten*, II, pp. 43 and 162.

obliterated the provincial Italic versions of Ionic and Corinthian must surely have gained some of its strength from his buildings and his books.

Some time before 100 B.C. the engineering requirements of Rome result in extraordinary technical advances. Authorities agree that the present Mulvian Bridge (Ponte Molle), just north of Rome, dates substantially from 109 B.C.[1] Its arches have the unprecedented span of 60 feet (our widest Gothic vault, over the Lady Chapel at Ely, is a mere 46 feet across). It is entirely of stone, but held together by a tough lime mortar and marked by differentiation of material according to purpose—tufa for the core, travertine for the voussoirs on the faces of the arches, Gabine stone (peperino) for the rest of the facing. Roman concrete was only just beginning, and first appeared in a certainly datable context in the foundations of the Temple of Concord (121 B.C.)[2]

4. THE FIRST ROMAN STYLE, 80–30 B.C.

In the last fifty years of the Republic, Roman architecture came into its own. Its works represent in some ways the culmination of pure Hellenistic building, as concrete, still too brittle for large spans, was required to perform merely the function of cut-stone vaults farther east. Inside Italy there were special reasons for magnificent building in the attempts of generals to curry popular favour. Outside it, war and oppression were continuous; and nothing need detain us except at Athens.

The Temple of Fortuna at Praeneste (Palestrina), we now know for certain, was in many ways the most splendid ever erected in Italy. It dates from about 80 B.C., when Sulla settled his partisans in this desirable town. On the very steep southern slope of a limestone ridge, about 30 miles east of Rome, it commands a breezy view over a wide plain east of the volcanic Alban Hills. The goddess Fortuna gave her oracles here from at least the third century, and must have had a noble temple when Carneades visited Praeneste some time after 168 and declared that nowhere was Fortune more fortunate. But the present building, which underlies all old Palestrina, is apparently of one piece, and Sullan. Enormous and magnificently terraced, it comprises a lower, closed,

---

[1] See Delbrueck, I, p. 4.
[2] See Blake, *Construction*, p. 329. The substance in the foundations of the Aqua Marcia of 144 B.C. is still, according to Blake (p. 327), 'pseudo-concrete'.

colonnaded court flanked by a basilica on the right and a partly natural grotto on the left, and a much larger upper temple, presumably approached by broad staircases either side of the lower temple and itself consisting of terraces and crescents all built around a gigantic central covered staircase. For the lower court, Delbrueck remains the authority. The upper temple, revealed by an American air raid, has just been published.[1]

The lower court itself rests partly on cellars, the fronts of which, built of large polygonal blocks, formed a firm base for the open colonnaded screen, which seems to have enclosed it on the south, in a fashion quite popular under the later Republic.[2] Along its north side a colonnade of two stages masked the sheer rock of the hillside. Delbrueck makes the lower storey very Greek, the upper an arcade on very plain piers. But this seems unlikely, and not only because of Pergamene analogies. For the architect here was fond of trabeated façades and used the arch sparingly on the exterior, generally employing only single arches, and those in important places.[3] The best attested examples are the two large arches under the wings on the highest level. But the magnificent intermediate tiers present in the Pergamene manner a largely trabeated front, like the Stoa of Eumenes at Athens.

To the left (west) of the lower court was the cave, trimmed and tidied and presented about 80 B.C. with a magnificent mosaic floor, apparently a view of Alexandria from the sea.[4] To its right was the apsidal basilica (see Fig. 87), a hall 74 by 47 feet internally,

[1] By F. Fasolo and G. Gullini, *Il Santuario della Fortuna Primigenia a Palestrina* (Rome, 1953). They have defied all previous authorities, and dated the ensemble to about 160 B.C. I hope to recapitulate some of the more obvious arguments against them in the next few pages.

[2] For instance in the Porticus Octavia(e), in its present form Severan, but probably modelled on a Republican or Augustan plan (see p. 316). Here the central portion is treated as a propylon, with pediments but no gate wall. When Pevsner says of Adam's open screen at Osterley that it had no precedent in antiquity (*Middlesex*, Harmondsworth, 1951, p. 128), he shows his ignorance of these screens. Pevsner passes too many over-confident remarks on the architecture of peoples outside his own limited field.

[3] For Delbrueck's reconstruction, see Delbrueck, I, Taf. XIV. The remains of an arch over the extreme eastern opening of this arcade provide in reality no evidence for the others, as it was not visible from the Court (Delbrueck, II, Taf. I), but opened on to the east arcade (Delbrueck, I, Abb. 44). Gullini retains Delbrueck's arches, but cumbers the court with buildings up to the full height of the ground floor—on what evidence, I cannot see. On one terrace, according to Gullini, a row of arches appeared externally. I am somewhat doubtful of this. See below, p. 271, n. 4.

[4] For the date, see Blake, *Pavements*, pp. 140–1.

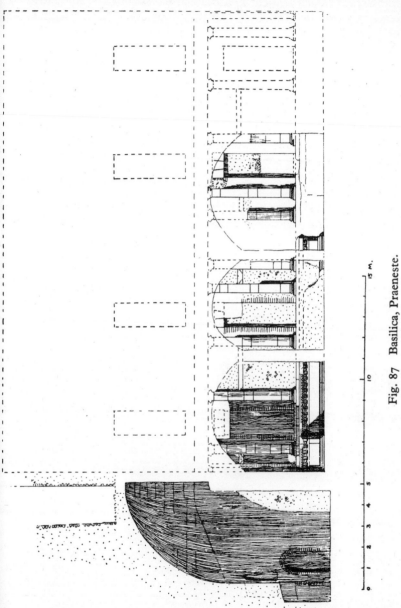

Fig. 87   Basilica, Praeneste.

excluding the semicircular apse, and strangely recalling some early Christian basilicas.[1] A projecting podium, with a complete Hellenistic entablature,[2] ran right round the interior, interrupted only by the entrance of the apse and the door from the court in the middle of the west side, although opposite this door it was partly cut away into a segmental niche extending its full height and perhaps designed for a cult-statue. The architect made the most of this cross-axis. For the large Corinthian order, which occupied the whole height of the walls above the podium, consisted of

Fig. 88   Roman model of a stage-building.

alternate engaged columns and pilasters; and, while he maintained this sequence, he spaced them most irregularly to give a large composition symmetrical about the niche and the west door. Short of the jambs of the northern apse he stopped the order altogether, so that with its tunnel-vaulted niches it formed an arcuated interruption. The design thus perpetuates in a very interesting way the old prejudice against the arch. A similar

[1] For pagan religious 'basilicas', see further Robertson, pp. 245–6. Note also the Kabeireion at Samothrace (Conze, *Samothrake*, II, p. 29).
[2] See above, p. 259.

interrupted order occurs in the ancient architect's model of a stage (see Fig. 88), discovered and published by Benndorf.[1] The floor of the apse, level with that of the main hall, contained the celebrated mosaic of the Nile,[2] a companion to that across the court.   Around the basilica, half-way up the wall, ran a subsidiary cornice, carefully broken before it reached each column, below which the wall in the wider spaces was treated as a slightly sunken panel.   Niches and windows appear above it.   The identity of this three-dimensional architecture and the Second Pompeian Style of 80–50 B.C., not only in principle but in detail, would seem complete.[3]   The actual plan is almost as elaborate as those of the cellas at Baalbek.[4]   The south external façade is even more remarkable, with its four engaged columns supported on brackets in a way not seen again till nearly four centuries later, on the Golden Gate of Spalato.[5]   In the two smaller side intervals are arches of masonry, but we do not know what filled the centre.

The lowest stage of the upper temple was a long and narrow terrace, supported on the south by a retaining wall of massive polygonal blocks laid in the Greek manner.   Here worshippers assembled for the ascent of the great double 'Persian' ramp,[6] the only Classical example, it seems, of any size, but sketched and 'restored' during the High Renaissance and so perhaps an influence on the 'Palladian' staircase.[7]   Unlike the stairs at Persepolis, it

[1] *Jahrbuch des Oesterreichischen Instituts*, 1902, p. 188.

[2] Blake, *Pavements*, pp. 140–1.

[3] For the resemblance see Winter, *Kunstgeschichte in Bildern*, p. 162.

[4] See below, p. 327.

[5] Gullini builds out the basement below, and turns these engaged columns into the responds of projecting aedicules.   But, as Delbrueck saw, the basement wall is an external wall, and neither extended vaults nor aedicules are possible.

[6] For this term, see above, p. 217.

[7] This is a complex matter, and my term probably begs several questions.   This type of stair is found in Palladio's designs for villas, notably Pl. 40 of his *Second Book of Architecture*.   His Villa Repeta, at Campiglia, furnishes us with a small but choice example of it (G. K. Loukomski, *Villas des Doges de Venise*, II (Paris, n.d.), Pl. 24).   In the works of English Palladians it occasionally runs riot, as at Chiswick House.   Palladio himself tells us (*Architecture*, I, 28 ad fin.) that he and many others have 'taken example' from an ancient double staircase up Monte Cavallo (the Quirinal) to a temple that he considers (IV, 12) the Temple of Jupiter.   IV, Pl. 25 shows on plan the substructure of this magnificent approach.   The temple we now know to be that of the Sun, erected by Aurelian after the Conquest of Palmyra (Lanciani, *Ruins*, pp. 430–4).   The oldest examples of such stairs we saw to be eastern (perhaps they even go back to ziggurats), and their rare appearances in the west could perhaps be ascribed to eastern influence.

was roofed, and had continuous Doric colonnades.[1]   The architrave shared the slope of the ramp, about fifteen degrees, and the abaci were actually tilted to follow suit (see Fig. 89)—an arrangement again probably unique in Classical architecture.

The landing in front of the next terrace, where the two ramps met, was roofed, it seems, on piers,[2] against which the Doric colonnades of the ramps ended in half-columns.   Below the landing, and in the middle of the south face between the ramps, was an enormous but fairly shallow arched niche, entered from the lowest terrace but with no access from those above.   Allowing room for only a narrow entrance on to the terrace to left and right of the landing, the staircase now proceeded in a single flight at right angles to the ramps, over a small intermediate terrace, to a wide court in front of the crowning hemicycle.

The terrace at the top of the double-ramp is magnificent and well preserved.   Each half is backed by an Ionic hemicycle between two Ionic stoas.   The colonnades, in fact, are broken back at the hemicycles, where in later, imperial work they would have run across them and masked them.   But a wall does cut off internally each of the stoas from the hemicycle, so preserving a slightly Greek feeling of measurable units.

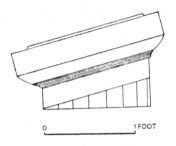

Fig. 89   Tilted capital, Praeneste.

Colonnades and hemicycles were all vaulted with long coffered tunnels, anticipating in character some famous Renaissance works,[3] and the backs of the straight stoas were divided into arched recesses (see Pl. 19). All this vaulting necessitated a blind storey above the Ionic columns on the south façade.   The resulting composition is Greek, with a proportion between open colonnade and blind storey of five and three.[4]   But the details are late Hellenistic,

---

[1] The main upward path, itself open to the sky, was hemmed in to the south by a thin colonnaded building above the outer wall of the ramp. Awkwardness was thus avoided at the junction of ramp and terrace.   But I cannot reconcile myself to the blank windowless south wall Gullini gives this building.

[2] It could have had arches between engaged columns.   Gullini leaves it roofless.   The evidence seems inadequate for any real decision.

[3] The Pazzi Chapel, for instance, and the Villa Giulia.

[4] See above, pp. 200 and 249.

mostly of local character. The bases are Attic. The shafts, as in all three Orders here, have an encircling fillet immediately below the Capital, found elsewhere in the first century B.C.[1] The Ionic capitals have the vertical palmette.[2] In front of the beautiful stylobate and the shallow gutter outside it, the terrace has a neat herringbone pavement of small terracotta tesserae, typical of the early first century. Before either hemicycle is a circular Hellenistic Doric puteal, one a real well-head, the other an altar[3]; and dignitaries will have gathered around each, as in the apse of a Christian church, if we may judge from the continuous benches, supported on beautiful brackets, along the back walls of the hemicycles.

The next terrace was narrow and its rear colonnade low, only about as high as the blind storey of the last. The two hemicycles, moreover, ate largely into its space. Arched niches occupied the entire length of its rear wall, even above the hemicycles, and there was no space for grand ceremonies.[4]

But the next court and central hemicycle worthily crowned the whole building. The plan of the hemicycle dictated the shape of the Palace of the Colonna, that now occupies its site; but only its vaulted substructure, with a straight façade along its diameter, appears to survive today. This façade has two short, shallow wings, each with a single arched opening framed inside two Corinthian pilasters and a complete entablature, forming a bay nearly square on elevation. It is an early specimen of the Roman 'arched order', so common later and originating naturally, as Baldwin Brown saw,[5] from a wish to apply the Orders to the tunnelled substructures of theatres and other buildings. The flanks of the wings are now obscured, but had apparently engaged Corinthian columns, the foremost carefully designed to meet the outer pilaster of the front. The repertory of Roman and Renaissance motifs is complete.

Almost the whole of Praeneste, including the walls of the

---

[1] For instance, on the Tabularium (Delbrueck, I, Taf. IX).

[2] For this, see above, p. 259.

[3] Gullini's plans put that of the eastern hemicycle off centre; but the authorities in charge of the actual remains do not yet seem to have made up their minds.

[4] Gullini believes that no colonnade existed on this terrace, unlike those below, in front of the arched niches. I am not certain he is right, as I found here no traces of the customary Praenestine drain, beautiful in itself and invaluable as evidence for the line of the façade.

[5] *JRIBA*, 1889, p. 144.

basilica, the engaged columns of the lower temple and the vaults and blind storeys of the upper, is concrete faced with quasi-reticulate 'opus incertum', which serves to date it rather closely. The first concrete, of *c.* 130 B.C., had an aggregate of rough stones about the size of a fist, and facing-stones of exactly the same sort. These were soon arranged more carefully to form 'opus incertum', and by Sulla's time approximated to a lozenge in shape (quasi-reticulate). The neat lozenges of real 'opus reticulatum' appear first, among dated buildings, on the Theatre of Pompey in 55 B.C. These various facings, of course, were always concealed with fine stucco. At Praeneste, moreover, the free-standing columns and their stylobates, the voussoirs of the arches and the bases and capitals of pilasters and engaged columns are of a hard bright limestone. Materials, in fact, are neatly differentiated according to position, though not so elaborately as in some other Sullan buildings. Marble, the favourite imperial facing-stone, has not yet appeared. Although in its details this temple shows none of the grossness of much imperial work, we already find at Praeneste a power of architectural combination that would do credit to the best of the later designers. It is unique among Roman buildings.

Other Sullan temples, as those of Jupiter Anxur at Terracina and Hercules at Tivoli, show the same technique and detailing as Praeneste on a less splendid scale.[1] The round 'Temple of the Sibyl' at Tivoli, whose details come very close to those of Praeneste, has a structural core of concrete, with concrete cella walls merging into the concrete of the podium and perhaps originally, though Delbrueck doubts this, a concrete dome above.[2] The Doric temple at Cori is a puzzle. It is delicate but barbarous, with mutules inside the pediment. On the whole it suits this date best.[3] At Rome the late Republican temple of Fortuna Virilis beside the Tiber is a degenerate little building, tetrastyle, with Ionic columns of travertine, that help to date it,[4] and a cella so broad that it reaches the side colonnades. The resulting engaged columns make the building pseudoperipteral, perhaps the earliest known

---

[1] See Blake, *Construction,* pp. 233–5. Gullini, to justify his early date for Praeneste, would wish to spin out the building of these Sullan temples over the century 160–60 B.C. He has not, I think, established his case.

[2] See Delbrueck, II, pp. 16–22.

[3] Delbrueck, II, pp. 23 ff.

[4] Travertine under the late Republic was used as a facing where the Empire used marble. See, e.g., Blake, *Construction,* p. 45.

East Curtain, Aigosthena

Plate 17

House of the Faun, Pompeii

Decoration in Second Pompeian style, House of Livia, Rome

(Reproduced from *Monumenti Inediti, pubicati dell' Instituto.*)

Plate

instance of this unsatisfactory and architecturally insignificant device.[1]

One would like, if one could, to assign to this period the far more interesting temple at Vienne.[2] Like the 'Corinthian-Doric' temple at Paestum and the Roman Republican temple at Gabii,[3] it has free-standing colonnades down the sides and an engaged order only at the rear, where the architect has varied pilasters with half-columns in an unsure but thoughtful, seemingly Republican way. Its cornice has the new invention, modillions,[4] but no dentils, so is lighter than known Augustan cornices. It shows intelligence and experiment, not yet the stereotyped refinement of the Augustan Maison Carrée.

In secular building, the Roman Theatre and the Roman Thermae emerge as definite types. Pompey, the first to build a wholly stone theatre, in 55 B.C., was forced by the flatness of the site, the low-lying Campus Martius north-west of the Capitol, to raise the auditorium on a vaulted concrete substructure. Here for the first time appears the good hydraulic concrete of reddish volcanic pozzuolana responsible for the extraordinary vaults peculiar under the Empire to the buildings of Rome and central Italy, in fact for the metropolitan style of Rome. This innovation is more important than alleged resemblances between the theatres of Pompey and of the Greek city, Mytilene.[5] The plan of the Roman Theatre is best postponed to the Augustan period.

The best-preserved Thermae are the Stabian Baths at Pompeii (see Fig. 90), in their present form of the Sullan Age, but already completely changed from their prototype, the Greek palaestra. The practical Italian mind has already invented, in place of braziers, furnaces (hypocausts) under the floors, to give a controlled heat.[6] These naturally made planning easier and smoother. From the colonnaded exercise-court, now subsidiary to the bath buildings, a vestibule leads into the rectangular apodyterium, or undressing-room, off the front portion of which the cold bathroom (frigidarium) opens, a domed circular building with four niches and a thick wall, giving a plan externally square. A central opening admitted light and air through the roof, as in the Pantheon. Designed

---

[1] For this temple, see Robertson, pp. 211–12.
[2] See the interesting note in Robertson, p. 340.
[3] See Delbrueck, II, pp. 5–10.
[4] See below, p. 278.
[5] Plutarch, *Pompey*, 42.
[6] About 100 B.C. See Pliny, *Natural History*, IX, 168.

for a large swimming-pool, this room undoubtedly inspired the earliest Christian baptisteries. On re-entering the apodyterium, one takes another door in the rear for the tepid bath (tepidarium), the hot bath (calidarium) next door to the main furnace. The whole arrangement, with the apodyterium at the cross-roads, was retained in the great Imperial Thermae. They improved, of course, on Pompeii in size, in symmetry and in their provisions for an easy and elegant circulation. But the type was already fixed in 80 B.C.[1]

The Tabularium, or Record Office, was rebuilt under Sulla on the east slope of the Capitol. As a building-type it naturally had few descendents. But as a work of at least three storeys using

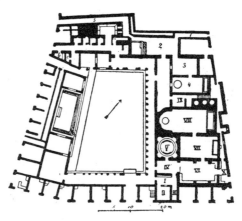

Fig. 90   Stabian Thermae, Pompeii.
Nos. 1–4 = Women's Bath and V = Cold Bath; VI = Changing-Room;
VII = Tepid Bath; VIII = Hot Bath; IX = Furnace.

concrete vaults it is as important and novel in its way as the Temple at Praeneste. It used the arch less sparingly on the exterior, and its top floor is faced with a 'Roman Order' of the sort described at Praeneste,[2] Doric, with upright oblong bays of proportions 9 by 7,[3] representing, however, not the ends of a succession of tunnels but the fenestration of a line of square compartments, each vaulted with a flattened and shapeless lid, running parallel with the façade. Again the architect varied his materials according to position, and—another Roman characteristic—avoided intricacies

---

[1] For the Stabian Baths, see Mau-Kelsey, pp. 186 ff.
[2] Above, p. 271. This arched order is further discussed below, pp. 309 ff.
[3] Robertson, Fig. 101.

of vaulting. Instead of the difficult sloping tunnel-vault, the stairs have a series of short horizontal tunnels at various levels. No tunnels intersect on the same level.[1] After all, most Roman labourers were slaves; and their employers did their best to avoid works like intersecting vaults too difficult for the servile intelligence. The shortcomings of the workers and the virtues of pozzuolana later made for clumsy pendentives. The usual long series of recesses, vaulted in concrete, opens off the rear wall of the gallery.

The most elaborate private house known, the Villa of the Papyri at Herculaneum (see Fig. 91), is still entirely Hellenistic. Excavated in the mid-eighteenth century, when it yielded papyri of the Epicurean philosophers, it has now again disappeared and is known only from the plan of Weber.[2] It almost certainly belonged

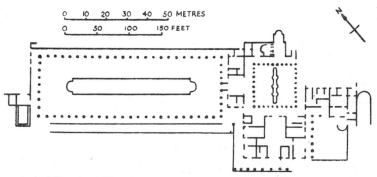

Fig. 91   Villa of the Papyri, Herculaneum: after Weber.

to the family of Piso, eminent in the Ciceronian Age. It ran from south-east to north-west, and had, to judge from the plan, a second-century nucleus, a villa typical of Campania, with a Tuscan atrium 48 feet by 34 feet internally, nearly as large as the best Pompeian examples, and a tablinum facing southwards with a view of the sea. This seems clear from the position of the alae. The Pisones turned the atrium round, converting the tablinum into a vestibule, added a peristyle on the north with a new tablinum on its west side, and then, west of this addition, constructed a further immense peristyle some 300 feet long, surrounded by rooms of

[1] See Delbrueck, I, Abb. 32 (Robertson, Fig. 100).
[2] Conveniently reproduced in E. R. Barker, *Buried Herculaneum* (London, 1908), Plan 7. A decimal point is misplaced on the scale, and makes the villa one-tenth of its real length.

choice shapes, interspersed with elegant statues and commanding various views of the sea. To the east of the original atrium and the smaller peristyle they added baths and domestic offices. This is the most lavish Hellenistic house we know, and the native Italian forms are almost submerged. Hellenism as strong as this marks much art and literature in the Ciceronian Age.

At Rome, the 'House of Livia' on the Palatine, which we are told once belonged to the famous late Republican orator, Hortensius, has some exquisite rooms of about 50 B.C. in the 'Second Pompeian Style'. But neither here nor elsewhere can one see much of the general plan. A Hellenising trend is apparent in the numerous peristyles with marble columns, which ancient writers seem to suggest were common at this time.

The competing generals now disposed of many engineers and workmen and, when playing for political power, would promise to settle their veterans in new towns ('coloniae') and curry popular favour with schemes of urban improvement. Lugdunum, or Lyons, for instance, was a colonia of 43 B.C., and Roman Carthage and Corinth were both inaugurated by Julius Caesar. Coloniae, being military camps, showed a general uniformity under the Empire, and are best postponed to our survey of that highly static society.

In Rome, Pompey combined his theatre with a large colonnaded enclosure, or 'porticus', for bargaining and lounging. Julius Caesar, more practically, laid out a forum for the relief of the overcrowded Forum Romanum, on its north side near the western end—the first of the series of imperial fora completed only under Hadrian. It is simple and rectangular, with at most one small hemicycle, perhaps because its architect was Attic, Athens being now the centre of the academic conservatives.[1] Julius honoured Athens, too, with a forum, a rectangular enclosure running east and west and entered from the classical Agora on the west through a Doric propylon of great purity.[2]

But Andronicus of Cyrrhus, probably one of its architects, showed himself more original, and recalls us from Roman organisation to Greek art. A typically Hellenistic scientist and theorist, he designed the Tower of the Winds, a combined water-clock and

---

[1] Cicero writes to Atticus in July, 45 B.C. 'What a disgrace! A compatriot of yours is enlarging our city, which he first saw only a year ago!' (*Ad Att.*, XIII, 35). A different work from the Forum, but revealing.

[2] See Stuart and Revett, I, Chap. I.

sundial near the east end of this forum. Vitruvius, who quotes him extensively in his first book and may even have worked under him for Caesar, thus acquiring his strong Greek bias, suggests that he would have wished to place this tower at the centre of an

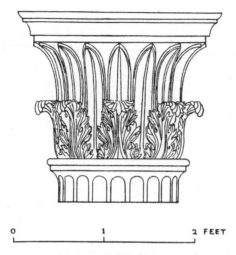

Fig. 92   Tower of the Winds, lanceolate capital.

octagonal city with a radiating street plan.[1]   Such a design, never carried out in antiquity, shows that under the late Republic Greeks retained some vitality.   The details of the Tower are equally original.   It is an octagon, with two small distyle porches and a small apse.   Each side faces a point of the compass and has a

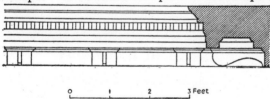

Fig. 93   Tower of the Winds, internal cornice.

relief of the appropriate wind.   The Corinthian columns of the porches have no bases and simple lanceolate capitals, that is, capitals where a ring of smooth spear-shaped leaves replaces the volutes and flowers of the upper half of the bell (see Fig. 92).   Andronicus

[1] Vitruvius, I, 6.

perhaps invented the type, popular in Roman Greece for at least five centuries.

Half-way up the inside of the Tower a small horizontal cornice, little more than a string course, with no corona but with small dentils immediately under its false sima, is supported by brackets almost suggesting modillions.[1]   Now the modillion, from the time of Augustus, becomes the distinctive mark of the Roman cornice. On several of his temples it has the shape of a console, like those on the door of the Erechtheum but fattened and tilted forward 90 degrees (see Fig. 96), and immediately supports the corona.[2]   With the dentils and their bedmould below, modillions swell the Roman cornice to an excessive size.   But in our small cornice of Andronicus the places of dentils and modillions are reversed.   A more Roman entablature, where modillions surmount dentils, crowns the main door in the Lesser Propylon at Eleusis (48 B.C.).   Near Rome, a cornice like that on the Tower of the Winds, but without the dentils, seems to have adorned the 'Tomb of the Claudii' at Bovillae.[3]   Even more orthodox, though again without dentils, is the cornice in the Pompeian dining-room (second quarter of the first century?) mentioned above.[4]   In fact, we know the modillion appeared at this time, but whether first in the Greek or Roman world it would be rash to decide.[5]

The Lesser Propylon of Eleusis (see Fig. 94) was commissioned by a Roman, Appius Claudius Pulcher, in 48 B.C.[6]   But its taste is Greek, though it resembles no other propylon.   It is unroofed and has a deep forecourt, with columns, just free-standing, in front of the side walls.   Their order was normal Greek Ionic and their entablature apparently unbroken, as at Bassae.   The cross-wall had originally one large door, protected in front by a Corinthian portico, distyle and prostyle, of remarkable beauty,

[1] Stuart and Revett, I, Chap. III, Pls. IV and IX.

[2] Robertson, Pl. XII (a).

[3] Illustrated in Rivoira, *Architettura Romana* (Milan, 1921), Fig. 4. The tomb is supposedly Republican, but no certain evidence exists for its date or attribution.

[4] See above, p. 262, n. 5.   The dentils are large and well formed.

[5] Delbrueck (II, Abb. 110) figures an Indian example from the Gandaritis, which he assigns to the second century B.C., and Foucher (*L'Art Gréco-Buddhique du Gandhara* (Paris, 1905)) shows many more. But experts tend these days to assign this art rather to the second century A.D., when it would offer no proof that modillions originated in some central tract, say Seleucid Syria, about 200 B.C.

[6] The evidence comes from an inscription on the frieze and two references by Cicero in his letters to Atticus.

that projected into the court. The hexagonal capitals of the two
columns had faces of the same exquisite design as those on the
antae behind them. Behind the cross-wall was a much shallower
court, and here the projection of the centre portal made use of
Caryatids. The order of the cross-wall is, rightly enough, on a
larger scale than that of the lateral Ionic order, whose columns
must have reached to about two-thirds of its height. Perhaps
they stood on a high podium, like those in the Lower Gymnasium

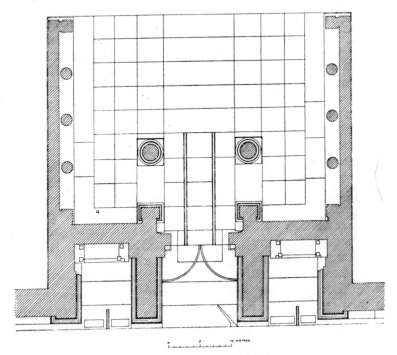

Fig. 94   Lesser Propylon, Eleusis.

of Priene mentioned above.[1] The architect seems to derive his
ensemble from the cella of Bassae, particularly if that was unroofed.
In any case his building, however novel, appears Greek.[2]

[1] Above, p. 262.
[2] Reconstructions of the propylon now have to depend (cf. Dinsmoor,
p. 286) on the beautiful engravings in *The Unedited Antiquities of Attica*
(Society of Dilettanti; London, 1817), Chap. III. Hoermann (*Die Inneren
Propyläen von Eleusis* (Berlin, 1932) attempted to discredit the Dilettanti,
but is refuted, in my view, by Dinsmoor, p. 286. He assembled, however,
the evidence available on the ground today.

The last Greek building of note is the famous catacomb of Mex, near Alexandria, a very symmetrical group of square chambers with niches on all sides so wide and deep that each room seems almost cruciform. The cross-passages give long axial views, detached columns flank the niches and the roofs, saucer domes sliced vertically by the transverse arches, give the whole an early Byzantine appearance remarkable for a date so early, if Delbrueck is right, as the mid-first century B.C.[1]

One may summarise this half-century by saying that the superiority in wealth, numbers and technique had passed tardily and almost by accident to Rome. It now required a Roman to initiate any scheme of real importance. The quality of concrete in central Italy was improving. By long experiment the Romans had come to employ pozzuolana, indispensable to all their achievements in the City, without in this period ever discerning its real nature. For even Vitruvius never suspected that the 'pit sand' dug east and north of Rome, the best for concrete, was in fact the same material as the volcanic dust of Puteoli (Pozzuoli) already used for water-proof moles and jetties in the Bay of Naples.[2] There is no doubt, too, that the Romans now differentiated their materials more skilfully and had begun to veneer more scientifically than their contemporaries. In the second century the Council-House at Miletus, a building with a core of hard gneiss, had been given a skin of marble. But the Romans had the materials and the means for far more careful differentiation.

In taste, however, Rome perhaps still lagged. The frescoes in the 'House of Livia' are superior, indeed, to almost everything of their own time at Pompeii. Pompeii, however, particularly under its Roman colonists, is not Alexandria. And the mosaic pavements, at any rate, even of Pompeii have no rivals in Rome. Miss Blake thinks it safe to propound the general rule[3] that a design found in pre-Sullan Pompeii reaches Rome about the middle of the first century B.C., and is carried northward during the reign of Augustus. Some exquisite Hellenistic patterns, like the Alexandrian rosette mosaic, found several times at Pompeii, never appear farther north in Italy.

[1] See Delbrueck II, pp. 78–9, and p. 102 which reproduces Napoleon's illustration.

[2] Miss Blake (*Construction*, p. 313) has most skilfully demonstrated this from all the evidence, including Vitruvius, III, 4, iii. Nothing shows better the empirical foundation of the building sciences.

[3] Blake, *Pavements*, pp. 79–80.

It is only under Augustus that Rome gathers into her hands most of the strings of artistic patronage that she is to hold for three centuries. Only under him can she organise for the use of hundreds of thousands those skills so painfully acquired in the three centuries after Alexander. We are at last ready to study Imperial Rome.

CHAPTER VIII

THE CHARACTER OF ROMAN ARCHITECTURE

I. THE ROMAN EMPIRE, 31 B.C.–A.D. 330

THE main events and phases of Imperial history can be fairly briefly summarised. The difficulty lies in their interpretation.

Augustus was carried to power by the yearning of the world for peace. Generals had fought each other for seventy years. As at the end of our Wars of the Roses, very small forces were engaged at the last decisive battle of Actium (31 B.C.), but everyone acquiesced in the result. Augustus, after murdering most of the nobility ten years before, had cleverly pretended to be fighting for the old Roman aristocratic ideals and the spread of the best Italian culture, and for most of his reign commanded the loyalty of great poets and artists in building a new and Italian world. While his power as 'imperator', or 'emperor', rested in 31 B.C. on the legions behind him and on their capable commander, Agrippa, he scrupulously observed the old Republican forms, nursed the senate and, by holding with his friends a succession of the chief legal offices, slowly added to his actual power the half-spiritual 'authority' always exercised at Rome by a magistrate of experience and judgment. He finally acquired at death the deification henceforward bestowed on good emperors.[1]

His slow, dispassionate, longsighted statesmanship recognised that mere military power would never suffice. The world was still far from the moral ruin of, say, the Europe of our own day, and still expected him to use his power reasonably. His dynasty

---

[1] The spirit of the Augustan principate, as it appeared to its Roman victims, is most brilliantly recaptured by Tacitus in the opening chapters of the *Annals* and by Gibbon in the third chapter of the *Decline and Fall*. Most modern students of the subject have devoted their time to correcting this impression, and have revealed the principate over most of the empire as a good, paternal government, with high administrative standards. One can bring against it only the criticism, which will seem either unrealistic or devastating according to personal taste, that it allowed small scope for individual genius.

appeared firmly rooted at his death, after a reign of forty-five years.
But his successors, weaker men and sometimes madmen, unable to
acquire his 'authority' over the better Romans and compelled to
fall back on military force, mostly met violent ends themselves,
or were disgraced by not being deified. Fifty years later, in A.D. 68.
Nero's follies brought his house to extinction. Yet even then
his spirit was still working to save Rome. He had built more
firmly outside his own family. He had worked hard through all
his reign, devoting the army to the protection of distant frontiers,
painfully 'rationalised' along the Rhine, the Danube and the
Euphrates, and educating his immediate subordinates in Roman
habits of industry and obedience. So during the anarchy of
A.D. 69, the year of the four emperors, only one frontier, the Rhine,
saw any real disaffection, most generals showed a decent moderation and the conqueror, Vespasian, the first Flavian emperor, had
not only compromised with a powerful rival in Syria but was a
complete stranger to nervousness or arrogance. In his earth-
bound way, he imitated the propaganda of Augustus—perhaps, as
his buildings show, with the populace, rather than the Senate, in
the foreground. When his unattractive son Domitian grew old
and nervous and cruel and was assassinated in A.D. 96, the great
magistrates carried the Empire without bloodshed through
another serious crisis. Nerva, a mild, weak senator quickly raised
to the purple by the assassins, could not have survived without
adopting Trajan, commander of the Rhine legions, as his son and
successor. But from that moment until the death of Marcus
Aurelius in A.D. 180 the Roman Empire enjoyed its greatest extent
and the Ancient World its 'Indian Summer' of prosperity under
Trajan, Hadrian and the Antonines.

The emperors themselves resembled at this time our better
Indian viceroys, the senators our privy councillors. Adoption
and succession to the principate, until Marcus chose his miserable
son Commodus, proceeded by merit. The chief task of the emperor was to maintain the framework of the empire. Augustus
had divided it into large frontier provinces with legions directly
under himself and his nominees, and older, peaceful provinces,
such as Narbonensis (Provence) and Asia (the rich western coast of
Asia Minor) under governors chosen by the Senate. The emperors
of course made the adjustments required from time to time between
the two kinds of province. They reserved Egypt for themselves,
because of its natural wealth, population and autocratic traditions,

and also because they had to organise a supply of Nile corn for the enormous city of Rome.

All campaigns were conducted by the emperor or in his name by his immediate subordinates, and his military provinces served not only as a bulwark but as a springboard for punitive or aggressive warfare. The chief, most of them organised under Augustus, were Upper and Lower Germany, strips along the Rhine, Pannonia, Dalmatia and Moesia, all three south of the Danube, and Syria. Claudius in A.D. 43 added Britain, Romanised under the Antonines as far as the Forth, Vespasian Judaea in A.D. 70, after reducing the Jews, and Trajan Dacia (the modern Rumania) in A.D. 105. Two regions caused the empire continual trouble, Central Europe and Mesopotamia, the former uncivilised but suffering endless pressure of population from the Steppes, the latter the seat of the half-Hellenised Parthian Kingdom, the heir of the Seleucids and the only civilised state contiguous to Roman provinces. However well organised, the Roman army proved too small to annex Mesopotamia, so very far from the centre of Roman power, especially at a time when, for whatever reason, Classical culture was receding in the East, as we see from Dura Europos and the very solid ruins of the Parthian outpost of Hatra. But the Rhineland and even Syria still witness in their Roman remains to the efficiency and splendour of their imperial organisation.

In the rest of the empire, shielded behind these military provinces, hundreds of autonomous cities administered their own small territories like the Greek cities of old—with one difference, that their constitutions were all of a largely identical pattern, their governments oligarchies and their chief magistrates Roman citizens. For so Rome could reconcile local independence with imperial cohesion. The emperors reserved to themselves the maintenance of an imperial highway and posting system, the minting of nearly all gold and silver coin, the official protection of certain manufactures and trades and the food and water supply of Rome. The aqueducts across the Campagna and above all the warehouses and granaries of Ostia, the port at the mouth of the Tiber, show imperial efficiency at its highest. How different from these were the poor, private work turned out by the autonomous cities, the caddis-fly architecture of mixed materials, nearly always inferior, that marred the last days of Pompeii, the exedrae and theatres lavished on Greece by her private fairy-godfather,

Herodes Atticus! Nor, in many cases, did the emperors them-
selves fare much better when they quitted the domain of public
utilities, in which one must include the great Baths and even the
Colosseum, and indulged such private whims as the 'City of
Hadrian' at Athens or the hideous trophy of Adamklissi, in the
Dobrudja.[1]

So well was the Empire now managed that, as Gibbon observes,
it had no history during the whole reign of Antoninus Pius. Its
government at this time truly represented the educated classes, and
could command the gratitude of all for the numberless material
benefits it had bestowed. The general fairness in the system of
promotion, the common sense of the higher officials and the
imperial monopoly in matters of the first importance all seemed
to promise an indefinite duration of the Antonine Age. One
might have discerned, however, a few warning signs. The ruling
class was perhaps at times taking its way of life too much for
granted, and was losing sight of the profundities of Greek culture.
We are entering an age of abridgements and anecdote libraries.
Even in the first century the young Agricola, for showing an
excessive interest in philosophy, had been removed from his
university at Massalia. In addition, the life of the local oligarchs
was becoming in many places almost monotonously easy and
enervating—a round of spectacles and ceremonies, and their
recording on honorific inscriptions. When civic rivalry in loyal
extravagance had led to overspending, no one but the central
government had the experience or competence to set things right.
We know from the correspondence of Pliny and Trajan how chaotic
the finances had become in the cities of Northern Asia Minor by
A.D. III. Worse still, these cities were prepared to seize the
chance of Pliny's presence and to appeal to him for decisions on
the most trivial matters. Readers of de Tocqueville, when they
see such helplessness as this, will fear the worst for the future of
the stricken community.

The third century, on the whole, was very poorly served by its
first historians. It is difficult to know, on the evidence available,
why the misdemeanours of Commodus led to a sequel so terrible
as the century of anarchy from 190 to 290. But many events

---

[1] Earlier imperial trophies had shown somewhat better taste, for
instance that of Augustus at La Turbie, in the Maritime Alps (O. Brogan,
Roman Gaul (London, 1953), Fig. 45b). But even here one finds ill-
proportioned projecting pedestals of the sort that spoil the Temple of
Vesta (below, p. 328).

seem to indicate that the traditional ruling class was now only thinly represented in the army, and not always, therefore, respected by the emperors whom the army created. Yet such was the position of the army and such the nature of the principate, despite its respectable Augustan façade, that no emperor could rule for a moment without military goodwill. At the same time, Roman military strength, never much more, perhaps, than a quarter of a million men, was drained away in wars between the rival claimants, while the real enemies, the Germans, were coalescing into larger groups, hurled against the Roman frontiers by pressure from farther east.

For a few years around 200 the rot was stayed by Septimius Severus (193–211), a sensible African general. But fifty years later, the barbarians at last broke through and did untold damage to Gaul and to the towns on the Aegean, including Athens. In the 'wretched reign' of Gallienus (260–68) the empire was parcelled out among thirty pretenders, while the father of the emperor, Valerian, was himself a prisoner of the Sassanid Persians, the new and fanatically eastern rulers of Mesopotamia. Palmyra under Odenathus and Zenobia (261–73) usurped the role of Rome as the protectress of Syria. For the whole period from 249 to 286 the empire was fighting for its life, and survived only in a very altered form.

As reorganised by Diocletian (286–305) it had lost most of its freedom. Farmers were tied rigidly to their land, townsmen to their trades or manufactures and all classes to their quotas of taxation. Barbarians who had settled inside the frontiers held their land almost feudally of the emperor in return for military service. In such a state of almost permanent siege Rome ceased to be convenient as a capital, and one emperor seemed insufficient for the task. Diocletian grappled with these problems, but only Constantine (312–337) had the genius to solve them. In A.D. 330 he founded Constantinople, 'New Rome', at the confluence of the main trade-routes and on a site then impregnable. He thus ensured the division of the empire into East and West, and a long lease of life for it in the east. But by his action he abruptly ended the Imperial Roman style of architecture. The basilica of his unsuccessful rival, Maxentius, is the last of those enormous axially-planned buildings, vaulted in pozzuolana and peculiar to central Italy under the pagan emperors.

Seeing the necessity of a faith, for lack of which the old society, for all its civic splendour, had perished, Constantine came to terms in A.D. 313 with Christianity, then the chief of those oriental religions filling the gap caused by the decay of classical thought and morals. By so doing, he undoubtedly prolonged the life of the empire in the west and perpetuated in a large degree the culture for which it had stood. His reign shows a sudden remarkable revival in art, to be followed soon by a revival of Latin letters. But since Christianity in A.D. 300 was wrapped in the language of Greek philosophy, and since, for whatever reason, only parts of the East, such as Egypt and Syria, had escaped the sterility of the earlier third century, we should not be surprised that the most impressive immediate result of his action is to be found in the new Byzantine civilisation of the Eastern Empire. Constantine had seized almost at the last moment the opportunity of wise, far-seeing statesmanship still available, though the empire was dying, to the universal emperor. As a maker of history, he is worthy to stand near Julius Caesar himself.

2. ROMAN BUILDING METHODS

In our bureaucratic age Imperial Rome has come into her own. Her cities approached in size the capitals of modern Europe; and the highly static government of the High Empire, in all those minutiae, the study of which so rewards a certain type of research-worker, is understood and envied by the harassed administrator of today. Indeed, if Europe is now to turn once more into a few conscientious shepherds and a multitude of sheep, what can we not gain from the study of Roman culture? We in modern London have provided little for our own half-educated masses beyond featureless flats and offices and disjointed halls of entertainment, all haphazard, few of much merit and none related to their surroundings. What a difference from Trajan, whose enormous forum by itself supplied the shops, markets, promenades, law-courts, libraries and places of worship required by the time, as well as an imposing new thoroughfare, a thousand feet long, from one crowded quarter to another—and all this on so grand a scale that the crowds could go about their business in perfect comfort! Were we to perish, could our modern buildings exert upon our successors the fruitful influence of Roman Provence upon the builders of the Romanesque or of Rome itself upon the Cinquecento?

In grand axial planning, as in construction, the Romans excelled. Indeed, the history of architecture teaches us that, where the planning of buildings is bold and rational, the means of constructing them are most often ready to hand. If the Romans had only possessed in addition the artistic sense of the Greeks, their architecture would have been the grandest the world has ever seen. But they relied too much on others. They were patrons rather than artists, content in most cases to import artificers from other countries, chiefly from Greece, to carry out their ideas. For this reason, perhaps, Roman buildings often lack the artistic completeness and sense of absolute fitness in all their parts which distinguish the masterpieces of some other schools. Their decoration, though generally lavish, lacks refinement and often even finish. But the planning is superb, the scale magnificent—qualities shown not only in the buildings themselves, but also in their approaches and surroundings, which are mapped out with a supreme disregard for short-term economies, and with a truly grand feeling for architectural effect. The scale on which they built was recalled in many countries besides Italy for many centuries after their empire had ceased to exist. In such towns as Albi and Avignon in the south of France, Autun in Burgundy and Trier in Germany, and in many an eastern city, the love of size inherited by the people from their former masters is strongly perceptible: and even the enormous bays of some Italian Gothic cathedrals are best explained by the prompting of the old Roman spirit.

During the Empire certain changes took place in architectural style, but not to the extent we might have expected. The fact is that the Romans followed Greek traditions fairly closely when dealing with religious buildings, for which precedent existed in Greece; but in others of a secular character, such as their theatres, amphitheatres and baths, to which Greek construction and planning were not wholly suited, they had to devise their own technique. Thus, on the one hand, the Theatre of Marcellus, of 13 B.C., is arched throughout in a design closely similar to that of the Colosseum but nearly a century older: on the other, some late temples, such as that of Faustina in the Forum (*c.* A.D. 145), are still entirely trabeated.

The greatest purity of detail is found under Augustus, whose reign saw an enormous programme of building—he claims to have 'restored', in most cases rebuilt, eighty-two temples

Terrace above
Great Ramp,
Praeneste

Plate 19

Pseudo-pendentives, Baths of Caracalla, Rome

Temple of Concord, Rome; interior, restored

Plate 20

alone.[1] Under Nero, after the famous fire of A.D. 64, much of Rome had to be rebuilt; but we have too little of his work to judge its style. The smaller buildings of the Flavians, such as the Temple of Vespasian and the Arch of Titus, approach the Augustan in delicacy; the larger, like the Colosseum, are grand and simple, but coarse in detail. Under Trajan and Hadrian (97–134) the Romans reached the height of their ability to model walls and vaults in concrete, as shown by the Pantheon and the Villa of Hadrian. The Antonines, by contrast, produced pedestrian work like the Temple of Faustina in the Forum. After their time grand buildings appear erratically and under isolated emperors, such as Caracalla, Gallienus and Maxentius; but the detailing of these always shows a sad deterioration, and it is not too much to say that in them the Romans had at last virtually abandoned their attempt to press their concrete arcuation into the trabeated mould of the orders.

So, after considering in this chapter the various Roman methods of construction and decoration, and in the next the types of building erected in the High Empire down to A.D. 200, we shall conclude with the slow abandonment of classicism between Severus and Constantine.

The Greeks used many and small points of support, the Romans, as a rule, few and large, because they required big unencumbered floor spaces. These spaces they covered with concrete vaults or domes, needing massive piers for their support. During most of the Empire basilicas, treated as purely trabeated buildings with timber roofs, disobeyed this rule[2]: otherwise the Romans to their credit preferred the more architectural and durable construction in concrete. They still used columns freely in interiors, but subordinated them to the concrete piers and placed them at the sides of rooms, where they were out of the way—for instance in the Throne Room of Domitian (see Fig. 95) or the Temple of Venus and Rome.[3] Thus columns became decorative features more than structural necessities. In addition, they gave scale. Now that most of the large halls in Rome are robbed of their columns, it is difficult to apprehend their size, but where columns

---

[1] *Res Gestae Divi Augusti* (ed. F. Gagé; Paris, 1935), Appendix 3.

[2] Small religious basilicas, like that near the Porta Maggiore (see *CAH*, Pl. IV, p. 180) might be vaulted even under the early Empire: but commercial basilicas abandoned their classical character only in the late third century A.D. (see below, p. 363).

[3] See below, p. 325.

19—I

still remain, as in front of the niches in the Pantheon, their valuable scale-giving properties at once appear, and must have appeared yet more strongly before the wretched 'baroque' saints, far larger than life, were permitted to dwarf the lower courses of the building. The Byzantines learnt this treatment of columns from the Romans, and turned it to excellent account in S. Sophia and other large churches.

Granted these habits, load-bearing colonnades or walls entirely of ashlar are rare in Roman work. The wall enclosing the Forum of Augustus provides a splendid example. They also appear in

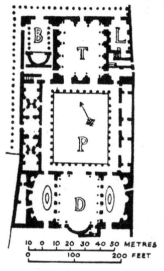

the small Hellenising temples of Augustan times, such as that of Castor in the Forum. Even in ashlar the Roman makes a practical contribution to construction. He joints the frieze in such a way as to turn it into a discharging arch between each pair of columns and so relieve some of the weight on the unsupported stretches of the architrave (see Fig. 96), a trick repeated in the later, Roman colonnades of the Forum at Pompeii.[1] Most good masonry of this period is found in Syria and Provence, but modifies only slightly the forms developed at Rome in concrete.

Fig. 95   Rome, Throne Room
of Domitian.
B = Basilica; T = Throne Room;
P = Peristglar Court; D = Dining
Room; L = Lobby.

Concrete was the principal building material of the Romans; and without its aid their most characteristic and interesting work could not have been carried out. It would have been sheer waste of valuable material to build great piers and thick walls solid in marble or stone, and neither could have been used for vaults of Roman span. Concrete formed an excellent and inexpensive substitute. Its ingredients were easily obtainable, and no skilled labour was required to lay it, so that it could easily be entrusted to slaves or pressed workmen, of whom the Romans always had thousands at their command. It was economical because its

---

[1] For the earlier, Hellenistic colonnades, see above, p. 251.

aggregate ('caementa')[1] could consist of the chips and waste from polished facing-blocks; and, being monolithic, it permitted those niches, apses and other re-entrants so exciting in Roman work, particularly in the show-buildings of Rome itself, and so long

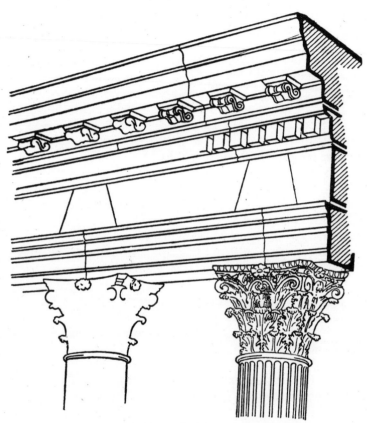

Fig. 96   Rome, Temple of Castor, entablature.

desired but so imperfectly achieved by the Hellenistic architects in dressed stone.[2]   Besides concrete, the Romans used stone and

[1] Note how completely the word 'cement' has changed its meaning in English.

[2] These, and many other advantages of concrete, as that the large, unskilful gangs necessitated large, simple, noble rooms, are lovingly developed by Delbrueck (*Hellenistische Bauten*, II, pp. 51 ff.) on the theme that 'all things work together for good' when the plan is simple and bold.   He is very ingenious here.

brick for ordinary facings, and for decoration granite, marble, porphyry, alabaster and bronze. Stucco, of great strength and thickness, though lacking the fineness of the Greek purely limestone stuccoes, was applied to most walls, external as well as internal, except those faced with ashlar or ornamental stone.

The chief building-stones in Rome were tufa and peperino, both of volcanic origin, and travertine, a hard semi-crystalline limestone formed in water and quarried at Tivoli.[1] The great period of the tufas, bad weathering stones, had passed with the second century B.C. Travertine and peperino were used as external facings and in positions where considerable strength was required. Travertine, a strong stone, has a beautiful texture and warm honey colour, but flakes badly in a fire. Peperino is as strong and withstands fire, so that it enjoyed a new popularity after the great fire of Rome in A.D. 64,[2] but has a texture so hideous that one is forced to plaster it over. The Romans, when they used stone blocks, liked them big—some of the travertine blocks on the Colosseum are 15 feet long—and many an arched opening, which otherwise would have no merit, owes its dignity to the size of its voussoirs. They showed to the full that scale is nearly always more effective than ornament. In ashlar-faced walls the stones are sometimes bedded in mortar, sometimes cramped together in the Greek manner. The face is generally worked smooth, but in some instances the margins only of each stone are drafted, the centre being left as a raised panel.

Roman bricks were of two kinds, sun-dried and kiln-baked. The former, as we saw, had been used by the Greeks from the earliest times. But ordinary tenements in Rome soon became too lofty for their employment, as we learn from Vitruvius[3]; and after an attempt, which he condemns,[4] at the end of the Republic to substitute inflammable wattle, walls of concrete with brick

---

[1] Many encyclopaedic accounts exist of Roman building-stones and their properties, with which the modern architect should make himself as familiar as possible. One of the best is by Middleton and Stuart Jones in the introduction to the article 'Rome' in the *Encyclopaedia Britannica* (1910 edition). Another, even more detailed, appears in the second chapter of M. E. Blake, *Ancient Building Construction in Italy* (Washington, 1947). For evidence on the marbles and their systematic exploitation in large quantities by the emperors from the early second century onwards, see J. B. Ward Perkins in *JRS*, 1951, pp. 89–104.

[2] Tacitus, *Annals*, XV, 43.

[3] Vitruvius, II, 8.

[4] Vitruvius, II, 8, xx.

facings became universal on large private buildings. No walls
in Rome were ever built of brick throughout; even in partitions
not more than 7 inches thick the facings alone are of brick, the core
of concrete (see Fig. 97). The Augustan city wall of Turin
provides an early example in the provinces of brick-faced concrete.[1]

It was long before builders learnt to eliminate 'through-
courses' from their walls. They appear, for instance, in the Baths
of Trajan.[2] In each section of ten courses in the wall of Turin,
the ninth and tenth were bonded through. In the provinces the
mortar is less good, but good bricks are dearer. Those available
are used on through-courses in walls of small dressed stones. So
in the wall of Roman London we find 2 or 3 feet above the ground
three courses of brick 'throughs' together, then five or six courses
of stone followed by two of brick, then six of stone, and so on for as

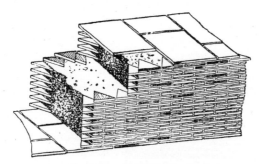

Fig. 97   Brick-faced concrete.

high as the wall is preserved.[3] The third-century wall at Richborough has fewer bricks.[4] But at Paris, as shown by the surviving bath buildings beside the Cluny Museum, the builders
could dispose of more, in three courses at a time to five of stone.
These through-courses of brick, levelling the wall at intervals,
have a tile-like appearance, which is hardly strange, for in Rome
itself the bricks applied to early concrete walls were simply tiles
some 2 feet square on plan and about 2 inches thick split in half
along the diagonal, deprived of their flanges and laid horizontally

[1] For this, see Ian Richmond in *Papers of the British School at Rome,*
XII, pp. 52 ff.
[2] Lanciani, *Ruins*, p. 363.
[3] See Gordon Home, *Roman London* (London, 1948), Chap. IX;
W. R. Lethaby, *Londinium* (London, 1923), pp. 68–9.
[4] Bushe-Fox, *Richborough* (Oxford, 1949), Pl. 17.

with the hypotenuse along the outer face of the wall.[1] Rectangular bricks were specially made for through-courses from Augustan times onwards, and were about 1 foot by 1½ feet by 2 inches. As Ashby shows,[2] the later bricks were even thinner than the Augustan split tiles; so that the thinner the courses and the thicker the mortar-joints, the later a wall is likely to be. Fewer through-courses, too, characterise later work. In pozzuolana they are unnecessary, are indeed points of weakness, as Middleton shows[3]: but the Roman could not bring himself to abandon tradition.

Concrete was now in general use for walls and roofs, and by the time of Nero builders were mixing the pozzuolana in the proper proportion. Their concrete has set extremely hard, harder than the Augustan. Nearly every concrete wall that was meant to be seen was faced with stone or brick. Coarse stone facings were now always of 'opus reticulatum', very popular under Augustus, where pyramidal stones, each with a base about 3 inches square, are laid with their apex embedded in the concrete core (see Fig. 98). On the face the square bases are placed lozenge-wise, forming the 'reticulate' or 'net-like' pattern. The arches and quoins are sometimes of stone, more usually of brick, and at regular intervals of from 3 to 5 feet through-courses are introduced of thin bricks about 2 feet square. Consequently, walls are generally some 2 feet or a multiple of 2 feet in thickness.

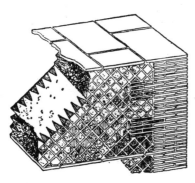

Fig. 98   Opus reticulatum.

Brick arches over openings (see Fig. 99) are constructed in a similar manner to the walling. Most of their bricks tail only 5 or 6 inches into the concrete behind, but every sixth or seventh is a 'through', extending to the other face. The arch behind the facing is thus divided into boxes, which are filled with concrete. This, no doubt, was done to keep the concrete in position and to

[1] Blake, *Construction*, p. 293.
[2] Anderson-Spiers-Ashby, *Architecture of Ancient Rome* (London, 1927), p. 33.
[3] J. H. Middleton, *Remains of Ancient Rome* (London, 1892), p. 58.

prevent it from slipping on to the haunches.   For the same reason, in many arches of the Colosseum some of the brick voussoirs are taller than others.

By the third century, reticulate work had grown rare, and brick facings had replaced it outside and inside buildings.   While reticulate work was always to be hidden, bricks were meant very occasionally to show, at any rate on exteriors.   We find deliberate polychromy in the so-called Temple of the Deus Rediculus on the

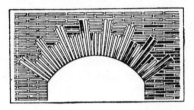

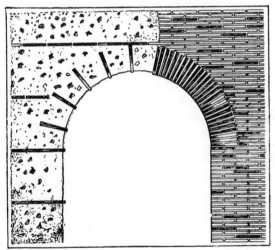

Fig. 99   Brick arches.

Appian Way[1] and in some of the details at Ostia, where much brickwork is of a high order.   Where concealed, the bricks must surely have given a better key to the plaster than would the surface of the concrete core.   Vitruvius in his seventh book well shows the pains taken by the ancients to ensure the most perfect foundation for the upper coats of plaster and pigment, and prescribes

[1] Anderson-Spiers-Ashby, Pl. XI.

cavity walls, their inner division wholly of tiles, for the preservation
of plaster on damp sites.[1]

Roman vaults are nearly always of concrete and constructed
to form one homogeneous mass, which, after it has once set,
exercises no lateral thrust.   This is the secret of their success.
Had their construction been different, had they been built of
brick and stone in the medieval manner, their thrusts would have
increased the difficulties of erection tenfold.   It must not be
forgotten that their spans are far greater than those of Gothic
vaults.   A method of construction suitable for a span of 40 feet
may be quite unsuited to one double that width, and some Roman
vaults are wider still.

Two kinds of vaults were popular with the Romans; the tunnel,
and the intersecting, or groined (see Fig. 100).   The latter was
generally employed on the baths and other wide halls.   It is
formed by the intersection of two equal tunnel vaults cutting one
another at right angles, and the lines of intersection are termed
groins or arrises.   It has two great advantages over the tunnel
vault; its weight is concentrated at certain points and it facilitates
the lighting of interiors.   For windows can be placed high up
immediately under the crown of the vault, whilst in tunnel vaults
they must come below the springing line.   As we saw,[2] the
groined vault was apparently a Hellenistic invention in cut stone.

With his numerous but unskilful workmen, the Roman architect
was required to design large and simple shapes.   His knowledge
of solid geometry was quite rudimentary; for where he made the
transition from a polygon to a hemisphere (see Pl. 19), he could
never hit on the correct shape—a spherical triangle—for the
transitional member, called the pendentive.[3]   For a long time he
avoided even the groined vault and the sloping tunnel above a
staircase.   In the Tabularium short stretches of horizontal
tunnelling succeeded one another in a stepped series above the
principal stairs,[4] and good care is taken to carry the long tunnel
vault of the gallery at a level clear of the tops of windows and cross-
tunnels, and thus to offer the labourers no unnecessary difficulties.
In the two lowest storeys of the Colosseum intersecting vaults are
similarly avoided, although, according to some restorations, more

[1] Vitruvius, VII, 4.
[2] Above, p. 247.
[3] See above, p. 228.
[4] Delbrueck, *Hellenistische Bauten*, I, Taf, VI.

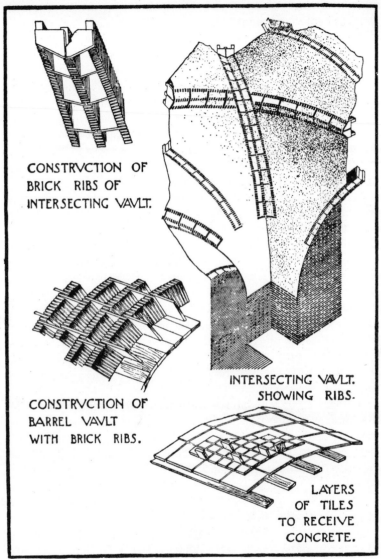

CONSTRVCTION OF
BRICK RIBS OF
INTERSECTING VAVLT.

CONSTRVCTION OF
BARREL VAVLT
WITH BRICK RIBS.

INTERSECTING VAVLT.
SHOWING RIBS.

LAYERS
OF TILES
TO RECEIVE
CONCRETE.

Fig. 100   Intersecting vaults (from Choisy).

common higher up the building.[1] As appears from other
amphitheatres, notably Pozzuoli, not to mention the vast
substructure of the Baths of Caracalla, the Roman builder

[1] See, e.g., that of Durm (Robertson, Fig. 118a).

was rather more willing to allow the intersection of a lower tunnel with a higher, forming what the Germans call a 'monastic vault'.

Tunnel vaults, according to Choisy,[1] were built as follows. Brick rings were generally placed about 2 feet apart, and were joined together at regular intervals by brick lacing courses. These divided the vault into a series of rectangular compartments, filled with concrete of no great thickness. The brickwork was supported on light wooden centering, and allowed to set before the concrete was added. Sometimes the rings were much farther apart, in which case planks were laid between them to support the first layer of concrete. When that had set, it was more than sufficiently strong to carry the second; and the more that were put on, the stronger the vault became. A thorough wetting on the back of each, before the next was applied, ensured that the whole should set into one solid mass. Sometimes, according to Choisy,[2] another plan was adopted. Above a light centering of wood, large square tiles were laid flat and bedded in cement; and after these had set, a second layer of somewhat smaller tiles was laid on top. Some of the latter were bedded vertically, to give a better hold to the concrete. These two thicknesses of tiles, assisted as they were by the centering below, formed a bed sufficiently strong to carry the first layer of concrete; and afterwards the different layers were applied as shown above.

In intersecting vaults much the same method was adopted. At the lines of intersection ribs were built first, consisting of tiles specially made to the required shape, with a course of tiles a little distance apart on either side. The three courses were joined together by lacing courses and formed permanent diagonal ribs, which, after they had set, were sufficiently strong to carry the wet concrete in-filling without the aid of further centering. As employed in vast buildings like the central hall of the Baths of Diocletian,[3] they offered a further advantage. It is difficult to get a sharp, clean arris in concrete, particularly in a large vault like this, 80 feet across. A preliminary rib would obviate the need;

---

[1] *L'Art de Bâtir chez les Romains* (Paris, 1873). Choisy, a constructional engineer, was the first and is still the most eminent of those who have sought to discover a consistent structural purpose in the systems of tiles embedded in Roman concrete vaults.

[2] Choisy, *op. cit.*, p. 76 and Fig. 43.

[3] Choisy, Pl. IX.

and most respectable groined vaults have a rib of this sort on the arris, with or without flanking-ribs.[1]

In domes the construction was much the same. Tile ribs started at the springing, and met at a circle round the centre. The ribs were connected by lacing courses, which were often horizontal. The dome of the Pantheon has a structure probably more complicated, but not well ascertained. Whether or no it has in its lower part a ring of brick relieving-arches to give a framework for the concrete while setting, and whether or no it consists for the rest entirely of concrete,[2] it certainly exercises no more thrust than one monolithic concrete lid. In these huge vaults and domes the expense of wooden centering would have been a serious item, and this to a great extent accounts for the methods of construction adopted.

Economy in centering seems, further, to have dictated the form of those stone vaults erected outside the region of pozzuolana. Many remain in Syria, and one exists at Nîmes in a building known as the Temple or Baths of Diana. All have reduced the necessary centering to a minimum. In most Syrian examples, a series of transverse arches spans each hall or aisle, and every arch is built up to give solid half-spandrels and a horizonal extrados to support the large slabs of a horizontal ceiling.[3] At Nîmes, on the contrary, the slabs of the ceiling rest directly on the voussoirs of the transverse arches (see Fig. 101), giving the appearance of a stone vault with flattish transverse ribs—a type surely not without influence on the later Romanesque schools of Toulouse and Burgundy.

In building these transverse arches, like any others, some wooden centering was required. In the Temple of Diana, it was easy to rest this on the continuous internal cornice, from which these arches were set back. But in buildings like the Pont du Gard,

---

[1] The Arch of Janus Quadrifrons, a very bad work of Severan times, has no rib on the arris according to Choisy, Pl. VII, 2. At present I am inclined to put this down to sheer unintelligence. One would wish to see other examples. But Rivoira, who might have known them, is not greatly interested in the matter (*Architettura Romana*, pp. 180–1), and adds nothing to Choisy's instances here, beyond one rough cellar on the Via Latina.

[2] For its structure, see Robertson, pp. 251 and 266 (note).

[3] For Syrian buildings, see Robertson, Figs. 99 and 133. The 'Temple of Diana' (Robertson, Pl. XV) has now been studied by C. Callmer, who makes the attractive suggestion (*Opuscula Archaeologica*, III, 1944, p. 178) that it was a library.

without an order and so without a cornice, some voussoirs project
from the soffit of each arch at a point about one-third of the way
up.   The centering for the upper part rested on the ledges so
formed.   Again, since each arched opening consisted in fact of
several thin parallel juxtaposed arches unbonded to each other,
the builders could use one very thin segment of centering and
move it horizontally inside any one opening from arch to arch.[1]
Other ledges remain on the face of the Pont du Gard, on which
the scaffolding was placed.   Elsewhere the Romans set back the
arch from the face of a plain pier to leave room for centering, on
whose removal they filled the space that resulted between the soffit
and the offset.   Hence the characteristic vertical sides and segmental head of the later imperial lunette.[2]   The arch receives

Fig. 101   Stone barrel vault, Baths of Diana, Nîmes.

massive support at the haunches and an appearance of prosaic
strength.
    Roman timber roofs have all vanished.   The most renowned
example was on many counts that of the Diribitorium, a building
used for ballots, and standing, thinks Ashby, on the site of the
present Gesù.[3]   The tree trunks used here were 100 feet long,
though only 18 inches thick at the small end.[4]   The last example
of any size to remain was the bronze-plated roof on the portico
of the Pantheon, melted down for cannon in 1626 by Pope Urban

[1] See Robertson, p. 237.
[2] See the diagrams in Middleton, I, Pl. 11.
[3] Platner and Ashby, *Topographical Dictionary of Ancient Rome*
(Oxford, 1929), *s.v.* Diribitorium.   I should like to rummage for the
Diribitorium.
[4] Pliny, *Natural History*, XVI, 201.

VIII.[1] Serlio gives a sketch of it,[2] showing that the four inner columns of the portico supported two walls dividing it into three compartments and extending up to the principal rafters (see Fig. 102). The central compartment was the largest, about 40 feet wide. Its truss, according to Serlio, was of the triangular tie-beam type, with two diagonal braces, firmly fixed in the two walls, supporting the tie-beam each about one-third of the way along. Choisy, although he does not name his source, or names it wrongly as Serlio,[3] actually prefers a sketch of it by Dosio, now accurately

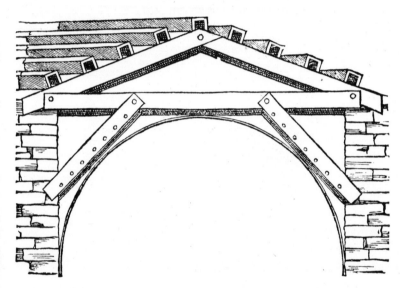

Fig. 102 Portico of Pantheon, roof according to Serlio.

reproduced by Lanciani,[4] which shows a king-post definitely in tension and strapped to the tie-beam, and moves the braces to points where they would be less useful, very near the ends of the tie-beam (see Fig. 103). As Dosio's sketch makes the whole

[1] His party dared to pretend, when he found he needed the cannon less urgently, that he had meant to give the Pantheon a better, viz. leaden, roof. See Lanciani, *Ruins*, p. 482. He belonged to the Barberini: hence the squib mentioned in the preface to this book.
[2] Third Booke, Fourth Chapter, Folio 3 Verso in the English Serlio (London, 1611).
[3] Choisy, *Histoire de l'Architecture*, p. 531.
[4] Lanciani, *Ruins*, Fig. 188.

compartment too narrow, he must be inaccurate with some of the beams—I think with the two braces among others.   Compare the position of the braces in a commonsense medieval roof, like that on the porch of Heckington.[1]   But in either picture, Dosio's or Serlio's, the size of the tie-beam and its relation to the other timbers imply that the builders already understood the principle of the true triangular truss.

Of certain vanished roofs the span was sufficient to make such a truss nearly certain.   Based as it is on the triangle of forces, it has all its members in tension; and 'once tie-beams are in tension, as they are in a true carpentry, they can be made of several pieces'.[2]

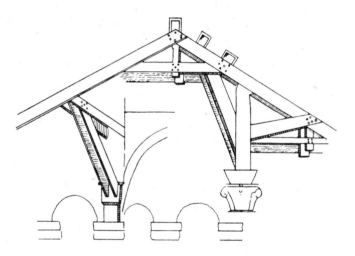

Fig. 103   Portico of Pantheon, roof according to Dosio.

True, the Diribitorium itself used beams 100 feet in length.[3]   But the first Christian basilicas in Rome, of the earlier fourth century, had slender tie-beams and straps with several joints; for instance, Old St. Peter's.   The Lateran, as shown by Pinturicchio in the Piccolomini Library at Siena, has cross beams too massive for normal ties.   But the shape of its truss reminds us of those on

---

[1] Francis Bond, *English Church Architecture*, II (Oxford, 1913), p. 791.
[2] Atkinson and Bagenal, *Theory and Elements*, pp. 209–11.   They seem, however, to imagine the Romans would find it difficult to collect timbers even 80 feet in length.
[3] See above, p. 300.

commercial buildings of the early nineteenth century.[1] The Lateran had been shattered and burnt during the Middle Ages. But so different does this roof seem from a normal medieval truss, that I am inclined to believe it had been patched up on its original antique pattern to appear as it does in Pinturicchio's version of it.

Of course, we cannot at present date the introduction of the tie-beam truss. We cannot say that Vitruvius knew it in the Augustan Age, for the roof of his basilica at Fano, as he describes it,[2] could have either bearer-beams or tie-beams. Again, the long larches and silver firs favoured by the ancients could conceivably have served as bearer beams. For they do not give, and they will support a large load without breaking. This would make a tie-beam truss less necessary. And that silver firs, with their straight trunks, were in high favour we have the word of Theophrastus, who considered theirs the strongest of all timbers. The oak, because it tended to warp and split more than silver fir and bore stresses less easily, had by no means acquired its medieval popularity.[3]

We can hardly doubt that in carpentry, as in other branches of building science, the Romans had reached the limits of knowledge attainable before the Industrial Revolution.

3. ROMAN ORNAMENT: THE ORDERS

Having erected their structural shells, how did the Romans proceed to civilise them? For they were not content, like their twentieth-century Roman successors, with mere engineering shapes, as inhuman in texture as in scale.

Marble was in great demand for decorative columns and veneers. The few Republican and Augustan temples of solid marble had a negligible influence. At first only Greek marbles, such as Pentelic and Hymettan, were available, but about the time of Augustus the quarries of Luna (Carrara) began to furnish an alternative supply of white marble. Roman taste, too, was soon running to

---

[1] For Old St. Peter's, see P. Letarouilly, *Vatican*, I (1882), Pl. 5. For Pinturicchio's fresco, see Ricci, *Pintoricchio* (London, 1902), pp. 196–201. For nineteenth-century market halls, see Bruyère, *L'Art des Constructions* (Paris, 1823), especially Vol. II, Figs. 15 and 71. I suspect Pinturicchio has rendered jointed tie-beams in the Lateran roof as massive bearer-beams.

[2] Vitruvius, V, 1, vi.

[3] For the virtues of silver fir, see Theophrastus, *On Plants*, V, 1, v ff., and for the defects of oak, V, 5, vi ff.

coloured marbles, such as cipollino (a streaky green and white marble from Euboea), red Phrygian or Numidian (giallo antico), not to mention the serpentines, such as the verde antico from Thessaly, and the alabaster, porphyry, basalt and red and grey granite all transported for several centuries from the inexhaustible quarries of Egypt.

Most Roman columns are monolithic and unfluted, like those of granite in the portico of the Pantheon or the cipollino columns on the front of the Temple of Faustina.   In not fluting them, the Romans combined good taste with economy.   To flute so hard a material as granite is very costly, while a marble with strongly marked veins, like cipollino, is better unfluted, when the full beauty of the figure can show.   White marble columns, however, used especially on Augustan temples like the Temple of Castor, may still be fluted and, if of any size, constructed of several drums in the Greek manner.   To the end the Romans fluted them, as we know from the white Proconnesian marble columns on the Basilica of Maxentius.[1]

Facing slabs of marble for the outsides of walls were still under Augustus of considerable thickness (5 to 8 inches) with bonding courses of greater depth at intervals; but in the second and third centuries they became often a veneer less than an inch thick. The marble was fixed to concrete walls by long metal cramps, but was also generally backed by cement.   Interiors, of course, served more often than exteriors for experiments in marble polychromy; and the remains of the Temple of Concord,[2] with four different marbles in the four lowest courses of the cella, show not only a sumptuous development of the earlier 'encrusted' style but an anticipation of the banded and patterned marble veneers on the walls of Byzantine churches (see Pl. 20).   We even find occasionally the thin frames of hard limestone raised to enclose the slabs of marble, by a technique almost wholly Byzantine—as, for example, in the luxurious barracks figured by Middleton.[3] Little, unhappily, remains of such decoration, as most of the marble was cut up in the Middle Ages for what one must confess to be the exquisitely beautiful pavements of the Cosmati.   But more ordinary examples survive in some private houses at Ostia,

[1] The last two survivors perished only in Renaissance times.   See Lanciani, *Ruins*, pp. 405–6.
[2] See the section given in the *Encyclopaedia Britannica* (1910), *s.v.* Rome, Fig. 4.
[3] *Remains of Ancient Rome*, I, p. 86, Fig. 14.

where one can study the patterns and techniques of later imperial marble wall-veneers, not to mention the marble pavements of 'opus sectile'[1] with which they were designed to harmonise, humble and somewhat indirect ancestors of the Cosmatesque masterpieces.[2]

Bronze was sometimes used constructionally, but was valued chiefly for decoration. We are uncertain as to the amount originally used in the roof-truss over the porch of the Pantheon. But the coffers of the ceiling were undoubtedly of bronze and of considerable thickness: for when Pope Urban VIII removed them, enough was obtained to cast eighty cannon for the Castle of S. Angelo and leave 40,000 lb. for other papal needs.[3] The roof-tiles also were of bronze, like those on the Temple of Venus and Rome. Presumably in a climate even slightly more rigorous than the Greek, marble tiles of Greek elegance would have succumbed all too often to the frost. Most impressive today are the bronze doors, partly recast, of the Pantheon, with their massive bronze pivots and the decorative grille of bronze openwork between the leaves and the lintel. In all this the Romans were conservative enough, as sumptuous buildings had had thresholds, pivots and door-leaves of bronze for centuries.[4] They also followed precedent in using bronze for applied lettering and festoons.

But we cannot understand Roman decorative treatment until we have discussed the Roman use of the Orders. The Greeks used them structurally, the Romans as decoration. It has long been the fashion to admire the clean lines of Roman utilitarian buildings like the Pont du Gard or those great shells like the Baths of Caracalla from which the applied decoration has fallen away. It is true that Roman construction has its own beauty. Yet for a true civic or religious building, as opposed to a mere work of engineering, the Roman continued to think the orders indispensable. Why? Was he merely hidebound and perverse, as it is

---

[1] I call them this, though they appear at this date to be wholly of marble, and according to Miss Blake the true 'Opus sectile' of Pompeian times included some limestone, besides being of smaller slabs and finer workmanship than the Ostian (Blake, *Pavements*, pp. 37 ff.).

[2] Of these we have a famous example in England, in the sanctuary of Westminster Abbey. This has deteriorated, owing to the use in it of some English stones: but it is a pity that it should not be more visible than it is.

[3] For particulars of this destruction, see Lanciani, *Ruins*, pp. 483 ff.

[4] And Roman poets thought of them as traditional. One remembers, for instance, Virgil, *Aeneid*, I, 448–9 (where 'cardo' means 'pivot').

the modern fashion to think him? Greek architects, notably at Pergamum, had already discarded the Orders from parts of their buildings: and they had as yet devised few of those extraordinary apses and vaults destined in Roman architecture to fit so awkwardly into the framework of the Greek post and lintel. We have already noticed the scale a columnar order imparts [1] and the reluctance to interrupt its shapes that was felt by the Greeks themselves. [2] Some more reasons for its retention may possibly transpire from the following pages and our descriptions of particular buildings; but this is a question no one, perhaps, is likely to settle.

The Romans used the three Greek orders, the Doric, Ionic and Corinthian, but altered the proportions of all three, especially the first. In addition, they are generally said to have added two more, the Tuscan and the Composite; but a consideration of Roman work will show that the differences between some of these so-called 'orders' are of little importance. The mischief was done at the time of the Renaissance, when men not only insisted on these divisions but also framed arbitrary proportions for all the parts, however small, of each order. In Roman work (see Fig. 104) these hard-and-fast rules did not exist.

We have already seen [3] the Etruscan modification of Greek Doric, used almost exclusively on timber temples—'Tuscan' temples, as Vitruvius calls them. We have also seen the Hellenistic versions of the same order at Pompeii [4] and elsewhere. The later and coarser essays in it that adorn Imperial Rome have a strong family likeness to each other, whether, like the Theatre of Marcellus, they contain triglyphs on the frieze, with perhaps some degenerate Hellenistic bulls' skulls (bucrania) and dishes (paterae) in the metopes, or whether, as on the Colosseum, the frieze lacks carving of any kind. Renaissance writers, without a shred of ancient evidence, considered the former Doric, the latter Tuscan. But both are forms of Imperial Roman Doric.

Less change took place in the Ionic order than in any other. The Roman version is naturally less refined than the Greek. The capital with diagonal volutes on all four sides was always intruding from the third century B.C. onwards. Though resisted in periods

[1] Above, pp. 289–90.
[2] Above, pp. 245 ff.
[3] Above, pp. 223 ff.
[4] Above, p. 251.

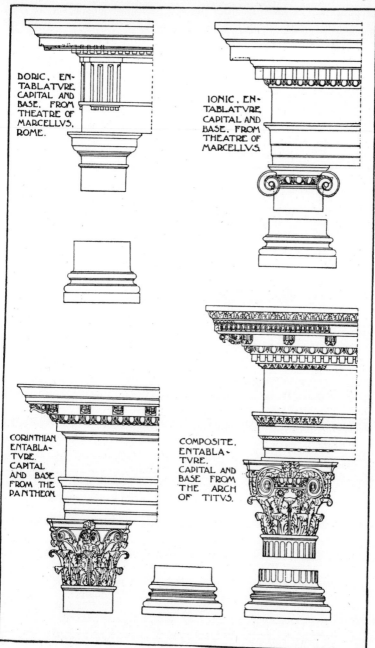

DORIC, EN-
TABLATVRE,
CAPITAL AND
BASE, FROM
THEATRE OF
MARCELLVS,
ROME.

IONIC, EN-
TABLATVRE,
CAPITAL AND
BASE, FROM
THEATRE OF
MARCELLVS

CORINTHIAN
ENTABLA-
TVRE,
CAPITAL
AND BASE
FROM THE
PANTHEON

COMPOSITE,
ENTABLA-
TVRE,
CAPITAL AND
BASE FROM
THE ARCH
OF TITVS.

Fig. 104   The Roman orders.

of good taste, like the late Republican and Augustan Age, it reappears on a few late examples, such as the Severan Temple of Saturn in the Forum, and would have occurred on more, but for the invention of the yet more barbarous Composite Capital. It was usual to reduce the three fasciae of the architrave to two, and to hold these apart with elaborate and misplaced moulded strings.

The Corinthian was emphatically the favourite order of the Romans and the one that they used, together with its sister the Composite, for most of their temples, triumphal arches and public buildings. Under Augustus, a form of it much nearer to the Classical Greek, with firmly modelled acanthus leaves, a well-knit structure and diagonally fluted cauliculi (see Pl. 21), everywhere replaced local varieties, including the Italian,[1] and is sufficiently recognisable everywhere to indicate that Baalbek in Syria, where it appears, was probably begun in Augustan times.[2] But it had travelled far from its early days, when it served as the rare and precious embellishment of a few sumptuous interiors; and in the circumstances one could hardly hope to find it improved. The Romans certainly elaborated it, by this means obtaining a general richness of effect not possible with Doric or Ionic exteriors. But not one of their capitals can compare in grace and refinement with the Greek example from Epidaurus. Those on the Temple of Castor, in some ways the most beautiful of all,[3] have ornamented abaci, structurally speaking a mistake. The best Roman examples of the order are the earliest, as on the Temple of Concord or the Great Temple of Baalbek in Syria,[4] or on some of the Provençal Roman buildings, like the Theatre of Orange. In these the modelling is very bold, and is enhanced by the large horizontal modillions, now prominent on almost every cornice and causing it to dominate the entablature. At Baalbek, furthermore, vertical brackets, like modillions turned through 90 degrees, appear on the frieze as supports for the front parts of lions and bulls, one below each modilllon of the cornice. Far more often a rich, monotonous Roman scroll fills the whole of the frieze. Despite the protests of Vitruvius at this barbarism, the dentils and modillions appeared,

---

[1] See above, p. 259.

[2] On the Corinthian capitals at least I find myself persuaded by E. Weigand, 'Baalbek', *JdI*, 1914.

[3] And called so by Peruzzi (quoted by Lanciani, *Ruins*, p. 273), but now most scandalously neglected by their Italian guardians.

[4] Weigand's Augustan date is supported by the classical name for Baalbek, which indicates that it was founded under the Julian family. The contrary statement of John Malalas is probably worthless.

usually vertical despite the slope, on the raking cornice also. But most early imperial works have sufficient plain surfaces for the richer parts to tell. Later, when every single member was carved, the over-elaboration of detail, of course, destroyed the very effect it was intended to produce; for, with no plain surfaces to enhance the richness of others, ornament loses most of its value. Besides, hard incision and undercutting had begun to replace the soft, warm plasticity of Augustan work. The Gate of Hadrian at Athens exhibits in its pilaster capitals some early examples of the decline. In the Lower Empire, after 200, the drill was used everywhere to get deep, hard shadows quickly. It requires, of course, little skill to work. Its artistic advantages rested for the most part unperceived, except, perhaps, in the Forum of Lepcis Magna,[1] until the fifth century A.D.

The only difference of any moment between Roman Corinthian and the so-called Composite Order is an alteration in the capital. An attempt was made to crown the lower tiers of acanthus leaves of the Corinthian capital with the Ionic echinus, canalis and volutes, always, of course, in a four-cornered, diagonal version. In purer examples, like the capitals of Aezani in Phrygia,[2] the volutes remained horizontal. But in Rome, in the great Baths of the third century, they give the illusion of growing from the echinus and, instead of being linked by a canalis, were held apart by vertical flowers in the Corinthian manner. This is the true Roman composite, and it is this that probably misled Renaissance blunderers, like Inigo Jones, into designing Ionic capitals with vertical volutes diagonal on plan. The new Regent Street shows us, further, that there is no end to this barbarism. The Arch of Titus at Rome (*c.* A.D. 81) is the earliest extant building to exhibit composite capitals (see Pl. 21).

Some of the most characteristic Roman buildings—basilicas, theatres and amphitheatres—exhibit on the exterior a very Roman combination of constructive arches and purely decorative columns and lintels. In Greek work columns are supports; they stand free and carry everything above them. In Roman they are attached to the face of piers, projecting only a half or three-quarters of their diameter, and, although they appear to support the entablature over them, they really do nothing of the sort.

[1] See J. B. Ward Perkins in *JRS*, 1948, especially Pl. VIII. At the same time, the drill could be shockingly abused at Lepcis (*ibid.*, Pl. XI).
[2] Robertson, Fig. 94.

For it is tailed into the wall in separate pieces of stone, and is supported, together with the wall, by arches thrown across from pier to pier.   One could remove the columns without impairing the strength of the building; while the entablatures are mere string courses dividing or pretending to divide one storey from another— on the Colosseum, at least, they do not exactly correspond to the divisions of the storeys behind them.   In Greek work, the length of the lintel dictated the extreme spacing of the columns.   The Romans were governed only by the proportions of the intervening arch, and in the better examples observed fairly constantly a column eight lower diameters in height and a column-spacing of about five lower diameters from centre to centre.[1]   The Tabularium and Theatre of Marcellus observe this proportion, and the bays of the two middle tiers on the Colosseum also approach it, with the aid of pedestals.   We saw[2] the alleged origin of the treatment in the external façades of tunnelled concrete substructures.   We should also remember that in Augustan times the true strength of concrete was still unknown, and it seemed simple wisdom to give it an ashlar facing as close as possible to the traditional forms.

Hard names have been given to this arrangement.   Fergusson calls it 'a useless network'.   But although it is responsible for much that is bad in the work of the last four centuries—chiefly because it destroys the plain wall surface which is so valuable in design—when it is carried out on a sufficiently large scale and with much repetition of parts, as in the Colosseum, it produces remarkably grand effects (see Fig. 105).   To tell as it should, it requires bays of ample size, engaged columns and an unbroken entablature.   Pilasters, as on the Theatre at Ostia, give too little modelling,[3] entablatures broken over the columns, as at Nîmes, too much.   Pettiness of scale, as often found in England, results in absurdity.   The Colosseum best combines amplitude of scale, an unending entablature and an impressive depth of shadow.

Having many buildings several storeys high, the Romans placed tiers of columns one above another on the façades.   A regular sequence is always observed.   The strongest order comes at the bottom, the most slender at the top.   So, in the Colosseum, the

---

[1] These proportions approach the famous 'golden cut', for the possible use of which in antiquity see J. Bousquet in *RA*, 1953, pp. 45 ff.

[2] Above, p. 271.

[3] At the same time I must admit I find the Amphitheatre of Pola, with its pilasters, most impressive.

ELEVATION SECTION

111' 4"
157' 6"

10 0 10 20 30 40 50 60 70 80

Fig. 105 Colosseum, elevation and part-section.

ground floor is Doric, the first floor Ionic, the second Corinthian and the top composite. In early buildings, like the Theatre of Marcellus, the Greek rule still appears to obtain, of making an upper column no greater than the upper diameter of the column below. But in the Colosseum the columns have the same width on all storeys.

Fig. 106   The Fourth Pompeian Style.

Interior decoration, where marble veneers were not used, continued for the most part the motif of the Orders—more freely, because here the medium was painting. For the first century of the Empire the Pompeian styles continued, and embraced to the very end the two main elements of a central picture, like the emblema of a mosaic pavement more important than all the rest, and an elaborate architectural surround, now in several storeys and painted in something resembling perspective. The Augustan Age saw the arrival of the Third Pompeian Style, with its sprinkling of Egyptian detail and general effect of implausible architecture, seen, for instance, in the engaged columns of bamboo-stalks suspended in mid-air. It seems to be this style against which Vitruvius protests in his seventh book.[1] Under Nero and the early Flavians a saner style, the Fourth Pompeian, prevails. The architecture remains wiredrawn, but recovers at least its canonical members

[1] See above, p. 239, n. 2.

and some sense of gravity (see Fig. 106). Although few remains exist of ancient decoration from between the Eruption of A.D. 79 and the first Constantinian mosaics, we have no reason to believe that the architectural framework ever lost its importance. While harmonising each room with the surrounding structure, it gave a spaciousness unattainable by any other means.

Great care was taken to make these paintings as brilliant and permanent as possible. As the seventh book of Vitruvius reveals, the architect played a large part in preparing the wall surfaces for them, and in many ways they formed an integral part of the architectural design. They were executed direct on plaster in fresco, tempera, oil or caustic, the last being the most brilliant and most durable method. In it, the medium used was wax, which was heated to make it liquid, and then mixed with the pigments.[1] Special protection was given wherever there seemed the slightest danger from damp. Vitruvius recommends an alternative method of building the wall, with provision for the circulation of air; and in the House of Livia on the Palatine the plaster is applied to a vertical layer of tiles, which is separated from the outer wall by a cavity.

The Ancients seem nowhere to have anticipated the rich ceiling-frescoes of the Renaissance. They covered their vaults, however, with plaster of fine quality and, when tired of coffering, either modelled this in low relief or painted it.[2] Good examples of modelled ceilings survive in the private baths of Hadrian at his Villa near Tivoli. But some research into the painted decoration of Roman vaults, especially possible ancestors of the magnificent mosaic-encrusted vaults of the first Christian churches, seems long overdue.

[1] The Elder Pliny haphazardly presents us in the thirty-fifth book of his Natural History with many of the details of ancient technique. Maiuri in the most valuable section of his new book (see above, p. 239, n. 2) shows how little we still know about the technique of Pompeii.
[2] See the splendid examples figured by E. Wadsworth in *MAAR*, IV (1924).

CHAPTER IX

THE BUILDINGS OF THE HIGH EMPIRE

I. CIVIC BUILDINGS

ROMAN cities conformed all over the Empire, even in Greek lands, to one general type—one which, with the addition of amphitheatres, comes very close to the city prescribed in the first and fifth books of Vitruvius—and their buildings aped, as closely as the absence of pozzuolana might allow, the large domed shapes and masking colonnades developed in the capital. As each city, moreover, had an oligarchy on the Roman model and a mob with broadly the same pleasures as the Roman, it will be possible to take examples of any type of Roman building we please from any city where they may happen to be preserved. Other cities, in their provincial way, follow, if they can, even the passing fashions of the capital. Under Augustus, when detail is pure at Rome, it is pure at Pola or Baalbek; when, in the later second century, free-standing columns replace engaged columns as a facing for triumphal arches in Rome, they replace them simultaneously at Timgad.[1]

The Romans never grew tired of long symmetrical vistas; witness their Herculean efforts to improve the hilly and crowded localities of Rome itself. When founding new cities they followed the plan adopted in their camps, of two straight roads crossing at the centre. Little variation was theoretically permitted in the size and nomenclature of the various divisions, laid out as they were by a semi-religious body of experts, the gromatici.[2] The forum was generally placed at the crossing of the main streets, and round it were the chief buildings of the city. The centre of Pompeii, under the Empire fully Romanised, contains all those

---

[1] The earliest surviving arch to show this feature in Rome itself is that of Septimius Severus. But perhaps Trajan's arch there had made the innovation. The so called 'Arch of Trajan' at Timgad seems to be later than was generally supposed. See Ashby, p. 118.

[2] For these, see H. Stuart Jones, *Companion to Roman History* (Oxford, 1912), pp. 16 ff., and *The Oxford Classical Dictionary* (Oxford, 1949), *s.v.* Gromatici.

normally found. At one end of the long narrow forum is the Temple of Jupiter, behind which are public baths; at the other the basilica and court houses; while along the two sides are more temples and public buildings.

In many eastern and southern cities the principal streets were lined by covered colonnades, which allowed the inhabitants to traverse the town sheltered from the fierce rays of the sun. Remains of these exist at Palmyra, Damascus, Gerasa and Timgad. In Rome colonnaded streets were less essential, as the many 'porticus' and fora answered the same purpose and provided the necessary shelter. In northern towns, such as Lincoln, one finds a certain number of colonnaded walks, built as a protection against the rain.[1]

The oldest and most famous of the fora, the Forum Romanum, originated as a central open space like the Greek Agora, triangular in shape, its base along the east side of the Capitol. It served on ordinary days as a market place, and hence as the scene of litigation. But here also the citizens met in their tribes for political assemblies and elections. On the west side were the rostra, for addressing these assemblies. On the north was the 'Curia', or senate house, for meetings of the ruling oligarchy. The forum lay, moreover, between the two centres of the official religion, the Capitol, the gods of which protected the State, and the Temple of Vesta, who protected the hearths of individual Romans. Through it and up the Capitol wound the Sacred Way, the processional road along which victorious generals led their prisoners and spoils in triumph; and here, from 264 B.C. onwards, were long held those gladiatorial battles that enlivened the celebrations and funerals of eminent Romans. So the Colosseum itself, to the east, is merely an extension, for one particular purpose, of the ancient forum.

By the second century B.C., at latest, the vegetable market and cattle market (forum holitorium and forum boarium), each with its group of small protecting temples, had been laid out beside the Tiber to the west of the Capitol. These two trades, a nuisance in the main Forum, could thus benefit from the nearness of the river. The meat market of Republican times probably occupied the site

---

[1] The remains at Palmyra were beautifully illustrated by Wood, *Palmyra* (London, 1758). They are now published by T. Wiegand, *Palmyra* (Berlin, 1932). For the 'porticus' at Rome, see below, p. 316. For the colonnade in Bailgate, Lincoln, see the plan by Loehr in *Archaeologia*, 1899, p. 371.

east of the Forum where now stands the Basilica of Maxentius—a less convenient place than that for the cattle market, and ill connected with the others.[1] Only under Nero were the butchers given a more splendid and permanent meat market (macellum) to the south-east, on the Caelian Hill.[2]

In the second century B.C., also, the Forum was given its surrounding basilicas, large covered market halls, with compartments for magistrates' courts either appended or included. But all these improvements still failed to meet the needs of Rome. The Campus Martius, the flat neighbourhood north-west of the Capitol where the Pantheon and most Renaissance palaces stand, was developed for the first time under the late Republic and devoted to buildings of recreation, like theatres, and to porticus (porticoes). The porticus were large. That of Octavia,[3] the most famous, was a court surrounded by open colonnades externally about 400 by 370 feet, and had, in the centre of its south-west face, a splendid propylon with a double colonnade and no gate-wall. It also contained a library and a lounge. Built originally to enclose two temples, it reminds us that porticus had a less commercial character than fora and lacked the basilicas found in most of the latter.

The Forum Romanum was still very congested at the beginning of the Empire, and it took the emperors a century and a half of building to relieve it of the crowds. The Capitol closed its western, the Palatine its southern side. Only on the north and east could it be extended, and on the north only by demolishing slums and excavating the rock—hence the high walls enclosing the Imperial Fora in a fashion unknown to the Forum Romanum and apparently the porticus. Julius and Augustus attached their new

---

[1] See Lanciani, *Ruins*, p. 204.

[2] Rebuilt three centuries later on the same plan, it was converted a century after that into the church of S. Stefano Rotondo (Lanciani, pp. 358-9). As a clumsy mid-fifth-century adaptation of a deserted meat-market, this seems of very minor importance in the history of early church-planning, though E. H. Swift (*Roman Origins of Christian Church Architecture* (New York, 1951), p. 44) takes it seriously.

[3] Platner and Ashby (*Topographical Dictionary of Ancient Rome, s.v.* Porticus Octaviae) say the Porticus of Octavia was not an Augustan rebuilding of the earlier Porticus Octavia (begun *c.* 168 B.C.). They admit, however, that the latter 'has left no traces'. I believe there was only one building, the Porticus Octavia(e), the present ruins of which date from A.D. 200 but probably adhere closely to the Augustan plan. In seeing only one building here, I follow Dio Cassius (XLIX, 43) and Lanciani (p. 472).

fora to its north-western end, Vespasian and Nerva continued these extensions along the whole of its north side, and Trajan finished the task by enormously enlarging the newly won space on its west side and linking it at last to the Campus Marius itself.[1]

Of the imperial fora the most interesting are those of Augustus and Trajan. The former set the fashion of slicing down the rocky face of the Quirinal north of the Forum Romanum, to the main axis of which it stretches roughly at right angles, with an overall dimension of 390 by 285 English feet. A lofty wall of peperino with travertine string-courses, an example of pure masonry rare in Imperial Rome, enclosed it on the east and west and masked the northern rock face. Inside, it comprised the usual rectangular court, with a colonnaded walk in front of shops and with a central gate in the south façade. Better organised than the earlier forum of Pompeii, it had a temple at the northern end orientated north and south, its back to the rock and its front facing down the forum with good effect directly to the gate. This was the splendid temple of Mars the Avenger, which Augustus built as a military shrine, consecrating there the Roman standards recovered from the enemies of Rome. Behind the east and west colonnades of the forum and towards its northern end were large hemicycles. Although almost aligned with the sides of the temple, they were not allowed to tell in the general effect of the court, but were completely masked by straight colonnades across their fronts —a very early instance of this general imperial practice, less poetic in effect than the Republican treatment at Praeneste.[2] In later fora, where they masked hemicycles of shops, screening colonnades had some aesthetic use. But the hemicycles of Augustus, designed to display the statues and trophies of Roman triumphatores, should surely have told in the general views of his forum. For full recognition of the beauty of such curved shapes one has to wait for the great Byzantine buildings of Justinian.

The masonry of this forum is excellent, an object-lesson in the intelligent use of varying stones. Under Augustus marble was placed at points of special strain, like columns and keystones, where travertine had appeared under the Republic. A little after

---

[1] For a good plan of the Forum Romanum and the Imperial Fora, see Anderson-Spiers-Ashby, Pl. XCIII. The plan in the *CAH*, XI, opposite p. 774 shows only the fora of Nerva, Augustus and Trajan.

[2] See above, p. 270.

Augustus, skill in masonry became less important, as pozzuolana revealed its true powers and purchasers demanded only the thinnest and most economical veneers of marble.

Trajan planned his forum at right angles to the Augustan, from which it was entered through a triumphal arch. The forum proper, reached first, was a vast open space about 280 feet wide, between covered porticoes to north and south with double rows of columns. Each portico screened a vast hemicycle, much larger than the Augustan, designed for shops and offices and several storeys high. Along the whole western side of the forum stretched

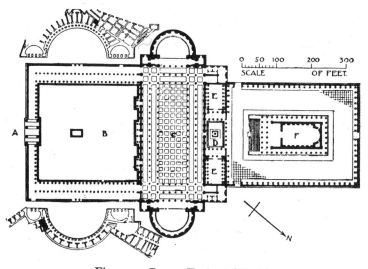

Fig. 107 Rome, Forum of Trajan.
A = Triumphal Arch; B = Main Court; C = Basilica; D = Trajan's Column;
E = Libraries; F = Temple of the Divine Trajan.

the Basilica Ulpia, the largest Roman basilica, described below, and west of this was a small peristylar square, dominated by Trajan's Column and flanked by two small libraries, one, it is assumed, for Greek, the other for Latin books.[1] The column, excluding the pedestal and measuring to the top of the abacus, has, like its copy, the Column of Marcus, a height of exactly 100 Roman feet. With the pedestal it seems to mark, as its own inscription and Dio both declare, the greatest height of rock sliced away

---

[1] Not one of the ancient authorities cited by Platner and Ashby (*s.v.* Forum Traiani), not even Dio, actually tells us so much. It is a mere guess of modern scholars.

from the Quirinal to make room for the markets in the forum.[1]
The room inside the pedestal probably contained an urn with the
ashes of Trajan. West of the peristylar square another large
rectangular enclosure, with a temple of the deified Trajan on the
axis of the forum, was built by Hadrian to complete this noble
group of buildings, and to give a proper approach from the
Campus Martius. Today everything west of the column is
covered by mean houses and churches, which choke the centre
of Rome and have forced successive Italian governments since
1870 to increasingly virulent solutions of the Roman traffic
problem.

Outside Rome the most impressive forum known is at Baalbek
in Syria. Considering its Roman plan, it seems fair to call it a
forum, although it has no basilica attached but had an altar in the
centre, and although, from another point of view, it represents
but one phase of those huge, immemorial bazaars belonging to the
wealthier temples of the east and already, as we saw,[2] so active
in the days of Sumer and Akkad. The platform on which it
stands recalls its eastern ancestors. The great temple of Jupiter,
nearly 180 feet wide on the stylobate, commands on the east a
space some 280 feet wide and over 300 feet long, entered on the
opposite side through a smaller hexagonal court from a grand
eastern propylon. The hexagon had some religious significance
at Baalbek.[3] But the larger court was surely given over, at least
in part, to commerce. It was enclosed on three sides by a
colonnaded walk, with a clear width of some 22 feet. This masks
a continuous series of large rectangular and semicircular rooms
internally as wide as itself. In dimensions it comes close to the
first court of Trajan's forum, where the clear space is very nearly
280 feet square. But though Trajan's architect Apollodorus came

---

[1] Dio 68, xvi, 3. Cf. Pauly-Wissowa, *s.v.* Rom, cols. 1047–8. Dio is
the only surviving ancient writer to give an unbroken narrative of the first
two and a half centuries of the empire. He took pains to chronicle the
erection of important buildings. To the student of Roman architecture
he is indispensable.

[2] Above, p. 9. P. Collart and P. Coupel (*L'Autel Monumental de
Baalbek* (Paris, 1951) have now stressed the size of this altar. But was
the whole forecourt occupied by religion alone? The adjustment of
religious, commercial and political activities in the centres of Hellenistic
towns has lately been studied by E. Gjerstad, 'Die Ursprungsgeschichte
der Römischen Kaiserfora' (*Opuscula Archaeologica*, III, pp. 40 ff.).
He concludes that the needs were first recognised, the grouping first
tentatively worked out in the Near East.

[3] See D. F. Brown in *AJA*, 1939, pp. 285 ff.

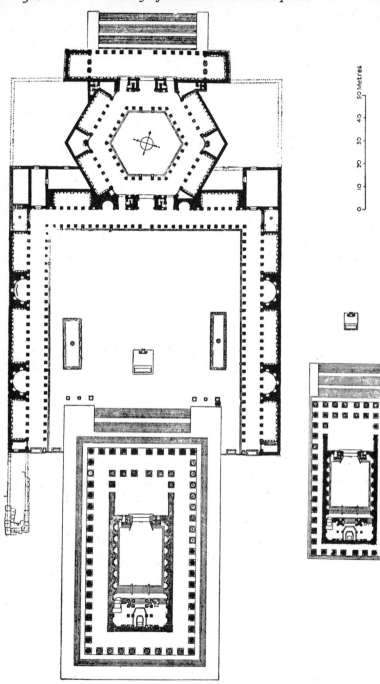

50 Metres

40

30

20

10

0

Fig. 108 The Great Sanctuary, Baalbek.

Arch of Titus, Rome

Plate 21

Pantheon, Rome

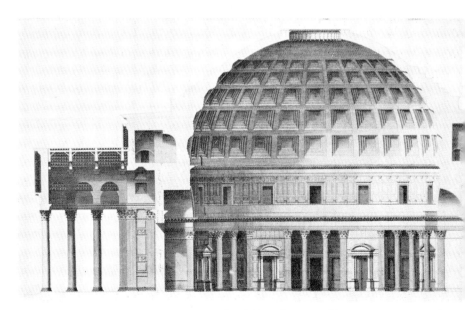

Profile of length of Pantheon at Rome

(Reproduced from Desgodetz, *Ancient Buildings of Rome*, 1795.)

Plate 22

from Damascus, next door to Baalbek,[1] there is otherwise little in common between the two ensembles—indeed the cross-basilica of Trajan's forum has few parallels in Rome or the East. On the oriental side, we may imagine the platform and forecourt of the Temple of Herod at Jerusalem as an enclosure similar to Baalbek; and we draw the conclusion that under the High Empire market places, with their dominating temples, were, *mutatis mutandis*, fairly similar all round the Mediterranean.

Another beautiful forum, this time with the temple in the centre, is the Caesareum (*c.* A.D. 6) at Cyrene. It owes its beauty to its magnificent entrance and its conservative Doric order,[2] very unusual in imperial fora. Its twin at Ostia, the Forum of the Corporations, behind the Theatre and devoted largely to mercantile agencies, possesses a notable pavement in black and white mosaic. Its continuous frame, designed to harmonise with the interior of the long surrounding colonnades, is clearly the work of the imperial architect. But the small centres, or 'emblemata',[3] in front of each shop were filled at the expense of the firms themselves—an admirable system of quiet and controlled advertisement.[4]

In Britain, Silchester had an interesting little forum and basilica.[5] On several northern sites, particularly in Gaul, where we see the usual appointments of a Roman town and no trace of private houses, we must assume the fora and basilicas were used only for occasional trading 'fairs' like those of the Middle Ages.[6] Of these 'fair-grounds', so interesting to the student of Romanisation, its successes and failures, we have examples near Compiègne and Poitiers. On them are found some of those strange Romano-Celtic temples,[7] on plan two concentric squares, now known to be

---

[1] For Apollodorus, see the Architectural Publications Society, *Dictionary* (London, 1887), *s.v.* and now also *Chambers's Encyclopaedia* (1950), *s.v.* The evidence comes mostly from Dio.

[2] See Hyslop and Applebaum, *Cyrene and Ancient Cyrenaica* (British Military Guide, 1945), Pl. VII. The building is now published in detail in the *Papers of the British School at Rome*, 1958.

[3] For 'emblemata', see above, p. 238.

[4] For this smallei forum, see G. Calza in *Bulletino Communale*, 1915, pp. 178–206. Laid out under Augustus and embellished under Claudius, it was disfigured under Commodus.

[5] See R. G. Collingwood, *The Archaeology of Roman Britain* (London, 1930), pp. 99–100.

[6] The village of Wood Eaton, near Oxford, seems to be a site of this kind. Excavations in 1952 revealed quite a big 'Romano-Celtic' temple. For the bronzes found earlier, suggesting a 'fair-ground', see *Oxoniensia*, 14 (1949).

[7] For an example, see *JRS*, 1950, p. 108 and Pl. VIII, 2.

fairly common in Gaul and Britain[1] but always too ill-preserved for us to restore the roof or even its inner supports.[2]   On one Gaulish site, Sanxay, two of these square temples, of identical orientation, are carefully aligned across a valley.   It is comic to see in so outlandish an example the Roman axial planning we have just observed at its most magnificent in the Forum of Trajan.

Of basilicas also the best example built under the High Empire was that of Trajan (see Fig. 109), called the Basilica Ulpia.   It surpassed the very similar Aemilian Basilica as rebuilt under Augustus on the north side of the Forum Romanum, still, when Pliny wrote (about A.D. 75), one of the 'three most beautiful

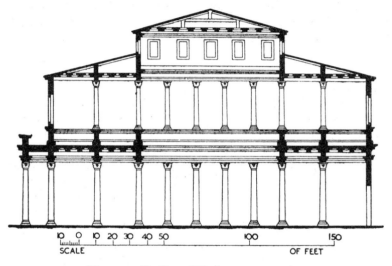

Fig. 109   Basilica of Trajan, cross-section.

buildings the world ever saw'.[3]   At this time all basilicas comprised central halls, with colonnades and clerestories of light construction, wooden roofs, one presumes of the long straight Roman larches, and lower enclosing aisles on all sides.   These

---

[1] British examples appear, among other places, at Caerwent and Colchester.   At Silchester is a circular building of similar type.   For a cluster of 'Romano-Celtic' temples at Trier see O. Brogan, *Roman Gaul*, Fig. 32.   For Sanxay, see J. Formigé, *Gallia*, 1944, p. 44.

[2] A circular temple at Périgueux has niches high on its exterior meant, it seems, for the rafters of a lean-to verandah.   See O. Brogan, *Roman Gaul*, p. 201 and Fig. 45a.

[3] *Natural History*, XXXVI, 102.   The other two were the Forum of Augustus and Vespasian's Temple of Peace in his own Forum.

aisles were double in the Basilica Ulpia; and the tribunals, of which one at Pompeii had occupied a kind of cage at the end of the hall, were here more conveniently relegated to two apses on the shorter ends masked by the returns of the aisles. The central hall measured 280 by 80 feet, and was enclosed by monolithic columns of granite, as opposed to the monoliths of Phrygian marble in the Aemilian Basilica. Vitruvius makes it quite clear[1] that the normal basilica had an upper aisle, separated from the central hall by an upper colonnade; and his own basilica at Fano, remarkable for having one giant order instead of two tiers of columns, itself had an aisle of two storeys. Between its roof and that of the hall he found space for a very open clerestory, broken by the great pier alone, some 12 feet high. Entrances and tribunals, provided they facilitated the main business of the building, might occupy any place the architect wished. His problem was simple, his solution flexible, utilitarian and seldom inelegant.

If the basilicas still savour a little of Greek architecture, the temples are the most Greek of all Roman buildings. Like the Greek, they were shrines, homes for deities, rather than congregational buildings. They were also used for many purposes which would appear to us decidedly incongruous. Thus, the Temple of Concord was frequently used for meetings of the Senate, and was especially noted for its collection of works brought from Greece, Egypt and the old Etruscan cities.[2] The Temple of Mars the Avenger contained a number of statues of famous generals. In the Temple of Saturn was housed the chief public treasure; and some part of the Temple of Castor was 'used as an office for the verification of weights and measures'.[3]

In all this the Roman practice was really the same as the Greek. State functions needed divine sanction, and the gods were useful chiefly for blessing and protecting the various departments of civic life. As in Greece, the surrounding court accommodated worshippers, while the altar usually faced the main front of the temple from outside. As, however, the Romans preferred a raised platform, or podium, for the temple, ascended only from the front, the altar was often incorporated in the front stairs or landing and so could not extend, as in Greece, for the full width

---

[1] V, 1, v.

[2] Pliny, in his thirty-fourth book, mentions a whole series of Greek bronzes of the greater Greek gods.

[3] Middleton, *Remains*, I, p. 281.

of the façade. The Romans also, as opposed to the Greeks, formally related their temples to fora or cross-roads, and therefore orientated them to give their fronts commanding vistas and prominent central positions in symmetrical groups of buildings.

Roman rectangular temples are not as a rule peripteral, but of the type called pseudoperipteral. In the pseudoperipteral plan the cella is extended so as to obliterate the side and rear peristyles and leave free only the outer halves of the colonnades, which thus appear as engaged columns.[1] But the front peristyle is deepened to about one-third of the length of the temple.[2] Occasional temples, such as the Temple of Concord, had a very wide cella and a total width greater than their length—a plan employed, according to some respectable authorities, in the original Pantheon of Agrippa.[3]

Whatever its shape, the Roman temple is raised on a high podium and approached by a wide flight of steps at the entrance, on each side of which is a dwarf 'cheek-wall', often supporting figures and groups of bronze or marble. It is usually of the Corinthian order; a few are Ionic, and only one or two are Doric. Some examples end in an apse, often concealed outside, especially in Hadrianic work. The cella itself is often walled and vaulted in concrete, and an internal division into nave and aisles is thus structurally unnecessary. Like their Greek prototypes, however, these Roman cellas had often free-standing columns placed very near the side-walls, to give scale without encumbering the floor space. The Temple of Venus and Rome (see Fig. 110) provides a well-known example.[4]

Of Augustan peripteral temples the most beautiful was that of Castor and Pollux (a building frequently but mistakenly identified since the Renaissance as the Temple of Jupiter Stator) on the south side of the Forum, a successor of the famous Republican temple and dedicated in A.D. 6. The plan of its entrance portico is unexpected and unique.[5] The columns are of excellent proportion and the capitals with their entwined volutes were considered by Peruzzi and Lanciani[6] about the best in Rome. The entablature,

---

[1] See above, p. 272.
[2] In the Republican temple of Cori, as in Vitruvius' Etruscan Temple, it was as much as half the total length. See above, p. 224.
[3] See below, p. 325.
[4] See Middleton, *Remains*, II, pp. 219 ff.
[5] See Robertson, p. 216.
[6] Lanciani, *Ruins*, p. 273. I suspend judgment on a recent view that they are Flavian.

not to mention its constructional ingenuity,[1] exceeds in delicacy
even the most careful later work. The three columns are now
much mutilated and the whole temple suffering (September 1952)
from strange neglect.[2]

The temple of Mars the Avenger in the Forum of Augustus
was dedicated in 2 B.C. It was fully peripteral, except at the rear,
where it abutted on the rock. The ruins include portions of a
fine coffered marble ceiling over the ambulatory, and part of the
cella-wall.[3] The latter is of peperino and was faced with thin
slabs of marble, with thicker marble bands at intervals. The most
interesting feature, however, is the semicircular apse at the end of
the cella. From simple halls without peristyles, such as the
examples at Samothrace and Praeneste, the apse has now invaded
the peristylar temple and has come to stay.

Peripteral temples now went out of fashion at Rome, until their
revival under Hadrian for temples to the Divine Trajan and to
Venus and Rome.[4] The latter temple, supposedly designed by
Hadrian himself, is a rather clumsy Roman version of the Parthenon, a double temple with two apsidal cellas placed back to back.
The side walls were continued so as to conceal the apses, and a
pseudodipteral peristyle surrounded the whole. Each cella
was about 70 feet square, exclusive of its apse, and was covered by
a barrel vault in concrete. Although extensively repaired under
Maxentius (*c.* A.D. 310), this temple has surely retained its Hadrianic arrangements. The bronze roof-tiles that rested directly on
the vaults, in a manner suggesting some tunnel-vaulted Romanesque churches of south-west France, were removed to the Vatican
by the famous heretical Pope Honorius I in the seventh century,
in time for the Saracens to loot them when they so boldly sacked
that suburb in A.D. 846. The vast level platform on which the
temple stood was surrounded by continuous stoas with gigantic
columns of porphyry and granite.

[1] See above, p. 290.
[2] I could nowhere find even one of the famous capitals preserved in a
safe place. All I found were half buried or wholly ivy-mantled, apart
from the three battered examples on the standing columns. Yet the
Italian authorities could have easily housed a few of them in the absurd
and at present useless 'Senate House of Diocletian', restored under the
Fascist régime at the expense of the Senate House of Julius Caesar (cf.
Blake, *Construction*, p. 153). A capital of this type, it may be noticed,
is preserved in the Soane Museum.
[3] See D'Espouy, *op. cit.*, Pls. 52–61.
[4] Vespasian's Temple of Peace, in his Forum of Peace (see p. 322 above),
could, from its situation, have been peripteral.

In the east peripteral temples remained very popular, and the largest examples, at Palmyra and Baalbek, are on a scale greater than any in Rome. The true admirer of classical architecture

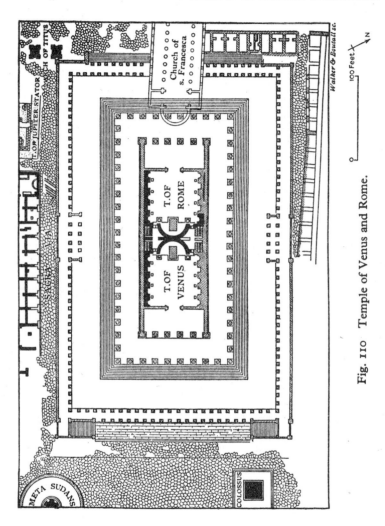

Fig. 110   Temple of Venus and Rome.

cannot surely be expected to describe the Temple of Bel at Palmyra, so cruelly does it debase his favourite forms. But the great temple of Jupiter at Baalbek, at least begun in Augustan times, and the smaller and later temple beside it are among the noblest Roman monuments. Much of their beauty is doubtless due to Greek artificers, whose forefathers had settled in Syria some centuries before. In their use of large stones and hair joints they outdo even classical Greek work; and the platform of the great temple contains three blocks which are probably the largest ever used on any building. Each is 12 feet high, 11 feet wide and over 60 feet long.[1] But the design of these buildings, as opposed to their technique, and their careful grouping are largely Roman (see Fig. 108). The Great Temple was a little shorter than Ephesus, the Temple of Bacchus alongside rather larger than the Parthenon. Unlike the 'factory chimneys' of Palmyra, the columns of the peristyles are sturdy and well proportioned. We have already described the bold brackets and modillions of the entablature.[2] They have a Roman self-confidence. Surviving doorways, too, have the Roman 'flat arch' for a lintel. The cella of the smaller temple probably copies with some fidelity the vanished interior of its great neighbour, and marks the triumph of that decorative scheme first employed in the Basilical Hall of Praeneste. In one respect it is unique. The side-pilasters of the nave are actually faced with engaged half-columns. With other features of the design, this had the effect, if Wiegand's restoration is right,[3] of diverting attention from the awkward internal corner pilasters, the continuous bugbear of Roman and Renaissance architects: but one is not surprised that the temple found no imitators. With no pozzuolana available, a stone roof for this cella was out of the question. So, like the churches of Constantine in the Holy Land, it had a wooden ceiling, whereas contemporary works in Rome were vaulted. Most differences between Rome and Syria are explained by this difference of materials, though it has been too often ignored by art-historians trying to find which is more 'advanced' or 'important' than the other.[4]

To turn to buildings which, in comparison with Baalbek, seem almost ridiculous, we have many examples of moderately sized

[1] See Brockedon and Roberts, *The Holy Land*, II (London, 1855), Baalbek, *ad fin.* This is twice the length of any stone Roberts saw in an Egyptian building, and exceeded by some of the obelisks and colossi alone.
[2] Above, p. 308.
[3] Reproduced in Robertson, Pl. XXII.
[4] This forgetfulness seems to me to pervade the pages of E. H. Swift (*Roman Origins of Christian Art*) on the fourth-century churches of Palestine. Because of their wooden roofs he thinks them poor copies of Rome. But we know that their iconography was not merely 'more advanced' than the Roman, but revolutionary.

pseudoperipteral temples, most famous of all being the Maison Carrée at Nîmes (see Fig. 111). Of undeniably precise workmanship, it fails as badly as most buildings of its type to impress the beholder with Roman grandeur.[1] There is something crude and bald in the way the cella fills up the rear; and, in addition, the provincial architect has made a cardinal error, rare indeed in Greek and Roman building, over the management of his ground courses. He actually places a full Greek krepis of three steps on top of a Roman podium, and has to continue the former at the front quite purposelessly along each of the 'cheek-walls'[2] and back again. Contrast the management of the single decent step in the Republican Temple of Fortuna Virilis at Rome.[3] But for none of these buildings is it possible to muster much enthusiasm, and one turns gladly to round temples, a form with which the Romans were happier.

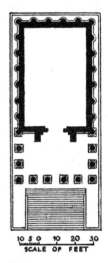

10 5 0   10   20   30
SCALE OF FEET

Fig. 111   Maison Carrée, Nîmes.

They are of three kinds, the pteron without a cella, the peripteral cella and the cella without a pteron. A famous example of the first is the little temple of Rome on the Acropolis of Athens, in its order a literal copy of the Erechtheum.[4]

Of the second we have already considered two famous Republican examples[5]; but the best known of all, the Temple of Vesta in the Forum, dates in its present shape only from the reign of Septimius Severus.[6]

It is an undistinguished building with meagre Ionic columns, each on a pedestal projecting on plan from the line of the podium. This, of course, ruins the scale. All

---

[1] I grant its surroundings are uncongenial—monotonous nineteenth-century Corinthian porticoes to the same scale as the temple (contrast the arrangement of Greek stoas, as described above, p. 201), and in the courtyard batteries of floodlights. Its restored cella, painted in a French ochre and used as a museum, savours too much of 'le monde où l'on s'ennuie'. Even the roof is ruined. The ancient tiles have all gone, and the edges of new clay tiles project above their sima, giving an impression of barbarism equalled only in the villas of Palladio.
[2] See above, p. 324.　　　[3] See above, p. 272.
[4] See G. A. S. Snijder, *RA*, 1924, pp. 223 ff.
[5] See above, pp. 264 and 272.
[6] It was re-erected in 1930 (*Touring Club Italiano*, Rome (Milan, 1934), p. 141). A publication of it seems hard to find.

through its history this temple had been circular. The ancients
preferred the form for a building containing the common hearth,
as the Tholos at Athens also shows. The Romans may have
given external domes to the cellas of round temples, as Vitruvius
perhaps prescribes,[1] instead of the Greek umbrella-roof of wood.
But none survives. Only once does the Roman builder success-
fully defy Greek tradition, in the little curved 'Temple of Venus'
at Baalbek, where he runs back the podium in a series of concavities,
one between each pair of columns on the peristyle, to so great a
depth that each just touches the cella-wall. The entablature
follows suit. It is very broken and undulating, and therefore
very pleasing to a Roman, and quite as 'advanced' formally as the
Hadrianic buildings of Rome and Tivoli.[2] The purpose was
wholly aesthetic, though Robertson supposes each sweep of the
entablature from column to column to serve as a horizontal arch,
an abutment for the vault of the cella. Hardly so, for it would fall,
having no proper abutment itself. Indeed, it is in a parlous state
over the columns, which it has dragged outwards.[3]

Only in the third class, of round temples without a peristyle,
does the Roman architect show his true calibre, and erect the
Pantheon (see Pl. 22 and Fig. 112). We owe this, the largest and
most wonderful of all Roman temples, to the Emperor Hadrian,
the greatest of all Roman patrons.[4] The tiles taken by Chédanne
from nearly every part of it all confirm its Hadrianic date. It
consists of three portions: the entrance portico on the north, an
intermediate rectangular member as wide as the portico but as
high as the rotunda, and the domed rotunda itself, to which it
owes its name. Like other nearly perfect ancient buildings, it
raises the hardest question of all, that of its original use. We do
not really understand it.[5] Its history, too, under the Empire is

[1] Vitruvius IV, 8, iii. His word, 'tholus', can mean many things.
[2] See above, p. 327. It is interesting to find the work at Baalbek so
good and so Roman. Someone should study the first-rate buildings
that set the fashions under the Empire.
[3] See Robertson, p. 265 and illustration.
[4] A good series of measured drawings is given by Desgodetz, *The
Ancient Buildings of Rome* (London, 1795), Pls. I–XXIII.
[5] It was certainly a temple, as Dio makes clear (LIII, 27), not a science
library, as alleged by Granger (*JRIBA*, 1932–3, pp. 57 ff.). Not to
mention Granger's hazardous readings and interpretations of Vitruvius,
his alterations of notes and his guesses about the political position of
Agrippa, I find his ideas of an original wooden Pantheon shaped like the
present building and his acquiescence in a coffered domical vault as a
presumably accurate sundial a train of thought it would be wrong to
pursue before dinner.

beset with problems.   We had better begin by describing it as it is.

The present portico looks like a rebuilding with the materials
of an older front.   The pitch of the pediment is steep, much
steeper than in Greek or even in other Roman buildings.   The
modillions, too, slope perceptibly inside the raking cornice.
Usually they are vertical in this position.[1]   The shallowness of the
tympanum is unexplained, unless we suppose it had a decoration
of bronze plates in harmony with the bronze of the roof now, alas!
all gone.   The shafts of the columns are chiefly of red and grey
Egyptian granite, unfluted and monolithic, and the capitals and
bases of white Pentelic marble.   An inscription on the front frieze
records the dedication of the first Pantheon by Agrippa in 27 B.C.
Others, in smaller letters, refer to restorations by Septimius
Severus and Caracalla.   None commemorates Hadrian.

The intermediate member has a flat roof level with the external
cornice of the rotunda.   Necessary aesthetically—for it prevents
the rotunda from overpowering the portico—it is clumsily executed.
Like the rotunda, it has several horizontal strings, which occur,
however, at a different level; so that the strings on either part
stop dead when they meet the other, making a rare tangle of the
junction.   Structurally, the rotunda and intermediate member
are nowhere connected.   But since the strings notice each other
in this way, and nowhere continue out of sight, one has surely to
agree with Robertson that the present design, however tangled,
was all carried out at one time.[2]   The junction of this member with
the portico is equally awkward.   The moulding on its face
designed to accommodate the roof of the portico wanders away
to meet the side strings some way above the two bottom corners.[3]
But internally it is useful and well designed.   For it provides two
side niches for shrines at the inner end of the portico and a tunnel-
vaulted vestibule before the great bronze doors described above.[4]

The rotunda, entered through a doorway 40 feet high and 20 feet
wide, has an interior 142 feet high and 142 feet wide, excluding
the recesses.   The surrounding wall is of concrete 20 feet thick,
but this is not solid throughout, as there are eight recesses on the

---

[1] There are, however, other exceptions, such as the Capitol at Ostia.
Desgodetz, *op. cit.*, p. 6, says of the Pantheon that 'The modillions are
plumb.'   This was not my impression of them.

[2] Robertson, pp. 247–8.

[3] The misdemeanours of the central member appear very clearly on
Pls. III and IV of Desgodetz.

[4] Above, p. 305.

ground floor, five rectangular (of which one forms the entrance) and three semicircular (see Fig. 112). Besides these, other vaulted niches exist at ground-floor level and also above, which are walled off from the interior. This honeycombing shows how completely the Romans trusted their concrete, how monolithic

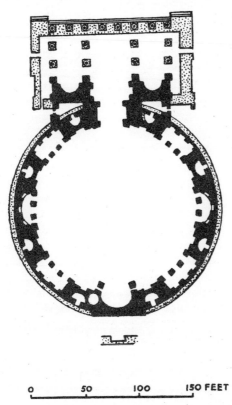

Fig. 112　The Pantheon and its predecessor.
Dotted areas are Augustan.
Black areas are Hadrianic.

they could make their construction at the time the Pantheon was built.[1] Between the recesses are aedicules; and each recess,

[1] According to the latest American reports, the architects of Sta Sophia attempted a similar hollowing—which failed, of course, at once in a building of brick and stone. If so, we have yet another instance of the part tradition plays in the building-crafts, in the hope of the Byzantines that brick might behave like the concrete of their Roman ancestors. But I have not seen this published, and owe my knowledge of it to the late Mr. Fletcher, of Campden Hill.

except the entrance and the semicircle directly opposite, is masked by two marble columns between 'Pompeian' corner-pilasters.[1]

The masking columns are not evenly spaced, being 8 feet 4 inches apart and only 7 feet from the pilasters. The wider central space produces an admirable effect. They have little structural value, as over each pair, but hidden from view, is a strong discharging arch, which carries the weight of the wall. Their chief value is that they give scale. Without them the Pantheon would not look half its size. This effect of scale is spoilt at present by the big 'baroque' saints and even more by some absurdly large and bare empty niches, with stupid pediments, in the storey above, inserted in 1747, against all the protests of Piranesi, by Pope Benedict XIV. As we see from drawings of Piranesi,[2] Desgodetz and others, this storey originally contained pilasters about half the height of the columns below, grouped in quadruplets and with a small niche between each group and its neighbour—something like an inversion of the outer peristyle on the dome of St. Paul's. Every niche came over an aedicule or the centre of a large niche on the ground floor. This design again most cleverly enhanced the scale by exaggerating the effects of perspective. In its execution and details it offered interesting analogies to Byzantine work. Similar stumpy pilasters with marble panels between them reappear in the chancel of San Vitale at Ravenna. So Viollet-le-Duc was wide of the mark to pronounce the original decoration of the Pantheon perfunctory and only half considered.[3] Indeed, its wall-design had a good influence on such careful Renaissance churches as S. Andrea, Mantua.[4]

Half the height of the Pantheon internally is vertical wall, the other half is dome. This suggests bad proportion; but such is not the case, as the division between the two is not strongly marked, and, by an optical illusion, the wall does not look vertical, but appears to curve slightly inwards, as though the dome started at floor-level. The dome itself is deeply coffered, with square panels and frames in mock perspective, at one time enriched with stucco mouldings, painted and gilded. A bronze flower once

[1] See above, p. 262.

[2] Rivoira, *Architettura Romana*, Fig. 132.

[3] *Lectures* (English edition), I, pp. 113–16. The original design has now been restored on one bay of the Pantheon—too small an area for its effect to tell. The result is now almost as irritating as the one completed face of Brunelleschi's dome at Florence.

[4] See Wittkower, *Architectural Principles in the Age of Humanism* (London, 1949), pp. 47 ff.

occupied the centre of every panel. Only the plain fasciae now remain, but we may doubt if the effect was ever finer than at present, when the sharp shadows falling on the recessed fasciae and panels and the charming play of light and shade all over the dome more than compensate, one might think, for the loss of distracting enrichments. However, the details that do remain give us every reason to trust the good taste in all matters of their consummate designer.

The noble appearance of the interior is due in a great measure to the method of lighting adopted. Only one opening, and that a circular one at the crown of the dome, about 28 feet wide, lights this vast hall. The amount of light it gives is ample, and, what is of equal importance, is evenly distributed over the whole building. No scheme of side lighting, however ingenious, could produce so fine an effect. The surface of the marble floor is slightly convex, perhaps to counteract the curve of the dome above, which would make it look concave were it quite flat, or perhaps merely to drain off the rain that enters through the eye.

The exterior of the rotunda, which was not originally much seen, is far less satisfying than the interior, and is fairly likened by Robertson to a full gasometer. This is because the outer wall is carried upwards, to weight the haunches of the dome—a precaution hardly necessary considering its homogeneity with its supports.[1] Those Byzantine builders who carried the wall up higher still and provided an outer timber roof produced one solution of this particular problem. But then their domes are proportionately much higher, and have in the centre, in place of the sky, the colossal figure of Christ the Ruler of All.[2] The visible part of the dome on the Pantheon rises at first in steps, and is curved only near the top. Once it was all covered with tiles of bronze, which survived until A.D. 663. Then, notwithstanding the consecration of the building as a church only half a century before, they were stripped by Constans II, who was conveying them to Constantinople when he lost them to the Saracens at Syracuse. The survival of the dome after such treatment well shows the hydraulic virtues of true pozzuolana. The external wall, which is about 100 feet high, is of brick-faced concrete and

[1] Perhaps, however, a roof of classical pitch was meant to disguise the dome.

[2] 'Nature I loved, and, next to Nature, Art.' The inferiority of 'mannerist' and 'baroque' domes to these early conceptions in simplicity, seriousness and sublimity is too obvious to call for comment.

is divided into three stages by brick strings. The two upper stages were covered originally with stucco, but there is some evidence that the lower had a facing of white Pentelic marble.[1]

In the two upper stages of this wall we can now see semi-circular brick arches at regular intervals all round the building. It still seems uncertain how deep they go and how closely they are tied to the similar internal arches, which appear, at any rate on the first floor, to correspond exactly with them in level and size. But reason would suggest a whole system of arches was first built to serve as a frame, and that the liquid concrete was then poured over them in the manner envisaged by Choisy.[2] The dome itself has no hidden arches and no tile facing, and must have been built in some other way, not exactly known at present.

The Pantheon is unique, certainly among temples. A smaller, derivative example at Ostia, very ill preserved, dates only from Christian times.[3] Closest to it in size and shape was the great circular room in the Baths of Caracalla; and it has not, of course, escaped notice that the Pantheon adjoined the Baths of Agrippa.[4] Vitruvius, moreover, recommends a central opening in the dome of one room, the 'laconicum', in the baths he prescribes[5]; and we have noticed a frigidarium of the sort in several early Thermae.[6] But all this is mere coincidence. Concrete in the time of Agrippa was not sufficiently good for him to dream of such a dome.[7] Besides, his main bath-building was south of the Pantheon, Caracalla's on the north side of the domed room. So early scholars like Scamozzi were compelled to turn the Pantheon into a mere entrance-vestibule. Dio calls it a temple, and indeed it could have no fitter form for the worship of all the gods of heaven.

But what form did it take at the hands of Agrippa? We saw that its present octostyle portico appears to have a pediment too compressed for the stones of which it is made. If so, its predeces-

[1] See Middleton, *Remains*, II, p. 135. He praises the surviving marble veneer on the intermediate member: but illustrations of this are not easy to find. Strack, *Die Baudenkmaeler des alten Rom* (Berlin, 1890), Blatt 4, shows something.

[2] See above, p. 298.

[3] See C. G. Brigg, *Memorials of the American Academy in Rome*, VII, p. 161.

[4] See O. B. Scamozzi, *Les Thermes des Romains* (Vicenza, 1785), pp. 14–15; Middleton, II, p. 126.

[5] V, 10, v.

[6] See above, p. 273.

[7] Blake, *Construction*, pp. 265–6. On p. 345 Miss Blake shows how timidly concrete was used under Augustus.

sor can only have been decastyle. Lanciani in fact publishes a massive substructure of travertine underneath the present portico and extending beyond both its flanking colonnades (see Fig. 112). Its extent and apparent date (early Imperial) both seem to bear out the surmise that the stones and inscription of Agrippa have been reused on a new foundation. Lanciani also sees evidence, in a fairly thin reticulate wall buried under those of the existing rotunda, of an open space that originally existed between the Baths of Agrippa on the south and his Pantheon facing them on the north. Hadrian's architect, by a bold flight of genius, later turned the space into a temple, the temple into a porch. Until then it must have resembled in its dimensions and proportions the wide, shallow Temple of Concord.[1] This theory, so ably expounded by Lanciani, appears to me as attractive as any.[2]

Why, however, has Hadrian left us no official inscription? He was not, according to the Augustan History, in the habit of inscribing his buildings. But conceivably the present porch is not his. Severus in his inscription says he found the Pantheon burnt. After Hadrian, the porch, one would think, is the only part that could burn; and a Severan rebuilding might explain some, though not all, of the roughnesses and discrepancies we have noticed on the porch and intermediate member.[3] Its boldness and the brilliance of its interior make the Pantheon, like Sta Sophia, one of those rare works of genius too original for close ancestors, too daring for even a single imitation. With it, we fittingly end our account of Roman temples.

A triumphal arch would often decorate the forum, when not serving as the main gate of the town, and would sometimes occupy, especially in eastern towns, the crossing of the four chief streets. In the last position it would have four equal faces, like the Arch of Janus Quadrifrons in Rome.[4] But official imperial arches have usually two main fronts, and observe a few thoroughly Roman laws. The arched opening must be flanked by engaged or (later) detached columns, always Corinthian or Composite, standing on a podium or pedestals. An engaged entablature must enrich the building just above it, and a tall attic must crown the whole. Usually erected to commemorate a military victory, triumphal

[1] See above, p. 324.
[2] Lanciani, *Ruins*, pp. 473 ff. Admittedly Dio (LIII, 27) implies that Agrippa's Pantheon was circular.
[3] This is the theory of Cozzo, for which see Robertson, p. 248.
[4] See Strack, *Die Baudenkmaeler des alten Rom* (Berlin, 1890), Blatt 32.

arches might also mark the completion of a great public work, like a new road or a colonia of settlers.

It was Augustus who set the fashion of building them every-where, and the earliest to survive are of his reign. The earliest of all are simple, with the arch itself formed of separate voussoir blocks, as at Susa, near Turin, and at Verona, but in few later examples.[1] But by the end of the reign the builders had antici-pated almost every later form. The 'Arch of Tiberius', for instance, at Orange, dedicated in A.D. 21,[2] is too elaborately carved for our taste, but must impress us as a masterpiece of clever architectural modelling worthy of Lutyens himself (see Fig. 113). It has three openings on each long side, a feature rare at this early date, and—yet more remarkably—two attics, together half the height of the main order. Fiechter made the inevitable German suggestion that the upper attic is a later addition: but one glance at the elevation of the short sides—in this arch given an unwonted importance—should convince the student that the whole building was designed at once. On these, a continuous podium supports four engaged columns. The entablature above the centre intercolumniation is slightly recessed, but the pediment is unbroken, although largely filled with a plain arch over the recessed space. Designs of this type very soon occupied the theorists of the Renaissance, who studied this very arch quite carefully.[3] The long sides, where pediments crown the central arches, are fairly normal, except for the Lutyens-like vagaries of the upper attic.

Later arches, even in Rome, are rather more sober. Of the single-arched type a good example is the Arch of Trajan at Ancona, but the best is the Arch of Titus, erected at the eastern end of the Forum to honour Titus and commemorate the conquest of Jerusalem, and finished by Domitian about A.D. 87. The proportions are excellent and the detail is extremely good (see Pl. 21). The piers on each side of the opening are wide enough to form excellent abutments, and the real and apparent stability of

[1] See Blake, *Construction*, pp. 205 ff. Because it bears the name of M. Vitruvius Cerdo, the Arch of Verona was at one time considered a work of Vitruvius himself. But, though simple and rather dull, it has dentils and modillions in the raking cornices, a practice we know our Vitruvius abominated (see Vitruvius, IV, ii, 5).

[2] See Robertson, p. 294. It is now considered a work of Caesar, rededicated under Tiberius, but without structural alteration. See Brogan, *Roman Gaul*, pp. 44 and 164.

[3] Wittkower, *Architectural Principles in the Age of Humanism*, pp. 45–6.

Amphitheatre of Pozzuoli

Plate 23

Cortile in Insula of Serapis, Ostia

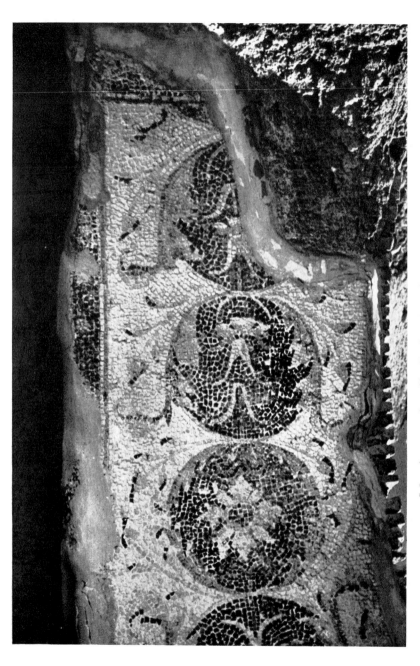

Mosaic on arch-soffit, Baths of the Seven Sages, Ostia

Plate 24

the whole is greatly assisted by the lofty attic, which occupies about a quarter of the height.   The lettering on this is fine in scale, and is a standing proof of how truly decorative lettering can be when properly treated.   On the jambs of the opening are sculptured panels representing the triumph, including the famous relief of the seven-branched candlestick.

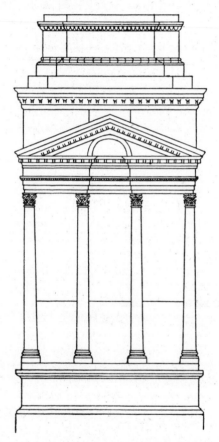

Fig. 113   Arch of Orange, short side (not to scale).

Of the arches with three openings the best, as a composition, is that of Constantine, near the Colosseum.   It is a clever pastiche of reused sculptured roundels and columns, most of them lifted from a building in honour of Trajan.   As the columns stand free in front of the piers, it seems doubtful whether they came from a

Trajanic triumphal arch: for in the surviving arches of Trajan they are still engaged, and break free on known examples only about A.D. 200.[1] Without this feature, one is bound to say one would consider the whole building an actual arch of Trajan rebuilt, especially since the few crude sculptures here certainly made for Constantine sufficiently show that his own men could not do good work, even when they had excellent models before them. The Arch of Septimius Severus, though all genuine work of A.D. 200, is infected in every part with the showiness and heaviness so inevitable in a monument of this sort in a period of declining art.

2. BATHS

Outside the fora, the places most generally frequented were the great thermae, or baths, the most sophisticated buildings of antiquity. We have seen earlier[2] how they arose from the Greek palaestra, with an additional and very soon a dominant series of rooms for hot and cold bathing. They were to the man of leisure what the basilicas were to the man of business, and formed the general meeting-place of those who had no work to do, or whose work for the day was over. As normally interpreted, the great imperial Thermae are a triumph of complicated axial planning, and the inspiration of the more rational architects of the last two hundred years. Unfortunately, they have just received a thorough reinterpretation at the hands of a German student, Miss Broedner, whose theories can now command the weighty support of Professor Ian Richmond.[3] The reader will pardon me, I hope, if I first expound the traditional view, as found, for instance, in the work of D. S. Robertson, and only later examine the new alternatives.

The following built large thermae in Rome: Agrippa, 21 B.C.; Nero, A.D. 60; Titus, 80; Trajan, 110; Caracalla, 206; Diocletian, 295; and Constantine, 320. Those of Caracalla and Diocletian have left important remains, splendid examples of the symmetrical planning and bigness of scale so conspicuous in all

[1] See above, p. 314.
[2] Above, p. 273.
[3] See his review in the *Antiquaries' Journal*, 1952, pp. 214–15. He says that there can be no doubt Broedner's main point is proved (that the courts generally thought to be open palaestrae were in fact covered basilicas), and that it is of fundamental importance.

J. B. Ward-Perkins has also reviewed this book, less sympathetically, in the *Journal of Roman Studies* (1953, pp. 210–12), and has made some telling points against it.

Roman works. The former accommodated 1600 bathers, the latter twice that number.[1] Their construction, too, is typically Roman; and in no other buildings can the Roman method of few and large points of support, combined with concrete vaults of wide span, be better studied.

The latest baths, or Central Baths, of Pompeii (see Fig. 114) had discarded the earlier system of separate suites for men and women. Whatever the distribution of the smaller compartments, only one existed of each of the larger bathrooms.[2] This single suite of large rooms is also what we find at the centre of the great imperial Thermae. If we draw the obvious analogy from the plan of the last Pompeian baths to the Thermae of Caracalla (see Fig. 115), the

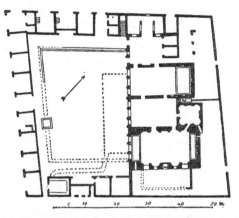

Fig. 114   Central Baths, Pompeii.

most perfect surviving in the capital, we shall conclude that the latter contained a large central oblong changing-room, or apodyterium, reached by two long, wide vestibules from the northern entrance front, a cold swimming pool (frigidarium) to its north, and to its south the tepidarium, a moderately heated vestibule to the hot swimming bath, or calidarium, built projecting from the south front to catch as much sunlight as possible. These rooms all reached the full height of the building, and the frigidarium was probably unroofed. The surrounding apartments are lower, and too ill-preserved on the whole for us to know whether they had

---

[1] See Middleton, *Remains*, II, p. 177.
[2] See Mau-Kelsey, p. 209 and Fig. 94; R. C. Carrington, *Pompeii* (Oxford 1936), p. 57 and Fig. 10.

terraced roofs or upper storeys.   To east and west of the changing-
room, and separated from it by lower, but still magnificent halls,
were open courts, or palaestrae, for exercise, with arcades on three
sides: and between each and the north entrance (but badly placed
as a thoroughfare) was a room about 40 feet square giving on to a
staircase, apparently the only important approach to the upper
parts of the building.   The remaining rooms on the south, east

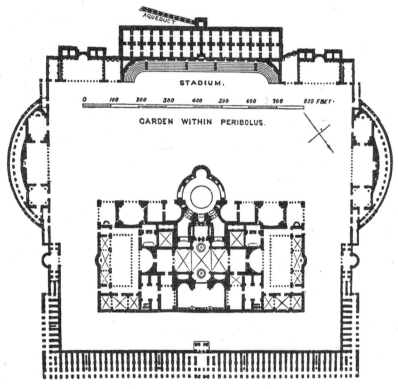

Fig. 115   Thermae of Caracalla.

and west sides were apparently devoted to steam baths, dry
sweating rooms and the numerous apartments of varying tempera-
ture required for the processes of 'Turkish' bathing.   We are
hindered in our conjectures for the Baths of Caracalla by the
absence of any published plan that shows the surviving hypocausts[1] and water-pipes, though there is no lack of clever and

[1] See above, p. 273.   The heat from these furnaces rose through the
tiled floors and up special flues in the walls.

elaborate perspectives of the restored ensemble. Admittedly, no architect could gain this information at present, as the whole building is used for, of all things, an opera house! But the sequence of rooms mentioned by Pliny in the private baths of his Laurentine villa substantially confirms the picture we have drawn.[1] He had a single frigidarium, and then a series of hotter rooms, including the calidarium and its wonderful hot swimming-pool, from which bathers could look southwards over the sea. Near this was his ball-court ('sphaeristerium'), designed to catch the sun at the end of the day. Whether this corresponds to our open palaestrae is disputable: but at any rate the bathers needed a place for exercise, seemingly in the open air, as near the baths as possible.

The central changing-room was 180 feet long and 78 feet wide, and roofed with an intersecting groined vault of concrete in three bays, still coffered but no longer classical in feeling. The upper face, or extrados of this vault, like those in the private baths of Hadrian at Tivoli, was thickened where necessary to give each of the long sides the appearance of three low-pitched classical roofs, designed to intersect one continuous longitudinal roof of the same height. Abutting on the long sides, their apex some 35 feet below that of the high vault, were three tunnel roofs, fairly shallow (only about 25 feet long) and serving to buttress the walls below the springing of the central groins. Between these tunnels, buttress-walls were continued up to the haunches of the high vault. Here, then, we have a complex of arched roofs designed to counter mutual thrusts, a system as far as possible from the trabeated. In fact, it is here that the attempts of the Romans to give their style a trabeated disguise begin to wear hopelessly thin. The ceiling only distantly recalled classical forms, and was perhaps given coloured mosaic in places, anticipating the Byzantine manner: while the columns, carved with the drill and therefore palpably 'late',[2] appear only as attachments to the fronts and sides of the great piers. Those in front, standing out in the central hall, have each an isolated fragment of entablature above, which has to stop dead at the face of the pier; for it would be impossible to carry it round the building. In its isolation it looks very bald and clumsy; so that one of the most curious facts in the history of architecture

---

[1] Pliny the Younger, *Letters*, II, 17.

[2] See above, p. 309. To me the design of these columns and chunks of entablature, aesthetically unconnected with the masonry behind them, seems fairly close to the Severan Forum of Lepcis, figured by J. B. Ward-Perkins in *JRS*, 1948, Pl. VI, 1 and 3.

is the way this objectionable feature was blindly copied by the later architects of the Renaissance.

The great calidarium in the middle of the south side was probably a complete circle. With a diameter of 116 feet, not much less than that of the Pantheon, it had far flimsier supports, coupled piers, between which room was perhaps left for small piscinae, or swimming-pools; and Middleton denies that it originally formed a circle or projected from the south front. He admits that at some time a wall did complete the circle, and had itself a small apse off its southern side. But all is at present obliterated under the seating for the opera. A surviving pier contains one of those arched squinches that form in the fifth-century Baptistery at Naples the transition from a polygonal chamber to a crowning cupola. It is interesting to see it so early, and to ask why a room of circular plan required it at all. But inspection is now fruitless amid the batteries and lighting-gantries that disfigure hereabouts the 'gigantic mechanism of the Roman structure'.[1]

These buildings occupy merely the centre of an enormous platform raised 20 feet above ground-level and covering an area about 400 yards by 350. The aqueduct met it on its south side, on its north side were shops and slipper-baths, while on the east and west it supported large ranges of buildings for exercise and discussion, buildings remarkable for the pendentives, however crude and experimental, of some of their domes.

Miss Broedner interprets the Bath Building as follows.[2] There were two large halls for cold-bathers, the north room or swimming-pool (natatio) and the great central room (our 'changing-room'), which she considers the frigidarium or cold bath proper, with four smaller plunge-baths in its side aisles and a large central space (180 feet by 78 feet) designed to look grand to persons half-way through their bathing. The tepidarium and calidarium are where we had put them; and the spaces we had thought open palaestrae were in fact used for exercise, but were entirely covered by a light, suspended, flat roof of bronze plates designed to catch the sunlight for the benefit of the athletes below. The roofs of the three surrounding arcades served as open sun-terraces, so that the structure of the central roof, over 60 feet wide, and wider still in the Baths of Diocletian, had to rest on poles or other flimsy

---

[1] Viollet-le-Duc, *Lectures*, I, p. 116.

[2] E. Broedner, *Untersuchungen an den Caracallathermen* (Berlin, 1951).

supports fastened to their inner edges. Such a room, she says, was the 'basilica of the baths' (a term for which ancient authority may exist), and the two together (or either) were what the Augustan History meant when it praised the 'sunny cella' of Caracalla with its 'large bronze grille supporting the vault, repeated nowhere later'.[1] It was called 'sunny' from the sun-terraces. The square room in front of the staircase served not as a crush-lobby, but as a changing-room. Presumably at the height of the bathing, just before sunset, when sixteen hundred people were disporting themselves in the Thermae at once, each of these rooms 40 feet square was expected to hold the garments of some eight hundred people and provide a thoroughfare to the sun-terraces. But the magnificent central hall of the whole composition, most naturally interpreted as a grand concourse from which clients in their hundreds could move unhurriedly to any of the suites they required, and long the inspiration of great architects faced with the problem of collecting and directing a crowd,[2] is now to be reduced by the German mind to purposelessness and nullity.

One must leave the detailed refutation of Miss Broedner to an investigator patient enough to endure the opera. One may, however, point out that the changing-room in the Pompeian Baths corresponds in size and position to our central hall[3]; that changing-rooms were described in antiquity as sumptuous apartments, adorned with work of art[4]; that we have no real literary evidence for the 'natatio' as a bath separate from the frigidarium (which is indeed often described as itself containing the 'piscina', the usual Latin word for swimming-pool); that according to the Augustan History Caracalla's 'cella soliaris' had found no imitator, when it was perhaps being imitated, if Broedner is right, at that (?) very moment by the writer's own patron Diocletian—for the plan of the rooms in question is almost the same in the two Thermae, of Caracalla and Diocletian; that the History mentions one cella soliaris, not two, but that there must have been two, according to Broedner, in the Baths of Caracalla;

[1] Augustan History, *Life of Caracalla*, IX, 4–6. The writer informs us that the roof baffled the experts of his own day.

[2] The Pennsylvania Railroad Station is, of course, the most famous example.

[3] See above, pp. 273–4 and 339.

[4] Ancient passages are cited in Middleton, *Remains*, II, p. 169. In the Baths of Caracalla, water tanks apparently existed under the side tunnels. But they are not quite unprecedented in a changing-room (see Mau-Kelsey, Fig. 94).

that the word is 'soliaris' or 'solearis', not the same as the common word 'solaris', or 'sunny' (itself not likely to be corrupted in a MS.); that it might mean many things ('solium', for instance, can mean a bath-tub, 'solea' a sandal in Latin); and that the word used to describe its roof, 'cameratio', meant, as we saw,[1] a vault, which is just what Broedner's 'Basilica of the Baths' could never have supported.

The Baths of Diocletian (A.D. 302–5) are very similar in plan. In the sixteenth century Michelangelo converted their great central hall into the nave of the church of S. Maria degli Angeli, raising the floor some 7 feet and giving the columns false bases, ruinous to their proportions, at the new level. Further meddlers in the eighteenth century formed a façade in the remains of the calidarium and a vestibule in the circular chamber, probably the tepidarium, south of the central room; the net result of which is to turn the main entrance of the Baths right about. The modern shops opposite the new entrance occupy the site of the great hemicycle, which bounded the artificial platform on the south side. At two corners of the enclosing wall were circular buildings, one of which remains as the Church of San Bernardo. Its interior, with the old coffered dome, is extremely effective; the only light coming, as in the Pantheon, from a central eye, now covered by a sixteenth-century cupola.

The Thermae of other Roman cities, such as Trier, while occasionally magnificent, add little to what we can glean from the examples in the Capital.

3. PLACES OF AMUSEMENT

Few Romans, apart from Nero, regarded the drama with the religious seriousness of the Greeks. But the plays of Euripides, Menander and their imitators, all plays where the plot was neat and the chorus could be omitted, remained everywhere very popular. Many new theatres were erected and older Greek theatres altered for the performance of this type of play; and the results correspond pretty exactly to the 'Roman Theatre' of Vitruvius, who prescribes a stage 5 feet high and a semicircular orchestra twice the depth of the stage for the seats of 'senators'.[2]

---

[1] See above, p. 246.
[2] Vitruvius, V, 6.

With the chorus, the parodoi have gone into disuse and are replaced by tunnels under the auditorium for the wealthy occupants of the orchestra—the choric revels of the Athenian Old Comedy are spiritually and physically impossible in this respectable and somewhat petrified society—into which they debouch under massive boxes. The plan is not quite the same in the Greek parts of the Empire, where during the first and second century A.D. the stage was often rather higher, like the Hellenistic stage,[1] and the orchestra rather deeper and apparently kept empty of seats. For one would need to sit well back to see the action on a stage even 7 feet high. But in the west the Roman plan obtains, notably at Vienne, Orange and Arles; and in both east and west the stage is backed by a scaenae frons of several storeys and, unlike the Greek skene, the full height of the auditorium—which, according to Vitruvius, improves the acoustics of the theatre.

This scaenae frons represents a palace, so is meant, one presumes, chiefly for tragedy, and has the advantage of at least precluding realistic scenery. Vitruvius lays down the conventional meaning of an entrance through each particular door. The niches and aedicules it contains recall the treatment of the hemicycles in the Forum of Augustus. The broken and sometimes segmental pediments are playfully disposed over columns sometimes just engaged, more often just free of the walls. Nowhere, amid all this fanciful architecture, does one encounter coupled columns, so popular at the Renaissance, but not, it seems, used before then with the true Classical Orders.[2] Indeed, these elaborate walls are an artistic blind alley, the excesses of an old style, not, like the earlier niched tombs of Alexandria, the germ of a new. Above the whole came a timber ceiling the full width of the stage and sloping downwards and backwards on to the scaenae frons, the weight of whose upper portion held its main joists in position.[3] In some buildings, as, for instance, the Odeum of Herodes Atticus in Athens (despite its name a true Roman Theatre of about A.D. 150), an awning, or 'velarium', swung from poles around the

[1] I never understand why the Hellenistic stage was made so high, particularly when the old choric drama was still performed. But I refer the student to pp. 297–319 of Dinsmoor, if he can understand them.

[2] The only possible exception is a gate at Palmyra, figured by Wood (*Palmyra* (London, 1753), Tab. XIV), but quite absent from Wiegand. The coupled columns of Sta Costanza at Rome (*c.* A.D. 325) represent for me the beginning of the Middle Ages.

[3] Robertson, pp. 281–2.

parapet, perhaps extended during performances over the whole auditorium. Robertson[1] assumes a similar velarium at Orange.

The Romans in their wide empire often found themselves building on sites much flatter than those available to the Greeks. In most of Provençe, for instance, the land is only mildly rolling. Consequently from the beginning they built themselves auditoria on radiating vaulted passages, with frequent stairs and vaulted approaches to all levels of the seating. This is another reason why the Greek parodoi, such important entrances to a cavea on a solid hillside, so soon dwindled in the true Roman theatre.

The Theatre of Marcellus, begun by Julius Caesar and finished by Augustus in 13 B.C., is one of the oldest and most famous of stone-built theatres. It is still difficult to recover its complete design, as the low-class shops and houses, which occupied it for so long, still leave their mark upon it and give its façade a certain charm. But we can see from this façade (part of the outer wall of the auditorium) that while in general design it closely resembled the Colosseum, in proportion and detail it far surpassed it.[2] The lower storey is Roman Doric, the upper Ionic. The travertine with which the whole was faced was covered, like Greek masonry, with hard white stucco.

The Rhone Valley, already highly civilised at the beginning of the Empire, boasts at least three theatres of that early date at Vienne, Arles and Orange. At Vienne we see very clearly the niched front, only some 4 feet high, of the actual stage, at Arles the groove for holding the curtain, lowered out of sight during performances, and at Orange the whole back wall of the stage, with the colonnaded scaenae frons of three storeys restored at a few points to its original grandeur. The elaborate compositions here and at Aspendos,[3] on the south coast of Asia Minor, the remains of which rival those of Orange, never acquired a real architectural unity. Niches and projections are patchily disposed. At Orange, which seems Augustan, one can understand this. The architect still shrank, like the builders of the basilica at Praeneste, from decorating large arches with architraves and archivolts. He would rather stop the orders dead where they met the voussoirs, like the architect of Benndorf's model stage.[4] But even at

[1] Robertson, *ibid.*
[2] See also above, pp. 271 and 310.
[3] One of the restorations of Aspendos (which vary considerably in detail) is given by Robertson, Fig. 117.
[4] See above, p. 269.

Aspendos, over a century later, where the entablatures carry through, the effect is childishly flat. These theatres, indeed, are provincial work, and lack the grandeur and subtlety of buildings in Rome herself and her more splendid colonies.

Far commoner than the theatres are the amphitheatres, gigantic oval buildings with central arenas, where lowbrows could glut their endless passion for gladiatorial contests and scenic displays. Indeed, no Roman town of any importance was thought complete without one. Even Britain, which has only one known theatre and that very tiny, at Verulamium, has fairly impressive amphitheatres at such places as Silchester, Dorchester (the 'Maumbury Rings') and Caerleon. Only in the Greek east were there still cities with sufficient culture to eschew them.

The most important remaining are at Rome, Verona, Capua, Pozzuoli and Pompeii, in Italy; at Syracuse, in Sicily; at Pola, in Jugoslavia; at El-Djem, in Tunisia; and at Nîmes and Arles, in the south of France. They are mostly later than the theatres: for in the early days of the Empire the crowd watched the gladiators either in fora or in amphitheatres of wood. Tacitus records the collapse of a wooden amphitheatre in A.D. 27.[1] What with this and the danger from fire, stone and concrete began to oust the more perishable material; and Tacitus notices with some disdain the careful foundations Nero laid for an amphitheatre in A.D. 57.[2] The largest and most famous, the Colosseum, was built a few years later, by the Flavian emperors, on the site of the lake belonging to Nero's 'Golden House', and was opened for use in A.D. 80. It had to be restored several times, for instance under the Gordians (*c.* A.D. 240). But even on its fourth storey it still appears to retain its Flavian design.

Like all other amphitheatres, it has an elliptical plan (see Fig. 116). It measures about 620 by 500 feet, and the space for the arena, which is also elliptical, measures about 290 feet by 180. The tiers of seating are supported by vaults of concrete on piers of stone. The angle of slope must have approached 45 degrees. For we see that the auditorium had a width of about 160 feet, which is almost exactly the height of the building at its outer edge. Each portion had its separate entrance, which opened into a wide corridor running all round the building. In fact, the circle of

[1] *Annals*, IV, 62–3.
[2] *Annals*, XIII, 31.

entrances leading upwards, downwards or horizontally, each to its own section of cavea, forms an unbroken arcade on the inner side of the corridor; and there are two similar encircling corridors with similar inner sides on the two storeys above. A building so designed, however vast, can be emptied in a few minutes. Each separate division, each tier and each seat could be numbered or marked, more smoothly even than the seats in the Albert Hall.

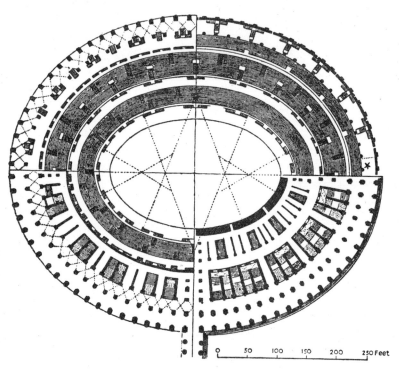

Fig. 116 Colosseum, plan at four levels.

Corridors and staircases were vaulted with concrete tunnels, enriched with mouldings and panels of stucco. Under the arena were numerous corridors disposed with equal neatness to connect the rooms for gladiators, the dens for wild beasts and the chambers for scenery and other paraphernalia. A low wall or metal grille protected the audience from the arena. Whether or how they were protected from the sun is a more difficult question. It is hard to imagine a velarium large enough and yet light enough to be slung across the whole space: but the exterior certainly supported a ring of masts.

Ruined as the interior is, nothing in existence gives such an impression of imposing size; and, apart from all sentimental interest, the power of this building, both inside and out, makes an unforgettable impression. The exterior is four storeys high, and is built of travertine stone in large blocks, held together by iron cramps. The design of the three lower storeys was discussed above.[1] They observe the usual superimposition of orders, and on each are eighty arched openings, all alike. The entablatures sweep, as we saw, in unbroken lines round the building, and it is to these fine sweeps and the reduplication of its parts, far more than its mere size, that the imposing aspect of the Colosseum is chiefly due.

The fourth storey is different from the others, as it is not arcaded, and has pilasters instead of three-quarter columns on the wall. It is sometimes stated that this storey is too high, and that it spoils the general proportions. On paper this appears to be the case,[2] but it is not so in reality; for the projecting stone corbels, on which the masts rested, seem in perspective to form a continuous band and to divide this storey into two parts.

The architect has skilfully got over the difficulty, which always occurs when two or more orders are placed above each other, of keeping his top entablature proportionate to the pilasters below, and yet at the same time making it a worthy crown for the whole building. The entablature is divided as usual into cornice, frieze and architrave, but in the frieze are corbels, which bind the three parts together and produce the effect of one big cornice.[3] Indeed, from the lower ring of corbels, half-way up this storey, to the highest point of the corona, the effect is virtually that of one great main entablature, measuring about one-ninth of the total height of the building (see Fig. 105). No style so exercises the mind as the classical.

The face of the wall on the first floor is flush with that below,

---

[1] Above, pp. 309 ff.

[2] Indeed, on paper it strikingly resembles in the proportions of its bays and its relation to the storey below the addition by Michelangelo to the Cortile of the Farnese Palace. It was more obviously copied by the architect of the Cancelleria Palace.

[3] Bramante and others used this corbelled cornice in similar positions and for the same reason. It is misused on the Palazzo Bevilacqua at Verona.

but the wall above is set back about 2 feet. The top storey is nearly flush with the second, but owing to the use of pilasters instead of columns a top-heavy appearance is avoided, and the whole building has a slightly pyramidal effect, which is excellent. Of the faults of the Colosseum it is easy to speak, but they are chiefly faults in detail. Delicacy would be lost in such a mass; but apart from the Ionic capitals on the first floor, which are unpardonably rough, the mouldings and other details are fairly good.

Of provincial amphitheatres, that at Pozzuoli, near Naples, affords, better than the Colosseum, an excellent idea of the working arrangements of these buildings, as, although the upper part is in a somewhat ruined state, the chambers and passages under the arena level are in a perfect condition (see Pl. 23). The plan of the arena floor is also complete. Forty-two trap-doors, each with its rebated stone curb, follow the curve of the arena on the outside, and other trap-doors are grouped round a long and wide central opening. The steps by which the gladiators and others reached the arena also exist; and altogether this is, after the Colosseum, by far the most interesting of the old amphitheatres.

Popular though they were—Lanciani lists five in the capital alone—circuses need not detain us very long. Designed for chariot-races, they contained one wide outward track and one back to the starting-place. The two were parallel and only a few feet apart, with a turning-post at the far end. The starting-line ran obliquely across the outward track, to equalise the distances covered, and there was, of course, eager and very dangerous competition to round the turning-post as closely as possible. Ancient Pharaonic obelisks from Egypt were set up as turning-posts and finishing-posts in the great days of the Empire, only to be transported yet again to the new papal squares in the Renaissance replanning of Rome. In the provinces, imitation obelisks might serve, like the famous example at Vienne. The seating, which followed the normal antique pattern, has now all disappeared, together with the adjacent buildings, such as the temples by the Circus Flaminius. Much disappeared only as late as the sixteenth century,[1] but we have now no real evidence of the effect the ensemble created. The Piazza Navona, about 700 feet long and 180 feet wide, replaces and seems from its outline to follow fairly closely the Circus of Domitian; and the Circus Maximus, the

[1] Lanciani, *Ruins*, p. 453.

oldest and largest circus, with a track once some 2,000 feet long, is now a dismal cleared expanse south of the Palatine.

Of Roman utilitarian buildings, like the enormous bridge of Alcantara, near Toledo, we have little space to speak. As everyone knows, they are excellent works of their sort. But their purposes are too limited, their forms too rigidly dictated by their functions, for the unprejudiced student to recognise the ability of their designers, undeniable in its kind, as strictly architectural. The great imperial grain-port of Ostia, so dramatically uncovered just before the last war, shows the simple manliness of construction and lucidity of planning to be expected of the best imperial engineers.[1] Over two-thirds of the area now laid bare was planned very efficiently on a grid. Its numerous granaries had wide entrances and simple rectangular colonnaded yards, quite as impressive as the Piece Hall at Halifax or the early nineteenth-century examples figured by Bruyère.[2] Around them were enormous rooms for grinding with hand-querns by multitudes of regimented slaves—which helps to explain why, with all their skill and for all their knowledge of screws and gear-wheels, these great engineers were never prompted to invent more than simple water-mills and mechanical toys.[3] The fronts of the granaries made the streets blanker and gaunter but far more impressive than those of imperial Pompeii. Their unrelieved coursed brickwork was varied only by an occasional brick relieving arch, sometimes of a different colour.

4. PRIVATE BUILDINGS

The most impressive private monuments, certainly the best known are the numerous tombs that line the approaches to many Roman cities. With them we may class even the tombs of emperors, which were in theory erected for them by their families as private citizens. Trajan's column, if it contained his ashes, was exceptional.

The oldest Roman method of disposing of the dead was by cremation, but about the second century A.D. this custom began

[1] One must give the excavators, too, credit for an efficiency nearly as great and remarkable under all the circumstances. Good résumés of Calza's discoveries are to be found in the *AJA* for the years up to 1941, when a very short summary is attempted (*AJA*, 1941, pp. 454 ff.).

[2] See above, p. 303, n. 1.

[3] See Vitruvius, Bk. X.

to die out amongst the wealthier classes, and the Egyptian method of embalming took its place.[1] The embalmed bodies were placed in sarcophagi of marble or stone, some of which are of rich design. Burial was forbidden within the walls of Rome. This accounts for the numerous tombs which line some of the roads outside the town for miles. Many are two storeys high, and are domed. The basement contained the sarcophagus, and the upper part formed a chamber in which the friends of the deceased could meet, as in the Egyptian tombs. The upper classes in Egypt had revived even the pyramid during the Hellenistic age; and so it is with little surprise that we see outside the Aventine at Rome itself the Pyramid of C. Cestius, with close similarities to some late pyramids in the Delta.[2]

The circular Imperial tombs resembled the old Etruscan ones in that the lower part of each was surrounded by a wall of stone, from which rose a large mound of earth. That of Augustus is said to have been planted with trees and laid out with walks as a garden[3]: only portions of the base remain. The most famous is the Mole or Mausoleum of Hadrian, commenced A.D. 135, which is now converted into barracks and known as the Castle of S. Angelo. It comprises a basement and circular superstructure, above which was either a mound, or else a conical marble roof, which made the total height about 300 feet, or nearly as high as the top of St. Paul's, London. The exterior was faced with marble and adorned with statues. The basement and super-structure are solid, as in the pyramids, except for the central chamber, which contained the sarcophagus of the emperor, and the surrounding passages which lead to it. In the Middle Ages other chambers were cut out of the solid concrete mass, and in the sixteenth century many rooms were added at the top.

In the East, the Romans followed the ancient custom of the country, and excavated their tombs in the sides of hills. A few exist at Jerusalem, but those at Petra are the most famous. The

[1] One of the first Romans to be embalmed was Poppaea, the wife of Nero (Tacitus, *Annals*, XVI, 6). Early sarcophagi besides that of Scipio (above, p. 259), of course, exist, but are few compared with the immense later imperial series. A certain number of house-tombs, recalling the Alexandrian (above, p. 241), were built for the wealthier dead.

[2] After the last royal pyramid, that of Ahmose (above, p. 39), the Egyptian upper classes seem to have used the form from time to time over the centuries. See I. E. S. Edwards, *The Pyramids of Egypt* (Harmondsworth, 1952).

[3] Strabo, p. 236 (Meineke).

fronts of many of these rise to over 100 feet in height, and are ornamented with columns, pediments, entablatures and other architectural features, which are, however, disposed somewhat fancifully, as though the artist felt that a licence was allowable which would have been impossible in an actual building.

The so-called Trophy of Adamklissi (Tropaeum Traiani), the most famous of the memorials occasionally set up by the Romans to mark their victories, resembled in its general outline and its large size one of the bigger imperial tombs. Trajan apparently set it up at this particular spot to mark the avenging of Fuscus, who perished here in A.D. 87. Its details are so barbarous, and the effect of the whole so provincial and uncouth, that it is better to say no more about it.

To find the really distinctive houses and tenements of the Empire we must go to Ostia. Most, as we see them today, date from the period between Hadrian and Severus. More under imperial control, it seems, than the capital, Ostia had comparatively few of those older single-storey atrium-houses which survived in great numbers in Rome as late as A.D. 200.[1] At Ostia, rich and poor lived in blocks of several storeys and of a surprisingly modern appearance. In their last days, as we saw,[2] the houses of Pompeii came to be masked by rows of shops along the streets. Certain quarters of Ostia continued still further this tendency, which Axel Boethius considers purely Italian, and which marks a departure from the classical Greek city, with its division into quarters purely residential or purely commercial.[3] True, shipping and trading agencies occupied a small forum of their own north of the theatre,[4] while the adjacent streets contained a number of granaries, on the sides of which shops could hardly encroach. But the more ordinary street would have continuous rows of open shops under several floors of tenements, anticipating in almost every detail those straight, commercial streets driven through so many towns in Italy during the clearances of the nineteenth century.

A block of tenement-buildings between four streets was called an insula, or island, which we know from imperial writers as a

[1] Above, p. 252.
[2] Above, p. 253.
[3] Above, p. 253, n. 4.
[4] Above, p. 321.

23—I

regrettably familiar feature of the capital.[1]   At Ostia, the main
staircases in these blocks generally led to the upper floors quite
independently of the shops; and the tenements had naturally
to be lit by windows on the streets, like modern flats, often with
built-out balconies of the sort surviving in the House of Diana.
Here the balconies have floors of brick-faced concrete.   What a
contrast to the patchy, variegated building of imperial Pompeii!

The threat of bad building and crowded conditions, of course,
necessitated building laws, some of them as old as Vitruvius, like
the law forbidding thick outer walls in the houses of Rome,
because the streets were already too narrow[2]; others imposed by
Nero and other emperors after one or other of the numerous
conflagrations.[3]   Thus Nero made regulations for the safe width
of streets and the proper fireproofing of blocks.   An earlier law,
quoted by Strabo,[4] limited the height of tenements to 70 feet.
Axel Boethius has collected the literary references to these
regulations.[5]   But the historian of architecture, who is concerned
mainly with successful and beautiful design, need surely do no
more than note their existence.   They are of necessity merely
negative things, intended to compel the profiteer and jobber, who
is not aiming at architecture, to produce moderately sound
buildings.   Or else they are meant to subdue architectural effect
to the pressing animal demands of an inflated population.   Either
they do not concern the artist, or they hinder him.   It is probably
true that, as Tacitus says, the most corrupt state has the most
laws; and numerous building laws help the society, whose vices
they cannot restrain, to debase and degrade its national architecture.   Fortunately, Rome escaped their tyranny on the whole.

Amid the tenements of Ostia a few large houses survive with
arcaded courtyards, anticipating this time the palaces of the High
Renaissance.   The houses of Serapis (see Pl. 23) and the
Charioteers, separated by a thermal establishment in the centre of
their insula, provide two good examples, the Headquarters of the
Vigiles (or Fire Station) another, which was converted to its
public use soon after erection.   It is only fair to say that these

---

[1] 'You could buy the best house in Frosinone for the sum you now
give at Rome to rent a single year's darkness': Juvenal, III, 222.

[2] The builders of tenements got over the law by raising them on piers.
How typical, this, of irrational urban development!   See Vitruvius, II, 8.

[3] See Tacitus, *Annals*, XV, 43.

[4] Strabo, p. 235.

[5] *AJA*, 1934, p. 165.

houses had evolved no piano nobile on the first floor. The bottom arcade on the central court was by Renaissance standards far too high; and, besides, there was always on the ground floor one large and important room, whether for receptions or ritual is uncertain, either opposite the 'fauces' (entrance) or at one end of the central cross-axis of the court.[1]

These new types, the tenement and the 'palazzo', like the great Thermae of Rome, finally strained the Classical Orders to breaking point. Indeed, door-frames excepted, the builders made no attempt to apply pilasters or pediments. Boethius calls such blocks 'non-classical'; and they contribute one of those utilitarian reasons for discarding the orders, into the cogency and effects of which we must now enquire.

[1] For this type of house, 'the palazzo for all', characteristic of the second century A.D., see the *AJA* for 1941, pp. 456–8 and Fig. 8.

CHAPTER X

THE TRANSFORMATION OF CLASSICAL ARCHITECTURE

THE developed Byzantine style of the sixth century is classical in its spirit and in almost all its ingredients. If it is classical to place the human figure in the centre of a composition, to explore the proportions and moods of that figure and to impose its scale on the background, then, by any test, Byzantium emerges as triumphantly classical. Is her architecture, with its brick exteriors, flat domes, vault-mosaics and marbled walls, as natural and smooth a development from the buildings of Imperial Rome? Can we call it, as Swift in effect calls it,[1] the West Roman style of Byzantium? Is the technique, which has passed with so many as 'narrowly oriental',[2] simply the last phase of Roman marble veneering and mosaic, and of the large Roman vaulted hall, now transported outside the region of that pozzuolana which had made the construction of large but simple concrete vaults apparently so effortless?

We may notice first a few features in the buildings of the Parthians and of their successors, the Sassanian Persians, the only civilised peoples in her world that Rome had failed to subdue. The best-known Parthian cities today are Hatra, a royal capital in the second century A.D., and Dura on the Euphrates, which started life as an ordinary Hellenistic 'new town' and, while remaining a mercantile city, became in our period, until its capture by the Romans in A.D. 164, progressively more Aramaic in language and oriental in general appearance. The art of Dura, in the inept stiffness and frontality of its figure-drawing and the flatness of its patterning, is supposed by some[3] to show as early as the Augustan Age an anticipation of certain Byzantine trends.

---

[1] See especially Swift, *Roman Origins*, pp. 70–1.

[2] Past audiences of Professor Norman Baynes will remember with delight the play he made of this phrase (in French) while rallying the fashionable 'orientalisers' across the Channel.

[3] E.g., Breasted, *Oriental Forerunners of Byzantine Painting* (Chicago, 1924).

But it is only at Hatra (see Fig. 117) that we find architecture on any scale, or vaulting that begins to approach the Roman.[1] Unlike the Babylonian palaces, the halls here are of dressed

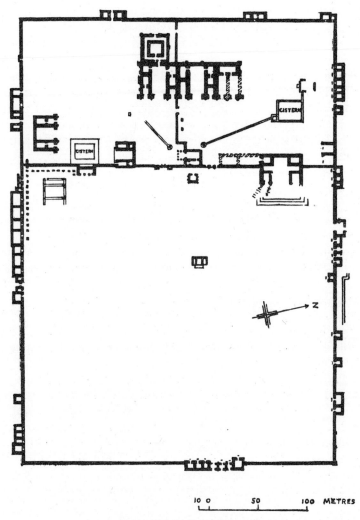

Fig. 117   Hatra, general plan.

[1] A good clear account of Hatra appears in F. Wachtsmuth, *Der Raum,* I (Marburg, 1929), pp. 122 ff.

masonry, of a rather Greek character. The cross-section in Wachtsmuth[1] shows a generally pseudo-isodomic type. Again, the arched openings are treated as Ionic archivolts, with at least two fasciae, although still enclosed by the hood-moulds and imposts already familiar from Assyrian work. In plan, Hatra is an agglomeration of buildings, nearly all of the old oriental type called the Iwan, which we noticed on north Syrian sites of the tenth to eighth centuries B.C.[2] Hatra, indeed, represents its culmination, with the large central tunnel-vaulted hall, here blocked at the back, running right through the building and much higher than the side rooms symmetrically flanking it. But, for

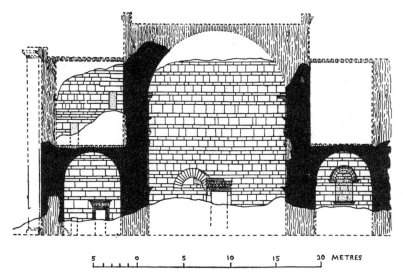

5   0   5   10   15   20 METRES

Fig. 118   Hatra, section through Iwan.

this very reason, it is most primitive and unsophisticated com-pared with the contemporary buildings of Rome. We have here no architectural grouping of units, only the old oriental sprawl. The vaults were simple undecorated tunnels each held together merely by thick side walls, with none of the subtleties of Roman abutment. The largest span was a mere 50 feet, compared with the odd 100 feet of Domitian's throne-room on the Palatine (see Fig. 118). The detailing, too, such as the plain half-columns between the entrances, remind us not of Pompeii or Rome but

[1] Wachtsmuth, Abb. 55.
[2] See above, p. 96.

Sumer and Akkad. An American scholar, Debevoise, has searched Mesopotamia for stucco ceilings of the Parthian period.[1] But the earliest he has found are of debased Hellenistic type, not earlier than A.D. 50. Pompeii can show large ceilings of good marbled stucco far earlier. We can conclude Parthia made no serious inroads on Classicism, and bequeathed nothing to Byzantium.

The Sassanian Persians, who succeeded the Parthians in A.D. 226, have a place in the history of architecture only because of a few scattered palaces.[2] At the very beginning they felt, like all these conquerors, the pull of Babylonia, and their first King Ardashir (A.D. 226–41) picked Ctesiphon, the old Parthian capital, near Seleucia and the still older Babylon, for his own administrative centre. Their palaces, even those, like Firuzabad and Sarvistan, in Persia itself, display the immemorial Babylonian tunnel vault of hairpin section, and are in this more reactionary even than Hatra. Unlike Hatra, but like Persepolis, they have a series of stepped or rectangular niches in the walls. At Firuzabad, probably the earliest palace, niches and vaults are plain, the external arcading simple and primitive and the architecture wholly 'old Asiatic', but for the square domed halls, with enormously thick walls, internally 45 feet across and 80 feet high. So Sassanian Persia perhaps deserves the credit for the earliest large example we know of domes over square halls. True, these rested not on pendentives in the normal Byzantine manner but always on squinches, which make them seem less experimental but also less influential than the earlier domes in the Baths of Caracalla.[3] Nor are the Persians known to have developed the masking and flanking columns for their inner niches or the tiers of rather barbarous blind arcading for their façades, limping imitations of the Hadrianic style, before about the fifth and sixth centuries, the probable dates of Sarvistan and the Arch of Chosroes at Ctesiphon. Nowhere in this hard, inartistic, narrowly palatial architecture can we see the slightest anticipation of Byzantium.

It is outside the province of this volume to consider the growth of the Syrian Christian style. We note merely that it developed no stone cupolas before the sixth century, and then on a section much steeper than the Byzantine, and that the churches built by

[1] *AJA*, 1941, pp. 45 ff.
[2] A good list is given in Wachtsmuth, *op cit.*, p. 142.
[3] See above, p. 296. There are some Byzantine squinches, perhaps as early as the Persian, in the Baptistery at Naples.

Constantine in Judea are Roman buildings of metropolitan style, but without the Roman roof of pozzuolana.[1]

So from all sides the evidence forces us back on Rome, who, to meet her own needs, abandoned the trammels of the orders and reduced both columns and entablatures to a few disjointed and relatively petty ornaments. The compromise between actual and apparent structure, responsible between Augustus and Trajan for the most characteristic Roman buildings, was breaking down under Hadrian. As we see his villa at Tivoli today, we cannot imagine its former columnar decoration; and yet one glimpse of its great brick vaults (see Fig. 119) is enough to convince us that it was the novelty and daring of their forms that engrossed the real energies of the imperial architect.[2] A classicist, perhaps, in Athens— though even here his principate is marked by a wholesale and unhellenic breaking of entablatures over single columns,[3] not anticipated even by the Propylon of Appius Claudius[4] — at Tivoli he abandons even the old practice of coffering vaults to imitate ceilings, and revels in umbrella half-domes over apses, their thin segments alternately flat and concave, as in later Byzantine work,[5] or else contrives such fantastic structures as the Piazza d'Oro. This octagonal building, with a central space 35 feet across, eight piers, four entrances and

Fig. 119   Hadrian's Villa, semi-dome.

[1] See Swift, pp. 43–6. Of course, by this date the metropolitan style is just becoming that of the Court rather than the old capital. Yet Rome can still boast about the finest example even of this age, in the Church of Sta Costanza.

[2] The size of the villa has hitherto baffled the scientific student. The last man to have attempted a proper survey of the whole was Piranesi. His plan is magnificent; but, of course, his was the most notoriously subjective spirit of a rather subjective generation. Attempts have been made in the *Memoirs of the American Academy in Rome* to restore some individual blocks of buildings.

[3] As in the Stoa and Library of Hadrian (Stuart and Revett, I, Chap. 5, Pl. III: W. Judeich, *Topographie von Athen* (Munich, 1931), Abb. 49 and Taf. 20).

[4] See above, p. 278.

[5] The Byzantines, of course, preferred full umbrella domes.

four apsed niches, supported what were in fact eight very high and tapering squinches of concrete, so close together that their divisions at the bottom resembled sharply-turned groins. No sooner had the squinches merged at the top into one dome, than this was pierced by a central opening, as in the Pantheon. This very interesting experiment with squinches, the earliest we know, left the emperor little room for any orders except eight attached columns at the inner angles of the piers.[1]

The villa shows another tendency equally fatal to classicism. Its niches and hemicycles are sometimes too deep for the thickness of the wall, and protrude externally. The example they set was followed in some third-century work like the 'Temple of Minerva Medica' (see Fig. 120), near the new Termini in Rome, now regarded as probably part of the Baths of Gallienus (c. A.D. 268).[2] This decagonal building, with its portico and nine apses, has an exterior at first sight as restless as a Gothic chevet—until one reflects that the ten piers are merely the supports of a concrete lid, while the exedrae are structurally harmless. One can hardly doubt that the exedrae around the sixth-century dome of San Vitale at Ravenna are directly descended from Minerva Medica. They have no structural importance, are in fact mere niches of a sort once found in concrete walls and surviving when the walls themselves were no longer employed.[3]

The few Antonine buildings A.D. 138–192 are conventional and classical after Hadrian, but the Baths of Caracalla reduced the orders to a humbler role than they had played even in Hadrian's Villa. The richly-coffered vaults of plaster and bronze, the marbled walls below them, panelled, we may be fairly sure, in the manner of Byzantine churches, and the coarse but garish marbles and mosaics of the floors together made a far greater impression than the corrupt Composite of the few single columns appended to the great piers. Some years before, a thermal establishment at Ostia[4] had been given a vault with coloured mosaics, whose pattern, a Roman Scroll, looks backwards to earlier carvings and

---

[1] Robertson illustrates this hall from Durm (Robertson, Fig. 107).

[2] See Lanciani, *Ruins*, p. 403.

[3] For an excellent discussion of this feature, with, in my view, a most correct and judicious conclusion in favour of its Roman concrete ancestry, see J. G. Davies, *Early Christian Church Architecture* (London, 1952), pp. 59–62.

[4] Not yet properly published. I owe my photograph of this detail from it to J. B. Ward-Perkins.

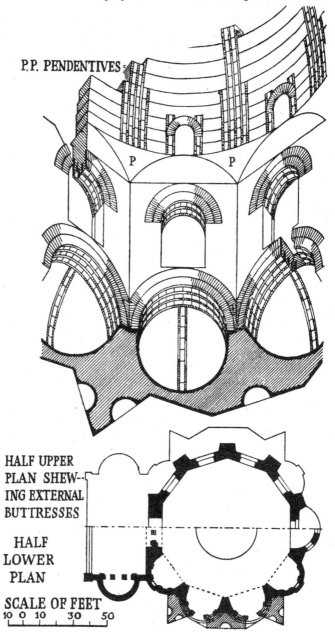

P.P. PENDENTIVES

P   P

HALF UPPER
PLAN SHEW-
ING EXTERNAL
BUTTRESSES

HALF
LOWER
PLAN

SCALE OF FEET
10 0 10   30   50

Fig. 120   Rome, 'Temple of Minerva Medica'

forwards to the closely similar soffits of mosaic-covered arches in the upper parts of Byzantine Churches (see Pl. 24). The court architects themselves used coloured mosaic on the vaults in the Palace of Diocletian at Spalato (A.D. 300), in no less a place than the grand domed entrance vestibule.[1]

We have in the third century not only great new triumphs of building science, but also a rapid decline of the educated classes. The wars of the third century placed them at the mercy of the army. All kinds of experiment reappear, which respect for Greek forms had driven underground. Now begins the great age of a new and most unhellenic material, the red porphyry of the Egyptian desert. Its hardness is fatal to subtlety, its numberless white specks equally fatal to texture; while its dark colour reduces to indistinctness most of the shadows familiar with Greek marble. It permits, however, a certain simple magnificence, free from late Hellenistic insipidity,[2] and therefore enjoys a certain popularity in the third and fourth centuries.

Arches again appear, as in late houses at Ostia,[3] resting directly on columns, for the first time since one or two minor examples in Late Republican Pompeii.[4] Again at Ostia, as in the House of Serapis, lofty square piers with the plainest of imposts support equally plain arches round the inner courtyards. The Roman is at last abandoning the effort, so long sustained, to give every wall its classical dress by modelling it in several planes, of which one at least shall be passably classical. He grows tired for a time even of the classical Basilica. When the Basilica Julia was rebuilt by Diocletian, it was given square piers in place of its earlier colon-nades[5]; and Maxentius planned and had nearly completed before 312 the famous basilica on the north of the Forum, that resembles no other we know. Dissatisfied with wooden ceilings, the architect lifted his design from the central hall of the recent, fashionable Thermae. He needed to modify the abutment-system in a few particulars, and was quite content to show an apse projecting from the short west end.[6]

---

[1] See Robertson, p. 319.
[2] Though capable of the most classical grandeur when used for his sarcophagus, now in Palermo Cathedral, by that extraordinary admirer of Pagan Antiquity, the Emperor Frederick II.
[3] Published by Becatti in *Case Ostiensi del Tardo Impero*, Rome, N.D.
[4] Two are illustrated by Rivoira, Figs. 114 and 115.
[5] Lanciani, *Ruins*, pp. 275 ff., Figs 105 and 106.
[6] Constantine later ruined the building by adding an apse and an entrance to the two long sides.

But the chief repository of new forms is, of course, the Palace of Diocletian at Spalato. The concrete used here is limited, and most of the work seems to be of masonry. Its plan need not detain

Fig. 121   Arcading in the Palace of Diocletian, Spalato.

us, as it belongs to a small ephemeral group modelled on the defensive military camps of the later empire; and it has been sufficiently described by Robertson.[1] It is a rectangular enclosure of over 700 feet from north to south and 600 feet from east to west, with three land gates and with a terrace 520 feet long above the sea on its south side. The royal apartments occupy the south front, and block the Cardo (or north-to-south street) like a military praetorium. The plan, then, is simple; but in the treatment the architect ranges at will (see Fig. 121). Mere corbels support columns on the face of the great north, or 'golden' gate. Colonnades may directly support an unbroken series of semicircular arches, treated with the mouldings peculiar to architraves, and therefore technically archivolts. Or one segmental archivolt may suddenly interrupt the horizontal architrave, although the interval between the two supporting columns may be no greater than usual.[2]

In fact, the Palace of Spalato shows not only the ignorance but the illogicality of these early fourth-century architects. Continuous war had led to a decline in the quality of the detailing—not, of course, in the use of pozzuolana, now a matter of engineering, but in the finer points of placing and proportioning.

The reign of Constantine sees a pause and a last hasty consolidation of the imperial resources. How will the new rulers and the new faith receive the inheritance of Roman architecture? There is no thought of deserting, only of cultivating for other purposes the fresh and always fertile demesne of classical Art. As we see from the early golden codices and from the fifth-century pavements of Antioch in Syria,[3] the true Byzantine style was created very slowly and carefully in the best classical schools. We have no remains in Constantinople of the architectural replicas of Rome supposedly bestowed by its founder on its new citizens and senators.[4] But if we remember the metropolitan style of central Italy during the centuries of the Roman Empire, we must surely admit that only here can we find the genuine ancestors of Sta Sophia.

[1] Robertson, pp. 316–21.
[2] Robertson, Pl. XXIVa.
[3] *AJA*, 1934, Pls. 21–25. These pavements have now been thoroughly published by Doro Levi in *Antioch Mosaic Pavements*, Princeton 1947. But I cannot myself see the 'complete break' with Classical art which he remarks in pavements of the reign of Constantine (*op. cit.*, p. 609).
[4] Gibbon (Chap. XVII) discredits the absurd stories of Codinus.

ARCHITECTURAL GLOSSARY

Note: Many of the more technical terms are explained in the text, especially in Chapter V, where the Greek Orders are considered in detail.

Abacus. The upper portion of the capital (*q.v.*) of a column, usually squarish on plan and flattened so as to support the weight of the architrave (*q.v.*).

Abutment. That which resists the lateral thrust of an arch.

Aedicule. A small tabernacle used as an architectural ornament and imitating the form of a house or temple.

Aisle. A division, usually a lateral division, of a columnar hall.

Ambulatory. Any part of a building intended for walking in. It often takes the form of a series of aisles or corridors enclosing at least three sides of a central space.

Anta (Gk. *Parastas*). The termination of a Greek house- or cella-wall, which received special architectural treatment. (See Chapter V.)

Ante-Chapel. The vestibule of a chapel, intended for certain preparations for services and also for less privileged spectators.

Apadana. The columnar audience-hall of the Great King of Persia, where he held his Durbars or levées-en-masse.

Apse. A semicircular or polygonal structure, seen as a recess internally, a projection externally, built out from one of the enclosing walls of a building.

Arch. A concave construction of bricks or small stones (voussoirs), so placed around one or more centres that they support one another.

Architrave. The lowest member of the classical entablature, which rests on the columns.

Archivolt. The outer face of an arch where it rests directly on columns of classical type and therefore receives the carving and moulding appropriate to a classical architrave.

Arcuated. Construction involving arches (*q.v.*), with consequent lateral pressures and eccentric loading. Often, in areas of small stones and poor supplies of labour, the only possible mode of construction.

Astylar. Without columns. Classical astylar buildings normally observe the general proportions of columnar.

Attic. That member or collection of members sometimes obtruded in Classical buildings between the cornice and the roof.

Base. The spreading member of a column on which the shaft rests, to be found in all Classical Orders but the Doric.

Basilica. A large oblong hall, used by the Romans for commercial and legal purposes. It was usually of light construction, with rows of internal columns, a clerestory and one or more apses.

Bay. A principal compartment in the arrangement of a building, the repetition of which determines the building's general design.

Bed. The bottom, less projecting part of a cornice on which the upper, projecting portion rests.

Buttress. A mass of masonry applied to the outer face of a wall at a point where the builders need to counter the thrust of an internal arch or vault.

Capital. The upper part of a column, normally projecting outside the line of the shaft and comprising an abacus and echinus.

Caryatid. Female figure used instead of a column to support an entablature.

Cella. The walled room for the cult-image, in the centre of a normal Greek peristylar temple. In small Roman temples, the cella tends to occupy the whole of the rear of the building.

Clerestory. An upper row of windows, providing direct light for the central area of a large hall.

Colonnade. A range of columns at regular intervals, supporting a horizontal entablature. Where the columns support arches, it is called an arcade.

Column. A slender, lofty, usually decorative member, of circular or polygonal plan, employed to support the entablature and roof of the normal trabeated building. The normal column comprises a head, or capital, a long central portion, or shaft, and a foot, or base.

Cornice. The uppermost, projecting member of the Classical entablature, originally intended to support the rafters and gutter (sima) of the Greek tiled roof.

Corona. The upper part of the cornice, which projects from the face of the bed and has a carefully decorated soffit (*q.v.*).

Dado. The continuous carved and decorated skirting along the lower part of a wall. Also the block of a pedestal at a corresponding level in a colonnade.

Diminution. The upward taper of a Classical column.

Dome. An hemispherical or approximately hemispherical roof.

Drafted Masonry. Masonry where the faces of the blocks are smoothed and sunk on either side of each joint, but are left with their centres projecting and (normally) roughened.

Architectural Glossary 369

Echinus. The 'cushion' of a Classical capital, which normally supports the abacus and spreads outwards from the sides of the shaft.

Engaged Column. A column attached to a wall and envisaged as partly sunk in it. Normally, rather more than half the column is visible.

Entablature. The sum of those horizontal members of a Classical order, which rest on the columns and support the actual roof. The normal entablature comprises an architrave, frieze and cornice.

Entasis. The slight convexity often present in the tapering sides of a Classical column.

Fascia. A flat continuous band, comparable in width to a board or plank.

Flat Arch. An arch of the normal wedge-shaped voussoirs, but with a horizontal soffit (*q.v.*).

Frieze. The middle member of the entablature, above the architrave. It normally contains the carved reliefs, in buildings designed for these. Hence, 'frieze' also comes to mean any band of continuous carved reliefs in almost any position but that of the dado.

Header. A stone extending through the thickness of a wall.

Hypaethral. Open to the sky.

Hypostyle Hall. Any large columnar hall. Usually, however, it is pictured as having more colonnades than a Roman basilica, and may have several clerestories and even a lantern.

Iconography. Scheme of decoration with a connected series of religious illustrations.

Impluvium. The sunk water-tank in the centre of a Pompeian front hall (atrium), which caught the rainwater through the central opening of the inward-sloping (compluviate) roof.

Impost. A simple block, usually rectangular, transmitting the weight of an arch or vault to a supporting member. An abacus is thus a special kind of impost.

Intaglio. A kind of low carved relief sunk slightly below the plane of the surrounding field.

Isodomic. In Greek masonry, walls with courses of uniform height are said to be 'isodomic'.

Lantern. A structure on the top of a roof, designed to admit light.

Lunette. A window of semicircular or approximately semicircular shape.

24—I

Mouldings.   The modelled surfaces used to frame the various architectural members or to emphasise their shapes.

Mullion.   An upright division between the lights of a window.

Order.   In trabeated architecture, one of the recognised methods of treating the upright column and the horizontal entablature that it supports.

Pediment.   The gable of a classical building, normally with a low pitch (15° or very little more).

Pendentive.   The spherical triangle employed to smooth the transition from a square or polygonal hall to a dome of circular plan.

Peripteral.   Entirely surrounded by an outward-facing colonnade.

Peristyle.   A colonnade (*q.v.*).   Also the space between a colonnade and a neighbouring, parallel wall.   Also an enclosing colonnade, and occasionally the area that it encloses.

Piano Nobile.   The most important floor of a building, in the Italian Renaissance the first floor.

Pier.   A mass of masonry, of any size or shape, used as a support.

Pilaster.   A column *flattened against* a wall, not merely *engaged* to it (*q.v.*), and having neither diminution (*q.v.*) nor entasis (*q.v.*).

Pilaster Strip.   A lofty, shallow projection from the outer face of a wall.   In some buildings, pilaster strips were ignorantly meant to serve as buttresses.

Pillar.   A detached support usually smaller than a pier, and different from a column in not necessarily having a circular or polygonal plan.

Plinth.   The flattened member, usually square on plan, that sometimes supports the base of a Classical column.   In Greek building, the blocks of an ordinary wall-course were also called 'plinths'.

Portico.   The colonnaded front or porch of a Classical building.   As used in the Greek and Roman sections of this book, the word 'portico' implies also a crowning pediment (*q.v.*).

Porticus.   The Latin for the Greek 'Stoa' (*q.v.*), sometimes applied to an architectural group of such stoas.

Prostyle.   Having a range of detached columns in front.

Pseudo-isodomic.   In Greek building, a wall having alternating courses of two different sizes is said to be 'pseudo-isodomic'.

Raking.   Inclined from the horizontal.

Respond.   A small projection from a wall, such as a pilaster, aligned on a colonnade or arcade and designed to take the last architrave-block or arch before it reaches the wall.

Return.   To turn through a right angle.

Sarcophagus. A stone coffin, often of large size and sometimes highly decorated.

Sima. The upturned lower edge of the outer tiles of some Greek roofs forms a continuous gutter or 'sima'. In Roman work the sima is often carved on the cornice-block.

Soffit. The visible underside of an architectural member such as an arch or corona.

Stoa. A Greek colonnaded walk, usually of some length and with a blank rear wall and side walls.

Stretcher. A stone placed with its greater length along the visible face of a wall.

String. A thin continuous horizontal moulding; *e.g.*, the Doric taenia.

Stylobate. The continuous step, especially important in Greek Doric, immediately supporting the columns.

Telamon. A male figure supporting an entablature. Also called 'Atlas' and 'Persian'.

Trabeated. A kind of construction where all the loads are vertical and directly countered by vertical supports. Post and lintel construction is trabeated, as are the Greek Orders. Suitable for areas with large stones and ready supplies of labour.

Vault. An arched roof.

Voussoirs. The small individual members, each usually wedge-shaped, comprising an arch.

INDEX

Note: This index is not exhaustive. But it does attempt to give those references which the student of architecture will find most useful. Famous buildings are more likely to be found directly under their own names, less famous under those of the towns which they embellish.

abacus, 44, 54, 130, 131, 141, 160, 161, 162, 169, 171, 182, 195
 (tilted), 270
Abu Simbel, 36, 39
Abusir, 19, 25
Abydos (Egypt), 16 n., 25, 26, 34, 35, 45 ff., 50
Acanthus, 216 n.
acanthus, 187, 195
acanthus column, 99
Achaememid Persia, 212 ff.
acropolis, 92
Acropolis of Athens, 113, 115, 117, 156, 179, 185, 208, 209, 328
Adamklissi, 285, 353
advertisement, 321
adyton, 120, 189
Aegae, 247
Aegean, 5, 10, 11, 12, 72 ff., 91, 101
Aegina, 118, 121, 131, 132, 155, 186
Aeolians, 108
Aeolis, 182, 184
Aezani, 309
Africa, 1
Agatharchides, 209 n.
agora, 108, 114, 121 ff., 196, 198 ff., 221, 235 ff., 251, 315
Agora of Athens, 115, 122, 198 ff.
Agrippa, 282, 324, 330, 334, 335
Ahmose I, 39
Ahmose II, 43
Aigosthena, 196, 197
Ak Alan, 222
Akhnaton, 11, 41, 54
Akkad, 7, 10, 58 n., 60, 319, 359
Akragas, 110, 145, 174, 181, 190, 243
akroteria, 125, 139, 146, 183, 184, 187
alae, 57, 255, 262
Alalakh, 10, 11, 72, 92, 93 ff.
Alatri, 226 n.
Albert Hall, 348
Alcantara, Bridge of, 351
Alexander Mosaic, 238
Alexandria, 43, 235, 238, 241, 246, 266, 280, 345
Alexandrian tombs, 241, 352 n.
Alinda, 247

altars, 117, 118, 121, 122, 243, 323
Altis, 200
Al 'Ubaid, 8 n., 9, 58 ff., 65
Al 'Ubaid Culture, 8, 56 n., 58
Amanus, 10
Amarna. See El 'Amarna
ambulatory, 28
Amenhotep III, 38
Amisus, 222
Amorites, 10, 12 n.
amphitheatres, 309, 314, 347 ff.
Amyclae, 186
Anagni, 99
anathyrosis, 150, 264
Anatolia, 5, 10
Ancona, Arch of Trajan, 336
ancones, 150, 154
Andronicus of Cyrrhus, 276, 278
Anfushy, 241
angle contraction (Doric), 134, 174, 184
Anglo-Saxon Art, 73
antae, 120, 121 n., 126, 141, 148, 153, 160, 167, 171, 175, 193, 202, 243, 263
antefixes, 138, 139, 187
anthemion ornament, 128, 192
Antioch, 235, 365
Apadanas, 216 ff.
Aphaia, Temple of, 115, 120, 121, 132, 139, 155, 186
apodyterium, 273, 339 ff.
Apollodorus of Damascus, 319 ff.
'apophyge', 160
apse, 251, 268, 269, 271, 277, 306, 323, 324, 325, 360, 361, 363 n.
Apulia, 2
Aqua Marcia, 265 n.
aqueducts, 284, 342
Arban, 95
arcades, 266, 340, 355, 359
Arch of Constantine, 337 ff.
Arch of Septimus Severus, 338
Arch of Titus, 289, 309, 336 ff.
Archaic Age, 108, 109, 139, 156, 175, 197, 216
'arched order', 271, 274, 309 ff.

arches, 50 ff., 68, 72, 84, 96, 100, 101, 223, 228, 235, 236, 244 ff., 260 ff., 266, 268, 292, 294, 332, 334, 335 ff., 363
architraves, 113, 132 ff., 139 ff., 151, 152, 154, 156, 158, 160, 163, 180, 182, 218, 221, 239, 262, 270, 365
archivolts, 262, 358, 365
arenas, 347 ff.
Argos, 109
Argos, Heraion, 132, 148, 182
Arles, 345, 346, 347
Armenia, 12
Arpachiyah, 9, 10 n., 81
arris, 131, 160, 296, 298
Arsinoe, Tomb of, 246
Ashur, 10, 65, 66, 67 n.
Asia, 1, 7, 14, 28, 93, 101, 158, 159, 168
Asia Minor, 10, 13, 89 ff., 128, 158, 191, 220 ff., 236
Asiatic base, 159, 191
Asiatics, 164
Aspendos, 346
Assos, 114
Assyria, 10, 12, 13, 56, 95, 96
Assyrian architecture, 62, 65 ff., 217
'astragalos', 126, 163
Athena Nike, Temple of, 159, 175
Athena Promachos, 264 n.
Athenian architecture, 74, 110, 171
Athenian sculpture, 109
Athenians, 47, 136, 140, 158, 187, 204, 209, 235, 345
Athens, 110, 115, 120, 122, 123, 125, 151, 159, 167, 168, 173, 174, 191, 196, 197 n., 208, 209, 233, 249, 252, 265, 276, 286, 360
'City of Hadrian', 285
Temple of Olympian Zeus, 264
Temple of Rome, 328
'Atlas', 99
Atreus, Treasury of, 82
atrium, 253 ff., 353
attic, 335, 336, 337
Attic base, 159, 170 ff., 243, 263, 264
auditoria, 122, 209, 345 ff.
Augustus, 234, 240, 260, 264, 278, 281, 282 ff., 288, 294, 304, 308, 316 ff., 321 n., 322
axial planning, 114, 217, 253 ff., 288, 338 ff.

Baalbek, 227, 234, 269, 308, 314, 319, 326, 327
'Temple of Venus', 329
Babylon, 10, 13, 14, 69 ff., 98 n., 101, 216 n., 245, 359
Babylonia, 58, 64, 216, 251, 357
Babylonian mathematics, 72
Balawat, 67

balconies, 69, 98, 354
baptisteries, 274
Barberini, 301 n.
'baroque', 31, 55, 234
Barry, Sir Charles, 75
Basilica Aemilia, 322
Basilica Julia, 363
Basilica of Maxentius, 286, 304, 363
Basilica Porcia, 249
Basilica Ulpia, 322 ff.
basilicas (secular), 64, 220 n., 249, 251, 289, 303, 309, 316, 321, 322 ff., 338 n.
(religious), 266 ff., 289 n.
(Christian), 79, 268, 302
Bassae, 130, 133 n., 140, 143, 154, 159 n., 170, 171, 181 n., 188, 189, 193, 278, 279
bathrooms, 86, 202
baths, 122, 309
Baths of Agrippa, 334, 338
Baths of Caracalla, 297, 305, 334, 338, 339 ff., 359, 361
Baths of Diocletian, 298, 338, 342, 344
Baths of Gallienus, 361
Baths of Trajan, 293, 338
bazaars, 319
Beaumaris Castle, 196
bedrooms, 204, 262
Black Sea, 2, 105, 222
Bloomsbury, 236
Boghazköi, 11, 89 ff., 94, 101
Bologna, 202
bonding (Egyptian), 29
bouleuterion, 121, 198
Bovillae, Tomb of the Claudii, 278
bracket capitals, 184 n.
Bramante, 349 n.
brickwork (Assyrian), 67
(Babylonian), 67, 70
(Egyptian), 50, 52
(Greek), 245
(Hellenistic), 64
(North Syrian), 96
(Roman), 292 ff., 334, 351
(Sumerian), 60, 64, 66, 100
Britain, 321, 322, 347
British Museum, 58 n., 66, 67, 85 n., 90, 98 n., 192 n., 222 n.
broken entablature, 310, 360
broken lintel, 49
broken pylon, 39, 43
bronze, 305
Bronze Age, 4, 47, 72 ff., 117, 118, 202
bucrania, 243, 306
Budrun, 161
building laws, 354
building science, 280 n., 287 ff., 363
Burma, 16
Bur-sin, 61
Busiris Vase, 167

Byblos, 6, 97
Byzantine architecture, 304, 317, 341, Chapter X *passim*
Byzantine art, Chapter X *passim*
Byzantines, 50, 112, 287, 290, 331 n., 333
Byzes of Naxos, 113

Cadachio. *See* Kardaki
'caementa', 291
Caere, 128, 222, 227
Caerleon, 347
Caerwent, 322 n.
Cairo, 6, 15
Calah, 66, 67 n., 68, 95
calidarium, 274, 339 ff.
Callicrates, 125 n.
Callimachus, 188 ff.
'camera', 246
'cameratio', 344
camps, Roman, 314, 365
Campus Martius, 273, 316, 317, 319
canalis, 160, 163
Cancelleria Palace, 349 n.
Canosa, 242, 248
capitals
  Babylonian, 70
  Composite, 308, 309
  Corinthian, 188 ff., 193 ff., 259 ff., 278 ff., 308 ff., 324
  Doric, 130 ff., 141, 148
  Egyptian, 25, 38, 44, 53 ff.
  lanceolate, 277
  Persian, 217 ff.
Capitol, 224, 225, 315
Capua, 347
Caracalla, 330, 338
caravanserai, 73
Carchemish, 95
Caryatids, 62, 98, 99, 102, 169, 243
Castor, Temple of, 290, 304, 308, 323, 324
cauliculus, 187, 195, 259
cavea, 210 ff., 346
cavetto, 103, 126
cavity walls, 296
ceilings, 28, 41, 60 n., 112, 114, 140, 141, 142, 152, 156, 158, 164, 166, 177 ff., 218, 219, 305, 325, 327, 341, 345
cella, 118, 119 ff., 125, 140, 142 ff., 159, 166, 174, 180, 183, 186, 188 ff., 193 ff., 224, 249, 263, 272, 324, 325, 327
cella-building, 117, 119 ff., 153, 155, 174, 186
'cella soliaris', 343 ff.
'cenaculum', 258
cenotaph, 82
Cervetri, 222
Chaldeans, 13

Chamaezi, 86 n.
chamber tombs, 81, 221
chamfer, 236, 264
cheek-walls, 324, 328
Cheops, 6, 21, 26
Chephren, 7, 21, 23, 25
Chersonese, Thracian, 107
chevet, 361
China, 4
'Chinese roof ', 136, 184
Chios, 113
Chiswick House, 269 n.
Chiusi, 248
Choregic Monument. *See* Lysicrates, Thrasyllos
chryselephantine statues, 125
circuses, 350 ff.
Circus Flaminius, 350
Circus Maximus, 248, 350 ff.
Circus of Domitian, 350
cisterns, 246
Civita Castellana, 225
clamps, 154
clerestory, 34, 43, 214, 219
Cloaca Maxima, 223
Clytemnestra, Tomb of, 82, 84
Cnossus, 73 ff., 80, 91, 97
  Little Palace, 77, 78
  Royal Villa, 78
  Temple Tomb, 80
Coffers, 140, 156, 166, 270, 305, 332, 361
Colchester, 322 n.
Colchis, 2
coloniae, 276, 336
colonnaded streets, 315
colonnades (Cretan), 73, 75 n., 77, 78, 79
  (Egyptian), 28, 31, 33, 34, 37, 38, 39, 43, 49, 55, 217, 218
  (Roman), 266, 290, 310, 317, 324, 365
  (Greek), 114, 118 ff., 130 ff., 143 ff., 158 ff., 167, 186, 247, 249
  (Hellenistic), 240 ff., 259 ff.
  (Persian), 216 ff.
  (Sumerian), 63
Colosseum, 227, 285, 288, 289, 292, 295, 296, 306, 310, 315, 347 ff.
colossi, 30, 70, 102, 118, 327 n.
colouring (Greek), 155 ff.
columns, 13 n., 69
  (Egyptian), 34, 53 ff., 126
  (Greek), 130, 149 ff., 156, 158 ff., 180
  (Minoan and Mycenaean), 75, 79, 84, 97
  (Persian), 214 n., 217
  (Roman), 289
  (Sumerian), 58, 101
  (Syrian), 97, 98

columns—*continued*
compluviate roof, 145, 254, 256
Composite Order, 306, 308, 309, 335, 361
Concord, Temple of, 265, 304, 308, 323, 324, 335
concrete, 3, 246, 265, 272, 280, 289, 290 ff., 324, 330 ff., 347 ff., 361
Constantine, 286, 327, 360, 365
Constantinople, 235, 286, 365
construction (Greek), 148 ff.
Cori, 99 n., 137, 225, 272, 324
Corinth, 156, 227
  Stoas, 201, 236 n., 238
  Temple of Apollo, 120, 131
Corinthian atrium, 256
Corinthian Order, 102, 170, 186, 188 ff., 193 ff., 263, 264, 268, 308 ff., 324, 335
'Corinthianesque' columns, 246
Corinthians, 139, 183
cornices, 126, 128, 133 ff., 151, 156, 163, 164, 221, 242, 273, 278, 349
Cosmati, 304
coupled columns, 345
courtyards, 354
crenellations, 66
Cretan architecture, 72 ff., 182 ff.
Cretan breastplates, 68
Cretans, 5
Crete, 5, 10, 11, 72 ff., 88, 98, 117, 182 ff.
Crimisa, 137
cross-axial rooms, 64 ff., 67, 90
Crusaders, 90
Crystal Palace, 101
Ctesiphon, Arch of Chosroes, 1, 96, 359
Cumae, Grotto of the Sibyl, 228
cupolas, 246, 342, 359
'Curia', 315
curvatures, 179 ff.
Cyclopean walls, 89
cyma recta, 126, 128, 164
cyma reversa, 126, 128, 136, 236
Cyprus, 70, 113, 222
Cyrene, 107
  Forum of Proculus, 321

'dactyliform' columns, 54, 79, 102, 161
dadoes, 62, 75, 159, 160, 166, 239
Damascus, 315
death-pits, 8, 59
Deir-el-Bahari, 16, 18 n., 27, 28, 36 ff., 44, 48, 49, 102, 103
Delos, 208, 232, 233, 238
  houses, 204, 252, 259, 260
  Hypostyle Hall, 200, 220 n., 249
Delphi, 113, 116, 117, 120, 146, 154, 155, 161, 168, 171, 197, 248
  Athenian Stoa, 167, 170, 199

Athenian Treasury, 130, 133, 153, 154
Clazomenian Treasury, 169
Cnidian Treasury, 169
Cyrenaean Treasury, 135, 174 n.
Massaliot Treasury, 99, 168, 169, 170
Naxian Sphinx, 161
'Sicyonian' Treasury, 133, 135, 185 n.
Siphnian Treasury, 39, 169
Temple of Apollo, 153, 188, 193
Temple of Athena Pronaia, 148, 184
Tholos (archaic), 133, 134
Tholos (classical), 189, 190
Demeter of Cnidus, 243
Demetrius of Phalerum, 238
Democritus, 245
Denderah, 38 n., 43, 44, 50
Dendra, 82, 84
dentils, 163, 164, 194, 218, 273, 278, 308, 336 n.
Deus Rediculus, Temple of, 295
Didyma, 117, 145, 159 n., 193, 195, 247
Dingle Peninsula, 228
dining-rooms, 238, 262
Dinsmoor's Law, 132, 175 n.
Dio Cassius, 318, 319 n.
Diribitorium, 300, 302
'displuviate' atrium, 258
Dodona, 117
Doganlu, 222
dolerite, 47
domes, 60, 81, 246, 273, 299, 329, 331 ff., 359, 360, 361
doors, 64, 67, 77, 84, 142, 153 ff., 176 ff., 193, 278, 305, 330
Dorchester, 'Maumbury Rings', 347
Dorians, 108
Doric mouldings, 128
Doric Order, 52, 84, 102, 126, 128 ff., 167, 187, 200, 236, 243, 249, 259, 306, 321, 324
  Origins of, 27, 84, 118, 120, 126, 137, 142, 147, 148, 157, 160, 183 ff., 221
Doric Temples, 39, 114, 119 ff., 125, 128 ff.
Dosio, 301 ff.
'Dragon House', 2 n.
Drah Abou'l Negah, 52
drains, 123, 223, 271 n.
draughtsmanship, 47
Dravidian Style, 31
Dreros, 183
drill, 309, 341
dromos, 81, 82, 92
Dugald Stewart, Monument of, 195
Dura Europos, 284, 356
Dystus, 204

Ecbatana, 66
echinus, 27, 130 ff., 148, 160, 161, 163, 169, 236
Edfou, 35 n., 43, 52, 54, 55
Edinburgh, George Street, 236
Egypt, 2, 4, 5, 6, 7, 9, 11, 15 ff., 42, 80, 89, 90, 100, 102, 103, 121, 156, 212, 240
Predynastic, 6, 52
Old Kingdom, 6, 7, 16 ff, 29, 53, 103
Middle Kingdom, 7, 23, 26 ff., 80
New Kingdom, 11, 23, 27, 28 ff., 43
Saite, 13, 42, 43, 100, 108, 245, 246
Ptolemaic, 15, 38, 42 ff., 55, 70, 259, 352
Egyptian cornice, 52, 103, 126, 216
Egyptian mathematics, 45 ff.
Egyptians, 126
Elam, 4 n., 13, 213
El 'Amarna, 15, 41, 47
Elamites, 8, 9, 19 n.
El-Djem, 347
Eleusinian limestone, 113, 176, 179
Eleusis, 110, 189
Eleusis, Lesser Propylon, 278 ff., 360
Elizabethan Art, 168
El Kab, 4 n., 38
El Kolah, 4 n.
elliptical arches, 50, 90, *see also* hairpin arches
Ely Cathedral, 265
embalming temples, 25
'emblema', 238, 321
'empolion', 150
engaged columns, 20, 58, 190, 241 ff., 248, 268, 272, 314, 327, 335
England, 114, 310
English, 47
entablature, 132 ff., 140, 141, 145 n., 151, 163 ff., 168, 180, 184, 219, 243, 268, 341, 349, 360
entasis, 141, 180, 181 n.
Ephesian base, 159, 170
Ephesus, Temple of Artemis (Diana), 116, 118, 145, 149, 158, 159, 160, 161, 163, 164 ff., 183, 185, 219, 327
Epidaurus
Stadium, 247
Temple, 193
Theatre, 155, 210, 211 ff., 259
Tholos, 190, 193 n., 194, 196, 259, 308
epikranitis, 140, 142, 156, 167, 169
Erechtheum, 115, 116, 128, 146, 147, 158, 168, 169, 171, 180, 189, 190, 192, 194, 328
Erechtheum accounts, 126 n., 152
Eridu, 7, 56 n.
Esneh, 43
Etrúria, 101, 128, 139, 212, 222 ff.
Etruscan Order, 223

Etruscan Temple, 95, 185, 324 n.
Etruscan Tomb, 222
Etruscans, 99, 222 ff.
Euboea, 2 n.
euthynteria, 129 ff.
exhibition architecture, 262
'fairs', 321
false porch, 119 ff., 186
Fano, 303, 323
Fara, 65
Farnese Palace, 349 n.
fasciae, 132, 135, 137, 139, 156, 163, 169, 216, 218, 221, 262, 308, 358
'fauces', 253 ff., 355
Faustina, Temple of, 288, 289, 304
Ferento, 263
Festival Hall, 34 n., 41
fire-platforms, 214
First Empire Style (French), 240 n.
First Pompeian Style, 239
Firuzabad, 359
Flamboyant Style, 31
Florence, 171, 258, 332
flutes, 131, 150, 159, 160, 241, 304
Foce del Sele, 135, 141, 157 n.
fora, 251, 253, 315, 316 ff., 324
'Forma Urbis', 252
fortification, 89
Fortuna Virilis, Temple of, 272, 328
forum boarium, 315
forum holitorium, 315
Forum of Augustus, 290, 316, 317
Forum of Julius, 276, 316
Forum of Nerva, 317
Forum of Peace (Vespasian), 317, 325 n.
Forum of Trajan, 287, 317, 318 ff.
Forum Romanum, 248, 249, 276, 315 ff.
foundations (Egyptian), 29
(Greek), 149 ff.
Fourth Pompeian Style, 312
frame and panel construction, 77
France, 2
Frederick II, 363 n.
'free planning', 70
French Gothic, 4
French Romanesque, 99, 325
frescoes, 29, 72, 74, 77, 86, 157, 239, 280
frieze (Doric), 102, 133 ff., 140, 141, 151, 156, 174, 202, 306
(Egyptian), 39
(Ionic), 39, 102, 158, 164, 168, 183, 187, 189, 192, 194
(Minoan and Mycenaean), 88
(Roman), 290, 306
(Sumerian), 64, 101
frigidarium, 273, 334, 339 ff.
functionalism, 204 n.

Gabii, 273
Gandhara Art, 278 n.
gargoyles, 35
Gate of Hadrian, Athens, 309
gates, 90, 101, 211
gate-towers, 28, 31, 90
gate-walls, 177 ff.
Gaul, 321, 322
Gerasa, 315
Gerzean Culture, 6, 9
giant order, 323
Gilgamesh, legends of, 9
Girgenti, 145, 146, 147, *see also* Akragas
Gizeh, 6, 17, 19, 21
Gla, 88
'golden cut', 310 n.
'gorge', Egyptian, 52, 103, 141, 216
Gothic architecture, 133, 148, 171 n.,
    187, 296, 361
granaries, 351
granite, 47, 304, 323, 325, 330
Granite Temple, the, 25, 47
Great Pyramid, 4 n., 21, 23
Greece, 2, 5, 100, 102, Chapters IV, V
    and VI *passim*
    Classical, 13, 79, 89, Chapters IV,
        V and VI *passim*
Greek Architecture, 27, 85, 99, 100,
    Chapters IV, V and VI *passim*
Greek Theatre, 206 ff.
Greeks, 3, 27, 41, 43, 52, 102, 103
    Classical, 12, 84, 98, Chapters IV,
        V and VI *passim*, 323, 324,
        327
    Hellenistic, 70, 101, Chapter VII
        passim
grids, town-planning, 206, 236 ff.
grilles, 120
groined vault, 247
gromatici, 314
ground-courses, 67
Gudea, 10, 61
guttae, 132 ff.
gymnasia, 116, 122, 205

Hadrian, 325, 329, 335, 336
hair-joints, 150
'hairpin' arches, 90, 359
half-timbering, 79
Halicarnassus, 161
Halifax, Piece Hall, 351
Hall of the Hundred Columns, 220
Hammurabi, 10
Hanging Gardens, 69
'harmonia', 154, 212
Hathor-headed capitals, 38, 55
Hatra, 96, 284, 356, 357 ff.
Hatshepsut, Queen, 36, 37, 38, 48
Hattusas, 11
Hauran, The, 1, 246
Hawara, Pyramid of, 23

hawksbeak moulding, 126, 128, 135,
    136, 137, 152
Heckington Church, 302
Heliopolis (Egypt), 19
Hellenistic Age, 122, 198, 231 ff.
Hellenistic Architecture, 64, 68, 69,
    89 n., 136 n., 200
Hellenistic Mixed Order, 241, 259
Hellenistic theatres, 207 ff.
hemicycles, 270, 317, 318, 344, 361
Hephaisteion, 133 n., 135, 140, 142 n.,
    146, 151, 153, 175, 187, 188,
    226
Herakleia on Latmos, 196, 197
Herculaneum, 189, 239, 254, 256
    Villa of Papyri, 275 ff.
Hermogenes, 249, 264
Herodes Atticus, 285
Herod's Temple, 321
Hetep-Heres, Egyptian Queen, 21
hexastyle façades, 200
hexastyle temples, 125, 132, 137, 151,
    175, 183
'Hilani', 93 ff.
Hippodamus, 206
Hittite Architecture, 89 ff.
Hittites, 5, 10, 11, 67, 89 ff., 101
'House of Livia', 239 n., 276, 280,
    313
houses
    Egyptian, 41 ff.
    Greek, 114, 123, 202 ff.
    Hellenistic, 236, 238, 252 ff.
    Mycenean, 107, 117
    Pompeian, 252 ff.
    Sumerian, 63 ff.
    Syrian, 246
Hurrites, 5, 10, 11
hut-urns, 225
Hyksos, 7, 11
Hymettan marble, 113, 303
hypaethral openings, 43, 143 ff., 189,
    190, 193
hypocausts, 273
hypostyle halls, 31, 33 ff., 41, 43, 48,
    55, 157, 200, 217, 220, 249

iconography, 327 n.
Iconostasis, 157
Ictinus, 125 n., 189, 190
Ilissus, Temple on, 188
Imhotep, 20
impluvium, 64, 145, 254
India, 4, 212
Inigo Jones, 224, 309
'insulae', 238, 353 ff.
Inwood's capital, 170
Ionia, 110, 118, 128, 158 ff., 227
Ionians, 108, 164
Ionic mouldings, 128, 139, 153, 165,
    166, 194, 243

Ionic Order, 74, 79, 84, 100, 102, 126, 132, 137, 139, 141, 158 ff., 186, 187, 200, 219, 243, 249, 306 ff., 324
Origins of, 74, 84, 99, 102, 137, 158, 160, 161 n., 164, 221
Ionic proportions, 173 ff.
Iron Age, 12
Ishtar Gate, 69
Isin Scribes, 8, 9
Isopata, 80, 81
Israel, 100
Israelites, 12
Italian Gothic, 288
'Italian House', 253
Italian Romanesque, 99
Italic buildings, 138, 225, 265
Italy, 107, 130, 131, 161, 222, 241, 251, 263, 286, 365
Iwan, 96, 358

Janus Quadrifrons, Arch of, 299 n., 335
Japan, 1
Jemdet Nasr Culture, 8, 58, 59, 62
Jerusalem, 336, 352
Temple of Herod, 321, *see also* Solomon's Temple
Jezebel, 97
Jupiter Stator, Temple of, 324
Jutland, 2 n.

Kabul, 102
Kalabshe, 43
Kalydon, 136, 138, 157 n., 184
Kara-Indash, 62
Kardaki, 128 n., 131, 133, 134, 136, 153, 185, 186, 259 n.
Karnak, 7, 15, 16, 27, 28, 29 ff., 37, 42, 48, 52, 217, 219
Kasanlik, 239 n., 242 n.
Kassites, 5, 10, 11, 27, 62
Khafajah, 58 n.
Khorsabad, 60, 65, 66, 67, 68
Kish, 7, 8 n., 9, 62, 65, 66, 69
Koyunjik, 66

Laconian roof-tiles, 183
Laconicum, 247, 334
Lagash, 7, 9, 10, 64
Lanceolate capitals, 277
larches, 303, 322
Larisa, 107, 128, 138, 163, 184, 202
Late Helladic II Culture, 82
Late Minoan, 73 ff., 81
Lateran, 302, 303
Laurel, 163
Laurentine villa, 341
Lebanon, 67
Legrain, 48
Lepcis Magna, 309, 341 n.

Lerna, 86 n.
Lesbian Leaf, 128, 161 n.
'Lesbian' masonry, 197
libraries, 316, 318, 329 n.
light-wells, 72, 73, 75
lilies, 156, 169, 186, 187, 260
Lincoln, 315
Lindos, Chronicle of, 143
'liwan', 96
Locri, 134, 161, 163, 167 n., 168
loggia, 42, 69, 91, 93 ff., 114, 184, 202, 216, 238
'loggia-building', 94 ff., 202, 214
London, 235, 287, 293
lotiform columns, 54
lotus, 27, 54, 67, 128, 161, 192
Louis Philippe, 30
Louvre, 216
Luna marble, 303
lunettes, 300
Lutyens, Sir Edwin, 181, 336
Luxor, 7, 16, 29 ff., 54
Lycia, 122 n., 159, 220 ff.
Lydia, 222
Lydians, 13
Lysicrates, Monument of, 137, 194 ff.

Macedonia, 111, 161, 168 n., 231 ff., 238, 242
Macedonian buildings, 220
macellum, 316
Machpelah, Cave of, 26
magazines, 77, 91
Magnesia, Temple of Artemis, 165, 264
Mallia, 81
Manetho, 6 n.
Mantua, S. Andrea, 332
marble, 148 ff., 303 ff.
Mari, 60, 62, 77 n.
Mars Ultor, Temple of, 195, 317, 323, 325
Martin, John, 114
Massaliot Treasury, 99
mastabas, 16 ff., 45
mastabas (royal), 17, 18, 52
mathematics (Babylonian), 72
(Egyptian), 45 ff.
(Greek), 109
Mausoleum, 102, 163 n., 166, 191 ff., 221
Mausoleum of Hadrian, 352
Maxentius, 286, 304, 325
Medes, 13
Medinet Habu, 30, 38 n., 39 n., 41, 49, 50
Mediterranean, 1, 2, 3, 108, 181
Medum, 19, 21
Megalopolis, 209
'megara', 2, 86, 88, 91 ff., 117, 120, 182, 202

Memphis, 6, 7, 15
Mentuhetep II, 28
Merire, tomb of, 47
Mesara, 81
Mesopotamia, 1, 4, 5, 8, 56 ff., 90, 91, 96, 245, 359
Messene, 196, 197
Metapontum, 'Church of Samson', 134
metopes, 125, 133 ff., 139, 141, 151, 153, 156, 177, 178, 185
Mex, catacomb, 280
Michelangelo, 344, 349 n.
Middle Kingdom. *See* Egypt
Middle Minoan, 10, 73
Miletus, 145, 159, 168, 193, 236
    Bouleuterion, 198, 243, 259, 260, 280
'Minerva Medica, Temple of', 361
Minoan Culture, 10, 11, 93, 97
Minoans, 52
Minyas, Treasury of, 82
Mitanni, 11
Mnesikles, 175, 177
models, 48, 66, 79, 86, 97, 138, 182, 225, 258, 269, 346
modillions, 262 n., 273, 278, 308, 330
modules, 132, 175
mortar, 21, 49, 64
Mortuary Temples, 16, 27 ff., 34, 36 ff.
mosaics, 157, 194, 238, 266, 269, 280, 313, 341, 361
mouldings, 52, 68, 171
    (Greek), 114, 125 ff., 138, 155 ff., 163, 165
    (Hellenistic), 236, 264
Mulvian Bridge, 265
mummies, 16 ff.
mutules, 135 ff., 185
'mutuli', 224 ff.
Mycenae, 2, 11, 25, 26, 86, 89, 216 n.
    beehive tombs, 82 ff.
Mycenaean Age, 82 ff., 92, 112, 117, 121
Mycenaeans, 118, 153
Mycerinus, 21
Myra, 221
mythology, 24 n., 65
Mytilene, 273

Nabu-apal-iddin, relief of, 59
Naopoioi, 120, 155
Naples, Baptistery, 342, 359 n.
Nagada, 18 n.
Naqshi Rustum, 214, 218
natatio, 342 ff.
Naucratis, 42, 161
Neandria, 13 n., 70, 182
Neapolis (Macedonia), 161, 168
Nebuchadnezzar, 13, 67
Nemea, Temple of Zeus, 152, 188, 193 ff.

Nemi, 138, 225
Nereid Monument, 102, 163, 165, 191, 221
Nero, 283, 294, 312, 316, 347, 354
New Kingdom. *See* Egypt
'Niles', 26
Nîmes
    Amphitheatre, 310, 347
    Maison Carrée, 273, 328
    Pont du Gard, 299 ff., 305
    Temple of Diana, 299
Nimrud, 62, 66, 95
Nimrud ivories, 67, 95 ff., 161
Nineveh, 66, 108
Nippur, 251
'non-classical' buildings, 355
Normans, 73
Norway, 4
Nubia, 36

obelisks, 18 n., 20, 30, 37, 38, 47, 48, 327 n., 350
Ocha, Mt., 2 n.
octostyle façades, 125
Odeion, 28
Odeion of Pericles, 115, 122, 200
Odeum of Herodes Atticus, 345
'oecus', 204, 238
offering temples, 22, 23, 25
Old Kingdom. *See* Egypt
Old St. Peter's, 302
Olympia, 116, 118, 136, 140, 146
    Echo Stoa, 200, 236
    Heraion, 118, 148, 153, 181, 183, 186
    Philippeum, 147, 194
    Stadium, 247
    Temple of Zeus, 130, 132, 135, 136, 152, 157, 194
Olynthus, 194, 204, 205, 206, 252
'opisthodomos', 120
opus Alexandrium, 194
opus incertum, 272
opus reticulatum, 272, 294
opus sectile, 305
Orange, 308, 336, 345, 346
orchestra, 122, 208, 209 ff., 344 ff.
Orchomenos, 82 ff., 88
Orders of Architecture, Chapter V *passim*, Chapter VIII, § 3, *passim*
Oropus, 207
orthostates, 62, 66, 73, 92, 96, 101, 142, 153, 179, 180, 183, 187, 198
Orvieto, 225, 227
'Osirid' piers, 25, 31, 36
Osterley, 266
Ostia, 259, 284, 295, 304, 310, 334, 351, 353 ff., 363
    Baths, 361
    Capitol, 330
    Forum of the Corporations, 321
    Tenements, 353 ff.

'oudos', 153
ovolo moulding, 126, 128, 133, 139, 160, 161, 163, 167, 171, 236

Paestum, 103, 108, 112, 126, 131, 133, 141, 152, 154, 161 n., 185, 227
Basilica, 141
'Corinthian-Doric' Temple, 259, 273
Temple of Ceres, 136, 152, 162 n., 177, 184, 185
Temple of Poseidon, 131, 134, 140, 141, 142, 143, 186
Palaikastro, 81, 83
Palatine, 239 n., 313
Palermo, 363 n.
Palestine, 327 n.
Palestrina, 128, 265
'Palladian Stairs', 66, 158, 217, 269
Palladio, 269 n., 328 n.
Palladium, 116
palmettes, 67, 70, 102, 128, 139, 156, 160, 161, 169, 170, 187, 192, 259
Palmyra, 315, 326, 327, 345
Panathenaia, 115, 116
Pantheon, 263 n., 273, 289, 290, 299, 300, 304, 324, 329 ff., 342, 361
Panticapaeum, 228
papyrus columns, 34, 54
'paradise', 220
'paraskenia', 211
Parian marble, 113, 156
Paris, 30
Roman Thermae, 293
parodoi, 209 ff., 345 ff.
Parthenon, 57, 110, 115, 116, 117, 120, 125, 130, 132, 134, 135, 138, 139, 142 n., 143, 146, 149, 152, 153, 173, 174, 175, 179 ff., 187, 188, 325, 327
Parthenon (pre-Periclean), 155
Parthia, 234, 284, 356 ff.
Parthian architecture, 356 ff.
Pasargadae, 214, 219
pastas, 114, 204 n., 252
Patras, 189
pavements, 67, 194, 271, 365
pavilions, 28, 31 n., 38 ff., 43, 44, 67, 69, 94, 118, 220, 240, 241, 242
Pazzi Chapel, 270 n.
pedestals, 285 n., 318, 328, 335
pediments, 121, 125, 136, 137, 145, 156, 164, 202, 216 n., 225, 330, 345, 355
Pekin, Temple of Heaven, 190
Peloponnese, 126, 141, 171
pendentives, 228, 275, 296, 359
Pennsylvania Railroad Station, 343
Pentelic marble, 113, 264, 303, 330, 334

peperino, 265, 292, 317
Pergamene architecture, 236, 247, 249, 264
Pergamene stoas, 249, 259
Pergamum, 231, 236, 238, 247, 249, 306
'periaktoi', 211
Pericles, 110, 122, 124 n.
Périgueux, 322 n.
peripteral temples, 39, 116, 117, 118 ff. 325
peristyle, 117, 118 ff., 130 ff., 139, 155, 162, 183, 185, 191, 204, 243, 253, 275, 324, 332
Persepolis, 14, 162, 202, 213, 214 ff., 221, 269, 359
Persia, 4 n., 8, 13, 14, 110, 161, 212 ff., 248, 356, 359
Persian architecture, 41, 212 ff.
'Persian' ramp, 269
Persians, 108, 110, 359
Peruzzi, 308 n., 324
Petra, 382
Phaistos, 73 n., 75, 77, 78, 85 n.
Pharaohs, 6, 39, 241
'Pharaoh's Bed', 38, 39, 44, 49
Pheidias, 117, 118, 124, 125
Philae, 38, 43, 44, 49, 53
Philo's Arsenal, 130, 172
Phoenicia, 100, 169, 222
Phoenicians, 6, 12, 108
Phrygia, 222
Phrygian marble, 323
piano nobile, 77, 355
Piazza Navona, 350
piers (Egyptian), 25, 27, 31
(Greek), 98
(Hellenistic), 239, 243, 247, 251
(Roman), 266, 289, 309, 336, 341, 361, 363
pilasters, 193, 236, 241, 243, 262 ff., 310, 332, 349, 350, 355
pilaster strips, 57
pillars, 74, 77
Pinturicchio, 302, 303
Piraeus, 130, 172
piscinae, 342
pivoted doors, 49, 67, 81, 153, 305
Place de la Concorde, 30
planning, 47, 77, 217
plano-convex bricks, 60
plaster, 102, 114, 241, 295, 313
Plataea, 206
Pnyx, 116, 198
podium, 39, 158, 159, 191, 222, 227, 243, 262, 268, 323, 324, 328, 335, 336
pointed vault (North Syrian), 96
Pola, 310 n., 314, 347
Polyclitus, 124
Polyclitus the Younger, 211

Polygnotus, 124
Pompeian houses, 252 ff.
Pompeian styles, 239 ff., 312
Pompeii, 64, 232, 233, 238, 239 ff.,
    258, 262, 263 n., 284, 314, 347,
    351, 359, 363
  Basilica, 249, 251, 323
  Baths, 273 ff., 339, 343
  Forum, 151, 167, 241 n., 251, 290
  House of the Centaur, 241
  House of the Faun, 238, 239, 256,
  House of the Silver Wedding, 256,
    262, 278
  House of the Surgeon, 253
'poros', 112, 156
porphyry, 325, 363
porticoes (Egyptian), 26, 43
  (Etruscan), 223
  (Greek), 114, 121, 186
  (Roman), 330
porticus, 315
Porticus Octavia(e), 266 n., 316
'posticum', 120, 180
pozzuolana, 273, 275, 280, 286, 294,
    318, 333, 356, 360
Pozzuoli, 297, 347, 350
Praeneste, 194, 264, 265 ff., 317, 325,
    327, 346
Priene, 101, 122, 198, 202 ff., 236 ff.
  Agora, 262
  Altar of Athena, 243
  Assembly Hall, 260
  Temple of Athena, 159, 164 ff.,
    173 ff., 192
  Lower Gymnasium, 262, 279
Prinia, 182, 183
pronaos, 120, 121 n., 131, 141, 157,
    180
proportions (Egyptian), 45 ff., 102
  (Etruscan), 223 ff.
  (Greek), 102, 128 ff., 159, 163, 167,
    168, 172 ff., 185, 192, 270
  (Hellenistic and Roman), 235, 259,
    270, 332, 349
  (Renaissance), 306, 349, 355
propyla, propylaea, 75, 86, 91, 121,
    130, 177, 202, 214, 217, 227, 260,
    276
Propylaea (Athenian), 110, 130, 132,
    135, 136, 140, 158, 169, 175 ff.,
    187
Propylaea (Eleusinian), 278 ff.
'Proto-Doric' Columns, 27, 54
Provence, 107, 236, 290, 346
prytaneion, 122, 198, 199
pseudodipteral temples, 186
pseudoperipteral temples, 272, 324
ptera, 118, 119, 328
Ptolemais in Cyrenaica, 241 n., 242 n.,
    263 n.
pulvinus, 28, 31, 36, 43, 49, 52

Puteoli, 280, see also Pozzuoli
Pydna, 242, 246, 248
pylon, 28, 31, 36, 43, 49, 52
  (broken), 39, 43
Pyramids, 4 n., 6, 16 ff., 28, 39, 40 n.,
    45, 352
Pyramid of Cestius, 352
Pyramid Texts, 7
Pythios, 192

raking cornice, 137
Rameses II, 16, 36, 54 n.
Rameses III, 40, 41
Ramesseum, 30, 31, 34, 51 n.
reed-building, 30
'refinements', 177, 179 ff., 193
Regolini-Galassi Tomb, 81, 227 ff.
regula, 132 ff., 142, 156
relief-carvings (Assyrian), 66, 69, 70,
    90, 94, 98, 220
  (Egyptian), 18, 29, 31
  (Greek), 159, 163, 171
  (Sumerian), 61
Renaissance Architecture, 179, 227,
    269, 306, 336, 342, 345, 354
Renaissance Art, 124, 141, 168, 313
reticulate work, 58
Rhamnous, 197
Rhamnous, Temple of Nemesis,
    133 n., 139, 151, 153, 154, 187,
    188
Rhineland, 284
ribs, 298 ff.
Richborough, 293
'rinceau' ornament, 139, 192
rockers, 48
roll, 126, 136, 185, 259 n.
Roman Architecture, 133, 158, 159,
    185, 220, 227, 228, 249, Chapter
    VII, § 4 passim, Chapters VIII, IX
    and X passim
Roman Doric, 136
Roman Emperors, 16, 282 ff.
'Roman Order', 274, 309 ff.
Roman Republic, 137, Chapter VII
    § 4 passim
Roman Scroll, 139, 308, 361
Roman Theatre, 211, 212, 273, 344 ff.
'Romano-Celtic' temples, 321 n.
Romans, 3, 43, 49, 55, 79
Rome (Classical), 147, 223, 228, 232 ff.,
    241, 248, 249, 259, 264, 265,
    Chapter VII § 4 passim, Chapters
    VIII, IX and X passim
  (Renaissance), 16, 30, 350
  Marble Plan, 252 ff.
  Temple of the Sun, 269 n.
Roofs, 1, 3, 28, 34, 73, 86, 101, 112,
    115, 121, 137 ff., 143 ff., 156, 165,
    182, 195, 201, 258, 300 ff., 341
roof-gutters, 126, 128, 138, 328 n.

roof-tiles, 3, 86 n., 109, 112, 113, 137 ff., 152, 225, 258, 305, 325, 328 n., 333
roof-trusses, 114, 146 ff., 301 ff.
Round Temple by the Tiber, 264
royal mastabas, 17, 18
Royal Stoa, 125, 200, 249
Russia, 3

Sahure, Pyramid of, 19, 54
S. Costanza, 345 n., 360 n.
S. Paul's Cathedral, 332, 352
S. Paul's, Covent Garden, 224
S. Sophia, 290, 331 n., 335, 365
S. Stefano Rotondo, 316 n.
Sakkara, 19, 20, 23, 27 n., 50
Salamis, 187
Samian base, 159
Samos, 118, 158, 162 n.
Samothrace
    Arsinoeion, 243
    Kabeireion, 268 n., 325
Sanctuaries, 35, 36, 49, 147, 157
Sandstone, 28, 41
Santorin, 2
San Vitale, Ravenna, 332, 361
Sanxay, 322
Sarcophagi, 23, 48, 259 n.
Sarcophagus of the Mourning Women, 162, 163, 192, 243
Sarcophagus of Scipio Barbatus, 259, 352
Sardis, 13
Sargon of Akkad, 7, 9, 10, 60
Sarvistan, 359
Sassanids, 214, 286, 356, 359
Saturn, Temple of, 308, 323
scaenae frons, 345, 346 ff.
scale-tiles, 137, 195
scamilli impares, 180
scotia, 126, 128, 170
screen walls (Egyptian), 39, 43
sculpture, 124, 125, 156, 165 ff., 185, 191, 220
Sea-raiders, 12
Second Pompeian Style, 240, 269, 276
Second Pyramid, 23 ff.
Segesta, 151, 155
Seleucia, 235, 245, 359
Selinus, 131, 185, 186
    Temple C, 128, 132, 134, 177
    Temple D, 137 n.
    Temple E, 146
    Temple F, 241
    Temple G, 143 ff., 185, 186
Senjirli, 12, 95, 96, 98, 99
Septimius Severus, 286, 330, 335, 338
serdabs, 18
Serlio, 301 ff.

Seti I, 34, 38, 40
Shatby, 241, 242
Shops, 236, 253, 318, 342, 353
Shrines, 28, 31, 75, 79, 88, 91, 95, 117, 323
Shubaid, Queen, 8
Shuruppak, 65
Sicily, 107, 134, 139, 156, 171, 185
Sicyon, 133 n., 208 n.
Sidi Gaber, 242
Signia, 224
Silchester, 321, 322 n., 347
Silsilah, 28, 41
Sima, 138, 139, 146, 152, 163, 169, 178, 183, 187
Siphnian Treasury, 39, 169
Siphnos, 113
Sisera, 97
skene, 209 ff.
Smyrna, Old, 54 n.
Soane Museum, 23, 40 n., 325 n.
'Sofa capitals', 126 n., 171
Solomon's Temple, 42 n., 95, 100
Spalato, Palace, 269, 363, 364, 365
Sparta, 107, 186, 196
Sphinx, 23
squinches, 342, 359
stadia, 174
stage, 210 ff., 269, 344 ff.
staircases, 49, 75 n., 94, 216, 217, 269 n., 296, 348
stairs, 58, 59, 74, 77, 92, 94
stave-churches, 4
stele (Egyptian funerary), 17, 18
step-pyramids, 18, 19
Stoa of Eumenes, Athens, 266
Stoas, 114, 122, 125, 157, 199 ff., 235 ff., 249 ff., 325
stucco, 272, 292, 334, 346, 359
stylobate, 130, 141, 149, 158, 173, 174, 175 ff., 199, 264, 271
Suk-el-Wardian, 241
Sulla, 233, 265
Sullan architecture, 241, 265 ff.
Sumer, 4, 5, 7, 9, 14, 50, 56 ff., 69, 100, 103, 319, 359
Sumerians, 10, 11, 42, 56 ff., 70, 72, 79, 101, 189
Sunium, 197
    Temple of Athena, 168, 188
    Temple of Poseidon, 130, 131, 137, 140, 148, 150, 152 n., 153, 154, 155, 188
Susa (N. Italy), 336
Susa (Persia), 9, 14, 213, 216, 217
Syene, 20, 37, 47
symmetry, 74, 95, 96, 114, 175, 181, 206, 236, 251, 254 ff., 268, 314, 338
Syracuse, 110, 115, 133 n., 134, 146, 206, 232, 259, 347

Syria, 1, 5 n., 6, 10, 11, 12, 13, 42, 69, 72, 93, 95 ff., 100, 103, 169, 184, 195, 216, 236, 246, 284, 290, 299, 327, 359
Syrians, 52, 95 ff.

'tablinum', 253, 256, 262, 275
Tabularium, 274, 296, 310
taenia, 132 ff., 139, 156
Taras, Tarentum, 170, 189, 232, 259
Tarkhan, 19 n.
Taxila, 235
Tegea, 113, 188, 190, 193 ff.
Tehuti-Hetep, tomb of, 54
'Telamones', 62, 99
Tell el 'Amarna. *See* el 'Amarna
Tell Halaf, 9, 10 n., 12, 67, 93, 95, 96 ff.
'temple oval', 58 n.
tenements, 292, 353 ff.
tent churches, 3
Teos, 264
Tepe Gawra, 56
Terracina, 272
tetrastyle atrium, 256
tetrastyle façades, 224
Theatre of Dionysos, 122, 208 ff.
Theatre of Marcellus, 288, 306, 310, 312, 346
Theatre of Pompey, 273
theatres (Greek), 93 n., 115, 206 ff., 309
Thebes (Egyptian), 7, 13, 28, 29 ff., 39, 43
Thera, 115
Therapne, 107, 117
thermae, 273 ff., 338 ff., 363, *see also* Baths
Thermon, 118 n., 151, 157 n., 183
Third Pompeian Style, 240, 312
Tholos (Athens), 329
Thothmes III, 28, 34 n., 39 n., 41, 161
throne rooms, 67, 70, 77, 78, 96
Throne Room of Domitian, 289, 358
Tibet, 93
Timgad, 314, 315
Tiryns, 11, 86 ff., 89, 91, 92, 118, 148, 184, 202, 227
Tivoli, 292
    Temples, 272
    Villa of Hadrian, 289, 313, 329, 341, 360 ff.
toichobate, 73, 130, 141, 153, 166, 183, 187, 198
Tomba della Pietrera, 228
torus, 126, 128, 159, 170
Tower of the Winds, 276 ff.
town planning, 122, 205 ff., 235 ff., 277
    (of Rome), 315 ff.
Trajan, 353
Trajan's Column, 318 ff., 351

transepts, 57
travertine, 265, 292, 317, 335, 346, 349
'Treasury of Atreus', 25
Trelleborg, 2 n.
Trier, 322 n., 344
triglyphs, 88, 133 ff., 139, 141, 152, 153, 155, 177, 178, 236, 251 n.
triumphal arches, 248, 314, 335 ff.
Troy, 10, 12, 79
trulli, 2
tufa, 265, 292
'Tufa Period', 232, 233, 239, 253, 258
'Tunnel of Pythagoras', 248
tunnel vaults (Assyrian), 65
    (Babylonian), 70, 245, 359
    (Egyptian), 29, 49, 50, 245
    (Hellenistic), 247, 262
    (Parthian), 355, 359
    (Roman), 270, 275, 296 ff., 330, 341, 348
    (Sumerian), 57, 60
    (Syrian), 96
La Turbie, 285
Turin, 293
Turner, J. M. W., 124
Tuscan Atrium, 256, 258, 275
Tuscan Order, 223 ff., 306
tympana, 125, 130, 136, 137, 139, 156, 165 ff., 177, 225, 330

Ugarit, 11, 12 n., 81, 92 ff.
umbrella domes, 360
Umma, 7
University College, London, 48
Uqair, 56 n.
Ur, 1 n., 5 n., 7, 8, 10, 14, 64, 65, 79, 82, 92
    Royal Tombs, 5 n., 59
    Ziggurats, 61
Urartu, 12, 13, 66
Uruk, 56 ff., 62, 100
Uruk Culture, 8, 56

Valley of the Kings, 30, 39
Varro, 228, 253
vaults, 101, 228, 236, 246, 262, 275, 296 ff., 306, 313, 356, 363
    intersecting (groined), 247, 275, 296 ff., 341
    'monastic', 298
    pointed, 96
    segmental, 27, 262
    See also tunnel vaults
Veii, 225 n., 226
'velarium', 345 ff.
Venice, S. Mark's, 194 n.
Venus and Rome, Temple of, 289, 305, 324, 325
verandah, 322 n.
Verona, 336, 347
    Palazzo Bevilacqua, 349

Versailles, 65 n.
  Trianons, 78
'vertical features', 31
Verulamium, 347
Vesta, Temple of, 255 n., 315, 328
Vetulonia, Tomba della Pietrera, 228
'via', 135
viaduct, 73
Vienne, 99 n., 159 n., 273, 345, 346, 350
Vignola, 195
Vikings, 2
Villa Giulia, 270 n.
Villa Repeta, 269
Vitruvius, 93, 99, 115, 120, 121, 131, 132, 135, 139, 159, 167, 168, 175, 179 ff., 186, 188, 200, 204, 208, 209, 211, 212, 223, 224, 228, 234, 235, 239 n., 247, 251, 253, 255, 258, 259, 264, 277, 280, 292, 295, 303, 308, 312, 314, 323, 324 n., 329, 334, 336 n., 344, 345, 354
volutes, 160 ff., 169, 192, 217, 251, 259, 309, 324
vertical, 70, 171, 182, 184, 195, 309
Vulci, 227

walls (Cretan), 79
  (Egyptian), 21, 29, 42, 49, 52
  (Greek), 119, 121, 148 ff., 196 ff.

walls—*continued*
  (Hellenistic and Pompeian), 240 ff. 269
  (Mycenaean), 89
  (Roman), 290 ff., 313, 317, 330 ff.
  (Sumerian), 101
Wen Amon, 97
Westminster Abbey, 305 n.
Westminster Hall, 88
Winchester, Corn Exchange, 224
windows, 102
  (Assyrian), 69
  (Egyptian), 42, 49, 97
  (Hellenistic and Pompeian), 240 ff.
  (Persian), 216
  (Syrian), 97 ff.
winter palace, 215 ff.
Wood Eaton, 321 n.

Xanthos, 122 n, 159, 163, 165, 221
Xerxes, 216

Yamkhad, 5 n.
York, Chapter Library, 133

Zeuxis, 124
ziggurats, 4, 19 n., 56, 60 ff., 65, 66, 269 n.
Zoroaster, 213
Zoser, 19, 20, 21